KU-466-929

James and
Jeannette Riddell

SKI HOLIDAYS IN
THE ALPS

PENGUIN BOOKS

Penguin Books Ltd, Harmondsworth, Middlesex
U.S.A.: Penguin Books Inc., 3300 Clipper Mill Road, Baltimore 11, Md
AUSTRALIA: Penguin Books Pty Ltd, 762 Whitehorse Road,
Mitcham, Victoria

—

First published 1961

—

—

Made and printed in Great Britain
by Cox and Wyman Ltd,
London, Reading, and Fakenham

Maps by A. Gatrell
Decorations by Adrian Bailey

CONTENTS

APPENDICES

To
A.R. *and* K.H.K.

AUTHOR'S NOTE

THE travels necessary for the compilation of the second half of this book alone have produced some curious and unusual statistics. In order to explore at first hand the vast amount of ski-ing that is now available to winter sports holiday-makers in the four major Alpine countries – Switzerland, Austria, France, and Italy – it is possible that my wife and I may have created something of a record.

We have together visited and skied at perhaps more than 250 centres and I doubt very much if anyone of any nationality, amateur or professional, can count more than one half this number to his credit. With certain few exceptions we have skied down every run in every centre. I have tried to work out the number of feet of uphill travel on the many forms of lifts and mountain railways that this activity has involved, and the answer comes out at a good bit more than 3,000,000 feet. This again has resulted in something like 5000 miles of pure downhill ski-ing – possibly more – seldom repeating the same descents more than twice.

The time required to produce such relatively astronomical figures – which, incidentally, involved no accident claims on insurance policies – was approximately twelve months, spread over a period of four winters. The total distance of Alpine travel, moving solely from ski centre to ski centre, works out at about 10,000 miles. Three quarters of this distance, say 7000 miles, was travelled by car – a small Fiat 600 Convertible with a ski rack on the roof – and not once on all the many passes, or in any of the manifold difficulties of snow and weather conditions on the Alpine roads, did this gallant little vehicle, shod with ordinary tyres and loaded to twice its unladen weight, fail to reach its destination. Chains were necessary on perhaps six occasions only.

Apart, however, from statistics, there are several other points I should like to make clear to the reader. The greater part of this book consists of information – first-hand, unbiased, and, I hope and believe, accurate – about a very large number of places where he may find good ski-ing. I cannot recommend one place or one area over and above any other for the simple reason that what suits one type of holiday skier does not necessarily suit another. All I can tell the reader is the type of ski-ing and the amenities each centre has to offer.

For my part, I like all ski-ing, and I believe that the beginner, going out to try ski-ing for the first time, will enjoy himself wherever he goes. Each place, however small, unknown, or undeveloped, has its own atmosphere and its own assets. Each place, however large, well-known, and possibly over-developed, is liable to have its defects. Each visitor, however rich or poor, has his own requirements and his own ideas of what constitutes a ski holiday.

There are countless highly-coloured brochures extolling the merits of literally hundreds of ski centres. These, very naturally, are equally 'highly-coloured' because of local prejudice and national pride, not to mention a well-developed commercial sense, and, strangely enough, they often do not tell the skier what he really wants to know. For this reason, and since the list of centres includes *all* the Alpine countries, in *one* volume – with each place separately assessed for its individual qualities from personal experience – it is probably unique.

Careful study of the individual descriptions should enable any type of winter visitor to the Alps, experienced or inexperienced, to discover which of the many ski resorts in the Alps have the right requirements for his own particular wishes.

The first section of this book consists of elementary but general information and advice for the potential skier – those, particularly the young and impecunious, who plan to try out ski-ing for the first time to find out what it is all about.

A very large number of words have already been written on how to ski and, together with complicated diagrams, on how to master each new technique. Many more will probably be written. Very little will be found on these subjects in these pages, for, however studious the reader, I do not believe that a beginner who has never stood on snow with a pair of skis on his feet can learn much from a book. Tuition on the snow, in all Alpine countries, has now reached such a high pitch of efficiency that it is in many ways a pity for a beginner to start out with his mind cluttered with wordy theory. Pre-ski exercises that can be done in this country beforehand are quite another matter, and are very much to be recommended. These are specially and meticulously designed to tone up the muscles used in ski-ing, and it is a pity to waste any part of your holiday through unfitness or possible injury.

This book, therefore, is strictly true to its title. It begins by telling the uninitiated a little of what ski-ing is all about and what a ski holiday involves, and a large section is devoted to telling everyone interested in ski-ing just how large a selection of resorts there is for ski holidays in the Alps and the facilities which can be found in each individual centre.

The reader will find that rather more detailed information has been given on the French and Italian ski centres than on those in Switzerland and Austria. This is partly because the former are less well known for ski-ing and certainly less publicized, and also because I have already written about the latter in considerable detail. Those who seek more details will find them in *The Ski Runs of Switzerland* and *The Ski Runs of Austria*, published by Michael Joseph.

JAMES RIDDELL

London 1961

INTRODUCTION

A FEW months ago I met an old ski acquaintance, a Swiss, at the top station of a big brand-new aerial cable-car system. This impressive installation, with a large car park at the bottom station, appeared – seemingly overnight, so quickly was it built – on the outskirts of a small Austrian town. The name of this little town, which lies within a few kilometres of the German frontier, does not, so far as I know, occur on any lists of well-known winter-sports centres, and I have not seen it advertised in this country. Previous to learning about this new *Luftseilbahn* I had not even heard of the place.

Our meeting was quite by chance, and similar to many another we have had in various corners of the Alps during the course of the past twenty-five to thirty years. Old ski acquaintances are accustomed to meeting in unlikely places – half-way down a glacier for example, or in some small out-of-the-way railway station buffet – and whereas the pleasure was in no way marked by surprise, we both had to admit that it was curiosity that brought us both to this little-known spot.

On this occasion we met at about 5700 ft above sea-level on a sunny terrace in front of a pleasant restaurant, half of which was in the open air and half in a cosy room behind big plate-glass windows. Having exchanged greetings and news we stood for some time watching the activity going on around us with no little interest.

'Two years ago', said my friend, 'there was nothing up here at all – nothing save those two old cowbarns down there in the hollow which have obviously been here a long time – and I doubt very much if anyone other than locals, and the odd enthusiast, ever climbed up here with a pair of skis in the wintertime. Look at it now.'

Down in the big sunny basin below us the snow was dotted with colourful figures of skiers struggling to learn the art of movement. Behind and to the right the slopes of the snow bowl mounted to a skyline ridge some thousand feet higher up, and all up and down these open slopes the zigzags of climbing tracks and the downward swirls of linked curves showed where many a more competent skier was practising his art.

'Next year', my friend continued, 'they plan to put ski lifts up that ridge. Save the climb. Open up more country. My bet, too, is that they will convert one of those old barns into a sort of hut restaurant.'

Just by our elbows a big signpost indicated the direction of various *piste* runs, and, below the snow platform on which we stood, the broad track of a prepared snow *piste* went curling away across the snow bowl to swerve down a long gulley and disappear over towards the steep slopes by the *Luftseilbahn* pylons. There was seldom a moment when small groups of the proverbial '*piste*-bashers' were not to be seen speedily curving their way down this highroad that led to valley bottom.

The terrace in front of the restaurant was alternately crowded and empty. As regularly as clockwork the two big cabins of the *Luftseilbahn*, sailing swiftly up and down over the tall pylons, controlled the traffic. Exactly six and a half minutes after an empty cabin left top station, its opposite number, crammed to capacity, came gliding smoothly up its altitude climb of 2660 ft to slow and sidle its way gently in between the sharply angled platforms. Two minutes for the upper cabin to disgorge its thirty-six passengers and for the lower cabin to fill up – and off they went again.

With each arrival our terrace became an active busy scene – skiers in gay pullovers and shirts, chatting and laughing, moved over to the snow to put on skis. This done, in ones and twos they launched off – most of them heading down the main *piste*, to run like ball bearings in a groove, all the way down (between four and five km.) to bottom station again. Then, for a few minutes there would be relative peace. So it went on. Thirty-six skiers at a time wafted up 2660 ft in six and a half minutes. Three hundred skiers an hour. Some of them would make the trip eight to ten times in the day – perhaps more – the fit and strong, particularly the good runners, thinking little of covering some forty km. and 25,000 ft or so of downhill ski-ing.

'Slight change', laughed my Swiss friend, 'since the days when you and I used to spend hours slogging uphill on skins in order to get any downhill running at all! What do you make of it all?'

'Make of it?' I replied. 'I can't see an end to it.'

'There won't be an end,' he replied, 'you mark my words – ski-ing is only just beginning. . . .'

*

In the relatively early days of the 1920s ('*le moyen âge*', I have heard them described as), I was one of a comparatively small handful of people – mainly British, and numbered then in hundreds – who were regular visitors to the Alps each winter: a handful that was looked upon quite erroneously by many as (*a*) very well-to-do, (*b*) slightly eccentric, and (*c*) foolhardy. Most of this handful were none of these things – but there were of course exceptions. We were merely the fortunate ones who, so to speak, happened to be in on the ground floor of one of the most astonishing phenomena of modern sport. Today those who still survive out of that small group can look around with both satisfaction and bewilderment at the immense popularity that ski-ing has achieved. The sport of a holiday on skis in the Alps, which started a mere fifty to sixty years ago, is now practised and enjoyed all round the world, anywhere where there are mountains and snow – in Europe, America, Canada, Scotland, South America, Russia, Japan, Australia, and New Zealand, and even in such unexpected places as Sicily, Cyprus, and the Middle East. With the growing ease and speed of travel it will doubtless spread to many an area considered now as too inaccessible for the average person – perhaps even to the foothills of the Himalayas.

Nothing, short of unforeseen (or even foreseeable) disaster, can stop this widespread growth for, as with the Frenchmen, several million people can't be wrong. That little handful of people now has the satisfaction of knowing that the joys it discovered in the winter snow and sunshine of the Alps are shared today by countless people of all nationalities who are no longer looked upon as well-to-do, eccentric, or foolhardy. In the 1920s and 1930s this same handful that witnessed, and in many cases was responsible for, so much – the development of ski technique and equipment, the formation of national and international ski organizations and clubs, the start and subsequent growth of the competitive Alpine events of downhill and slalom ski-racing, etc. – can look now, with some astonishment and pride, and even a little apprehension, at the tremendous advances and popularity that are today apparent. This same handful, which used to have to slog uphill for practically every foot of downhill ski-ing it enjoyed, can now look with bewilderment and often – let's face it – with a sigh of relief as well, at the immense and complex network of thousands of lifts and cableways – not to mention helicopters – that now transport the skier effortlessly to the high-altitude tops of countless lovely ski runs.

To use a British understatement, ski-ing is here to stay. It is today not only one of the biggest participant (as opposed to 'spectator') sports in the world (whose numbers of active supporters must almost rival that of golf), it is an industry in itself. It has, in short, greatly altered the pattern of life for huge numbers of people. It has in a very big way brought business to the tourist world: to hotel-keepers, to railways, air services, road transport; to manufacturers of equipment, fashion designers, and clothing factories; to travel agents, advertising agents, department stores, and ski shops; to engineers and transport construction companies; to the wood, plastic, steel, and engineering industries; to innumerable trades and professions right down – or rather up – to the new profession of ski teacher. The list is endless. Whole valleys and even wide areas that used to be moribund in winter now hum with activity, and with both employment and enjoyment, while remote places that used only to see the chamois and the eagle now see crowds of curious (a two-edged word) and happy human beings.

In a period of over thirty years of intense interest in ski-ing I have tried my hand – perhaps I should say feet – at almost all forms of this sport. I have taken part in ski-racing, both downhill and slalom; in ski-jumping; even in *Langlauf*; in *piste* ski-ing, in off-the-*piste* ski-ing, in ski wandering; in gentle touring, in high-altitude ski touring and mountaineering among the peaks and glaciers. For one long period during the war I was actively engaged in technical tuition and, although I have never turned professional, I think I must be the only amateur who organized and ran a ski school – a school which, even today, has probably not been matched in size, for its establishment of instructors numbered just over one hundred.* I have been fortunate enough to do extensive ski-ing in more than a dozen countries.

The intrigue of this entrancing game has never dulled or become stale – it has in fact increased. I have written books about it, not because I consider myself more qualified in any way than many others I could name, but because I suffer from an urge to communicate to others some of the joys that this sport has brought to me. This is my excuse, or rather reason, for this particular book, which will, I hope, save me and many another skier from the endless annual series of questions – of How? and Why? and When? and Where? – from those who have not yet become initiated or knowledgeable.

I once wrote: 'To ski is to enjoy being alive. It is to be conscious, for a change, that one's body is a mechanism competent to deal with movements more interesting, more complex, and more thrilling than walking on hard pavements, sitting in chairs, and driving mechanical vehicles. To ski, however well or poorly, is a reminder – whatever one may for a long time have suspected – that one is alive, and that living is tremendous fun.' To many people, however, this superb sport still remains something of a mystery. This, particularly in the way ski-ing is often presented by the press, is not altogether surprising. Even after many seasons of experience I have to make the confession that it is a constant source of wonderment and elation to me that anyone – I repeat, anyone – *should* be able to travel at speed down natural mountainsides that are often precipitously steep, wearing a seven-foot length of wood on each foot and bearing a stick in either hand; not only do this, but also, quite frequently, maintain control of movement, and, in a surprising number of cases, even rival the precision and grace of a bird in flight. Theoretically, taking into consideration the hazards – the angles, the changes in gradient, the bumps, rocks, gulleys, trees, fences, streams, rivers, chalets, paths, cliffs, bushes, and boulders, in fact all the natural and man-made hazards that even the lower mountainsides inevitably produce – the idea seems fantastic. Cover all these obstacles with varying depths of an extremely slippery, unpredictable white substance that is subject to infinitely subtle changes of stability, quality, and mood, and the

* The story of this strange wartime activity was described in *Dog in the Snow* (Michael Joseph).

theory looks impossible. This theory, however, is modern ski-ing.

Many a time, when summer's warmth has banished much of the snow up to the higher contours, I have stood at the top of long steep slopes and rocky hillsides down which I could not dream of running on my own two feet. The knowledge in my head that I, and thousands of others, have in wintertime skimmed down these self-same frightful places with the aid of a pair of skis still brings almost as much bewilderment as pride. It is small wonder that the uninitiated find it difficult to understand how such unlikely and cumbersome equipment, which in any work-aday environment would reduce the wearer to stupefied and laughable immobility, can bring such wonderful mobility and such joy. How can it? Well, it does. And if the several millions of people of all ages all over the world who have tried out this theory, and found it not only practicable but even highly en-joyable, are not sufficient proof of its basic soundness, then the game will have to remain an unsolved mystery in the future for as long as skis have been in existence in the past.

When did they start, these skis? For the answer to this one has to go back through the mists of time to the days when men drew primitive rock-wall pictures. In Scandinavia some of these drawings show figures wearing skis on their feet, and the famous Hoting ski, 1·1 m. long and 20 cm. broad, found in a bog in Sweden, has been dated at approximately 2500 B.C. It is hard to be exact about early dates but one thing is certain: no other sport, not even our hallowed cricket, is splendid enough to be able to boast of a god and goddess to watch over it. But ski-ing does. Dear, benign, and venerable Ull and Skade from the far north may once have thought that theirs was a limited responsi-bility. Now they have a global parish and countless devotees who consciously or unconsciously worship at their shrines. Perhaps this will give some clue as to the length of time that ski-ing has been practised.

The first beginnings thus took place in Scandinavia where the ski originated as utilitarian equipment to enable men to become mobile in snow, both in ordinary life and for military purposes. In the course of time, man being what he is, this led quite logically to competitive events, and the rolling snow-covered areas of these northern lands produced the oldest of all ski races – the *Langlauf* (lit. 'long run'), a cross-country event of long distance running. This, coupled with the more artificial but thrilling sport of ski-jumping on prepared hills, has long formed the Scandinavian contribution to the competitive side of ski-ing.

Ski-ing in the Alps is absurdly young by comparison. It was not until the closing years of the nineteenth century that the practice spread to Europe. To quote the greatest living expert on these matters, Sir Arnold Lunn,* 'The English can claim to have been among the first to introduce ski-ing to Switzerland.' In 1888 a Colonel Napier brought skis to Davos and in 1889 Sir Arthur Conan Doyle and Mr and Mrs Hugh Dobson began to ski in that same famous centre. In 1890 another Englishman, a Mr Knoker, introduced three pairs of Scandinavian skis to Meiringen. There was, one suspects, no small amount of scepticism from the stolid locals of these places, but, from these early beginnings, the game was on. He would have been a brave man, however, who could have forecast that the lone and historic snow signatures of these few skis in the hitherto trackless snowfields of the Alps would lead to the voluminous snow writings that today we call the '*pistes*'. In the light of the subsequent history of ski-ing the analogy of the snowball is hard to resist.

It was also in point of fact very largely due to the English, who in those days were sufficiently interested and enterprising to be considered mad, that first the sport of downhill ski-racing and later that of the slalom were originated and evolved. In 1928 the Ski Club of Great Britain (founded in 1903) had its rules for downhill and slalom racing provisionally accepted by the international authorities, and these two competitions have since 1929 been the 'Alpine events' in national and international ski competitions.

All big national and international ski meetings from the World Championships and the Olympic Games downwards now include the four events, the cross-country and jumping from Scandinavia and the downhill and slalom from the Alps, and all important competitions are controlled by the Fédération Internationale du Ski (FIS) which was founded in 1924.

Top-line ski racing, however, is all very well. In its modern form it has developed into an affair of such technical perfection and such audacity that it is very hard indeed for the non-professional even to approach the fringes of the International élite class. It does, however, as a spectacle, form part of the fun

* For all those interested in the complete history of this sport, the works of Sir Arnold Lunn, notably *The Story of Ski-ing* and *A History of Ski-ing*, are essential literature.

of a winter sports holiday. If there are any big race meetings or even one in which the local experts are taking part in or near your holiday centre, go and watch them. At the other end of the scale almost every ski centre, local ski school, and local ski club has throughout the season a busy programme of race competitions for visitors, both beginners and the relatively experienced, and these are very much part and parcel of a ski holiday.

In view of the phenomenal growth in popularity of ski-ing many of those who regularly take their holidays in summertime are quite rightly beginning to wonder why it is that so many people in so many lands deliberately choose to do the reverse and go off in the wintertime to seek the snows. What is it, in short, that this game of ski-ing has to cause the big attraction? Biased I may be, but to me the answer is quite simple. What other sport, in what other element, in what other surroundings, has quite so much to offer? Consider . . .

Apart from a pair of very long feet and two light sticks you play this game of ski-ing as *you*: entirely on your own, without any mechanical or animal aids; no engine, hull, or horse; no wheels, no wings, no sails – and yet with the equivalent of all!

You do it without any complicated arrangements involving others – like making up a tennis four or a cricket eleven. You do it alone, and yet in company. Gay company at that, for ski-ing is a thing of spirit as well as of movement. The frequent and wonderful combination of sunshine and snow creates an atmosphere that causes strangers, and even strangers with strange tongues, to make friends easily, and it brings, even to the learning of this game, companionship born of laughter. The exhilaration and gaiety of a ski holiday is not only confined to the snow slopes, for you play this game in picturesque places far removed from the humdrum headaches of modern city existence. The nightlife, whether in the big sophisticated centres or the simple little *Skidörfer*, often extends to the small hours of the morning. There is, moreover, some strange champagne-like quality in the air of a mountain village in winter that enables even the sluggard to enjoy both the snow slopes by day and the *après-ski* entertainments of the night-spots by night.

You play this game in all conditions, and in all weathers – but generally in bright sunshine – and you can, if you wish, play it all day, every day. You play it in wonderful surroundings of great beauty, and because it is the only real means of access to such surroundings; the more you learn the more you can explore.

You do it for the challenge: the challenge to yourself, your nerve, your muscle; and the challenge to the mountainside and nature. You do it because, even without competitive events, it is, in itself, competitive. You do it to compete with an infinite variety of ever-changing conditions of snow, slope, obstacle, and problem. You do it in spite of, probably because of, a certain amount of personal risk.

You do it for the tremendous thrill of speed and the content-ment of balance – and both combined. You do it either young or old, fast or slow, athletic or non-athletic, and it provides a level of enjoyment for all. You do it for the sensation of flight, for the beauty of free movement, and to seek the accuracy of such move-ment – and, however accomplished you become, you never cease to learn.

You do it . . . well . . . you do it because, once you have tried it and taken to it, there isn't any other game to compare with it in all the world.

Those who do not know these things – those going to the Alpine snows for the first time, as beginners – soon get a glimmering of the truth. A whole series of new, unexpected, and often hilarious adventures awaits them. Those who know a little, who are medium performers, go again to learn a little more. Those who know a lot, who are experts at the game, go back time after time because they know, quite simply, that to ski is to enjoy being alive.

*

Whether my Swiss friend was right or wrong in saying that ski-ing is only just beginning cannot be argued here. The fact remains however, that there cannot be much argument about the interest it causes. Whenever the subject crops up – which it does today with increasing frequency – there always follows a tornado of questions.

The answers to all the questions, even for those who have given long study to the matter, cannot be supplied in a few words, for the subject is immense and complex. A vast proportion of those who have recently taken to going out to the snows for two or three weeks each season do not, and cannot, have more than a very limited knowledge of all the aspects of this many-sided, many-splendoured sport. How then to explain it to those who have never been out? How can it best be described to those who, as yet, barely know whether 'ski' rhymes with 'thee' or 'sky'? (Since one has to start somewhere, please make it rhyme with 'thee'! Apart from this, save in the French language when the 'k' *must* be hard, it is largely a matter of personal preference whether you say 'ski' or 'she'. So far so good.)

I fully realize that no one can ever know all the right answers for everyone, but there would be little excuse for me if, by this time, I could not at least suggest answers to most of the questions of the uninitiated and the beginners who seek, in ever increasing numbers, to know the do's and don'ts – the hows, the whys, the wheres, and the whens – of ski-ing. This book, which will I hope give even the experienced a useful hint or two, is largely devoted to those who have not as yet tasted the joys of ski-ing.

ONE

Planning a First Ski Holiday

INTRODUCTION

THE obvious essentials for any holiday abroad – passport, travellers' cheques, etc. – need no extra emphasis here, save that it is a good idea to have spare copies of a passport photo. It is not unusual for these to be required for ski-lift or mountain-railway *abonnement* (or season ticket) cards.

The 'first-time' skier has to think much in the following way: When can I take my holiday and what is the best period to aim at? The family man will, of course, be limited to school holidays and many of the popular places are crowded during these periods. Any well-known, popular ski centre requires very early booking. Don't leave it late. Start thinking in the summer. There are, however, many small, less-well-known ski centres that are much more suited to beginners and are seldom so crowded in the holiday season. Beginners cannot really appreciate the full facilities of big centres until they are reasonably mobile on skis – so do not ignore the little places. Those not bound by school holidays have an infinitely wider choice. They can go to the Alps in the so-called 'low season' periods. Conditions are just as good; crowding is far less severe; prices are liable to be lower; and certainly employers will be glad to have employees taking their holiday in, say, January.

Is there any organization to which I have access that will help? In the first place, how many first-time skiers know of the full list of facilities offered by the Ski Club of Great Britain? Secondly, many a large company and commercial organization is now running its own summer and winter holiday parties. What about yours? The same thing applies to Government departments, youth groups, welfare associations, schools, universities, sports clubs, and so on. Party terms are generally the best bet financially. Many of these clubs and organizations are affiliated to the S.C.G.B.

Do not forget the travel-agency parties. Provided you go to reputable agencies – and check their offered centres – these are excellently run and give splendid value. Quite apart from joining any party, the travel agent will take care of any normal travel and hotel bookings.

The next questions will be: What do I need in the way of ski clothing and ski equipment? Do I as a beginner hire or buy this extra clothing and equipment? And what do I do about insurance? All this inevitably centres round the big question – how much is all this likely to cost, and can I afford it? There is, if you learn where to look for it, a ski holiday to suit every depth of pocket.

The final, and most important question of all is: Where shall I go? This is a question that taxes already keen skiers every bit as much as the uninitiated.

Suggestions to cover all these, and many more, questions will be found in the following pages.

THE SNOW SEASON

'WHEN shall I go ski-ing?'

Silly questions deserve silly answers – but they very seldom get them. Supposing I were to recommend the first week in June? Surely that's the time most people begin using tennis rackets and messing about in boats . . . ?

Two or three years ago I left London on 3 June in a party of four and went to Turin in Italy. We drove in a hired car through the hot sunny Val d'Aosta and on up to the village of Breuil-Cervinia at 6792 ft. There are cableway cabins here that waft one up to nearly 11,500 ft. Every morning for a whole week we had glorious ski-ing – runs of eight to nine km. in length and nearly 5000-ft descents – that took one, mostly on that joyful and easiest of snow conditions, spring snow, right down to our hotel in the village. Every afternoon we lay and sunbathed in deck-chairs on a terrace outside the hotel. Back in England, after nine days away, we found the daily papers fully occupied with a test match.

Silly answer? Some years it might well be a silly answer – but by no means always. In any case I can easily escape any charges of exaggeration for, in point of fact, there are today quite a number of places in the Alps – easily reached by modern lifts – where ski-ing is practised right through the summer and in fact all the year round.

All very well, you may say, but if things are so good when it's warm weather, why on earth go out to some high mountain in the depth of winter where it must be even more miserably cold than it is here?

The millions who only take their holidays in summertime generally connect the sport of ski-ing with the occasional figure seen hobbling about with a leg in plaster, and they wag their heads knowingly. But what about the ever-increasing quantities of people that suddenly begin to appear, at the office, in bus queues, and at cocktail parties, with shining, mahogany-brown, sunburnt faces in the very middle of all our winter gloom?

The average person in this country, to whom a pair of skis is merely two long comically cumbersome planks of wood turned up at one end, which cartoonists often draw so inaccurately, has almost as sketchy an idea of the Alpine ski season as he has of Alpine snow. Snow, when it comes to this country, is unpopular stuff and our winters bear very little resemblance to those they enjoy in the Alps. We English have long ago resigned ourselves to weathering a lengthy dismal period, between November and April – the main ski season in the Alps – when we expect to be submitted to anything from damp cold to heavy rain, from thick fog to wet snow – to conditions that are unenviably gloomy and which have little or nothing to do with sunshine.

Even today, with ski-ing as popular as it has already become, it is often still quite difficult to explain to the uninitiated that the inevitable mental association of snow with cold by no means always holds good in the Alps. It is even harder to convince the sceptical that ski-ing on a glacier – a *glacier* mark you – in March, at, say, 12,000 ft above sea-level, can easily prove hotter than lying on a south of France beach in August. Brilliant sunshine and snow, these unbelievers argue, cannot, by the very nature of things, go together. . . .

But they do. Without going into this matter too technically, suffice it to say that, for one reason and another – mostly to do with ground temperatures, altitudes, depths of snow, and angles of slope – sunshine and snow are frequently bosom friends in the Alps.

Let's take it then that the main snow season extends from the end of November to the middle of April. But, make no mistake, this cannot be guaranteed. It has been known for little or no snow to be delivered until the second week in January – and so little may fall in the season that ski-ing may begin to close down in early March. Equally there may be bumper snowfalls both early and late in the season.

The ski mountains of the Alps cover a very wide area and just because it may snow heavily in one quarter this does not mean that the coverage is universal. Just as season differs from season, so does area from area – and even centre from centre

in the same area. High altitude is frequently held to be a fair
guarantee for adequate delivery, but this is by no means always
so. Many a medium-height and low-altitude ski centre lies in
what is called a 'snow pocket' where snowfalls are liable to
occur when a high place may well be missed out. The Alps in
winter can be as temperamental as England in summer, and
by far the best answer to those who ask 'Will there be good
snow in Mittelalp just after Christmas?' is 'I'll tell you that if
you can assure me there will be a nice long spell of sunshine
at Tipsy-on-the-Water next July.'

Some people will say I am being unduly cautious and even
pessimistic. Maybe I am. Let me add with haste that however
bad conditions may be at the beginning and end of the odd
short season, ski-ing is always possible somewhere, and no
snow season is ever shorter than mid-January to early March.

A generalization of an average-to-good season might go
much like this: *

NOVEMBER and DECEMBER are the period of the first real
snowfalls – the falls which largely decide whether a season is
going to be good, average, or poor. These months provide the
'foundation', and a good foundation greatly affects the quality,
stability, and duration of snow. The ideal is to have the early
snowfalls interspersed with short periods of rain to allow for
good bonding and 'bedding down' on ground levels. Sufficient
must fall to provide good coverage of rocks and stony places,
and since snow falling on snow obviously lasts longer than that
falling on bare ground, a good foundation makes a tremendous
difference when the main winter snowfalls come. During these
early months the weather is seldom reliably good, but ski
conditions can be. The holiday rush begins about 20 December.

JANUARY and FEBRUARY are the months of the main
winter snowfalls. These are only very seldom continuous.
They come in periods ranging from twelve hours to four or
five days and are frequently interspersed with week-long (or
longer) sessions of wonderful, bright sparkling sunshine. The
average village temperatures during snowfalls generally range
from $+ 5°$ C. to $- 5°$ C., and during the bright sunny sessions

* For further details on snow conditions, see pp. 72–7.

the thermometer can fall much lower – sometimes down to
– 25° C.* Given no interference, these two months provide
lovely powder snow conditions. Interference comes in various
forms but mainly as wind – either warm or cold. The former,
known in German as *Föhn*, which often brings rain, has a
heavy, depressing effect upon both snow conditions and
spirits. The latter often destroys the smooth beauty of powder
snow ski-ing and can produce 'rough-sea' conditions of waves
and corrugations. Neither of these wind conditions necessarily
prevents ski-ing. Conditions may become unpleasant, but to
the true enthusiast they merely come under the heading of
'interesting'.

Too early for ski mountaineering and high-altitude ski-
touring, these are the main months for the dream ski-ing of
powder snow and for the interesting problems of all kinds of
varied snow. *Piste* ski-ing is generally at its best.

The 'holiday-rush season' ends about 10 January. Public
and school holidays being placed as they are, there is a definite
trend for centres to be emptier of visitors from 10 January for
approximately one month. The number of ski visitors begins
to increase about 10 February.

MARCH is the period of a second, lesser 'high season' –
which culminates in the movable feast of Easter and spills over
into April. Fewer snowfalls occur – but they can occur and
they can be heavy. Nights are cold but days warm. The sun
has gained a lot of strength and the weather is generally
wonderful. Powder snow is rare and of short duration. The
joy of spring snow conditions is the main attraction. Best
conditions occur before 2 p.m. – after that the snow becomes
wet and soggy, and sunbathing is more popular. Low-altitude
centres begin to lose their snow. Alpine huts begin to open and
ski touring comes into its own. The snowline recedes up to
about 5000 ft.

APRIL. Snowfalls are rare indeed. Many low-altitude centres
are empty. Others have plenty of room for visitors. Spring
ski-ing takes place earlier and earlier in the day, for melting
from hot sunshine occurs around noon. Skiers move higher.

* For Fahrenheit and Centigrade conversions, see p. 385.

Glacier and ski mountaineering is probably at its best. The snowline recedes up beyond 6000 ft.

MAY ONWARDS takes one into summer ski-ing – a pursuit that can rarely be performed at any normal ski centre but a pleasure much sought after by the enthusiasts who chase the snowline ever upwards.

This, I must repeat, is merely a generalization, and I have had to omit many factors and considerations. All things considered, perhaps the uninitiated can understand how difficult it is to give a straight answer to the question 'When shall I go ski-ing?'

If you can go out between the two main 'high seasons', then naturally you will find far less crowding. For the young, however, limited to school holidays, the period over Christmas and the New Year will almost certainly require advance booking – but how many parents think of taking their children out in the Easter holidays? Why not?

The ideal, but not always practicable, answer, if you can take your holiday when you like, is to keep yourself well-informed of the snow and weather conditions actually prevailing in the Alps, and to go out any time between 15 December and the end of March when things are good. In any case, keep an eye on the daily reports given in *The Times* and the *Daily Telegraph*. These reports, provided by representatives of the Ski Club of Great Britain – which also runs its own information service at its headquarters in London – are quite unbiased by propaganda and are of immense value to the keen skier.

As will be seen from the above, 'When shall I go ski-ing?' is also bound up with 'Where shall I go ski-ing?', and 'What kind of ski-ing do I want?' There is also the matter of costs. Holiday-rush periods, and high-season periods generally, mean higher prices than during emptier times. Study hotel price-lists with care and, particularly in the smaller centres, you will find considerable differences in high- and low-season prices. Certain highly popular and over-populous centres, which are nearly always fully booked, have largely given up low-season prices.

On the Continent itself there is a fairly loosely defined pattern as to which type of clientele is likely to take its ski holidays at which periods. In December it is mainly family groups and students; in January, when trade is less intense, business men of all categories but mainly of the non-executive type, employees, clerks, shopkeepers, etc.; in February, professional men – lawyers, doctors, etc. – employers, directors of businesses; mid-February to mid-March is the time favoured by the fashionable international set, the well-to-do. At Easter it is back to family parties and students again. Throughout the whole season, now that Mr Average Man of every class and income group has taken to ski-ing, any good week-end (with Sunday the big day) is liable to mean large numbers of people arriving at any ski centre where the snow conditions are in any way encouraging.

SKI HOLIDAY CLOTHES

'WHAT do I need? What do I wear?'

First-time skiers are immensely puzzled by the problems of clothing. After weeks of prolonged discussions with friends who 'know the ropes' they end up even less clear, and six out of ten spend too much money and take out twice as much as is necessary. There is need to be relatively thoughtful but no good reason to be puzzled. A ski holiday is no more compli- cated than any other enterprising sports holiday that requires certain essentials of specialist equipment.

So far as clothing is concerned it is well to bear in mind the wide range of conditions your body may well have to contend with. Those out-of-season, mahogany-brown faces which sud- denly begin to appear in England shortly after Christmas have not only been tanned by the sun, they have also almost certainly been exposed to several days of wind or cold, or both combined; maybe a blizzard as well.

Even on a day of bright sunshine and blue skies it can be bitterly cold work merely being pulled uphill on a ski-lift – and more so sitting in an open chairlift – particularly if it is wafting you up north-facing slopes through shade. Open-lift travel in deep winter (mid-December to mid-February) – particularly at high levels – can cause even the best circulation to work overtime.

Of all the geographical features of the world's surface mountains are the most temperamental weather-wise. Nowhere can smiling sunny gentleness change more suddenly into an angry display of temper, and the other way about. Mountains are mountains, and in no sense must they ever be treated with anything other than the greatest respect.

Regardless of weather, ski-ing very seldom stops. Really bad conditions may, very occasionally, shut down all activity – including even the uphill transport lifts – but it is very rare indeed that skiers prepared to face unusual conditions cannot practise on nearby slopes around the village. There is a great fascination in learning how to manoeuvre and navigate in bad

T – S.H.A. – B

weather. It is, in fact, an important part of ski-ing, for later on when you tackle any ski touring – or even go on some of the long *piste* runs – you must be able to cope with a wide range of problems. As with any other adventurous sport, such as ocean sailing, you must be prepared to deal with the rough as well as the smooth – and, properly prepared, the one can be just as instructive and just as much fun as the other.

Basic advice is: always be prepared for cold. It is easy to remove and carry clothing if you have too much on, but it is desperately difficult to put on something extra if you have left it behind. This blinding glimpse of the obvious may seem like a childish statement, but it is remarkable how many times holiday skiers have to prove it for themselves – the hard way.

By no means does all this mean that you have to go round looking like an arctic explorer; nor does it mean that you have to spend a lot of money; nor that you have to conform to any set of rules. A tennis player who turned up on the Centre Court at Wimbledon in full evening dress and a cloth cap might well cause a comment or two, but, as I have observed for myself, a bikini and ski boots on a glacier merely result in the usual interest that bikinis always cause.

Ski clothes are both functional and/or fashionable. Skiers dress more or less as they please. Some spend a lot of money and some very little indeed. Some look as though they have stepped straight out of a fashion plate in a glossy magazine, and others like clumsy parcels done up with insufficient string. Beginners would be unwise to attempt high-fashion effects, for it takes a reasonably good skier to remain tidy and unruffled for very long. Better be functional and comfortable. To achieve these ends the average, learner, holiday skiers – save for unusually large boots – mostly look like people comfortably, tidily, and colourfully clothed for a coldish week-end on a boat or in the country. Those who ski regularly each season can generally be picked out fairly easily. There is little uniformity about their appearance, for each one has merely developed some individually characteristic style best suited to combine his own ideas of efficiency and personality. There are, in fact, very few rules.

Extras there have to be, specialist items of clothing as well as equipment, but basically many of the clothes you wear for such occupations as sailing, hiking, golf, climbing, shooting, or cycling, or any outdoor activity, will fit into ski requirements. The development of ski clothing in the last thirty years or so has had a great effect upon ordinary sportswear and, particularly with *après-ski* clothing, even upon the fickle feminine world of *haute couture* and teenage fashions. As a result of this many necessary items such as windjackets or anoraks, big wool sweaters and heavy socks, tapered slacks, bootees, dufflecoats, etc., are fairly common articles in most wardrobes, male and female. Much of normal everyday clothing can be applied to ski-ing, so that, unless you feel like going to town on all the latest year-by-year designs, there is little need for much extra expense.

The one essential article of clothing that beginners of either sex are unlikely to possess is a pair of ski trousers.

The following is an unblushing exposure of what an average male skier standing at the top of a ski lift at say 8000 ft, on a coldish December or January morning, might well be wearing in the way of clothing and equipment: light under-vest; long-sleeved over-vest; shirt; light under-pants; long pants; one pair thin and one pair thick oiled-wool socks; ski trousers; one or two light sweaters; scarf; windjacket or anorak with hood; sun glasses or goggles; woollen ski cap or ear band; ski gloves; ski boots; bumbag (optional); skis and ski sticks. Let's break down this list and examine each item. (The figures given in brackets after each garment indicate the minimum number that you will normally need for a two-week holiday.)

Under-vest (2). Either normal variety or string. This latter, specialist garment is excellent value. Based on the 'thermos' principle of providing a layer of air between the wearer and his clothing, a string vest tends to keep him warm in cold weather and cool in hot.

Under-pants (2). Normal. Cotton or nylon. Nylon, being non-absorbent, does not suit everybody.

Long-sleeved over-vest (1). Soft, light, woollen type; a light sweater will do the same job.

Long pants (1). Matching sets of these soft and comfortable long pants and long-sleeved vests, in gay colours, are much in vogue for both male and female wear. Essential for cold conditions, these tight-fitting romper-type garments combine warmth and glamour with propriety and are eminently suitable, for example, for the somewhat intimate conditions of hut-living when ski touring.

Shirt (2). Normal sports, wool or cotton type, with long sleeves. No holds barred about gay check patterns and colours. In warm weather many a south-of-France type light material shirt is common, but long sleeves are always essential.

(From the shirt down to the skin bear this in mind. Laundry in the Alps is quick and efficient, but expensive. Drip-dry materials of the non-clammy type, or clothes you can easily wash yourself, are a great advantage.)

Ski trousers (1). These are generally smart specialist garments – called Vorlages or *Keilhosen* – serviceable only for winter sports. With elastic loops under the instep, they are specially tailored affairs that should be warm and reasonably water-repellent, made of smooth, tight-woven material which will not collect or hold snow. Worn fairly taut from hip to ankle to present a neat tapered appearance, they will, unless made of an elasticized material, quickly bag at the knees. Regarding width, comfort should not be sacrificed to fashion by over-exaggeration. Appearance and comfort gain by a little extra width and there will be less distortion. These can be bought ready-made in most size fittings. Some have them specially tailored either here or abroad, and in this case, for a man, twin hip pockets are highly recommended. Colours, even for men, can border on the gay, and for women anything goes, from red right through the spectrum round to something approaching ultra-violet. There is nothing against plus-fours, nor a more baggy type of long trouser, and many a beginner trying out the game is content to tuck ordinary trousers into his socks – but this can only be regarded as a temporary measure. A woman, quite naturally, has to be a good skier to wear a skirt – and very attractive it looks when she can.

Socks (thin wool, 3; thick oiled-wool, 1). One or two pairs of normal socks covered by one thick pair of oiled-wool ski socks is the best set-up. Two pairs of medium-thick wool socks is an alternative, but the natural oiled specialist pair tend to keep feet warm. Very few skiers wear only one pair of socks. It is both sensible and fashionable to wear socks inside the trousers – not outside and turned down over the tops of the boots. This latter practice causes permanently wet socks and it is liable to cause tripping through catching parts of the ski binding in the turndown.

Boots (1 pair). See Ski Equipment (p. 43). These are specialist affairs that can either be hired or bought and cannot reasonably be used for any purpose other than ski or mountain use.

Sweaters (2). One or two normal wool sweaters. Two light layers of wool are more efficient than one heavy one, and this makes it easier to cope with any rise or fall in temperature. An alternative to sweaters is the padded down jacket. This is a light, comfortable, hip-length coatee-type garment filled with down or nylon substitute. On the bulky side, it gives excellent protection and does not restrict free movement.

Scarf (1). Normal. An ordinary sports type collar and tie are not uncommon.

Windjacket (1) (parka or anorak). The normal modern type generally includes a hood – attached or detachable – and this is essential for cold weather ski-ing. (Without a hood, warm headgear must be carried.) The more pockets the better, and these must be provided with either zips or buttons. Made of windproof, water-repellent (but *not* waterproof) material, these garments can be either nylon or very close-weave natural fibres, and many consist of two layers of these materials. This can easily be of practical use for other sports, but it should be jacket length – to cover the seat and to avoid a damp patch at the waist. It can be worn tucked into the trousers but is preferably kept outside.

Bumbag (1). This curiously but descriptively named piece of equipment is a sophisticated development or refinement of its big brother, the rucksack. It consists of a convenient carrier (either cloth or leather) with built-in belt. Worn at the rear, just above the first syllable of its name, it can carry the skier's individual requirements such as: packed lunches, camera, waxes, spare glasses, earband, gloves, etc. Straps attached either to top or bottom (preferably both) allow for easy carriage of superfluous clothing – rolled windjacket or sweater – and climbing skins, etc.

Gloves (1). Many types: leather, wool, and proofed material are available. Those people with good circulation can wear fingered gloves which allow easier manipulation of ski bindings, etc. Mitt-type keep the fingers warmer. People with poor circulations should wear undergloves, in either wool or silk, but preferably the latter. All gloves, particularly the gauntlet type, must be sufficiently loose not to impair circulation. Some kind of cuff to overlap the sleeve end of the windjacket is desirable – especially for beginners. Children will require several pairs of easily dried gloves.

Caps. Earbands. Hoods. Many types available. A simple woollen skull cap or stocking type headgear is very popular, and easy to carry. Comfort, warmth, and suitability are purely individual matters.

So much for actual ski clothing. The relative prices of specialist items not likely to be in your wardrobe are given on page 42. For specialist ski equipment, such as skis, sticks, boots, sunglasses, etc., see pages 43–51.

Practically speaking all forms of accommodation at ski centres have radiators in the rooms. Wet clothing can be dried overnight, so avoid taking out too many spares. All clothing stays cleaner in the Alps for much longer than it does in this country.

Fashions of ski clothing change from season to season, and constant improvements both in materials and styles occur each year. The enthusiast knows what he wants, what to look for, and where to look for it. He or she goes to the department stores and shops that specialize in winter sports* – particularly to those that have ski experts in charge – where models of both home and continental clothing are available.

* See list of these, Appendix 16.

The uninitiated should do the same. They should seek out these experts, tell them of their requirements, indicate whether they wish to make expensive or cheap purchases, and listen to their advice.

Shopping for ski clothing is great fun, for this sport lends itself to a wide range of self-expression in both style and colour. The beginner would be wise, however, to concentrate on more sober, tried and true, functional clothing for his first effort. Once he has found out from experience whether he takes to ski-ing or not, and having once seen the wide range of sartorial self-expression on the slopes, then he will know how to plan his own clothing for the following season. All in all, it is probably best for beginners who are in doubt, and especially growing children, to hire specialist items for this first ski holiday – that is, of course, unless they can borrow from friends.

Some Special Advice for Women

You will find immense choice in all the shops, as regards price and shape, style and colour – and it is all too easy for the wide selection to lead you into wild extravagance. By and large a woman wears the same outer garments as a man – but most like to have more variation.

Be sensible. Think gaily but think interchangeably. Go for colours in shirts and jerseys that will go with your ski pants and your after-ski pants or skirt and will be of use to you at home.

Select your trousers first, then see what goes with them. It is always smart to have one layer of clothing to match – trousers and shirt, sweater or windjacket – then let fly with any other colour contrasts that are fun.

What to wear underneath? Avoid a girdle if you possibly can; this garment ruins the 'sit' of tight tapered ski trousers. (If you have not one of the fortunate figures that can do this, wear a pantie-belt instead.) Having discarded your girdle, remember that you will have nothing to keep stockings up, so you will require a pair of long wool pants. Remember too that you will have at least three layers of warm clothes (vest, pants, and tucked-in shirt) around your waist – so do fit your ski trousers with whatever underwear you have decided on.

Light, compact luggage is a great asset, so take your make-up in plastic bottles. Remember that the sun in the Alps in winter can burn and blister, so take some special sports preparation like glacier cream (good for men too) as a protection. Red is a sun-repellent colour; a greasy lipstick is sufficient except on the glaciers in spring.

Save on shoes. You won't wear many. Travel in your woolly booties, and then one pair of sandals to wear with your cocktail dress and one pair of flatties for after-ski skirt or Vorlages can be enough. Save on underwear. With the central heating and dry atmosphere nylon dries very quickly.

Après-Ski Clothing

The next puzzle for the beginner is what he will require for evening wear when ski-ing is over. Here again after-ski clothing need cause little anxiety. There is almost as much variety and self-expression off the slopes as on, and the general picture is one of comfort, common sense, and colour. In many small unfussy places you will see people sitting down to dinner, and even dancing in the night spots, in exactly the same clothing, boots and all, in which they have been ski-ing all day. Sensible people will, however, at least change boots and socks for less heavy footwear. At the other end of the scale some, women particularly, spend more money on *après-ski* apparel than on normal ski clothes, and the results of this are often startling, interesting, and amusing. Nowhere, however, will you find very much in the way of formality. Save in very few instances, such as Christmas time in big Palace Hotels in fashionable expensive centres, the dinner jacket and evening dress have long ceased to appear. Even when and where they do appear, the man in a normal lounge suit, or the girl in a cocktail dress, need never feel out of place.

In other words, almost anything goes.

Hotels in the middle and upper price ranges very sensibly

expect their guests to make some sort of an effort, and rightly frown on sweaty besweatered figures clumping around in boots. In any case, most reasonably civilized people prefer a change of clothing after heavy exercise. Even so, slacks and pullovers, colourful shirts and blouses can look both tidy and gay. Remember that by English standards hotels are very warmly heated.

Broadly speaking, my advice to men and women is as follows:

For men. If you want to cut luggage to absolute minimum, then travel out in the kind of clothes and shoes that will be suitable for tidy evening wear. Either a normal suit, or dark grey flannels and a blue blazer, will fill the bill. Many wear tweed jackets.

For women. More or less the same thing applies to travel kit. The lower half is generally coped with by a skirt, slacks, or fancy Vorlages, so take a variety of 'tops' – blouses, shirts, or sweaters to combine with any or all these. Don't forget indoor footwear to go with the trousers. Teenage fashions are by no means limited to teens. Go to town on colour if you feel like it.

For both. Cut down on shoes. You will find that you live either in ski boots or in what you want for dancing. Even though village streets are often slippery and frequently icy take shoes that will do for dancing. Rely on woolly-lined, rubber-soled bootees – almost an essential – or some form of overshoes or galoshes, for getting about the village in the evenings.

Travel out in, or with, a warm overcoat or dufflecoat. This is not only essential in the evenings, but can also be very useful on long open chairlifts (in which case they are returned down to bottom station for you).

All in all, the problems are not severe. Most people will find most of the clothing they require for a ski holiday already in their wardrobes and, unless they have very big ideas, everything they want for two weeks will easily go into one average-sized suitcase. For the specialist items beginners are unlikely to possess, here is a rough guide to costs involved:

	min.	max.
ski trousers	£4	£18
windjacket/anorak	£4	£12
ski socks	10s.	25s.
ski gloves	25s.	£4
rucksack or bumbag	30s.	£6
set of long-sleeved vest and pants	£4	£6
quilted anorak	£12	£18

SKI EQUIPMENT

'WHAT do I do about skis?'

If you are the sort of person who, deciding one day to take up golf for the first time, can go straight into a sports shop and buy a matched set of Bobby Locke golf clubs (with bag and all the trimmings) for £70–80, then you are in one way to be envied for your freedom of action but in no way for your sense of proportion or judgement. A superb set of golf clubs is no guarantee that you are going to be a good pupil or indeed that you are going to enjoy being one at all.

A more balanced approach is to hire a few suitable clubs from the course professional, or borrow some from a friend, and see how things go for a little. The Bobby Locke touch can come later. The same thing applies to all sports – and certainly to ski-ing.

There is nothing to stop you spending £50 on a pair of skis straightaway, if you feel so inclined. There will be plenty of people ready to purchase them off you second-hand for less than half-price a few days later.

There are literally scores of manufacturers, of all nationalities, making many ranges of different types of skis, out of all sorts of traditional and unexpected materials, and there are thousands of experts, in each of the several forms of ski-ing, busy commenting, favourably and unfavourably, on the performance of all these products.

The situation is not unlike that of the motor industry. Many different vehicles, for many different purposes, are produced for the multitudinous transport problems of vast numbers of very fussy, very opinionated, sometimes ignorant but often very knowledgeable, people of all manner of competence, age groups, position, and bank balances. It needs only a moment's consideration to realize how absurd it would be for any so-called motoring authority to attempt the nice tidy piece of advice that, before even learning to drive, all would-be motorists should avail themselves of one particular motor car which is able to meet all possible requirements – right through the range from touring with Grandma to Grand Prix racing.

To a limited degree much the same thing applies to skis and ski-ing. What goes for Grandma won't go for Friedl.

The main thing for the beginner is – not to worry. There is absolutely no sense at all in being fussy about skis until you know something about what it feels like to have a pair – almost any pair of your size – fixed on your own two feet. Leave all the heady technical discussions to those who have just weathered the experimental period and are now in the splendid position of being able to blame their skis for every mistake they make and for every fall they have.

Just get a pair of skis. How? To begin with, hire; or, if you can, borrow. Skis are not cheap to buy – modern pairs (new) range from £10 to £50 – and until you know how you feel about ski-ing it would be foolish to spend that much. The moment you find, as do the great majority, that ski-ing is all and more than you hoped it would be, then buy. By that time, you will know a little of what to look for and what type of ski is most likely to suit you best – and even if you don't you can soon find out from your ski school instructor.

The importance of owning your own equipment – whether new or second-hand – then becomes just as vital as it does for the tennis or golf enthusiast – not to mention the car driver.

Where do I hire? Either here or in the Alps. Preferably the latter – for there it is easier to cope with any necessary changes on the spot. (*Buying* skis is another matter. For all save the out-and-out specialist or the big-time ski racer, the selection to be found, say, at Lillywhites or Harrods is as good as anywhere.) The best bet in this country is to go to one of the several well-known sports shops or department stores that specialize – but do choose one where there is a ski expert to give you proper advice. In any centre in the Alps it is extremely unlikely that there will not be at least one ski shop dealing with equipment for hire. In neither of these cases are you very likely to be done down – but it never does any harm at all to indicate that, should the hired skis be good enough to encourage you to take up the game, you will be back either to buy that particular pair or a new one. If you have a knowledgeable friend with time to spare, ask him to go along with you.

Old, tired skis look old and tired, and even a novice at tennis would think twice about hiring a racquet that looked that way. On the other hand, a second-hand ski, a pair that has been 'broken in' so to speak, is easier for a beginner to handle than a brand new pair. The following are the main points to look for: Warping. The two skis must be a *true* pair. Put them together, side by side, and look down their length. Put them together, running surface to running surface, and see how they match both in arch and in points of contact. Even an unpractised eye will be able to detect any signs of distortion in either twist or loss of shape lengthwise. The 'arch' of a ski, together with its general flexibility, varies for all sorts of reasons, from pair to pair. To begin with choose a pair that is 'alive' but neither too stiff nor too whippy. Do not accept a pair that has lost its arch or shows any sign of cracks, or one where a break has been repaired. The best length for a beginner is one where the ski tip comes to approximately 3–8 in. above the head. Better to be a little short than a little long.

Armed with such elementary information no beginner should go far wrong. Your ski-school instructor will soon tell you if your initial flounderings on the nursery slopes are due more to some basic fault in your equipment than to your ability, and, if the skis are at fault, do not hesitate to return to the shop and ask for a better pair.

When it comes to buying your own pair – say for your second visit to the Alps – you will find an almost bewildering variety from which to choose. Modern skis come in all kinds of materials – in wood, in laminated wood, in plastic, in metal, in fibre glass, and in various combinations of these and other materials; and each type has its own qualities, its own purposes, and its own advantages and disadvantages. They also come in varying degrees of stiffness and flexibility – and naturally of length.

Save to the expert, or to the technically-minded, the construction of these highly-specialized instruments matters very little. All that matters is that the skis you choose must be able to cope with the demands you wish to make of them.

When you have graduated from your smooth nursery slopes to the various prepared runs known as *pistes* you will inevitably find out various things for yourself, but, just in case you are singularly unobservant, here are a few simple facts:

Whereas the flexible ski may be easier to turn, it is not so easy to control when running straight and fast on hard beaten or frozen surfaces. The importance of a stiff ski, with sharp steel edges, quickly becomes apparent – particularly on traverses. This requirement increases in direct ratio with the efficiency of your technique, the degree of angle of the slopes, and the speed at which you travel. If you do not believe this, have a look at any racing skier's equipment.

The short ski, which it may be easier to manoeuvre, is slower and has less fore-and-aft stability than the long ski.

Easy, you say, my pair will be long and stiff.

Ask even a good skier, however, wearing long stiff skis, to move away from a *piste* and to ski off in 'natural' snow. . . . More than likely he will at once look very unhappy. In almost any natural snow condition, where one is not actually ski-ing on the surface of the snow, stiff skis – both long and short – will tend to plunge and to refuse to ride normally. Soft snow, or variable snow, requires a resilient flexible ski.

So, you see, it all depends on the demands you wish to make of your skis. Stated very simply – if you want to become one of the thousands of happy '*piste*-bashers' the problem is relatively simple. If you decide to join the comparative few who never want to see a *piste* again the problem is equally simple. But what if you want to fulfil the true purpose of ski-ing and become an all-round skier who likes a bit of everything?

Surely there must be some brands of all-purpose skis? Of course there are. But here again there is a fairly wide range. Some are more efficient than others and some more popular than others, and it is difficult for an outsider to judge which kind will suit which style of ski-ing best. Maybe prices will help you more than anything else, for the top costs of all-purpose skis are higher than any other.

The best advice one can give is this: during your first visit have a good look at the skis the people around you are wearing, and go and study the ranges offered in the sports shops. You will soon form a pretty shrewd idea as to which skis are popular and which ones you can afford.

Basically, your problem will boil down to this: selection depends upon your potential ability; your ambitions; your inclinations and preferences concerning the various forms of ski-ing; your own observations; your pocket book; and your common sense. These are the best and only guides that will assist any expert you consult. Consult an experienced person you must – and preferably one who has seen you in action on your hired skis.

Sample (*approximate ski prices*)

Head ski	£44–48
Attenhofer A.15	£34
Hart Ski	£32
Rossignol 'Allais'	£48–50
Kästle	£23
Kneissl	£24
Norwegian	£15
Fischer	£13

Ski Boots

Believe it or not, boots are the most important part of your equipment. They are the essential link between you and your skis and they have to cope with all manner of stresses and problems. A good skier with good boots and poor skis will be only a little troubled, but a good skier with good skis and poor boots will be most unhappy. A beginner thus starting off with poor boots will suffer from a major disadvantage which may even discourage him from continuing.

A modern ski binding, whether of the cable or safety release type, has to exert great pressure on the sole of the boot to hold it rigidly on the footplate of the ski (see Release Bindings, p. 50). These pressures are immensely increased when the skier is in motion. The whole of the heels-down forward-lean – the 'vorlage' – position of normal running depends upon the rigidity with which the boots are stressed in the bindings. For maximum efficiency the expert technician must feel that the sole of his own foot through the link of his boot is one with the sole of his ski.

The first test of a good boot therefore is that the sole (strengthened internally with steel and often without a shaped instep) should be completely rigid and not subject to any torque. If you can bend or twist it at all the boot is of little value. It will buckle when under pressure in the binding.

When fitting your boots do so only with the ski socks you intend wearing. Guesswork as to size doesn't pay. Too big, and you will suffer from loss of control. Too small, and you will be miserable. Do not worry about boots feeling heavy – they have to be. Light boots are liable to lack sufficient strength. Remember that your feet, and particularly your toes, work very hard when you ski. They seldom get any credit for this – but they do. A big toe pressing against the boot end, or the front of the foot being in any way squeezed, will soon have you crying for mercy. There are few things more uncomfortable than an ill-fitting ski boot and, conversely, a proper fitting pair, once you have 'broken them in' and got used to their weight, is one of the most comfortable and comforting forms of footwear.

Even the most herculean of ankles could not, without support, stand up to the constant torsional demands of ski-ing. The uppers of ski boots provide this support and, here again, the fit is important. These uppers must fit the ankle very closely, and overstiffness of the leather is infinitely preferable to undue flexibility. Ankle support is greatly increased with boots that have two separate uppers and double lacing.

A well-made pair of ski boots will be as near waterproof as it is possible for leather footwear to be.

Finally, the boot must have a rubber sole with a tread that will allow non-slip walking and climbing on snow and ice surfaces. Never use nails.

Many are the shapes and designs of ski boots you will find on the market and many are the theories you will hear about which are superior and which inferior. Do not be unduly dismayed by all the complexity. For a start, as with skis – hire.

Bear in mind the above essentials and go to a sports shop either here or in the Alps. Make it quite clear to the assistant or the expert adviser that, although a beginner, you are fully aware that good boots are the first essential of ski-ing. It pays to be fussy. You will not necessarily get a new pair, but don't accept any pair that looks old and tired. These days no reputable shop will associate itself with second-hand equipment that is not serviceable. If, however, you do find, after trial, that your hired boots are in any way faulty, do not hesitate to go back and ask for a replacement pair.

Ninety-nine per cent of all regular skiers buy their own boots, and a fair proportion of these have them specially made to measure. You will be unlikely to find bootmakers in small centres who are expert at the complicated business of building a ski boot, but in many a large centre you will find family businesses that have become famous for their bootmaking. Look at the advertisements in the sports papers; look at the boots on show in the sports shops. Ask for advice. Here at home, go to a shop or store where there is a ski expert and consult him or her. Once you know a little of how a hired boot feels, and what you want of a ski boot, you will not find it difficult to choose a suitable type in a suitable price range.

Ski boots must be looked after. They are expensive items. Between seasons they should be kept in trees for shape. Both during use and storage ordinary boot polish should be used. Dubbin or oil, etc., over-softens the leather. High polish preserves leather and greatly improves the quality of waterproofing. Boots wet after use should not be dried on radiators or close to stoves or fires. The best method is to stuff them with newspapers and hang them up to dry in a warm room.

Sample boot prices (approximate)

Swiss	£12 15s. 0d.
French	£10 15s. 0d.
Italian	£9 10s. 0d.
Austrian	£8 17s. 0d.
English	£8 15s. 0d.

For average hire prices abroad for both skis and boots, see p. 53.

Safety – or Release – Bindings

In one form or another, these are an essential. Here again there are many different models on the market. The aim and object of these devices, designed to give the same control but to replace the inflexible fixture of cable and other bindings, is to release the boot from the ski should there be sufficient stress, either forward or rotational, in any fall likely to cause injury to the legs.

There is, to date, no such thing as an infallible safety release binding, but there are many models which can be used, either singly or combined, and which can, and do, cope with many of the stresses caused by forward or twisting falls.

Progress in the design of these bindings is being made from year to year. The only answer here is to consult the expert. The beginner, either with his own skis or hired skis, cannot be recommended too highly to make sure he has the best possible release binding from the word go. Evidence of the importance of this lies in the fact that his Insurance Policy will almost always grant him better terms if he fits a recognized binding to his skis.

Among the many types of release bindings on the market are: the *Cubco*, the *Alimonte*, the *Dover*, the *Lift*, the *Tyrolia*, the *Attenhofer A-95* (Securo), the *Marker*, the *Kandahar*, and a dozen or so other brands.

Some of these combine both rotational and forward release features. Others specialize in either rotational *or* forward release features, and these should, where possible, be used in combination.

The Accident Prevention Committee of the Ski Club of Great Britain keeps a constant and close study of the relative merits of all release bindings, and details of all developments and advice on this very complex subject are always available to members.

The best advice for non-members that can be given here is that they should consult the expert either at the shop or store they wish to patronize or at the ski centre in the Alps when they hire their skis.

It is most important to learn how to adjust release bindings and to keep them in good daily working order. The correct setting and maintenance is an essential – and do not forget to fit retaining straps so that you do not lose a ski once the release mechanism has operated on the slopes.

Ski Sticks

Not much problem here. Length of sticks is largely according to individual choice – if they reach up to armpit level on solid ground they are a good average height. The thing to go for is lightness and strength. Ski sticks are made with either cane or tubular steel tapering shafts, and the prices range from £2 to £5 respectively per pair.

Sunglasses and Goggles

Here again, many brands are available on the market. Various factors, such as the brilliance of the sunshine combined with the reflected glare from snow surfaces, make these essential. Equally, bad weather conditions and falling snow, etc., make them a necessity.

To ski without tinted or dark glasses of one sort or another is to invite serious eye strain and trouble – and possible 'snow blindness'.

THE £ s. d. OF A SKI HOLIDAY

'How much does it cost?'

This is somewhat like asking 'How long is a piece of string?' or 'How valuable is a cheque book?', and the inevitable counter-question must be 'How much do you normally allow for your two-week annual holiday?'

What the answer is depends on whether you own a yacht, a car, or merely your own two feet, but, steering a modest course somewhere between these extremes, I can say this with some certainty: If you can afford to go touring abroad – or even in this country – by car in summer; or go for a golfing holiday here in England; or even spend three weeks at the seaside just lying on the beach – then, without stinting yourself at all, you can certainly afford a fortnight's ski-ing in the Alps. With a little bit of stinting you can even do two weeks' ski-ing for exactly the same price – travel and all – as a two-weeks' stay at a holiday camp, say, in Scarborough. How this is done is hard to figure, but it is a fact that travel agents do now offer all-in terms at certain centres of their own choosing in Austria and Switzerland for sums in the region of £30, and even slightly under.

It is a fair bet, these days, that were you to be able to examine the pocket-book of Mr Average Man on his way to Blackpool or Brighton in July or August you would probably discover £75 to £100 tucked away for holiday expenses. Equally you would be likely to find Mr Average Skier returning from, say, Lenzerheide or Saalbach, with quite a bit of change out of a £100 allowance. It is arguable, therefore, that either of these Mr Average Holiday-makers is prepared to spend something between £40 and £80 for his fun.

Bearing in mind the many obvious variables involved, to attempt to make any accurate estimate of how much it costs to go ski-ing is to stick one's neck out very rashly indeed. Please allow me to do this and to offer here a sample budget for an average man – *going out on his own for the first time to a medium-priced ski centre to stay in a comfortable but inexpensive hotel, for a two-week holiday.*

Approximate costs

(1) Payable in this currency
<blockquote>
Return ticket (rail)   £15

Return ticket (air)   £25
</blockquote>

(2) Payable in foreign currency
<blockquote>
Hotel, full pension @
approx. 35s. for 13
days   £23
</blockquote>

2 weeks' hire of	
Ski boots	£1 10s. 0d.
Skis and sticks	£2 10s. 0d.
1 week ski school	£2 10s. 0d.
Ski lift tickets	£5 0s. 0d.
Skating, lugeing, etc.	£1 10s. 0d.
Extras (tea, coffee, drinks, entertainments, etc.)	£8 0s. 0d.

£59 0s. 0d.   £69 0s. 0d.

At many smaller centres these figures may be reduced to about £50 to £60. Travel-agency parties where large numbers are concerned will offer greatly reduced figures.

The beginner will, of course, use the uphill transports very little in comparison with the more advanced and good skiers.

Actual figures for hire of equipment vary from country to country and from centre to centre. The following indication however is reasonable:

Two weeks' hire of:

Skis and sticks	£2 8s. 0d.
Skis with safety bindings	£2 18s. 0d.
Metal skis	£5 10s. 0d.
Children's skis	£1 0s. 0d. – £1 15s. 0d.
Ski boots	£1 8s. 0d.

Children's ski boots	£1　1s. od.
Toboggans	£1　os. od.
Boots with skates	£1　1os. od.
Children's boots with skates	£1　7s. od.

As with any holiday either here or abroad, there are always ways and means of increasing or trimming any or all of the items of such a list. There is nothing to stop a wealthy man spending £100 in about the same number of hours. In some big Palace Hotels in certain big fashionable centres there is in fact everything to encourage him to do so. He will, however, be using the same practice slopes and runs as the impecunious student who is staying in the same centre, but living in a modest small room over the bootmaker's shop.

The range of possibility is wide indeed – but few people need to be instructed on how to spend money. Probably the best bargain for an inexpensive holiday is to go out in a party. Plenty of opportunity for this is offered by travel agents, and all you have to do is to ask one for the relevant brochures. But do remember two things: first, the choice of centres is often limited to those places where the agency has been able to obtain the cheapest terms, and this sometimes means that such centres may not have all the facilities you would like to find; second, the price of ski-lift tickets generally – but not always – has to be added to the all-in cost. Above all, choose a well-established agency that specializes in winter-sports holidays, study their suggestions well, and make yourself acquainted with the facilities available in the suggested centres. (See pp. 388–9.)

Equally, one can arrange one's own parties among one's own friends. Hotels very naturally offer better terms for bookings of ten or twelve people than for single visitors. Today it is becoming common practice for schools, universities, sports clubs, hospitals, industrial groups and factories, governmental departments, etc., to organize winter-sports parties for themselves. These are arranged either direct with the tourist bureau of any selected ski centre or through the services of a reputable travel agent. Such parties are very good value – particularly for young people.

Another way of doing things amusingly and on the cheap is to invest simply in a room with breakfast, in a small hotel or chalet, and to fend for yourself by feeding in local inns or by doing your own picnic shopping. Families or small groups of friends can often rent a flat or apartment, or a whole chalet, and even in relatively expensive centres it is not impossible to obtain such accommodation for as little as 7s. 6d. per head per night. In these cases catering and cooking for yourselves can be managed much the same as anywhere else.

In many places there are youth hostels where basic costs can be measured in terms of shillings per day.

Do not reject the idea of travelling out and back by car. Two to three people can share the driving and the expenses, and even with a night *en route* both out and back, this can come a good deal cheaper than return tickets. Apart from this, a car in the Alps is a great asset both for economy and variety. (See pp. 85–90.)

Travel costs, whether by air, rail, or car, vary of course according to how close or far your chosen centre happens to be, but the wise person will find out about the special snow-sport trains and snowflight air services organized by travel agencies and, in the latter case, by the Ski Club of Great Britain.

Currency exchange rates also affect the economics of ski-ing. These, and the cost of living in the various Alpine countries, cause some to be more favourable to the visitor than others. The actual differences are not so very great, but it would seem that the best terms, quite apart from facilities, follow the order: Austria, Italy, Germany, Switzerland, France. It would be a pity to allow this consideration to influence your choice – the main thing is to choose your centre, regardless of country, according to the facilities and the kind of holiday you want. In doing this, remember that the fashionable, lavishly equipped centres are liable to charge more for basic and extras – and rightly so. Places, whether large or small, that have many amenities such as a big range of ski-lifts are inevitably more expensive. The beginner contemplating his first visit would be well advised not to be bedazzled by famous place-names just because he has heard his friends raving about the wonderful big lifts and the superb long runs. Until he has learned a little and become sensibly mobile on his skis, he cannot possibly make full use of such facilities. Better by far to start your ski experience in one of the more modest centres where you can quickly appreciate both the ski country and the charges.

The moment a beginner has found out the extent of his liking for the game, and his potential ability, he will very soon find out two important things: which kind of centre he would like to graduate to the following season, and how to manage his accommodation and expenses according to his pocket. In the meanwhile, although there *may* be room there, don't start at the top.

One thing is very clear to me. Once bitten by ski-ing one cannot shy off. Whether I could afford it or not I always managed somehow. I have vivid memories of one visit – I must have been about eighteen at the time – when I was obliged to cross Switzerland, ticketless and horribly exposed, on the back buffer of an express train. I do not recommend this kind of solution to the £ s. d. problems – the sudden shocks of express passing express inside the many long dark tunnels is far too nerve-racking.

FITNESS AND THE EXERCISE OF SKI-ING

'Do I have to be very fit to go ski-ing?'

For the out-and-out expert, the competitor in international events, there can be few sports more demanding in the way of physical fitness. He knows, or should know, how to prepare himself for big-time ski-ing. But what about lesser mortals?

Basically, there are three very good reasons for persuading the beginner to get fit before going out to ski.

1. He will enjoy it much more.
2. He will learn much more quickly.
3. He will be far less likely to hurt himself.

Look at it this way. A beginner is going to spend a great deal of his early days either on his back or struggling to his feet. The blissful moments of actual movement on ski are apt to be punctuated at frequent and regular intervals with sprawling falls of one kind or another. These erratic activities cause a great deal of amusement not only to fellow beginners in the same ski-school class but also to the beginner himself. In the case of ski-ing, the old banana-skin joke, no matter whether you yourself or somebody else happens to be the victim, is so basic, so inevitable, and so comic that even the most serious-minded do an inordinate amount of laughing. This in itself is relatively tiring.

Have you ever tried spending a day on a soft, slippery, slanting surface, with two yards of wood on each foot, picking yourself up off the ground time after time after time? This may sound a strange way of spending a day, but this is what happens, and the majority of learners persist because, funnily enough, mastering the early rudiments of ski-ing is the very greatest fun. Even the young, who are generally fit anyway, find themselves pleasantly tired at the end of such a day. If you happen to be anywhere between thirty and fifty years old and spend fifty weeks of the year sitting either in an office chair or a motor car, your body will have quite a lot to say about such unusual and strenuous treatment.

Ski-ing will make you fit anyway, but it seems a pity to have to wait for your body to become reasonably accustomed to all the unusual exercise until the last few days of your holiday. In other words, it pays hand over fist to go out prepared to go head over heels – and to learn as quickly as possible how to avoid too many somersaults. Overtiredness, particularly when you first embark on doing short runs, can rob ski-ing of a great deal of its pleasure, and an overtired body is much more likely to hurt itself than one which is not so. And a fit strong body will learn the early rules of ski-ing much more quickly.

The arguments in favour of fitness are not unreasonable – and nobody knows them better than the insurance companies.

What about those who are not beginners? What about the large numbers of average-to-good skiers? Again, look at it this way. An average-to-good skier who knows his technique and is, most of the time, properly in balance, uses relatively little energy to go coasting down a prepared *piste*. But remember this: he will certainly use a 1500-ft lift at least four to six times a day and that adds up to between 6000 ft and 9000 ft and 16–24 km. of downhill running. He will, moreover, spend most of that running time at speeds between 20 and 40 m.p.h. and consequently when he makes his mistakes (not if, mark you, but when) his falls are liable to be far more impressive than those of a beginner travelling at 5 m.p.h.

The most I have ever heard of, in the way of downhill ski-ing done in one day, using one 2000-ft lift, is 43,246 ft over about 60 km. Such a performance must be very nearly unique, but a reasonably fit expert skier will think little of 12,000 ft and 30–40 km. Whichever extreme you consider – from bumbling beginner to racing expert – you must bear in mind that to one degree or another *all* the muscles of the body are working *all* the time and, if you feel much the same as the average man does after a five-mile walk on the level in the English countryside, then you will understand what these figures represent in terms of physical exercise.

Such is modern ski-ing. In the days gone by, before ski lifts were commonplace, one generally had to climb uphill for every foot of downhill ski-ing. This in itself was an excellent thing for fitness. It meant that, before, submitting one's legs to the stresses and strains of downhill running, the muscles were warm and exercised and ready. Today a man can get straight out of the train from England and have himself deposited, without effort, and probably cold, 2000 ft (or 6000 ft for that matter) above the village. However good a skier he may be, this is asking a bit much of legs that have taken very little exercise for the rest of the year.

The answer, of course, is to go out prepared.

There are many ways that you yourself can cope with this preparation but, first of all, there are a number of organized bodies waiting to help with regular sessions of pre-ski exercises.

The Ski Club of Great Britain in cooperation with the C.C.P.R. (Central Council of Physical Recreation) organizes dry ski training classes in many parts of the country. So do many of the leading stores who specialize in winter sports (e.g. in the London region, Lillywhites, Harrods, Gordon Lowe's, etc.) and travel agents (World Sport and Travel, etc.). Wherever and whenever these courses are available (which can be ascertained from the sources shown in Appendix 14), dry ski classes not only provide physical fitness, they also give elementary instruction in ski movement itself. This is of great importance. A beginner on the snow who already knows what it feels like to have skis on his feet and how to walk and do simple turning movements is at a great advantage over others.

Should anyone not be able to attend such classes, there is an excellent booklet entitled *Pre-Ski Exercises* obtainable, even by non-members, from the Ski Club of Great Britain for the modest cost of 3s. 6d.

This booklet gives simple pictorial instruction of a range of exercises that can be done at home. Designed by experts, these exercises indicate quite clearly that it is not only the legs that are important for ski-ing. In this game all the muscles of the body are involved. One does not have to be a gymnast to follow the instructions and many of the exercises will indicate the positions essential to ski-ing.

There are as well, of course, many other more obvious

methods of warning your muscles that you intend to use them rather more than normal. Try, for example, to spurn the push-button lift and to make more use of those old-fashioned things called staircases – up, as well as down. Leave the motor car or scooter behind when you have to walk a few hundred yards to go shopping or visit friends. Try going for a walk instead of spending the evening glued to the T V waiting for a Western you have seen, in one form or another, dozens of times before. Think more in terms of 'Have Bicycle, Will Travel'. Have the strings mended on that tennis racket and use it. Spend a little less on cigarettes and see if you can manage without 'one for the road'.

Advice such as this, I freely admit, is yet another blinding glimpse of the obvious and, as such, is only offered very shyly to those who, if ever they feel the urge for exercise, lie down until it passes off. For those who are naturally active, who play games and actually approve of keeping fit without any outside prodding, there is little need for further embroidery. Possibly one of the best forms of exercise, preparatory to ski-ing, is walking, running, and scrambling in hilly country. Zigzag traverses both up and downhill on steep hillsides, smooth and rough, will soon tickle up some of the muscles that ski-ing requires. Balance and coordination also improve. One international ski team, training in summer, makes a practice of doing this at the run on thickly wooded hillsides where the problems of dodging low-hanging branches and avoiding tree trunks make things even more spirited and comprehensive. Not everyone, however, can find such conditions readily available on their doorstep. The main thing is to do the best you can. The more strength and flexibility you can give to knees and ankles, and to calf and thigh muscles, the better off you will be. In this connexion, those who balance precariously on high-heeled shoes should try to spend at least part of each day wearing flat footwear.

There is one further consideration: a fit body means an improved circulation – and a good circulation is more able to cope with any cold conditions you may encounter in the mountains. Finally, whether in the end you take to ski-ing or not, if you do make some of these preparatory efforts you will probably notice an improvement in your general well-being, and you may even discover that it does not really require an Act of Parliament to instruct you on how to spend your leisure.

INSURANCE

No one wants to be a pessimist. Ski-ing like any other energetic sport is by no means a gentle game. To be quite brief and downright about the matter, it is pure folly not to insure yourself. The accident rate, since the advent of safety release bindings, has been very greatly reduced and it is nothing over which the beginner should lose any sleep. The general advance in all ski equipment and the efficient methods of early tuition in the ski schools have all resulted in making the game a great deal safer than it used to be in the early days of experiment and development. Ski-ing is, nevertheless, a game of such intrigue that self-daring plays a big part. The beginner is often tempted to try out manoeuvres that are beyond his limited technique and he is not always aware of the speed at which his skis are capable of moving.

There can be no argument. Insure yourself you must. There is no problem about this. The Ski Club of Great Britain has its own insurance scheme. So have the travel agencies. So have the insurance companies.

Skiers who wear recognized safety release bindings will find that the premiums offered are often reduced.

THE FORMS OF SKI-ING

WHEN one speaks of 'winter sports' the phrase itself covers a very wide variety of activities – from ski-ing, to skating, to lugeing and tobogganing, to bob sleighing, to curling, and to the various forms of these sports that use snow and ice for their surface. Holiday-makers in the Alps will find that facilities are laid on in many centres – by no means all, but certainly the big ones – for the various branches of winter sports, but, with skating a close second, the one sport that is universally catered for is ski-ing.

So much so is this the case that the phrase 'winter sports' is generally accepted as referring mainly to ski-ing.

As with skating – which includes many forms such as figure skating, racing, exhibition skating, and dancing, etc., all of which are well understood and practised in this country – so does ski-ing break down into various forms. These, perhaps, are not quite so well understood.

A quick survey of the various stages of ski-ing, to encompass an all-round knowledge of the various specialized forms of this sport, might well go as follows:

1. The early stages of tuition take place on the flat and on gentle nursery slopes where beginners learn the 'feel' of their unusual equipment and the art of simple movement. This 'nursery slope period' should *always* be undertaken in ski-school classes. In these classes the learner is taught such things as how to move about on the level, how to climb uphill, how to run straight on short descents, how to control his forward speed, how to stop, how to perform elementary turns, and, last but not least, how to pick himself up from a fall.

In passing, it would be wrong not to emphasize the fun of early ski-school classes. In these one always finds oneself among people of one's own standard. Whether you are slow or quick to absorb tuition matters very little – the ski teachers will quickly size you up and see that you are placed in a suitable class. Here, almost willy nilly, you will meet many people and quickly make acquaintanceships and friends – and, however seriously or light-heartedly you undertake the game, laughter is part and parcel of the whole affair.

2. Having mastered the short nursery-slope ski tows or ski-lifts the beginner graduates to longer lifts – lifts that will take him up say 500 to 700 ft in altitude and which will allow him to practise his early technique on short easy downhill runs. On wide, hardbeaten snow surfaces, similar to his nursery slopes, he gradually finds out how to link his elementary turns into continuous curving descents. It is rare indeed that even the most backward classes cannot accompany a teacher on short runs after two to three days on the nursery slopes.

3. The average beginner should be able to tackle the longer ski-lifts – those which rise a thousand feet and more – perhaps at the end of a week.

Uphill transport systems in every ski centre worthy of the name are always planned so that each ski lift provides a variety of descents for good, medium, and indifferent performers. In general the marked runs that swerve down close to the line of the lift itself are the shortest and therefore the steepest, but the 'beginners' routes' go curling far out on either side of the lift. These latter cover much greater distances and seek the easy ground.

Ski-school classes are soon taken on these 'family type' beginners' runs.

According to progress, the learner will soon find out for himself when he can tackle the more advanced runs. Study the large notice boards that are nearly always to be found at the bottom of every ski-lift and you will soon discover the categories and the degree of skill required for each marked run.

4. Once he has become reasonably competent at easy marked runs, the beginner should certainly go on any ski-school excursion run – a half-day or full-day ski tour – which involves easy cross-country terrain. Such outings, which are part of the weekly programmes, involve short climbs and ski-ing away from the normal marked *pistes*.

5. As early in his ski career as possible the beginner should try for his ski tests. In each Alpine country the national ski school organizes and runs standardized ski tests – Bronze

Medal, Silver Medal, and Gold. These are a great stimulant to progress and the badges of competence are eagerly sought.

The tests organized by the Ski Club of Great Britain are possibly the most eagerly sought of all. These are held very regularly at every ski centre where there are Ski Club of Great Britain representatives (see p. 378). The standards set by these tests, which incidentally were the first to be laid down by any school or club, are undoubtedly higher than those demanded by the Alpine countries. It is generally recognized – but seldom admitted – that a Swiss Gold, or First-Class, test, for example, is only a little more severe than a British Silver, or Second-Class, test. The British tests, particularly the First- and Second-Class tests, are designed through long experience to cover true all-round ski-ing in all conditions, and the award of either of these badges is a sign of real competence.

So much for early beginnings. Once you have learned the rudiments of ski-ing you will soon discover for yourself which forms of the sport suit you best and intrigue you most. Broadly and briefly speaking, the choice is as follows:

Piste Ski-ing. This, undoubtedly, is the most popular with the masses – fast, quick runs down highways marked with marker poles and with the snow beaten to as consistent a surface as possible. Often repetitive, *piste* ski-ing is 'mechanical' ski-ing – up by lift and down by ski – and the competent can build up thousands of feet of downhill running over very considerable distances.

Ski Racing. A direct relative of *piste* ski-ing. A first-class downhill race course is really a super *piste* – but the quality of technique required to be a successful competitor in a big event needs to be high indeed.

Very few from this country can, by the very nature of things, rise to the standards of the élite international racing class, but here again, as with the ski tests, races for all categories of skiers are regularly organized by clubs and ski schools for all classes at well-run ski centres.

The slalom race – a twisting, turning competition against the clock down through many pairs of flags set in a sequence of control gates – is again run on a beaten prepared snow surface.

T – S.H.A. – C

The giant slalom is a combination of both the above – a well-controlled short downhill race.

All these events are immensely popular with all grades of skiers. The modest performer will soon find out the flaws in his *piste* technique by taking part in downhill and slalom events.

Off-the-Piste Ski-ing. In other words, using any available uphill transport but ski-ing away from the marked and prepared ski runs. This non-competitive form of ski-ing involves greater all-round technique than *piste* ski-ing. It requires a study of every type of natural snow condition, however easy or difficult, and it brings great mobility, a wide range of exploration, and great joy to the adept.

Ski Touring. A direct relative of 'off-the-piste' ski-ing. In its simpler forms ski touring represents free movement both uphill and downhill well away from developed or 'mechanized' areas. In its more advanced forms, it becomes ski mountaineering, and includes high regions of peaks, glaciers, seracs, and crevasses, involving the use of ropes and specialized equipment and knowledge. Both of these forms are for the true lover of the mountains. Both will lead him to the splendours and the mysteries of a lovely upper world where he can experience the simplicity of hut life and escape from the shambles of civilization.

No list, however briefly or badly explained, of the various forms of ski-ing would be complete without including one or two slightly more specialized branches of the sport.

Langlauf – or Cross-Country Ski-ing and Racing. Far more popular in Scandinavia than in the Alps, where the rolling countryside lends itself to long distance travel, this form, which demands its own technique, is directly akin to cross-country running or racing on foot.

Ski Jumping. Even the relative beginner on his nursery slopes should experience the sensation of lifting himself off the ground over a small bump or a little prepared platform. Once he has experienced this he may well take to baby jumps of five to ten metres, and it will greatly improve his general efficiency if he does. The specialist, gradually increasing his interest, will find jumping hills of all sizes dotted all over the Alps. The spectacle of ski jumpers covering distances of fifty to eighty metres is one of the most enthralling of all winter sports events.

There are three or four outstandingly large jumping hills in the Alps where the sport has become 'ski flying' and jumps of between 100 metres and 130 metres have been recorded (well over the 100 yards).

Ski-Jöring (or ski towing). A specialized form of ski-ing where the skier is towed over flat surfaces by anything from a horse to a motor bicycle or a motor car – and sometimes even by an aircraft or helicopter. Something of a 'gimmick' and something of a spectacle.

The really keen skier will try his hand at all the various forms of the sport. The main thing to emphasize however is that, fully to appreciate exactly how much a pair of skis has to offer, the beginner should set himself to master 'off-the-*piste*' ski-ing as well as '*piste*' ski-ing. This is the key to free movement in the mountains in winter.

THE SEQUENCE OF TUITION

EACH national ski school claims its own 'method'. So far as the *ab initio* beginner is concerned the variations are of little import, and it is only when a skier reaches a certain degree of proficiency that the approaches to more advanced techniques begin to assume importance. These variations – or, rather, refinements – have themselves always been subject to alterations (almost from year to year) owing to the increase of knowledge and the constant improvement of equipment, and the popularity of any one national 'method' is often very largely based on the degree of success of any particular national ski team in the big international race meetings. Fashion very rightly follows success.

The beginner need not concern himself with fashion or the subtleties of advanced technique. He should concentrate on learning basic movement, and, broadly speaking, the principles of basic technique are the same whatever national classes he attends. There are, of course, inspired and uninspired ski teachers in every national school, and the sequence of lessons may not always be the same, but the beginner must remember that every teacher in every national school has had to pass a very severe test in order to gain his certificate.

When he joins the classes of a ski school, the beginner can expect to be instructed in the following subjects – in roughly the following sequence:

1. How to handle his skis; to put them on and take them off, and how to carry them.
2. How to stand on the level and turn to face any direction.
3. How to walk and slide on the level (German: *Geh und Gleitschritt*, French: *pas marché et pas glissé*).
4. How to climb uphill (German: *gehen am Hang*, French: *marche à la montée*). This will involve side-stepping (German: *Treppenschritt*, French: *pas en escalier*); herringboning (German: *Grätenschritt*, French: *montée en ciseau*); and the traverse climb (German: *Halbtreppenschritt*, French: *montée en biais*).

5. How to turn (German: *wenden*, French: *conversions*) when climbing; to do kickturns (German: *Spitzkehre*, French: *demi tour sur place*), both facing into and out from the hill.

6. How to position himself for easy downhill runs (German: *Fahrstellungen*, French: *positions de descente*). This will involve correct attitudes for straight running (German: *Fallinienstellung*, French: *trace directe*) and traverse running, or running across the slope (German: *Schrägfahrtstellung*, French: *descente de biais*).

7. How to pick himself up from falls both on the flat and on the hillside.

8. How to cross hollows and bumps (German: *geländefahren*, French: *traces directes dans les creux et les bosses*).

9. How to brake and stop forward movement by use of the snowplough or stem position (German: *bremsen durch Stemmen*, French: *chasse-neige, freinage, et arrêt*).

10. How to turn downhill by using the snowplough or stem position (German: *Stemmbogen*, French: *chasse-neige virage*).

11. How to link snowplough or stem turns into slow continuous descents on simple gradients.

12. How to sideslip (German: *bremsen durch seitliches Abrutschen*, French: *freinage par dérapage latéral*).

13. How to do stepturns (German: *Drehschritt*, French: *pas tournant*).

14. How to do stopturns on a traverse. The 'uphill' christiania. (German: *Kristiania zum Hang*, French: *christiania en amont*).

15. How to do stopturns from direct descent by developing the stem turn into the stop christiania and sideslipping to a standstill.

These, and various other movements, are often taught simultaneously as classes move up and down gentle nursery slopes. A reasonable understanding of these basic movements, which is less difficult than it sounds and is often achieved quite quickly, will allow the beginner to cope, slowly and within reason, with easy runs and short excursions. A sound understanding, which only comes with practice, allows the skier to move about a mountainside – albeit slowly – more or less wherever he wishes provided the problems of gradient, obstacle, and snow conditions are not severe.

The language problem, if your instructor speaks little or no English (more and more are becoming competent these days), is a disadvantage but by no means a discouragement. Mimicry plays a big role in learning to ski, and demonstrations can be universally understood.

Following basic tuition the learner skier must apply himself to increased problems – to more fluid movement, on more difficult ground, at increased speed. To achieve these things he has to learn two main lessons:

1. How to improve the steadiness of his straight-running both across the hill in traversing and straight down the fall-line in 'Schuss'.
2. How to streamline his turns from the slow control of the snowplough or stem turn into the more fluid faster forms of turn.

These two studies are closely interwoven for, as steeper gradients induce greater speed, the control of any skier on any ground depends upon his ability to turn smoothly and at will. Turning is, in effect, the means of controlling and checking forward speed.

The increase of fluidity in turning is achieved by a gradual elimination of the braking movement of the snow plough or stem position. The snowplough turn evolves logically into the stem christiania and this, in turn, finally crystallizes into the parallel swing. It is during the early stages of this period that the learner ceases to be a beginner and enters the realms of ski technique proper.

For the purposes of this book, which is primarily for beginners, this heavily curtailed version of the sequence of tuition must suffice, but it cannot be too strongly emphasized that the would-be skier will never graduate to any kind of advanced technique unless he has behind him a really solid foundation of the elementary early essentials.

Most of the early tuition takes place on easy prepared (i.e. beaten down) *piste*, but the beginner will find that the more attention he has paid to basic movements – particularly the groundwork of the snowplough and the stem – the easier will he be able to develop his stem-christiania turns in natural snow conditions.

The ultimate aim is to be able to link fast smooth turns, both long and short, more or less straight down the fall-line both on prepared *piste* and in natural powder snow conditions: to do this, and to negotiate the various bumps and undulations of steep hill-sides in a position of relaxed balance. Many and varied are the refinements of technique, of weighting and unweighting the skis, of body rotation and posture, that are applied to the mastery of advanced movement.

The skier must also learn to apply his technique to the more demanding and more difficult snow conditions (see Snowcraft, p. 72), and here, without solid mastery of the snowplough and stem turns – and an understanding of the jump turn (German: *Drehsprung*, French: *saut tournant*) – he will be completely at sea.

One of the greatest rewards in ski-ing is the confidence and the ability to tackle and manage *all* forms of snow.

Any beginner, with his eyes open, will be able to witness the technique of advanced skiers – both instructors and amateur experts – on the slopes around him, and he will begin to understand for himself what it means to do pure parallel swings and to 'tailwag' (German and universally known as *Wedeln*, French: *godille*).

To describe advanced technique in detail and in all its stages would require a separate book, and, as I have already said, I have yet to meet anyone who has learned to ski from a book. The beginner, beyond intelligent observation, should not concern himself with the refinements of advanced technique and should devote himself entirely to learning how to master the essential early lessons of basic movement.

SNOW CONDITIONS

'WHAT's the snow like?'

This is the main question that keen skiers are constantly asking – before going out to the Alps; directly they arrive; almost every day they are actually on the snow; any time. . . .

Surely, cry the uninformed, this is yet another example of a silly question sitting up and asking for a silly answer? Snow is snow – and any ass ought to know what snow is like.

Even the beginner, after only a few days' experience, will soon find out for himself that the question is both sensible and necessary. Snow in the Alps is not as we know it in this country – that nice decorative Christmas-card stuff that calls for tea-trays and snowball fights, or that occasional confounded nuisance that clutters up the towns and countryside.

Snow in the Alps is to the snow in this country as the Atlantic Ocean is to the village pond. Furthermore – and you must tell it not in Zürs and publish it not in the streets of Zermatt – the Master Mariner who knows every eventuality that the Atlantic can produce does not exist. Snow in high mountains can be every bit as temperamental as the sea – just as calm and peaceful, and just as rough and dangerous – and equally capable of many, many moods. The Master Mariner of the Alps, the fully qualified *Bergführer*, knows when to expect trouble and how best to avoid trouble but, being the philosopher he is, he would be the last person to boast that all his judgements are infallible.

None of this should in any way worry or alarm the beginner on skis. Snowcraft, in its fullest sense, will not concern him any more than seamanship concerns a rower on the Serpentine. As with sailing or swimming it is only when the inexperienced try to bite off more than they can chew that there is any cause for alarm.

In its fullest sense this word 'snowcraft' stands for a life-time study of the quality and the stability of snow – two aspects that are separate yet inextricably interwoven. Both of these are affected by many variables – temperature; altitude; time;

place; wind; sun; shade; structure; depth; consistency; direction; angle, and shape of slope; formation of ground surface; underlayers; bonding of layers; and even whether the snow is tracked or untracked. The list is very long, and the possible permutations of all the factors involved is so endless that even a lot of knowledge cannot always provide the right answers.

The non-skier sometimes reads of avalanche accidents and he cannot imagine why holiday-makers should willingly submit themselves to such perils. These perils do of course exist – but not for the beginner. Even for the fast and experienced *piste* skier, provided he obeys local rules, the hazard is negligible. Local standard runs are generally entirely safe, and should they at any moment show signs of becoming suspect they are at once controlled or shut. The non-skier does not read of the why and the wherefore of the avalanche nor does he realize that the average ski accident that results in a sprain or a broken bone is, more often than not, due to a lack of understanding of snow conditions.

In its lesser, everyday sense the word 'snowcraft' indicates an almost amateur understanding of certain factors that will enable a skier to distinguish and cope with the basic variations of good, bad, and indifferent snow conditions. It represents a relatively simple study of day-to-day changes and, in this instance, a little knowledge is far from being a dangerous thing. A little knowledge will greatly affect the enjoyment of a ski holiday and, once he has acquired a glimmering of what the many different forms are like, a skier is far less likely to cause himself an injury. He will, too, gradually learn where and when to seek out the best conditions.

Back to the eternal question: 'What's the snow like?'

The answers one hears are seldom technical. They range from 'Marvellous!' down through 'O.K.', 'Not too bad', and 'So so', on down to 'Lousy', 'Putrid', and various unprintable descriptive terms. A typical answer might be 'It was dreamy stuff on the chairlift side this morning but over on the ski lift, after lunch, it was absolute filth.' Others: 'There's powder up on the top bits but you keep running into great big drifts.' 'Absolute ice till you get round to the south slopes – then, oh boy!' 'The Standard's gone all treacherous. Keep breaking through into absolute pudding.' And so on, *ad infinitum*.

The intelligent beginner should always ask 'Why?'

The only preliminary warning that one can give to any would-be skier is that he must be prepared to find that the quality of snow is seldom constant. Even on his well-prepared, flat-beaten nursery slopes and on the well-patronized, short, easy runs he may well find day-to-day differences in running. Skis can run easily, jerkily, and sometimes barely at all. Watch out for the differences between sunshine and shade, for example. Push your way gently a few yards off the beaten slopes and you will find all sorts of other generally more difficult conditions. See how the snow on a north-facing slope compares with that on a south-facing slope. In other words, if you are going to try to understand ski-ing fully, as from the very first moment that you sprawl your way up and down the nursery slopes, you should figure out for yourself the why and the wherefore of every change. Any skier should always keep his eye on those two most important instruments – generally to be found at the hotel, but *always* somewhere in the village street – the thermometer and the barometer. Any beginner should always question his ski instructor about anything he cannot explain for himself and ask him to find and let him experience (albeit gingerly at first) different examples of different snows.

There are very few complete experts on snowcraft, but there are thousands who have acquired 'snowmanship' from intelligent observation while actually learning to ski. This is what the beginner must try to do.

The ultimate aim of the true skier should be to have sufficient knowledge to go – within reason – wherever his fancy takes him and not forever to be guided by the flags and markers of prepared runs. To accomplish this he must learn all he can about the manifold moods of snow and he must develop his ski technique so that he can safely cope with bad as well as good conditions.

Very few people ever learn active sports through reading books. They have to try them first before they even understand what the writer is talking about. Here, however, are a few basic facts.

The really joyful snow conditions for ski-ing are:

1. New, untracked powder snow (6 in. on hard foundation).
2. Hard-beaten cold *piste* snow.
3. Spring snow.

The medium conditions are:

4. Deep powder snow (over 1 ft 6 in.).
5. Unbreakable crust.
6. Hard wet snow.
7. Heavy snow.
8. Frozen *piste*.

Worst conditions:

9. Breakable crust.
10. Wind eroded snow.
11. Heavy 'sog' and 'rotten' snow.
12. Hard frozen, icy, and deeply rutted snow.

Alpine Ski-ing At All Heights and Seasons, by Arnold Lunn was the first systematic attempt to analyse snowcraft from the point of view of the skier and the ski mountaineer. In its French translation it had great influence on the development of French ski-ing.

SUNSHINE AND SHADE

So far as the beginner is concerned, the 'nursery-slope' instruction areas are, or should be, situated on sunny slopes
near the village. For the average and good skier, however,
sunshine and shade – or the general direction in which the
slopes in any one ski centre face – is of considerable importance.

Snow is temperamental stuff and it reacts like a difficult
patient to sunshine, shade, wind, and change of temperature.
Too much of any one of these conditions is not a good thing
for all-round ski-ing. Wind and change of temperature can
seldom be guarded against, but a good deal can be done about
selecting places where sun and shade are suitably available.

North-facing Slopes. These, very naturally, see little of the
sun – mostly only slanting rays. Wooded north-facing slopes
often stay shaded all day. This makes for cold conditions and
low ground temperatures. The principal asset of this is that
powder snow stays powdery for much longer periods and
makes for wonderful ski conditions. *Pistes* also remain in good
condition – save after any intervening period of thaw, when
icy conditions may prevail until further snowfall. Open lifts
(ski, chair, or *télébenne*, etc.) often mean bitterly cold uphill
travel.

South-facing Slopes. Being fully exposed to maximum sun
hours means that, unless weather is overcast, powder snow
conditions are only available during and immediately after
snowfall. In full winter – December to the end of February –
untracked south slopes are subject to unpleasant crust conditions which make for difficult ski-ing. Tracked or beaten
pistes, however, generally stay in reasonably good shape.
South-facing slopes come into their own in springtime when
hot sunshine by day and low temperatures by night result in
an overall hard surface that produces superb and easy ski-ing.
(This is known as 'firn' or 'spring' snow.)

East- and West-facing Slopes. For this purpose these may be
grouped together. The former are, naturally, sunny in the

mornings and shaded in the afternoons, and with the latter the programme is reversed. East- and west-facing slopes tend therefore to share both the assets and the defects of north- and south-facing slopes, but to a minor degree.

General Comments. Save in the instance of slopes that are obstinate about being north or south, few hillsides are predominantly hidebound about sun and shade. There is always sufficient variety of ground formation on east- and west-facing slopes to provide all conditions of sunshine and shadow.

Thus, if a ski resort has only *one* lift system up *one* ski area it is almost certainly preferable that the general direction should face either east or west. The ideal ski centre is one where hillsides can be found that face each compass point. *Sometimes* this can be achieved at places where there is only one ski area and one main uphill transport system. More frequently it happens that a ski resort requires at least two ski areas with separate lift systems. The ideal generally occurs where two or more ski areas, each with its own uphill lifts, are interlinked into a ski circus.

The keen skier should, therefore, look for places where two or more ski areas are available.

SKI TIPS

GOOD boots and average skis are better than average boots and good skis.

Never trust mountain weather. It is surprising how quickly a warm, windless day can turn into a miserably cold one. Where-ever and whenever you go ski-ing always take more clothing than you think you will require.

Two or three layers of thin wool clothing are warmer than one thick one.

However warm and springlike it may seem, never ski without gloves or with rolled-up sleeves – unless you are prepared to lose a lot of skin off your knuckles and elbows.

See that your boots are a good fit, and that they are *comfortably* tightly laced before doing a run. Loose boots reduce control. Tight boots reduce circulation.

It is folly to go ski-ing uninsured.

Wear safety release bindings. Remember however that no man-made mechanism is foolproof. Blame yourself, not your equipment, if you hurt yourself through trying something beyond your powers. The best insurance against injury is early determination to create for yourself as near faultless a basic technique as is possible.

Learn about your bindings before you attend ski school. How to adjust them and how to put skis on and take them off. Particularly so with release bindings. Otherwise you will be a nuisance to yourself and to everyone else in the class, and, failing a breakage, your teacher will soon tire of helping you.

When you first stand on the level on a pair of skis, move about as if you meant to – not as if you were anxiously waiting for someone to pull the rug out from under your feet.

Learn to carry your skis sensibly, comfortably, and without inconvenience to others. It is easy to break windows, decapitate people, and smash electric light bulbs if you are careless. Easy, but not very popular.

When walking you do not look at your feet. When driving you do not focus on the radiator cap of your car. When ski-ing do not stare at your ski tips.

Take your skis down every slope. Never let them take you.

Learn control – in the form of the stem and the stem turn – before everything else.

The one who 'shows off' is, sooner or later, shown up.

Never run fast over a blind horizon. There may be a body the other side. Don't make it two.

Ski-ing is more international than any other sport. One is constantly meeting, seeing, or hearing foreigners of all nations on the slopes, in the hotels, in the village, on the ski lifts, on the dance floors. You will find that you are judging these countries by the amount you like their representatives and by the way each group behaves. Remember that they are almost certainly doing the same with you.

A fall on a steep slope is generally safer than a fall on the flat.

The uppermost ski on any slope should always lead.

Never ski far away from a *piste* on your own.

Always lean down the hill, never back or into the slope.

Never disobey instructions, whether verbal or written, by local authorities. If a run is declared *gesperrt* (shut), treat it as *gesperrt* and go ski-ing elsewhere.

Yellow flags stand for danger. Treat them as motorists ought to treat road signs, otherwise you will only have yourself to blame.

Queueing for certain ski lifts and mountain railways is sometimes inevitable. Queueing is a bore. So are people who push and shove and behave as though they have just bought the place.

On a *piste*, if you stop on an easy place – watch out. Someone else, with perhaps a little less control than you, may well want to do the same. Leave room for him, or prepare to be felled to the ground.

Fast *piste* skiers are by no means always in control of their actions.

Legs that have walked a little way uphill are better prepared to go downhill.

Vorlage – the correct forward-leaning posture for downhill running – starts from the bottom, at the ankles, not from the bottom higher up.

You have no driving mirror. Learn to look around you when *piste* ski-ing. A faster skier may be overtaking you and any unexpected action on your part may result in a distressing misunderstanding.

Alcohol gives you a temporary feeling of warmth. It subsequently reduces your resistance to cold.

Alcohol gives you a temporary feeling of great bravery. It also reduces your resistance to gravity.

Always study the texture of the surface of the snow you are running on. Gradually you will come to learn how your skis will react to each change. This is the beginning of snowcraft.

Always study the way a slope is facing. Gradually you will learn the effects that sun, shade, and wind have upon the snow.

Bare patches, trees, and rocks are generally warmer than unbroken snow. Expect variation when you ski close to these.

When running downhill, if you are conscious of any one muscle being overloaded, then you are not in balance. Find out what is wrong by experimenting with your position and get in balance.

Packed lunches are popular with skiers. Litter looks terrible anywhere, but it looks worst of all on the snow.

Lengthen your wheelbase when riding bumpy ground.

It is easy to assess how seriously any hotel in any centre takes the ski welfare of its guests. One glance at the ski-room tells the whole story. Furthermore, to the discriminating, the skis in any ski-room, and the way they are treated by their owners, will tell you what kind of standard one may expect on the slopes.

The beauty of ski movement is that of relaxed balance.

Always look behind you before restarting after a rest or fall.

Never stand in the main *piste* to rest. Move over to the side. If you fall, sort yourself out quickly, and get out of the way. Someone else may want to fall just where you have.

Sound carries a long way in the mountains. You will almost certainly be able to hear interesting comments on your actions if you behave offensively or without thought for others.

Don't wait until you are at the top of some railway to see if your bindings are properly fitted and in working order. You may have to travel down by train.

Never follow too close behind another skier – even an expert. Always leave yourself room to avoid the leader should he make a mistake or hit some unexpected obstacle.

Never throw your skis to the ground before putting them on. Snow is slippery stuff, and flat-looking places are often deceptively angled. Skis are very quickly off the mark and they travel more directly and faster downhill without you than with you. Apart from the stupidity of losing your only means of transport, a runaway ski can cause a great deal of damage to some unfortunate person anywhere between you and the valley bottom.

Ski-ing is a high-spirited sport of quick reaction. High spirits and quick reactions sometimes foster loud behaviour and displays of temperament. Remember that self-control is the secret, as much as the acquisition of ski technique.

Use your eyes and find out where the various S O S posts, telephones, and sledges, etc., are located on the main runs. You may be present when someone hurts himself.

It is of little use to try to master parallel swings before you have learned basic technique. Certain fashionable methods of ski tuition attempt to short-cut essentials. Fashions will always change, but the early essentials such as control by means of 'snowplough' and 'stem turns' will not change.

Do not always follow your ski-teacher. Ask him sometimes to follow you. This will teach you a little of how to choose a line for yourself and allow the teacher better opportunity to spot faults in your technique. A running commentary from behind corrects these.

Once you think you have mastered some easy manoeuvre on an easy *piste*, move over a little and try it on untracked snow. This will soon reveal to you whether your theory is correct.

Never ask your legs to do anything too energetic before you have given them a chance to get fit and strong.

When ski-ing try to develop a one-track mind. Leave no tramlines behind you in the snow.

Never undertake a run that is either too long or too difficult for your own standard, simply for the sake of boasting you have done it. It may do you.

Do not spend too long telling other skiers about your own falls. The moment you pause for breath you will only get long-winded versions of theirs in return.

Any centre that is easily accessible to the big towns of the valleys is liable to be crowded on Sundays.

Study the tracks you leave behind you in the snow. Study those left behind by an expert. A little analysis of both will teach you more than many a ski teacher and all instructional books.

There is a big difference between winter and spring ski-ing. In winter (December to end of February) you have shorter days, less sunshine, and possibly very cold spells, but these disadvantages are offset by frequent periods of glorious powder snow conditions. By and large there is little serious ski-touring in winter. In spring-time (March, April) you have long, sunny days and frequently restricted hours for ski-ing. Hot sun often makes slopes unsuitable after midday. This is the best ski-touring period.

The time of least crowds and lowest prices is 5 January to 5 February.

In any description of a ski run, the use of the words 'bumps' and 'bumpy' is not derogatory. Bumpy ground is part of the fun of ski-ing.

When ski-touring, and using huts and their facilities, it pays to join the national Alpine Club.

In every way it pays to join your national ski club (e.g. the Ski Club of Great Britain). Information, good rates, party arrangements, tests, cheaper air travel, insurance, etc., are generally available.

Beginners should always submit themselves to the tender mercies and expert guidance of the ski school. Local branches of this exist at every centre.

If you can afford it, buy your ski-railway *abonnements* by the week. This means that, should poor conditions or over-crowding occur, you are at liberty to consider changing to another centre where things are better for the remainder of your holiday.

For all inquiries and problems to do with either accommodation or ski-ing, the man to approach in any centre is the director of the local tourist information office.

Be grateful, not angry, if your release binding opens in a minor fall. The trouble of putting your ski on again is infinitely preferable to an injury. Be as angry as you like with yourself if you have forgotten to use a retaining strap and the ski escapes down the slopes. That will be your own fault.

Skiers, whether beginners or experts, who have not taught themselves how to adjust (and keep adjusted) their release bindings properly, are a confounded nuisance to themselves and to anyone else with whom they may be ski-ing.

A fast skier whose binding releases itself from maladjustment rather than overstressing can suffer unnecessary and dangerous falls.

The keen skier likes to keep up with ski news all the year round. Apart from the S.C.G.B. publications, he would be well advised to subscribe to *The Skier*, published by Perigee Publications Ltd, 11 Spoutmouth, Glasgow c1.

CAR SKI-ING

A LARGE proportion of the huge number of Continental enthusiasts go ski-ing by car. Throughout the whole snow season,
from the very first high snowfalls in the hills until late in
springtime – almost no matter where you are in Europe, from
Brussels to Rome or Lyon to Vienna – a very high percentage
of the cars you will see abroad have skis on the roofracks.
This pattern goes for the annual holiday-maker, for the
public holiday crowds, for the weekender, for those on cross-
country business trips, and even for those with only a few
hours to spare who live close to mountain country. Ski-ing is
no longer localized to a dozen or so celebrated resorts – it goes
on everywhere where there are slopes and the likelihood of
snow, and, wherever this fortunate combination occurs, there
you will find the ubiquitous uphill transport lifts – and motor
cars.

Most of the winter sports traffic from these islands to the
Alps travels out by rail or air, and these are undoubtedly the
best methods for those with limited time – and certainly for
the beginner, who should stay in one centre while learning the
early essentials.

Holiday periods these days, however, are not always confined to ten days or a fortnight, and the averagely accomplished
skier can greatly extend his ski horizons, and his experience
and interest, with the use of a car. (In point of fact two or
three people sharing the driving can, if they wish, travel out
almost as quickly as by rail, and joint expenses will probably
be less. Touring on the Continent in winter can be just as
much fun as in summer and the roads in France at this time
are certainly less crowded.)

There are many areas in the Alps (see p. 384) ideally suited
for car-ski-ing. Careful choice of a good central base will allow
keen skiers to visit different ski centres and use different uphill
transport lifts almost every day of a holiday. The central base,
moreover, need not necessarily be a ski centre. No room at the
inn merely means that the car-borne skier can easily seek

accommodation elsewhere – at prices that will frequently be considerably less than in a crowded popular resort. He can, too, very much vary his *après-ski* life, and his lunches and dinners, by going further afield than his own hotel or the confines of one centre. Finally, two points: should the weather turn foul or the snow be scarce or unsuitable, he can always leave for more promising regions; should he for any reason want a rest or a change from ski-ing, then he can easily seek the fun of a day away from the snow in the valleys or nearby towns. This pleasure can be doubly appreciated in the Italian ski centres, where Milan, Turin, and Venice, with the Mediterranean and the Adriatic (not to mention the Italian lakes), are close enough to be easily accessible.

Driving a car in winter in the Alps does not present the problems that it used to do not long ago. The snow-clearance public-service organizations in all the Alpine countries, equipped with all manner of mechanical marvels in the way of snowploughs, are constantly at work throughout the entire snow season and it is very seldom indeed that any main road, or entry road up to any ski centre, or even many of the essential high passes, remains blocked for more than a few hours.

The question most often asked by those who have had no experience is 'What is it like driving in the Alps in all that snow?' My own personal answer to this is that it is great fun. That there are problems over and above normal driving is self-evident, but, as very largely with ski-ing itself, it is the problems, and the acquisition of technique necessary to overcome them, that makes for this fun.

This technique involves both car and driver.

So far as the vehicle is concerned, the modern motor car, generally speaking, is a tough reliable affair which, given the necessary attention, can stand up to harsh conditions of cold and exposure. Antifreeze treatment for water-cooling systems should allow for at least − 20° C., and this, together with a radiator muff to offset wind, and a *sound* battery – highly important this – to get things turning in the morning, will allow a car to stand out in the open, night after night, exposed to conditions at high altitudes that would cause great misery to any car owner. Garage it if you can, but do not be alarmed if the car, when parked outside, becomes partially covered, or even semi-buried, in a heavy snowfall or drift. Unless the car is required, leave the snow there – it will act as protection and insulation against both cold and wind.

So far as the driver is concerned there are several rules that one inevitably learns. By far the most important of these is the maximum possible avoidance of wheelspin or wheel-slip either when static or moving on the level, uphill or downhill. Various additional aids to prevent this, such as chains or snow-tyres, are sometimes essential – particularly on unsnowploughed roads where drifts and varying depths are encountered – but on roads that are habitually kept 'open' by snowploughs they are by no means always necessary.

Snowploughed surfaces are interesting. Allow me to digress for one moment. A driver with a slight knowledge of snow conditions or, as the ski-ing world knows it, of 'snowcraft', has a definite advantage over others, but even the inexperienced one who keeps himself reasonably acquainted with whatever the thermometer is recording in the way of temperature will soon learn what to expect. 'Cold' snow, either hard or soft, and 'cold' ice grip better than wet snow and wet ice. A normally well-swept snow road with the temperature around the zero mark provides a good crisp surface on which, with good ordinary tyres, even steep gradients can be safely tackled. Sometimes snow surfaces can be so surprisingly good that one is tempted to drive fast. Beware however of those innocuous looking white banks of snow on either side of the road – vertical banks set up by snowploughs. These are apt to become so solidly frozen that they are every bit as destructive to wings and bodywork as a cement wall. Beware, too, of warmer conditions, particularly if these are followed by evening cold. Shallow slush is not too bad, but when the road is well covered and only the upper surface is melted, then one can be in trouble. Frozen slush often produces nightmare networks of awkward and uncomfortable ruts of every depth and wheelbase width. Manoeuvring a small car among deep frozen ruts originally formed by huge pullman coaches or post-buses can produce many a surprising angle of travel, and passing other vehicles sometimes seems like two trams trying to squeeze by on only three rails.

In really poor or deep conditions chains often become a necessity. It is a wise move, if conditions look unpromising, to consult a garage at the foot of any pass or climb. For a small fee they will quickly slip on your own chains for you (if you are lazy and this is necessary) or, in many cases, hire you a pair of chains to navigate certain passes. Many a motorist relies solely on snowtyres, but these do have their disadvantages, when permanently worn, on long-distance travel on normal roads. Given suitable driving technique, ordinary tyres with good treads will perform quite adequately. The time, however, may well come, sooner or later, when chains are essential and it is the unwise motorist who does not carry a set. A chain-shod car can perform wonders in all manner of horrid conditions.

It is much easier to drive uphill on snow and ice than downhill – or even on the level. Passing and being passed on twisting uphill roads is infinitely preferable to the same manoeuvres downhill. There is an old wives tale that when climbing on these slippery surfaces one should stay in a high gear for as long as possible. I disagree with this and hold that one should drop down quite normally through the ratios, according to the gradient, always providing you avoid 'heavyfoot' and subsequent wheelspin. An unladen car climbs less well on slippery surfaces than one with a normal load over the driving wheels. Slippery downhill sections – sometimes covering long distances – must be treated with great care and attention. An obedient car can easily become a very disobedient toboggan. Use the brakes as little as possible and preferably not at all. Drop down through the gears and allow the car to 'lean on its own engine', and only touch the clutch when changing gear. You will, when conditions and gradients are tricky, be reduced to first gear crawl, but this is infinitely preferable to gaining speed unwillingly, probably in circles, with all four wheels locked. Watch out, too, for downhill corners – it takes only very little excess forward motion for the front wheels to lose their ability to turn the car. Never oversteer or jerk the steering wheel.

On the level, when ice is about, drive with concentration and circumspection and watch out for all sections of road that are habitually shaded – such as valley roads that lie close under northfacing slopes, and those that curl through thick woods, etc. Even a levelly parked car – let alone one on a slight up-gradient – can have difficulty in moving off. Never allow the wheels to spin on take-off. On ice this may work, but on snow – as in mud – the situation may develop from poor to hopeless as the driving wheels bog down. At the slightest sign of wheel-spin, it is preferable, if possible, to manhandle the car to a more suitable position.

If ever you are in doubt about the road surface over which you are travelling, stop in a suitable spot where restarting is certain, get out and try the surface on foot. Very frequently you will find that this will have a very sobering effect on your subsequent throttle pressure.

Surprisingly awesome-looking snowdrifts in exposed places can often be managed provided they are tackled with determination and continuity of power. Never allow yourself or your car to tackle such problems half-heartedly. Maintain impetus at all costs. Should this look like proving impossible, stop before you are forced to, and back or manhandle the car back and out without any wheelspin. If you are nearly through – try again. If not, retire.

One of the biggest problems in difficult conditions is finding the way blocked by cars that have themselves stuck. Never follow other cars too closely – either on up or down gradients. Use your eyes to watch the behaviour of cars in front of you and note whether they are shod with chains or snowtyres. Always leave plenty of room for self-extrication or retreat if the car in front gets into difficulties.

A second important point is to beware of various forms of snow, particularly wet snow, building up into a solid mass inside the wings around the wheels. In certain conditions this can not only affect the driving power of rear wheels, but, worse still, it can reduce your turning circle on the front to a

few centimetres, and at times one becomes aware of this limitation only when it is too late to do much about it. Taken in
time a few kicks, or prods with a ski stick, will generally loosen
wheel-cavity snow-blocks, but try never to allow these blocks
to turn to ice. Always clear out wheel cavities before leaving a
car standing out for the night, or even after sundown. It only
requires a very few degrees of cold to transform the snow
clutter round your wheel surrounds into solid ice. Such conditions can even occur in unheated garages so, even if your
car is under 'shelter', clearance of these self-forming blocks
is a must.

Some of the above paragraphs may make winter motoring
in the Alps sound a trifle hazardous and uncertain. Most of
the cases however will be seldom met with on main-road
systems that are kept open to traffic, and it is generally only if
one becomes exploration-minded on lesser roads or tracks
that the problems become either severe or impossible. A little
care, observation, and the gradual acquisition of snow and ice
technique will get the average driver most places.

'AIRLIFT' SKI-ING AND TOURING

'AIRLIFT' ski-ing is coming more and more into fashion, and it is a joy so dramatic and so novel that it is difficult to describe it with adequate balance.

In recent years a large amount of military and civilian experience in the use of light aircraft, fitted with ski undercarriage, for high-altitude landings on glaciers and upper snowfields, has been gained. In the last six years or so the helicopter has also been very successfully applied to mountain use.

Primarily devoted to rescue work, and discounting the military angle, the paying ski passengers soon became a necessary adjunct for the private operators to the financing of this laudable and highly efficient work – and all the signs and portents are that the keen skier is taking to this new and exciting method of uphill transport like the proverbial duck to water.

By no means yet within the reach of all, the pleasure and the fascination of airlift ski-ing is restricted by two factors – cash and individual competence. Firstly, the cost of a trip is, as yet, naturally on the high side; and secondly no skier with insufficient competence or confidence in himself wishes to be landed a long way away from home base on some unknown and untracked high mountainside or peak – even accompanied by a guide (who, in most cases, is of course an essential).

Costs, however, are by no means prohibitive, and the keen competent skier is quickly discovering that the joys are so great that the occasional splurge of £5 or £10 is very much worth while. Look at it this way: few people on any sort of holiday abroad do not, at some point or another, give themselves a similar kind of treat for the same kind of costs by, say, hiring a car for a day's outing or a motorboat for a day's excursion – or even by having a night out on some foreign town!

The experience of airlift ski-ing is directly comparable in price, and for those well and truly bitten by the full beauty of

snow mountains and the freedom of movement that is the gift
of the ski, the rewards are infinitely greater than almost any
other kind of expensive treat.

At the time of writing various kind of aircraft are in everyday
use at certain centres. There are the light two- or four-seater
aircraft which carry either one or three passengers and have a
fully loaded 'ceiling' of between 14,500/15,000 ft. The
famous Alpine pilot, Hermann Geiger, has already developed
a six-passenger plane, 'The Pilatus Porter', specially suited to
operate in mountains.

The main theatres of operation for conventional aircraft are
in the Valais (Zermatt, Sass-Fee, and the big glacier regions
that lead up to the Bernese Oberland giants); in the Bernese
Oberland (Grindelwald, Wengen, Mürren, etc.); and in the
Grisons and Upper Engadine (St Moritz, Pontresina, Davos,
etc.).

The enterprising private firm of Heliswiss in Berne began
to pioneer with helicopters in St Moritz some six years ago.
They now operate mainly in St Moritz, Davos, and Gstaad,
using Bell machines that carry two passengers and have a fully
loaded 'ceiling' of about 11,500 ft. The French also use helicopters (the Alouette for example) which operate notably in
the Mont Blanc area and Val d'Isère, etc.

The main differences between light aircraft and helicopter
performances are that the former demand a certain amount of
relatively flat snow surface and a fair approach (i.e. wide
glaciers or open cols) for their landings, whereas the latter can
perch, within reason, almost where they will – and that the
cost of helicoptering is rather higher than that of winged
aircraft.

Both services have their technical advantages and disadvantages and there is, very naturally, some controversy in
aeronautical circles as to which is the superior form of transport. Both however can perform such valuable services that
there is obviously plenty of room for development in the two
fields. The probability is that the near future will see considerably greater numbers of both types of aircraft in everyday
use, and, in order to bring down the costs, the passenger

carrying capacity will certainly be raised. From the 'ski-lift' angle the optimum capacity at the moment would appear to be the six passenger aircraft (a party of five plus one guide). More than this is difficult to organize for an ideal, well-balanced party of level standard skiers, and less means that the costs are inevitably steeper.

For good skiers who have limited time in the Alps the benefits of 'airlift ski-ing' are tremendous. To begin with the flight itself, especially seated in the glass bubble of a helicopter, is an experience no one can easily forget. The delight and intrigue of having an eagle's eye view of high Alpine scenery – of peak and pass, cornice, rockface, and snowslope, of peering down into the secrets of glaciers and lovely sunlit corners inhabited only by chamois, is something of such dramatic beauty that a lifetime of experience seems to be packed, like a dream, into the space of a few minutes. All this, over and above the actual ski-ing!

The aircraft skier can, of course, choose his own snow. Immediately conditions and weather prove right he can have himself transported in anything from six to fifteen minutes far from the madding crowds on the *pistes*, to some high point only to be gained otherwise by anything from four to six hours' slog uphill, where before his ski tips lies kilometre after kilometre of untracked perfection!

For those qualified to enjoy this latest addition to the sport of ski-ing an 'airlift' is a must!

INTRODUCTION

THE 'official' altitude of any given Alpine village is, or ought to be, taken from the height of the local church above sea level. In many cases, mainly for reasons of propaganda, altitudes shown in winter-sports travel brochures are seldom strictly accurate. There is a tendency, in the mistaken idea that it will attract more visitors, for many an information centre in many a ski resort to convert, say, 1890 metres into 2000 metres.

In compiling the following list of more than 165 ski centres in their order of altitude, I have been at some pains to combine accuracy with fair dealing. So far as ski-ing is concerned it is not always reasonable to follow this 'church' rule. The reason for this is that many centres, regardless of where the local church may be, spread upwards and downwards on their hillsides for as much as 500 to 800 ft. Examples of this are Arosa, Leysin, Bad Gastein, Courchevel, Méribel – to select but a few.

For reasons given below, and for the purpose of this comparative list only, I have in every relevant case taken the *uppermost* altitude of each centre. True altitudes showing the height differences existing – e.g. Arosa 5610 to 6200 ft; Courchevel 5643 to 6070 ft – are given on the pages where each centre is described in detail.

These maximum figures, together with the column showing the altitude of the highest (but often not the only) lift top station in each centre, show at a glance the maximum operational altitudes at which the holiday-maker lives and skis.

The purpose of this list is that people have very varied ideas about altitudes. Some do not like to be too high. Some cannot be high enough. Many believe the fallacy that there must always be more snow the higher you go. Many, equally wrongly, think that many centres, particularly in Austria, are too low for good conditions. A few experience minor discomfort in one form or another over certain heights – e.g. sleeplessness if the hotel is above, say, 5000 ft; or breathlessness if the top lift station is as high as 10,000 ft.

Many inexperienced people think that the higher the ski centre the tougher the ski-ing must be – and that the runs must automatically be long and only for the good performer.

There are, and there can be, no rules about altitudes so far as the *quality* of any given centre is concerned. Preferences, yes – but rules, no. The main difficulty in selecting the right conditions and the right amenities lies more in the lack of coordinated and comprehensive information than in anything else. It is hoped that the list of centres given here in order of altitude, to be read in conjunction with the individual characteristic description of the centres in each Alpine country, will provide this coordinated and comprehensive information, and solve many problems.

Basically, it is fair to say that no one should be either bedazzled or scared by pure high altitude. In any normal winter all the ski resorts mentioned will have sufficient snow to produce reasonable ski conditions during their seasons. Snowfalls are, of course, geographically variable. One area, however high or low, may at any time have more or less snow than another. The best way to keep abreast of information is to follow the snow and weather reports in *The Times* and the *Daily Tele-*

graph, furnished by the S.C.G.B., or for members to watch the notice boards at the Ski Club of Great Britain.

Nowadays the keen skier tends to search out the places that allow for big height differences of ski runs served from bottom to top by uphill transport. The beginner does not, and should not, seek the same amenities. Short lifts are better suited for learners. The keen skier should therefore note that the height of the top station above each centre by no means always gives the maximum ski altitude difference provided by the lift systems. The reason for this is that ski centres are certainly not always situated at the lowest limits of their ski terrain. Some are placed centrally in their lift systems and a few occur quite near their top stations (Kleine Scheidegg, Hochsölden, etc.). Here again the figures showing maximum height differences provided by local lifts are given in the descriptions of each individual centre.

The compilation of this list has caused me much intrinsic interest in spite of the fact that I know the centres personally. It may well cause an equal interest among keen skiers who only know a few centres personally. It is intriguing to find, for example, that Pontresina and Saas-Fee are very similar in altitude – as are St Anton and Cortina d'Ampezzo, and Auron (near Nice) and Zermatt. And that Lenzerheide is well over 1000 ft higher than Megève, and Innsbruck 700 ft lower than Lauterbrunnen. And so on.

It is also of considerable interest to find that many of the very highest places have little or no ski-touring and are, in themselves, ideally suited for beginner holidays. Equally a large number of low-altitude resorts provide not only extensive touring but also some of the toughest and most difficult ski runs.

Many interesting comparisons and observations will emerge from close study of this list. Among these is the generalization that whereas higher altitudes often indicate longer ski seasons, low altitude certainly does not indicate lack of snowfall. Kitzbühel at 2500 ft (No. 151 on the list), for example, certainly has a shorter season than Zermatt at 5316 ft (No. 39), but it often has at least as great a depth of snow during its high season. On the other hand the ski season of Stuben (No. 69) and even that of the Dachstein (No. 167) will often last far longer than that of Mürren (No. 37) and even that of Hoch-sölden (No. 2) and Arosa (No. 12).

Finally, this list is worthy of study in that it reveals the immensely wide choice and the tremendous variety that is available in the Alps to the lover of ski-ing. It shows, with the natural exception of Germany, that each of the four major Alpine countries has a fine selection of ski centres in each altitude group. It reveals that 113 centres out of 168 lie between 2000 ft and 5000 ft, and that an average of 12 centres each between 5000 and 7000 ft is equally shared by Austria, France, Italy, and Switzerland.

The skier-reader who grumbles about overcrowding at his favourite and very popular centre may well find that many a less well-known place offers equal or better facilities for his winter sport. The beginner will find that there is many a suitable unpublicized place where he can start to learn, the name of which has probably never even come to his attention.

The following points should be noted:

1. No attempt, beyond generalities, is made to give hotel prices. These, like fashions, are subject to change from year to year. Prices should always be obtained either direct from local information offices in any selected ski centre, or, more easily, from any reputable travel agency (see p. 388) dealing in winter sports.

2. In nearly every ski centre a doctor is either resident or easily available. S O S ski-accident services are widespread.

3. It is only in cases of extreme rarity that a ski centre has no local church.

4. Tobogganning, or lugeing, can always be practised in any centre. Prepared luge runs are, however, something of a rarity.

5. Skating rinks can generally be found at most centres but these are expensive items to maintain and smaller villages frequently do not have them. It is difficult to be categorical about the availability of skating, for in many of these small places there is a year-to-year decision about making or maintaining a rink.

6. New uphill transport lifts are constantly appearing. Indication is always given where projects are envisaged. Indication is also given wherever the local terrain is capable of future development. The general quality of the ski-ing available in any one area is not so subject to revision, for, if there is one unchanging thing in a changing world, it is a range of mountains.

7. Length of description of individual ski centres is no criterion of their good or poor qualities. Places that are sufficiently well known and publicized often have reputations that speak for themselves – even to the uninitiated. It is to the less well known but promising centres that lengthier descriptions are often necessary.

8. In judging the size and scope of any centre the statistics showing inhabitants and number of hotels and pensions, etc., are of importance. These, taken in conjunction with the number of ski areas and the altitude differences of the lift systems, should enable the reader very quickly to form an opinion of the nature of any centre and to compare it with any other.

9. 'Other accommodation' refers to the bed and breakfast trade of private rooms in chalets or boarding houses, etc.

10. Ski centres often tend to be placed in clusters. Reference is always given to indicate neighbouring places.

11. Apology must be made for the slightly staccato style of writing for the descriptions of individual ski centres. Limitation of space makes this a necessity.

I. SKI RESORTS BETWEEN 7000 FT AND 6000 FT

Place	Altitude of Highest Point in Centre	Country	Altitude of Top Station (Projects in brackets)
1. TIGNES, LAC DE See p. 227 and Val d'Isère	6890 ft (2100 m.)	France	8944 ft (11,647 ft)
2. HOCHSÖLDEN See p. 155	6857 ft (2090 m.)	Austria	7874 ft
3. BREUIL-CERVINIA See p. 274 and Zermatt	6792 ft (2070 m.)	Italy	11,470 ft
4. KLEINE SCHEIDEGG See p. 342 and Grindelwald and Wengen	6772 ft (2064 m.)	Switzerland	8055 ft Jungfraujoch 11,332 ft
5. SESTRIERE See p. 282 and Turin area	6677 ft (2035 m.)	Italy	8861 ft
6. ALPE DI SIUSI See p. 298 and Val Gardena	6578 ft (2005 m.)	Italy	Short lifts only
7. PASSO ROLLE See p. 293 and S. Martino di Castrozza	6463 ft (1970 m.)	Italy	7234 ft
8. KÜHTAI See p. 157	6454 ft (1967 m.)	Austria	Short lifts only
9. MELCHSEE FRUTT See p. 337 and Engelberg	6299 ft (1920 m.)	Switzerland	7420 ft

10. OBERGURGL See p. 153	6266 ft (1910 m.)	Austria	8655 ft
11. VENT See p. 154	6221 ft (1896 m.)	Austria	Short lifts only
12. AROSA See p. 320	6200 ft (1890 m.)	Switzerland	8704 ft
13. ST MORITZ See p. 325 and Pontresina	6135 ft (1870 m.)	Switzerland	9941 ft (10,807 ft)
14. LIVIGNO See p. 286 and Bormio	6135 ft (1870 m.)	Italy	No lifts (7630 ft?)
15. ALPE D'HUEZ See p. 232	6102 ft (1860 m.)	France	8858 ft (10,990 ft)
16. MONTGENÈVRE See p. 237 and Claviere	6089 ft (1856 m.)	France	8498 ft
17. VAL D'ISÈRE See p. 225 and Tignes	6073 ft (1851 m.)	France	9350 ft (11,112 ft)
18. COURCHEVEL See p. 222 and Méribel	6070 ft (1850 m.)	France	8885 ft
19. ST MARTIN DE BELLEVILLE See p. 224 and Courchevel and Méribel	6000 ft? (not yet built)	France	No lifts (9210 ft)

II. SKI RESORTS BETWEEN 6000 FT AND 5000 FT

Place	Altitude of Highest Point in Centre	Country	Altitude of Top Station (Projects in brackets)
20. SILVAPLANA See p. 330	5955 ft	Switzerland	(10,807 ft)
21. PONTRESINA See p. 330 and St Moritz	5938 ft (1810 m.)	Switzerland	8032 ft Diavolezza 9754 ft
22. SAAS-FEE See p. 367	5873 ft (1790 m.)	Switzerland	9416 ft
23. ST CHRISTOPH-AM-ARLBERG See p. 144 and St Anton	5810 ft (1771 m.)	Austria	9222 ft
24. BIVIO See p. 328 and St Moritz	5803 ft (1769 m.)	Switzerland	7181 ft
25. TURRACHERHÖHE See p. 187	5784 ft (1763 m.)	Austria	6588 ft (7000 ft)
26. CLAVIERE See p. 280 and Montgenèvre	5774 ft (1760 m.)	Italy	6748 ft
27. OBERTAUERN See p. 185	5702 ft (1738 m.)	Austria	6529 ft (7218 ft)
28. CELERINA See p. 325 and St Moritz	5676 ft (1732 m.)	Switzerland	9514 ft

29. OBERLECH	5643 ft (1720 m.)	Austria	7119 ft
See p. 141 and Lech and Zürs			
30. ZÜRS	5630 ft (1716 m.)	Austria	7999 ft
See p. 139 and Lech			
31. MÉRIBEL-LES-ALLUES	5610 ft (1710 m.)	France	8885 ft
See p. 220 and Courchevel			
32. VALBERG	5570 ft (1702 m.)	France	6270 ft
See p. 243			
33. LES DEUX ALPES	5446 ft (1660 m.)	France	8038 ft (9229 ft)
See p. 233			
34. TAUPLITZALM	5446 ft (1660 m.)	Austria	6434 ft
See p. 191 and Tauplitz-Klachau			
35. CHAMROUSSE	5413 ft (1650 m.)	France	7382 ft
See p. 231			
36. COLFOSCO	5397 ft (1645 m.)	Italy	7713 ft
See p. 302 and Corvara and Selva			
37. MÜRREN	5374 ft (1638 m.)	Switzerland	6956 ft (9500 ft?)
See p. 345 and Lauterbrunnen			
38. SELVA	5331 ft (1625 m.)	Italy	7713 ft
See p. 300 and Canazei			
39. ZERMATT	5316 ft (1620 m.)	Switzerland	11,175 ft
See p. 369 and Breuil-Cervinia			

Place	Altitude of Highest Point in Centre	Country	Altitude of Top Station (Projects in brackets)
40. AURON See p. 241	5282 ft (1610 m.)	France	7858 ft
41. PLAN See p. 301 and Selva and Canazei	5269 ft (1606 m.)	Italy	7349 ft
42. GALTÜR See p. 146 and Parthenen	5197 ft (1584 m.)	Austria	Short lifts only
43. CORVARA See p. 302 and Selva and Colfosco	5168 ft (1568 m.)	Italy	6339 ft
44. SAUZE D'OULX AND SPORTINIA See p. 277 and Sestriere	5135 ft (1565 m.)	Italy	8127 ft
45. MORIOND See p. 222 and Courchevel	5118 ft (1560 m.)	France	6800 ft
46. DAVOS DORF	5118 ft (1560 m.)	Switzerland	9262 ft } See p. 317
47. DAVOS PLATZ	5052 ft (1540 m.)	Switzerland	8497 ft } and Klosters
48. VERBIER See p. 364	5010 ft (1527 m.)	Switzerland	9918 ft (10,919 ft)
49. VALTOURNANCHE See p. 275 and Breuil-Cervinia	5000 ft (1524 m.)	Italy	5984 ft

III. SKI RESORTS BETWEEN 5000 FT AND 4000 FT

50. MADONNA DI CAMPIGLIO See p. 290	4993 ft (1522 m.)	Italy	6850 ft
51. HINTERTUX See p. 171 and Mayrhofen	4875 ft (1486 m.)	Austria	Short lift only
52. SAN MARTINO DI CASTROZZA See p. 293 and Passo Rolle	4856 ft (1480 m.)	Italy	7234 ft (7808 ft) Also Rosetta, 8537 ft
53. ENZINGERBODEN-WEISS-SEE See p. 179 and Lienz	4856 ft (1480 m.)	Austria	7605 ft
54. LENZERHEIDE (including VALBELLA and PARPAN) See p. 322	4840 ft (1476 m.)	Switzerland	8268 ft (8530 ft)
55. CRANS–MONTANA See p. 366	4823 ft (1470 m.)	Switzerland	8297 ft
56. CANAZEI See p. 294 and Campitello and Selva	4807 ft (1465 m.)	Italy	7677 ft (Marmolada 11,021 ft)
57. ARGENTIÈRE–LE TOUR See p. 214 and Chamonix	4790 ft (1460 m.)	France	7234 ft (10,827 ft)
58. LEYSIN See p. 361	4757 ft (1450 m.)	Switzerland	6683 ft (7085 ft)

Place	Altitude of Highest Point in Centre	Country	Altitude of Top Station (Projects in brackets)
59. CAMPITELLO See p. 294 and Canazei	4751 ft (1448 m.)	Italy	7828 ft
60. ANDERMATT See p. 337	4747 ft (1447 m.)	Switzerland	7700 ft (9700 ft)
61. LECH See p. 141 and Oberlech and Zürs	4744 ft (1446 m.)	Austria	7664 ft
62. COL DES MOSSES See p. 357 and Château d'Oex	4741 ft (1445 m.)	Switzerland	6140 ft
63. DAMÜLS See p. 137	4720 ft (1439 m.)	Austria	5320 ft
64. GARGELLEN See p. 136 and Montafon	4692 ft (1430 m.)	Austria	5604 ft (7218 ft)
65. VALLOIRE See p. 216	4692 ft (1430 m.)	France	7612 ft (10,600 ft)
66. SANTA CRISTINA See p. 299 and Selva	4682 ft (1427 m.)	Italy	6745 ft
67. SERFAUS See p. 147	4682 ft (1427 m.)	Austria	6601 ft (9843 ft)
68. PRALOGNAN See p. 218 and Courchevel	4626 ft (1410 m.)	France	7365 ft (7500 ft and other distant projects)
69. STUBEN See p. 138 and St Anton, Zürs, and Lech	4616 ft (1407 m.)	Austria	7756 ft (8297 ft)

				Short lifts only (Plus projects)

70. SEDRUN	4606 ft (1404 m.)	Switzerland	7808 ft
See p. 324 and Andermatt			
71. VILLENEUVE	4528 ft (1380 m.)	France	No lifts (7582 ft)
See p. 236 and Serre-Chevalier			
72. ISCHGL	4518 ft (1377 m.)	Austria	7014 ft
See p. 145			
73. BARCELONNETTE–LE SAUZE	4495 ft (1370 m.)	France	
See p. 239			
74. CESANA	4455 ft (1358 m.)	Italy	7336 ft
See p. 281 and Claviere and Sestriere			
75. ADELBODEN	4439 ft (1353 m.)	Switzerland	7326 ft
See p. 347 and Lenk			
76. MORGINS	4439 ft (1353 m.)	Switzerland	5589 ft (6500 ft approx.)
See p. 364 and Champéry			
77. SÖLDEN	4436 ft (1352 m.)	Austria	7874 ft
See p. 155 and Hochsölden			
78. SERRE-CHEVALIER (CHANTEMERLE)	4429 ft (1350 m.)	France	8137 ft
See p. 236 and Villeneuve			
79. MONTE BONDONE	4429 ft (1350 m.)	Italy	6877 ft
See p. 291			

Place	Altitude of Highest Point in Centre	Country	Altitude of Top Station (Projects in brackets)
80. HEILIGENBLUT See p. 187	4426 ft (1288 m.)	Austria	Small lifts only (6759 ft)
81. BERWANG See p. 150 and Reutte and Ehrwald	4383 ft (1336 m.)	Austria	5000 ft (5479 ft)
82. MACUGNAGA See p. 276	4354 ft (1327 m.)	Italy	6339 ft
83. BARDONECCHIA See p. 278	4305 ft (1312 m.)	Italy	8071 ft (9137 ft)
84. ST ANTON-AM-ARLBERG See p. 142 and St Christoph, Stuben, Zürs, etc.	4219 ft (1286 m.)	Austria	9222 ft
85. LANERSBACH See p. 171 and Mayrhofen	4219 ft (1286 m.)	Austria	Small lifts only
86. WENGEN See p. 343 and Kleine Scheidegg	4180 ft (1274 m.)	Switzerland	8055 ft Jungfraujoch 11,332 ft
87. CORTINA D'AMPEZZO See p. 306	4173 ft (1272 m.)	Italy	9836 ft
88. SAANENMÖSER (SCHÖNRIED) See p. 352 and Gstaad and Zweisimmen	4170 ft (1271 m.)	Switzerland	6303 ft

89. PONTE DI LEGNO	4127 ft (1258m.)	Italy	7874 ft
See p. 289			
90. BRAUNWALD	4115 ft (1254 m.)	Switzerland	6247 ft (6700 ft)
See p. 334			
91. VILLARS	4111 ft (1253 m.)	Switzerland	6890 ft
See p. 359 and Barboleusaz			
92. GERLOS	4098 ft (1249 m.)	Austria	Short lift only (Projects)
See p. 169 and Alpbach			
93. ORTISEI	4055 ft (1236 m.)	Italy	6578 ft (8260 ft)
See p. 297 and Alpe di Siusi and Selva			
94. COURMAYEUR	4016 ft (1224 m.)	Italy	7399 ft (9186 ft), also Col du Géant 11,254 ft
See p. 270 and Chamonix			

IV. SKI RESORTS BETWEEN 4000 FT AND 3000 FT

95. BORMIO	3993 ft (1217 m.)	Italy	7890 ft
See p. 286 and Livigno			
96. BARBOLEUSAZ	3973 ft (1211 m.)	Switzerland	6628 ft
See p. 359 and Villars			
97. MALLNITZ	3931 ft (1198 m.)	Austria	6109 ft (8550 ft)
See p. 186 and Bad Gastein			
98. KLOSTERS	3908 ft (1191 m.)	Switzerland	7992 ft (8737 ft)
See p. 319 and Davos Dorf and Platz			

Place	Altitude of Highest Point in Centre	Country	Altitude of Top Station (Projects in brackets)
99. SEEFELD See p. 164 and Mittenwald	3872 ft (1180 m.)	Austria	6890 ft
100. KANDERSTEG See p. 346	3858 ft (1176 m.)	Switzerland	5988 ft
101. AIROLO See p. 339	3855 ft (1175 m.)	Switzerland	(6775 ft)
102. GRIES-AM-BRENNER See p. 163 and Steinach and Colle Isarco	3822 ft (1165 m.)	Austria	Small lift only (6913 ft)
103. LES CONTAMINES See p. 208 and St Gervais	3819 ft (1164 m.)	France	7218 ft
104. LES GETS See p. 202 and Morzine	3816 ft (1163 m.)	France	5900 ft
105. LES DIABLERETS See p. 358 and Gstaad	3780 ft (1152 m.)	Switzerland	6234 ft (6814 ft) (Also 9748 ft)
106. HINDELANG AND BAD OBERDORF See p. 253	3773 ft (1150 m.)	Germany	5085 ft
107. NOTRE DAME DE BELLECOMBE See p. 229	3720 ft (1134 m.)	France	5906 ft

108. BAD GASTEIN	3707 ft (1130 m.)	Austria	7323 ft
	See p. 182 and Mallnitz and Bad Hofgastein		
109. MEGÈVE	3652 ft (1113 m.)	France	6421 ft (6562 ft)
	See p. 205 and St Gervais		
110. WILDHAUS	3600 ft (1100 m.)	Switzerland	5518 ft
	See p. 332 and Unterwasser and Alt St Johann		
111. SCHLIERSEE–NEUHAUS	3600 ft (1100 m.)	Germany	4856 ft
(SPITZINGSEE)			
	See p. 257		
112. COLLE ISARCO	3599 ft (1097 m.)	Italy	6234 ft
	See p. 304 and Steinach and Gries		
113. FLIMS	3543 ft (1080 m.)	Switzerland	8858 ft
	See p. 323		
114. LENK	3504 ft (1068 m.)	Switzerland	6400 ft
	See p. 349 and Zweisimmen and Adelboden		
115. GRINDELWALD	3500 ft (1067 m.)	Switzerland	8055 ft
	See p. 341 and Scheidegg and Wengen		Also Jungfraujoch 11,332 ft
116. CHAMPÉRY	3491 ft (1064 m.)	Switzerland	6378 ft
	See p. 363 and Morzine and Morgins		
117. GSTAAD	3450 ft (1052 m.)	Switzerland	6375 ft (9748 ft)
	See p. 354 and Zweisimmen, Saanenmöser, Château d'Oex, Les Diablerets, etc.		

Place	Altitude of Highest Point in Centre	Country	Altitude of Top Station (Projects in brackets)
118. STEINACH-AM-BRENNER	3438 ft (1048 m.)	Austria	5414 ft (6890 ft)
See p. 162 and Gries and Colle Isarco			
119. CHAMONIX	3422 ft (1043 m.)	France	8284 ft and Aig. du Midi 12,474 ft
See p. 211 and Courmayeur, Les Houches, and Argentière–Le Tour			
120. ST CERGUE	3422 ft (1043 m.)	Switzerland	4400 ft
See p. 362			
121. PARTHENEN	3369 ft (1027 m.)	Austria	5742 ft
See p. 135 and Silvretta			
122. MORZINE	3320 ft (1012 m.)	France	5906 ft (7200 ft)
See p. 201 and Les Gets and Champéry			
123. LIMONE PIEMONTE	3314 ft (1010 m.)	Italy	6757 ft
See p. 285			
124. SAALBACH	3291 ft (1003 m.)	Austria	5312 ft (6621 ft)
See p. 180 and Zell-am-See			
125. LES HOUCHES	3281 ft (1000 m.)	France	6070 ft
See p. 210 and Chamonix and St Gervais			
126. ENGELBERG	3281 ft (1000 m.)	Switzerland	7261 ft
See p. 335 and Melchsee-Frutt			

No.	Resort	Altitude	Country	Top
127.	EHRWALD	3268 ft (996 m.)	Austria	4167 ft (6234 ft) Also Zugspitze 9252 ft
	See p. 149 and Lermoos and Garmisch-Partenkirchen			
128.	LERMOOS	3264 ft (995 m.)	Austria	6950 ft Also Zugspitze 9252 ft
	See p. 148 and Ehrwald			
129.	ROUGEMONT	3264 ft (995 m.)	Switzerland	7087 ft
	See p. 355 and Gstaad and Château d'Oex			
130.	GASCHURN	3215 ft (980 m.)	Austria	4869 ft (6400 ft)
	See p. 134 and Schruns			
131.	ALPBACH	3192 ft (973 m.)	Austria	Short lifts only (chairlift project)
	See p. 168 and Wildschönau			
132.	CHÂTEAU D'OEX	3182 ft (970 m.)	Switzerland	5739 ft (5915 ft)
	See p. 356 and Col des Mosses, Rougemont, etc.			
133.	ZWEISIMMEN	3087 ft (941 m.)	Switzerland	6588 ft
	See p. 352 and Lenk, Saanenmöser, and Gstaad			
134.	OBERAU	3071 ft (936 m.)	Austria	4058 ft
	See p. 166 and Niederau			
135.	MITTENWALD	3018 ft (920 m.)	Germany	4528 ft (7220 ft)
	See p. 255 and Seefeld			

v. SKI RESORTS BETWEEN 3000 FT AND 2000 FT

No.	Resort	Altitude	Country	Top
136.	UNTERWASSER	2973 ft (906 m.)	Switzerland	5518 ft
	See p. 332 and Wildhaus			

Place	Altitude of Highest Point in Centre	Country	Altitude of Top Station (Projects in brackets)
137. TAUPLITZ–KLACHAU See p. 191 and Tauplitzalm	2923 ft (891 m.)	Austria	6434 ft
138. ALT ST JOHANN See p. 332 and Unterwasser	2920 ft (890 m.)	Switzerland	4760 ft approx.
139. AUFFACH See p. 166 and Oberau and Niederau	2871 ft (875 m.)	Austria	Short lift only
140. IGLS See p. 160 and Innsbruck	2854 ft (870 m.)	Austria	6404 ft (7375 ft)
141. BAD HOFGASTEIN See p. 184 and Bad Gastein	2815 ft (858 m.)	Austria	6447 ft
142. REUTTE See p. 151 and Berwang	2802 ft (854 m.)	Austria	6299 ft
143. OBERSTDORF (and KLEINES WALSERTAL) See p. 252	2766 ft (843 m.)	Germany	6824 ft
144. KIRCHBERG See p. 174 and Kitzbühel	2749 ft (838 m.)	Austria	5290 ft (6667 ft)
145. MUTTERS See p. 161 and Innsbruck	2723 ft (830 m.)	Austria	5279 ft (6000 ft)

146. NIEDERAU See p. 166 and Oberau	2700 ft (823 m.)	Austria	4692 ft	
147. ST GERVAIS See p. 207 and Megève, Les Houches, and Les Contamines	2648 ft (807 m.)	France	6014 ft	
148. LAUTERBRUNNEN (STECHELBERG) See p. 344 and Mürren, Wengen, and Scheidegg	2612 ft (796 m.)	Switzerland	8055 ft (9500 ft?) also Jungfraujoch	
149. KAPRUN See p. 179 and Zell-am-See	2579 ft (786 m.)	Austria	5069 ft	
150. WESTENDORF See p. 176 and Kirchberg	2576 ft (785 m.)	Austria	5168 ft	
151. KITZBÜHEL See p. 173	2503 ft (763 m.)	Austria	6440 ft	
152. TEGERNSEE (ROTTACH-EGERN) See p. 256	2487 ft (758 m.)	Germany	5577 ft	
153. ZELL-AM-SEE See p. 178 and Saalbach	2487 ft (758 m.)	Austria	6444 ft	
154. CHIOMONTE See p. 277	2444 ft (745 m.)	Italy	6873 ft	
155. GARMISCH-PARTENKIRCHEN See p. 254 and Ehrwald	2362 ft (720 m.)	Germany	5791 ft Also Zugspitze 9383 ft	

Place	Altitude of Highest Point in Centre	Country	Altitude of Top Station (Projects in brackets)
156. SAMOËNS and ARACHES See p. 203	2329 ft (710 m.)	France	6930 ft (8450 ft)
157. SCHRUNS See p. 132 and Tschagguns	2261 ft (689 m.)	Austria	6224 ft (7819 ft)
158. TSCHAGGUNS See p. 133 and Schruns	2244 ft (684 m.)	Austria	6224 ft (6880 ft)
159. LIENZ See p. 189 and Weiss-See	2208 ft (673 m.)	Austria	7260 ft
160. ST JOHANN-IN-TYROL See p. 175 and Kitzbühel	2165 ft (660 m.)	Austria	5210 ft
161. MAYRHOFEN See p. 170 and Hintertux	2060 ft (628 m.)	Austria	6611 ft
162. HOPFGARTEN See p. 176 and Westendorf	2041 ft (622 m.)	Austria	5026 ft (6001 ft)
VI. SKI RESORTS BELOW 2000 FT			
163. INNSBRUCK See p. 159 and Igls and Mutters	1903 ft (689 m.)	Austria	7402 ft
164. SCHWAZ See p. 161 and Innsbruck	1765 ft (538 m.)	Austria	6168 ft

165. WANGSPIZOL (BAD RAGAZ) See p. 333
166. BERCHTESGADEN See p. 258
167. OBERTRAUN–HALLSTATT (DACHSTEIN) See p. 192
168. BAD REICHENHALL See p. 257

165. WANGSPIZOL (BAD RAGAZ)	1755 ft (535 m.)	Switzerland	7284 ft
166. BERCHTESGADEN	1739 ft (530 m.)	Germany	5906 ft
167. OBERTRAUN–HALLSTATT (DACHSTEIN)	1677 ft (511 m.)	Austria	6821 ft (9160 ft)
168. BAD REICHENHALL	1542 ft (470 m.)	Germany	5548 ft

Of the selected ski resorts of the Alps listed above, the breakdown into countries and altitude groups works out as follows:

	AUSTRIA	FRANCE	GERMANY	ITALY	SWITZERLAND	TOTALS
Above 6000 ft	4	6	0	5	4	19
6000–5000 ft	7	6	0	7	10	30
5000–4000 ft	14	6	0	13	12	45
4000–3000 ft	12	7	3	3	16	41
3000–2000 ft	18	2	3	1	3	27
Below 2000 ft	3	0	2	0	1	6
Totals	58	27	8	29	46	168

Mention of various ski centres not listed above may be found by reference to the Index

THREE

Austrian Ski Centres

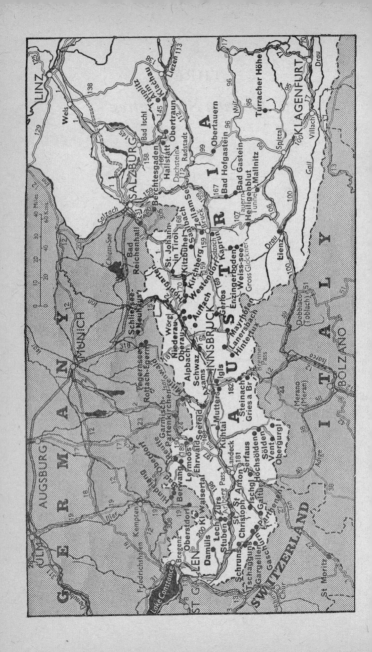

CONTENTS

THE INNSBRUCK AREA — TYROL

THE WILDSCHÖNAU AREA — TYROL

THE ZILLERTAL AREA — TYROL

THE KITZBÜHEL AREA — TYROL

THE PINZGAU AND HOHE TAUERN AREA — SALZBURG

THE GASTEINERTAL AND RADSTÄDTER TAUERN AREAS — SALZBURG

CONTENTS

INTRODUCTION

ANY national booklet advertising the ski resorts of this highly popular Alpine country will indicate a vast number of centres – well over two hundred maybe. In one sense this is quite correct and in another not. There are very few places in Austria where one cannot ski, and few Austrians who do not ski. More than any other nation, regardless of class or pocket, the Austrian people love ski-ing, and the inevitable pairs of ski that you will find in every garage, back yard, front hall, or cupboard are used by every age group. The Austrian scarcely has to 'go' ski-ing. He skis wherever he is and whenever there is snow, for practically speaking every town and village has its own ski fields close to its own doorstep. It is for this reason that the standard of ski-ing, both with the masses and in the ski schools and the élite racing groups, is universally very high.

On the other hand many of the villages listed as ski centres scarcely live up to the standards expected by foreign visitors. At least two-thirds of a full Austrian list will only serve for weekend or day ski visitors, or as a base for ski-touring expeditions. The remaining third however is very large. There are, for example, some sixty ski centres listed in this book – as opposed to Switzerland's forty and France and Italy's thirty each. Of these, approximately one dozen are either large, or popular, thriving, international centres – and among these there are the famous names, such as St Anton, Zürs, Kitzbühel, and one or two others, where the ski-ing can rival the best of any other part of the Alps. Even in the bigger centres you will very seldom find the large architecture of the 'Palace'-type hotel (Bad Gastein is an exception) for few of these Austrian ski centres have ever been other than naturally formed small towns and mountain villages which have happened to cater, almost casually, for summer visitors. Most of the large buildings of this nature, for either tourist or health visitors, were built some time ago, south of the main Alpine barrier in Süd Tyrol, which now – sadly for the Austrian – lies in Italy.

Thus most of the ski centres in Austria consist of medium- and small-sized hotel buildings – inns rather than hotels – grafted on to, or in to, workaday mountain and valley villages and even towns. A few places, such as Hochsölden, Zürs, etc., have been specially created as ski centres. There is, to a degree, a sense of sharing life with a local community when you stay in many an Austrian village centre.

The standard of living in Austria is not so high as that of Switzerland (or for that matter of France – it is similar in some respects to that of Italy) and the cost of a holiday is, save in the big international centres, generally cheaper. The currency is not so strong as the Swiss Franc and salaries are lower. Add to this the fact that many a modern hotel and many a lift system has been heavily subsidized since the last war by American aid.

All of this tends to make for economical winter-sports holidays in extremely pleasant surroundings. The traditional regional architectural styles, which are colourful, cosy, and gay, have been faithfully perpetuated in most modern hotel and 'chalet type' building.

In considering the 'atmosphere' of an Austrian ski centre, consider for a moment the character of the Austrian himself. He has little of his Teutonic cousin's efficiency and fixity of purpose, and almost none of his military regimentation. The Austrian is to the Swiss as the lightweight boxer is to the heavyweight – as the willow is to the oak. Steadier and less temperamental than the Italian, he has, nevertheless, rather more than the fleeting understanding of the spontaneity of the Latin mentality than one might expect. The average Austrian is a disarming person capable of charming the birds off the trees. He is gay and informal. No business man on paper, he likes to accept any excuse to escape from his desk or office, but, increasingly in these last years, he has learned to charge and mind the pennies. He loves music and he loves to dance. He demands little of life and does not expect to subscribe much in return. He is, so to speak, 'impromptu' – delightful; willing; able when it pays to be able and lazy when it doesn't; and, taken all round, he is delightfully but sometimes maddeningly unpredictable.

Apply these characteristics to an average Austrian ski centre and you have some of the answers. You will find friendliness and gaiety that is seldom over-organized. You will find comfort that is simple rather than sophisticated. You will find food that is adequate but never inspired – and, all too frequently, stodgy and just plain dull. There is about an Austrian village a happy-go-lucky air, and an enthusiasm for the enjoyment of the moment, which goes ill with dull routine and well with carefree holidays.

The Austrian loves his mountains – even more for themselves than for their commercial possibilities. Although there are in this country many hundreds of ski-lifts, large numbers of Austrians are just as happy and as adept at ski-touring and 'ski-wandering' as they are at the modern mechanical downhill-only game. The country is admirably suited to both forms of sport. In consequence, whereas you will find the well-equipped expensive forms of *téléférique* in the big centres, many of the lesser villages are only equipped with small inexpensive lift systems, and some with barely any transport at all. Rather too many of these small lift systems are slow, open, and cold, but provided the liftman does not himself want to go ski-ing they usually work.

The Austrian ski school organization is remarkable, but perhaps not quite so universally thorough as the Swiss. In character with all things Austrian, it reaches high points and low points. In places like St Anton, Kitzbühel, and other highly developed and mechanized centres, the teaching is inspired, and not to be paralleled anywhere. In many of the smaller places the tuition is more lackadaisical. High point or low point, however, the Austrian ski teacher always makes his lesson fun. *

* For more comprehensive information and fullest details of all the Austrian ski centres, the reader is referred to *The Ski Runs of Austria* published by Michael Joseph Ltd.

THE MONTAFON–SILVRETTA AREA

A REWARDING, but relatively little publicized, area containing five ski centres: Schruns and Tschagguns, which are
adjoining; Gaschurn and Parthenen further up the valley; and
Gargellen, considerably higher to the south-west of the main
valley. Easily accessible, this 'Alpenpark' valley lies close to
the Swiss–Austrian frontier. Mainly low in altitude, and well
wooded, it provides a good variety of *piste* ski-ing, with adequate ski transport (and more to come). It is better known,
perhaps, as the main entry from the Vorarlberg side up into
the lovely ski-touring and ski-mountaineering regions of the
Silvretta and Rätikon Mountains on its south and west sides,
and the Verwall group to the east. The Montafon is separated
from the Davos–Klosters area by the former, and all these
mountain groups, which are amply provided with fine huts,
are immensely popular in springtime. (A car is an asset in the
Montafon valley, but bus services connect all five centres and
link with Bludenz.)

*Centre 157**		Altitude
SCHRUNS	Province: Vorarlberg	2261 ft

Description. 2300 inhabitants, 13 hotels and pensions with 386
beds. Other accommodation, 350 beds. Language German –
very little English spoken.

Very attractive, low-altitude, large village on the Ill River,
busy with its own affairs, unsophisticated and unspoilt, situated
on sunny side of wide section of attractive Montafon Valley
directly next to Tschagguns. No over-large hotels. Buildings
decorative and suitably modernized, maintaining typically
Austrian style. Pleasant valley scenery with fine views of Silvretta and Rätikon ranges from top of lifts.

Ski facilities. One ski area served by one main chairlift system going up eastwards in two sections to 6224 ft. Ski areas also

* Each place description is numbered according to the Altitude List,
pp. 104–21.

at Tschagguns, 1 km. distant. Baby lifts on village nursery slopes and at top station.

The Hochjoch ski area gives runs of 4 to 6 km. and 3800 ft descent. Small open gentle playground at top, with restaurants. Densely wooded upper section with two well-designed, beautiful, cleared glade *pistes*. Meadow slopes lower section. Steep in places, but with suitable *pistes* for beginners throughout. Slopes range from south-west-facing, through west round to north.

Ski touring. Negligible in immediate vicinity. Short climbs possible above present lift system. Good touring at neighbouring Tschagguns. See General Comments.

Amenities. Ski teachers. Skating rink. Good shopping centre. Three sports shops for equipment, etc. Cinema. Dance bars.

Life in centre. Gentle friendly village life. Costs moderate. Extras cheap. Food national, unpretentious but good. Few or no English guests. Nightlife restricted to simple holiday fun in small hotels and dance bars, etc.

Specialities. Well-known health resort. Mineral waters, baths treatment, sauna, etc. Good walks for non-skiers in and around valley. Locally made furniture. Celebrated dairy cattle.

Accessibility. Train: 40 mins. Bludenz (main Arlberg Express halt). Road: 30 mins. bus Bludenz. Good road, always open. Airport: Zürich.

General comments. Well worth short visit. Easy access Tschagguns provides variety. Ideal if car-borne for daily visits to Gargellen, Gaschurn, Parthenen, all of which are entry points for widespread and wonderful ski touring in the Silvretta, Rätikon, and Verwall mountains. (Projected lift from present system to 7819 ft will provide 5558 ft of descent.) Good for family parties and groups of modest performers.

Centre 158   Altitude
TSCHAGGUNS   Province: Vorarlberg   2244 ft

Description. 1700 inhabitants. 5 hotels and 2 pensions with 238 beds. Other accommodation 200 beds. Language German, almost exclusively. Immediate neighbour of Schruns. Smaller. Basically simple, but with addition of big hydro-electric works which do not assist upper scenery but which provide main lift system.

Ski facilities. Two adjoining ski areas served by two lift systems.

(1) *The Hochegga Area.* Two-section (chair then ski) lift, giving rise of 2759 ft up to 5167 ft. Capable of further development. Runs of between $3\frac{1}{2}$ and $5\frac{1}{2}$ km., mostly on northish-facing slopes. Easy, fast, open fields with clumps of woodlands.

(2) *The Golm Area.* Two-section – bus to 3258 ft then open funicular to 6224 ft, giving total rise of 3980 ft. Ski lift will continue to 6880 ft. One main splendid and variable run – the Golm Abfahrt – mainly on north-east slopes, of between 7 to 8 km. Good beginner fields at bottom.

Ski touring. Excellent entry points from top of both transport systems into widespread touring of Rätikon and Silvretta regions.

Amenities. Modestly equipped but sharing those of Schruns. For remainder of description, see Schruns (p. 132). The ski-ing and the general life of both Schruns and Tschagguns can be shared by a visitor staying at either centre, but the average guest will probably prefer to be based in Schruns.

Centre 130   Altitude
GASCHURN   Province: Vorarlberg   3215 ft

Description. 1000 inhabitants in area. 1 hotel and 3 inns providing 150 beds. Other accommodation 140 beds. Language German.

A small, picturesque, and genuine village. Comfortable, traditional hotel amid pleasant surroundings. Sunny situation. Sheltered. Little known, unpretentious, and peaceful.

Ski facilities. One medium to small ski area served by ski-lift giving rise of 1581 ft up to 4869 ft. Excellent little selection of amusing and good ski runs, mostly on open east-facing slopes, of between 2 and 3 km.

Given the finance, much upward development could be achieved, but for the moment the good ski-ing of the Gantekopf has to be gained by climbs of $2-2\frac{1}{2}$ hrs.

Ski touring. All the splendid Silvretta–Rätikon and Verwall mountain groups easily accessible nearby. See also Parthenen, 7 km. distant.

Amenities. Ski teachers available. Small rink. Village shops only. All Schruns and Tschagguns amenities available by bus (12 km).

Life in centre. Village life. Unhurried and gentle. Hotel and small bar dancing. Inexpensive.

Accessibility. Post-bus from Bludenz (1 hr 20 mins.) on main Arlberg line. Airport: Zürich.

General Comments. Not for the 'Ski-tiger' or the international set, but ideal for small parties who like a quiet life, and for easy going parents with energetic small children.

Centre 121	Altitude
PARTHENEN Province: Vorarlberg	3369 ft

Description. 600 inhabitants. 5 inns providing 350 beds. Other accommodation 250 beds. Language German only.

A strange, plain little village, somewhat overpowered by big hydro-electric works. Deep valley situation at head of Montafon, at the start point of the Silvretta High Alpine Road (closed in winter). Simple but scarcely picturesque.

Ski facilities. One ski area served by hydro-electric works funicular giving rise of 2297 ft up to 5742 ft. One main run, carved out of heavily timbered steep hillside, approx. $2\frac{1}{2}$ km. long. Ski-lift at bottom for beginners.

Longer run available (5–6 km.) from end of tunnel (see below) down route of the Silvretta High Alpine Road.

Ski touring. Direct access on foot from top of funicular via initial 2-km.-long tunnel and galleries, to open slopes leading up to the Silvretta Hotel (6667 ft) which lies in the heart of the Silvretta ski-touring area. Almost endless choice of ski touring and ski mountaineering.

Amenities. Ski teachers. Small rink. Village shops.

Life in centre. Small valley village life intertwined with hydro-electric works activities. Inexpensive living. Little excitement.

Accessibility. Post-bus from Bludenz (1 hr 35 mins.) on main Arlberg line. Airport: Zürich.

General comments. Of interest for a week-end or day visit, but mainly recommended as a base for ski touring. Even better base is the 'upstairs satellite' of the Silvretta Hotel at Bielerhöhe.

Centre 64   Altitude
GARGELLEN   Province: Vorarlberg   4692 ft

Description. 80 inhabitants. 6 hotels with 310 beds. Other accommodation 90 beds. Language German – some English spoken.

Very charming, popular, picturesque, and peaceful small resort. Beautifully situated near top of sunny valley surrounded by pleasant mountain scenery. Little car traffic. Activity revolves round ski-ing without much local village life. High, pleasantly remote, reliable for snow. Medium and small chalet-type hotels. Friendly atmosphere. Efficiently run.

Ski facilities. Mainly touring. One chairlift. Baby lift on nursery slopes.

Present short chairlift allows for two or three modest but good descents of between 1 and 2 km. and 912 ft. Local ski mountain, the Schafberg, requires 1½-hours climb from top station. (Projected lift here will go up to 7218 ft.) Excellent, safe, open snow slopes.

Ski touring. Wide selection of very good short and long ski tours including expeditions over into Switzerland and throughout Rätikon and renowned Silvretta mountains.

Amenities. Ski school. Guides. Visitor races. Two sports shops for equipment, etc. Dance bars.

Life in centre. Simple ski-holiday-resort atmosphere. No glamour. Medium prices. Nightlife modest and what you make it, with hotel dance band and several dance bars. Lone skiers will quickly make friends.

Specialities. Unique instructional ski school organization to encourage touring.

Accessibility. Train: nearest station Schruns (23 km.).

Road: bus 45 mins. Schruns, $1\frac{1}{2}$ hrs Bludenz. Small steepish road kept open. Chains advisable. Airport: Zürich.

General comments. Main emphasis on all grades of ski touring. Little joy for standard '*piste*-tigers'. Good for beginners and for all who seek natural ski-ing without a welter of lifts.

VORARLBERG

Centre 63	Altitude
DAMÜLS Province: Vorarlberg	4720 ft

Description. 4 hotel/pensions giving 145 beds. Other accommodation 185 beds. Language German.

A small settlement of buildings surrounded by scattered chalets, set on a small ridge amid sunny and pleasant scenery. Very small and new to ski-ing, but adequate for learner skiers.

Three small lifts (maximum rise 600 ft) allow for open easy ski-ing on both north- and south-facing slopes. Small ski school. Small village shops.

Quiet existence. No frills. Nothing for the proficient skiers; but safe, suitable, and inexpensive for the *ab initio* beginner.

Accessibility. Bus: 3 hrs Feldkirch.

THE ARLBERG AREA

THIS is certainly one of the premier and probably the best of the Austrian ski regions. The ski-ing to be found here can rival the best in any Alpine country. It consists of half a dozen ski centres, all of which are rightly well known, clustered round the Arlberg and Flexen Pass roads. Of these, Stuben, Zürs, Lech, and Oberlech are in the Vorarlberg, and St Christoph and St Anton in the Tyrol. All these centres have their own characteristics and each embraces a wide variety of ski terrain. The distinctive feature is that all these varied ski areas are sufficiently close to abut on one another and form an interlinking circuit – a gigantic five-ring circus in fact – and a visitor to one can sample the ski-ing of all. Some twenty-five major uphill transport lifts (with more to come) serve the whole region and act as trapezes to move from one area to another. Bus and small taxi services also allow easy intercommunication. A car is a great asset, but not a necessity.

The stations of Langen and St Anton, one on each side of the Arlberg tunnel, serve all centres and the whole is easily and speedily accessible from either east or west on the famous Arlberg Express, or over the passes by road.

Centre 69   Altitude
STUBEN   Province: Vorarlberg   4616 ft

Description. 70 inhabitants. 3 hotels with 145 beds. Other accommodation 105 beds. Language German – some English spoken.

A charming old village, crouching under steep surrounding mountainsides at western foot of Arlberg Pass, not enhanced by heavy main-road traffic through narrow village street. Small, compact, and friendly, it can boast of superb ski-ing but of none of the frivolities of more developed resorts. Hotels traditional, simple, and comfortable. Prices moderate. Valley unimpressive and frequently shaded. For fine views and sunshine go to the top of the lift system.

Ski facilities. One large ski area served by one main chairlift system in two sections giving a total rise of 3133 ft and a fine selection of north-facing runs of from 3¾ to 8 km. (to Langen). One medium ski-lift on sunny nursery slopes by village.

The Albona chairlift system was a bold conception. Cold travel in winter but lovely in springtime, this long open chair-lift (21 mins.) has opened up superb steep ski country for the competent skier. The area, mostly above the tree line, is indivi-dualistic, specialized, and unusual, suited mainly to solid technique, and capable of producing dangerous conditions off the marked runs. Beginners will be neither happy nor capable of coping, moderate skiers impressed and often exhausted, good skiers delighted.

Ski touring. 45-mins. climb to Maroikopf (8297 ft). Projected lift up this from Albonagrat. Easy access (2½-hrs climb) into the Kaltenberg ski-touring area.

Amenities. Ski teachers. One small sports shop. One dance bar.

Life in centre. Glamour absent. Simple traditional Austrian inn life with little local activity.

Specialities. Excellent spring ski-ing. Latest season in whole Arlberg area.

Accessibility. Train: nearest station Langen (3 km.), Arlberg Express halt. Road: bus 10 mins. Langen. Main road Inns-bruck 112 km. Zürich 168 km. Airport: Zürich.

General comments. Easy bus or car access to Zürs and Lech. Car, taxi, or train to St Anton. Daily ski potential in these places limitless. In general Stuben is at its best from mid-March till May.

Centre 30	Altitude
ZÜRS Province: Vorarlberg	5630 ft

Description. 60 inhabitants. 6 hotels and 2 pensions with 600 beds. Other accommodation 60 beds. Language German – most other continental languages spoken.

A collection of pleasant, comfortable, modern hotels built for ski visitors, and situated amid lovely snowfields in sunny open valley just over summit of Flexen Pass (5820 ft). Small, but not unattractive, this world-famous specialist centre, without any normal village life, is uniquely devoted to ski and *après-ski*. Sophisticated, gay, and on the expensive side, it is excellent value and rightly very popular. Advance booking essential. Visitors international, smart set included, but all active and keen skiers.

Ski facilities. Two ski areas served by two main lift systems. Other lifts, two; plus one project. Nursery lift one.

(1) *Hexenboden Area* (east side of valley). Ski-lift giving rise of 1818 ft and four main *pistes* of 2½ to 5 km.

(2) *Mahdlochjoch Area* (west side of valley). Two-section chairlift (middle station also reached by ski-lift) giving rise of 2369 ft and four main *pistes* of 3 to 5½ km. Top station at 7999 ft is start of ski link with Lech (6 km. and 3255 ft descent).

Splendid, compact ski-ing. Surprisingly wide variety of open treeless slopes suitable for all grades of skiers. Medium-sized local runs always return you home.

Ski touring. Good full-day ski expeditions above and behind both areas.

Amenities. Excellent ski school. Restricted but good shops. Sports shops. Hotel dancing and dance bars. First-class garage for 200 cars. S.C.G.B. representative.

Life in centre. Lively, gay, sophisticated nightlife both in hotels and dance bars.

Accessibility. Train: nearest station Langen (main Arlberg Express halt). Road: bus 35 mins. Langen up impressive Flexen Pass; occasionally closed by adverse conditions. Car chains advisable. Airport: Zürich.

General comments. Excellent place for young people to learn and enjoy ski-ing. The ski link with Lech makes the two places into one big circus and all the Lech ski-ing (see opposite) is easily reachable. Easy car access to Stuben and St Anton. Whole area much to be recommended.

Centre 61 and 29   Altitude
LECH   Province: Vorarlberg   4744 ft
OBERLECH   5643 ft

Description. Lech: 720 inhabitants. 6 hotels and 4 pensions with
500 beds. Other accommodation 720 beds. Language German
(adequate English). *Oberlech:* 48 inhabitants. 3 hotels and 1
pension with 192 beds. Other accommodation 70 beds.

A truly delightful, picturesque, and sunny workaday
Austrian village, astride the river Lech, which because of its
surroundings has developed into a thriving, friendly, and very
popular ski centre. Slightly less expensive than Zürs but by no
means cheap, Lech's hotels are of traditional style cleverly
designed for modern comfort, and bookings must be done in
advance. The upstairs annexe of Oberlech, reached by cable
car, sprawls on a sunny shelf. Surroundings are varied and
beautiful – the neighbouring ski fields can be seen from the
village and the mountains never overpower.

Ski facilities. Two ski areas served by two main lift systems.
Other lifts three (plus two projects) at Oberlech. Baby lifts two.

(1) *Kriegerhorn Area.* Two-section – ski-lift then chairlift-
system giving rise of 2411 ft and good selection of runs of $2\frac{1}{2}$
to 4 km. Several subsidiary lifts to, at, and above Oberlech.
Oberlech area for beginners. Kriegerhorn for all standards,
with south- and north-facing slopes. Unpisted descent, both
steep and gentle, to nearby village of Zug (return sleigh 3 km.).

(2) *Rüfikopf Area.* Cable car giving rise of 2940 ft provides
two difficult runs of approximately 4 km. back to Lech for good
runners, and the easy ski link run of 5 km. over to Zürs.
Access to lovely spring ski-ing area.

In general there is a fine selection of short varied runs. Little
woodrunning; few awkward places. Ideal for all grades,
specially for beginners, family groups, etc.

Ski touring. Good selection of uncomplicated and rewarding
short and long day excursions in immediate vicinity.

Amenities. Good ski school. Ice rink. Cinemas. Coffee houses.
Dance bars. Good shops. Sports shops. Pleasant valley walks
and sleigh rides. S.C.G.B. representative.

Life in centre. Friendly holiday atmosphere. Much gay activity by day, evening, and night. Easygoing, lively, and pleasantly sociable guests from all nations. Plenty of evening entertainment including special events.

Specialities. All round winter-sports-holiday activities.

Accessibility. Train: nearest station Langen (12 km.). Main Arlberg Express halt. Road: bus 50 mins. Langen, via Zürs. Car chains advisable. Airport: Zürich, 4 hrs train.

General comments. Much sought after and well recommended – with good winter and spring ski-ing, and excellent, well-organized facilities. Never a dull moment for the young and enterprising.

Centre 84
ST ANTON–AM–ARLBERG   Province: Tyrol   Altitude 4219 ft

Description. 1800 inhabitants. 10 hotels and 12 pensions, with 1100 beds. Other accommodation 900 beds. Language German – English and all continental languages widely spoken.

Famous in ski history, this fashionable centre is today a large straggling main-road village, of little individual charm, situated at eastern end of 10-km. main-line tunnel under Arlberg Pass. Architecture unimpressive; valley somewhat dull. Superb views from tops of lifts (good restaurants). Popular and populous, generally crowded owing to easy access (constant trains and countless cars and buses); devoted almost entirely to ski-ing.

Ski facilities. Three big adjoining ski areas served by separate, but interlinking, systems of cable-cars, chairlift, and ski-lifts. Total number of lifts, including St Christoph, four cable-cars, two chairlifts, and five ski-lifts (three projected lifts).

(1) *Gampen–Kapall Area.* Two-section chairlift giving rise of 3307 ft and runs of 4–5 km.

(2) *Galzig Area.* Cable-car giving 2529-ft descents and many runs of approximately 4 km. (See also St Christoph.)

(3) *Valluga Area.* Cable-car from Galzig giving 4353-ft

descents to St Anton, also to St Christoph, Stuben, and ski link with Zürs, all ranging from 8 to 9 km. in length.

The whole represents big, widespread, serious, and superb ski-ing of every kind. Slopes of all gradients from gentle to very steep, orientated to face all compass points, mostly open but some timbered, can be found and chosen as required. Immense linkage of *pistes* and lifts which can always return you to your doorstep. World-renowned ski country – and rightly so.

A project, which may be effected by 1963, consists of a cable-car system up the Gamberg directly facing St Anton village.

Ski touring. Not basically a touring area. Limitless variations for those who seek 'off-the-*piste*' ski-ing on a big scale – but beware of avalanche conditions.

Amenities. Probably best ski school in the world – catering for *every* class. Good nursery slopes. Ice rink. Cinema. Good selection of shops including specialists in sports clothes and ski boots. Hotel dancing. Coffee houses and dance bars. Sauna. Garages. S.C.G.B. representative.

Life in centre. International atmosphere. Village life largely overwhelmed by ski visitors ranging from the smart set to impecunious enthusiasts. Certain air of ski snobbery without much of its social counterpart. Accent throughout on active sport which is extremely well organized. *Après-ski* life suffers from overcrowding with insufficient restaurants and nightspots to cope with large percentage of bed-and-breakfast trade. Many small pensions allow for relatively inexpensive living in this expensive centre. Ski transport, being big and extensive, can be costly.

Specialities. Long, fast, and immensely varied *piste* running. Ski school emphasis on modern technique for medium, good, and expert skiers. Famous runs include the Arlberg–Kandahar race courses – old and new. Late season possible owing to upper lift linkage systems.

Accessibility. Train: main-line Arlberg Express $4\frac{1}{2}$ hrs Zürich, 1 hr 50 mins. Innsbruck. Road: Arlberg Pass (5892 ft) kept open (chains advisable). Train car ferry through tunnel if pass temporarily closed. Road access to St Christoph guaranteed. Airport: Zürich.

General comments. All that the knowledgeable skier dreams of. Ski standards extremely high. Visiting 'experts' quickly apt to be cut down to size. Sensible beginners should plan elsewhere and visit when properly able to appreciate. Important to obey notice boards which announce closure of runs due to avalanche possibilities.

Centre 23	Altitude
ST CHRISTOPH Province: Tyrol	5810 ft
—AM—ARLBERG	

Description. 35 inhabitants. 5 hotels with 300 beds. Language German – English spoken.

A picturesque little cluster of small modern hotels with restaurants and dance bars. Open, sunny situation, surrounded by good nursery slopes, close to summit of Arlberg Pass, 6 km. on main road up from St Anton with which it is closely integrated in every way. This medium-priced little centre, where snow is reliable, is crowded by day and gay in a self-contained simple way after ski-ing. It is excellent for beginners and for those who wish for the big St Anton ski-ing from a small base.

Ski facilities. Two ski areas served by two main lift systems. One baby lift.

(1) *Galzig Area.* Cable-car giving rise of 1352 ft providing local runs of 1½ to 3 km. This lift gives access to the entire St Anton ski country and lifts. Also served by ski-lifts.

(2) *Brunnenkopf–Peischlkopf Area.* Present ski-lift gives rise of 787 ft. Projected extension will continue up to Peischlkopf summit at 7914 ft. This fine area links with that of Stuben (see p. 138).

Amenities. For all other details, see St Anton (p. 142).

THE PAZNAUN–SILVRETTA AREA

The long Paznaun valley leads south-westwards from Land-eck right up to the Silvretta mountains. Here it curls round to the north to join the Montafon valley (see p. 132) passing close under the Austrian–Swiss frontier.

This Paznauntal, rather more primitive and wild than most Austrian valleys, has little to offer the modern up-and-down *piste* skier. The two centres, Ischgl and Galtür, in spite of a lift project in the former, are more for early beginners and for the proficient, who like to climb on skins and explore the untracked mountains. For these latter there is plenty to explore, and this valley, which is the main Tyrol entry into the Silvretta as well as the Verwall and Samnaun groups of mountains, is rightly very popular with ski-touring enthusiasts of all categories.

Centre 72   Altitude
ISCHGL   Province: Tyrol   4518 ft

Description. 800 inhabitants. 3 hotels and 5 inn pensions pro-viding 300 beds. Other accommodation 300 beds. Language German.

An unassuming, not unattractive, simple little valley village, surrounded by nursery slopes above which the mountainsides become steep and wooded and largely unsuited to ski-ing. Short trainer lifts on village slopes. Sunny sheltered place for beginners.

Projected *Luftseilbahn* (50 person cabins) up to Idalpe Plateau at 7546 ft should be finished by 1962. Mountain hotel here open all year round. Runs of 4–6 km. and over 3000 ft. Cable-car extension planned up to Viderjoch at about 9055 ft will open up fine ski fields between Parditschergrat and Vider-joch.

Many short half-day and day tours are available for graduates to touring, and for the true enthusiast vast areas of the surround-ing ranges will answer all the ski tourist's dreams. Steep ski-ing for the springtime is available directly above the village (the

Madlein Abfahrt) but you have to climb for it – 3 hrs up to
about 9200 ft.

Life and amenities in Ischgl are modest and village-type, but
parties here do not lack gaiety and prices are equally modest.

Accessibility. 1½ hrs post-bus from Landeck on main Arlberg
Express line.

General Comments. Once developed mechanically Ischgl will
grow in importance.

Centre 42		Altitude
GALTÜR	Province: Tyrol	5197 ft

Description. 500 inhabitants. 5 hotels, 4 inns, and 4 pensions
giving 400 beds. Other accommodation 400 beds. Language
German.

A small, attractive, old (dating from A.D. 1000), high-altitude
village lying in the wide junction of two valleys. Cosy atmosphere combined with feeling of remoteness, in uninspiring but
not unfriendly mountain scenery. A collection of pleasant
small buildings in exposed but sunny open situation, surrounded by good gentle nursery slopes.

Ski facilities. Short trainer lifts plus one small lift giving
rise of 400 ft.

Excellent value for parties of beginners who can soon graduate to a fine selection of short (2–3 hrs) and day excursions.

Ski touring. Galtür is primarily a centre for the ski tourer
and ski mountaineer. It is only 3½ hrs on ski from the Silvretta
Hotel at Bielerhöhe (see Parthenen in the Montafon, p. 135) and
is centrally placed amid all the splendid variety of the Samnaun, Verwall, and Silvretta ranges.

Amenities. Ski school. Guides. Village shops, etc.

Life in centre. Friendly, unpretentious, simple life. Family
atmosphere and small village life. Tom will meet Lisa and there
will be gay evenings. Folklore events. Easy access to Ischgl.

Accessibility. 2 hrs post-bus from Landeck on main Arlberg
Express line.

THE UPPER INN VALLEY AREA

THE little town of Landeck, on the main Arlberg Express line from central Switzerland through to Innsbruck and Vienna, lies close to the threefold frontier of Austria, Italy, and south-east Switzerland. Landeck is the station for Serfaus on the road that curls up south-westwards towards the lower Engadine.

Centre 67   Altitude
SERFAUS   Province: Tyrol   4682 ft

Description. 600 inhabitants. 4 hotels and 5 pensions providing 236 beds. Other accommodation 400 beds. Language German.

A friendly, simple, true village, of Roman origin, situated on a sunny shelf facing south-east across the Upper Inn Valley towards the Glockturm Kamm. Traditional farm houses and buildings converted and enlarged into comfortable modern hotels. Considerable building in progress.

Ski facilities. One medium-sized ski area served by a new *Seilbahn*, giving a rise of 1732 ft up to about 6600 ft. Open and woodland ski-ing, never difficult and often easy. Runs of $3\frac{1}{2}$ to 6 km. Various small lifts. Ski country faces mostly north-east and south-east.

Plenty of room both round village and top station (Kölner Haus) for uphill transport development. Several ski-lift projects in view, with ultimate aim to reach Furgler Gipfel (9843 ft).

Ski touring. Plenty of good short day tours and longer excursions in immediate neighbourhood.

Amenities. Ski school. Village shops. Small hotel and bar dancing. Folklore events.

Life in centre. Easy-going sunny existence, amid village life. Little excitement or glamour, but well organized for normal holiday pleasures. Inexpensive and genuine.

Accessibility. $1\frac{1}{2}$ hr post-bus journey from Landeck on main Arlberg Express line.

General comments. Good value for parties of inexperienced skiers, who should get reasonable terms. Ski standards medium to low. Great possibilities for future development.

THE AUSSERFERN

THE Ausserfern contains four ski centres, two well known – Ehrwald and Lermoos, which are almost adjoining – and two less well known – Berwang and Reutte, some 25–35 km. further to the north-west.

This long, semi-enclosed, and twisting valley consists of the upper section, north of the Fern Pass out of the Inn Valley, of the ancient trade route between Innsbruck and Bavaria. The whole is situated close to the southern frontier of Germany and can be approached from either north or south. It contains much variety and many pleasant surprises for the keen skier. A car is a great asset.

Centre 128		Altitude
LERMOOS	Province: Tyrol	3264 ft

Description. 700 inhabitants. 3 hotels and 6 inns providing 420 beds. Other accommodation 200 beds. Language German.

A picturesque little village, set openly and sunnily at the foot of the Grubigstein, faces eastwards across a wide plain to the village of Ehrwald (2 km. distant) crouching beneath the magnificent western end of the Wetterstein Range whose highest rock walls form the Zugspitze massif. No peak altitudes much over 9000 ft but scenery dramatic and fine.

Ski facilities. One ski area served by two-section chairlift giving initial rise of 1161 ft up to 4442 ft. Open, with scattered tree clumps, these slopes face generally to the east. Invariably quickly beaten after snowfalls, they provide amusing and varied ski-ing for medium skiers and easy ways for the beginner. This chairlift has now been extended up to the Grubigstein, at about 6950 ft, which greatly increases variety with descents of about 3500 ft over 4½ to 6 km.

Various small trainer lifts close to village.

Easy bus service allows Lermoos to share the ski-ing of Ehrwald and the Zugspitze (see pp. 149–50).

Amenities. Ski school. Ice rink. Sports shops. Village shops.

General winter-sports facilities. Hotel and small bar dancing. S.C.G.B. representative.

Life in centre. Compact and friendly place. The atmosphere is gay and friends are easily made. Much activity for the spectator. Evening entertainments modest and what you make them. Folklore events. Considerable traffic at week-ends. Costs very reasonable.

Accessibility. 40 mins. post-bus from Imst on main Arlberg Express line. 3 hrs train from Innsbruck via Garmisch-Partenkirchen. 2½ hrs train Munich (Airport).

General comments. Good ski-ing in immediate vicinity and plenty of variety easily accessible nearby at Ehrwald and the Zugspitze. Recommended for parties of beginners and those around medium standards. Lermoos is expanding rapidly and increasing in popularity.

Centre 127		Altitude
EHRWALD	Province: Tyrol	3268 ft

Description. 2480 inhabitants. 9 hotels and 18 inns providing 700 beds. Other accommodation 750 beds. Language German – English available.

A sizeable village of considerable charm. Old and new hotels of traditional style and many scattered chalets. Popular with visitors of many nationalities, it is a friendly, workaday place, situated in lovely surroundings, where village and holiday life are pleasantly intermingled. Only 2 km. distant from Lermoos, it shares the ski-ing and the amenities of that village as well (see p. 148).

Ski facilities. Two ski areas, one modest and the other big, served by ski-lifts and a big *téléférique*.

(1) *The Ehrwald Area*. On the big apron of snow slopes that sweep down from the final cliffs of the Zugspitze, and on the Ehrwalderalm, there are one or two gentle lifts that give a rise of about 700 ft. West-facing slopes suitable for beginner tuition. A project plans to reach 6234 ft giving descents of about 2800 ft. A second, and important, project consists of a lift up towards the Sonnenspitze (Coburger Hut) which will open up

much fine long north-slope ski-ing. Considerable development possible in Ehrwald area.

(2) *The Zugspitze Area.* (15 mins. by bus from Ehrwald, shared also by Garmisch-Partenkirchen.) *Téléférique* to 9203 ft. West-facing runs of $3\frac{1}{2}$ to 6 km. from Pylon IV give descents of up to 3500 ft back to Ehrwald. Suitable for good and medium skiers. Tunnel from top station crosses German frontier through to upland ski area of the Zugspitze Platte, a big basin of permanent snow where there is a network of small lifts giving total rise of about 1700 ft. Suitable for all types of skier, this enclosed and limited area allows for late and summer ski-ing. Superb viewpoints. Passports required. Big hotel, the Schnee-fernerhaus, comparable to that at Jungfraujoch. Cog railway connexion with Garmisch-Partenkirchen.

Ski touring. Good possibilities (springtime) in close-by Mieminger Range.

Amenities. Ski school. Ice rink. Ski jump. Cinema. Sports shops. Good selection of village shops. Coffee and dance bars. Local folklore entertainment, etc.

Life in centre. Gay, friendly, completely 'unstuffy' atmosphere. No artificial glamour. Accent on fun rather than stern ski-ing. Standards low to medium. Prices very reasonable.

Speciality. One long downhill run, from the Zugspitze, via the Gatterl, right round and back to Ehrwald is a fine experience. Reputed to be 18–20 km. long with some 6000 ft of downhill ski-ing. Passports required.

Accessibility. Same as for Lermoos (see p. 149).

General comments. Much recommended for parties of all ages who seek a combination of ski and restful village holiday in lovely surroundings at reasonable prices.

Centre 81		Altitude
BERWANG	Province: Tyrol	4383 ft

Description. 600 inhabitants. 2 hotels and 6 inn/pensions providing 380 beds. Other accommodation 250 beds.

A charming, picture-book, Christmas-card village interested in cattle and farming. Small, compact, and friendly, the ski-ing is equally small, compact, and friendly. Sheltered position close to a small pass.

Ski facilities. Village area only. Short lifts rising to approx. 5000 ft giving north-facing descents of about 800 ft.

Chairlift gives 525-ft rise on sunny south-facing slopes. Capable of extension up to 5479 ft, this will provide easy descents of about 1180 ft.

A small ski school gives adequate tuition. The general amenities, including a skating rink, are modest and picturesque. Small village shops and simple but comfortable small hotel life. Difficult not to make friends.

Eminently suitable for children and beginner family parties, this is no place for the *piste*-tiger or the ski-tourer. An hour or two of easy ski-ing, plenty of food and wine, and a deck-chair in the sun is more the line at Berwang.

Centre 142		Altitude
REUTTE	Province: Tyrol	2802 ft

Description. 4200 inhabitants. 3 hotels and 6 inns providing 407 beds. Other accommodation 1200 beds.

This busy and pleasant small market town is situated in a wide flat basin surrounded by some six small villages (total population 8000) and encircled by picturesque mountain scenery. Interested in textiles, metal, breweries, timber, and glass. The construction of a nearby (4 km. distant) cable-car system has recently brought Reutte into the list of ski centres. Worthily too.

Ski facilities. The Reutte Hahnenkamm area. This long north–south-running ridge has a fine variety of east-facing slopes. Centrally served by a quick new *Seilbahn* that rises 2661 ft in 6½ mins., there is a good selection of enterprising ski-ing, with runs ranging from 4 to 7 km. Top station has open sunny upper ski area provided with ski lifts extending up to ridge top at 6299 ft. Total height difference 3245 ft. Considerable off-*piste* exploration possible. Also considerable development envisaged along ridge side in neighbouring gullies and upper basins.

Plenty of places for beginners to practise, but ski-ing in general is for medium and good performers. The *piste*-basher will accumulate a lot of downhill running and, if he wants to, find a lot of problems.

Amenities. Small ski school. Bus services to ski area. Car parks. Ice rink. Cinemas. All the shopping facilities of a small town.

Life in centre. Little of the feeling of being in a ski centre. Pleasant atmosphere of small workaday town community not yet fully adapted to providing winter visitors with special holiday entertainment.

Accessibility. Train: Innsbruck 3 hrs, Munich 3 hrs. Airport: Munich.

General comments. Unorthodox as a ski centre, Reutte is unspoilt, unsophisticated, and capable of much further development. The nearby ski-ing is, however, already very good and hotel building will probably soon occur close to this area. A car is an asset (particularly with Ehrwald and Lermoos only 35 km. away) and a visit will not be a disappointment.

THE ÖTZTAL AREA

THE name of this 50-km.-long valley is famous for both beauty and ski-ing. The Ötztal contains four popular ski centres, which can only be reached by road transport. They are Obergurgl, Vent, Sölden, and Hochsölden (the last two, technically, are one). With the exception of Vent, there is an adequate amount of uphill transport at the others to guarantee a reasonable amount of the mechanical, 'downhill only' type of *piste* ski-ing that is the modern requirement. This, however, in comparison even with many less well-known centres in the same country, and also in France and Italy, is strictly on the limited side. The skier who is accustomed to the *pistes* of, say St Anton, Zermatt, Val d'Isère, or Cortina d'Ampezzo will look in vain in the Ötztal for similar qualities.

It is the wonderful ski-touring possibilities that are, and always have been, the high point of Ötztal ski-ing.

Centre 10		Altitude
OBERGURGL	Province: Tyrol	6266 ft

Description. 200 inhabitants. 7 hotels with 700 beds. Other accommodation 200 beds. Language German – slight English spoken.

Reputedly the highest parish in Europe (but St Veran in France at 6693 ft is higher), this famous little peasant settlement at the head of the Ötztal, until recently a remote and somewhat bleak entry-base for splendid glacier ski touring, has now developed into an easily reached, thriving, and even cosy little ski centre with lifts and *pistes* of its own. With real 'Alpine village' atmosphere, the pleasant hotel buildings are sheltered but sunny in a valley-end situation. The views become much more spectacular from the top of the lift system, where a fine array of many peaks and many glaciers explains the visual and ski intrigue of this well-known centre.

Ski facilities. One ski area served by two-section chairlift system with one subsidiary ski-lift near lower half.

The Gaisberg–Höhe Mut area gives a total rise of 2382 ft with north-west-facing runs of 3–5 km. Big upper Höhe Mut section – open, steep, and enterprising. Lower Gaisberg area, including wide playground region called Schönwies, easy and ideal for beginners. Abundant nursery slopes.

Limited but highly interesting, the 'mechanical ski-ing' is only one side of the facilities.

Ski touring. The time-honoured entry into the justly-famed Ötztaler Rundtour area where many tours, both short and long, from hut to hut, attract enthusiasts who love to wander and explore. (See also Vent, below)

Amenities. Ski school. Guides. Visitors' races. Tobogganning. Small village shops, including sports shops. Hotel dancing. Cafés.

Life in centre. Simple, unpretentious, not expensive. Organized mainly for ski-ing. Easy-going but lively. No smart *après-ski* but plenty of spontaneous gaiety. Folklore events. Small village life with international guests. Popular with English.

Specialities. Long reliable snow season – starts early (November), ends late (May). Glacier ski-ing from Hochwilde and Ramol Huts, etc. (9426 ft and 9862 ft), continues almost throughout year.

Accessibility. Train: nearest station Ötztaler Station on main Arlberg–Innsbruck line. Road: bus, via Zwieselstein, 2 hrs (53 km.). Cars require chains, later section to Obergurgl steep – buses four-wheel drive. Airport: Munich.

General comments. One of the relatively rare small places that combines good *piste* ski-ing and excellent ski touring. Much to be recommended for those who like to 'find their legs' before going off into the mountains.

Centre 11   Altitude
VENT   Province: Tyrol   6221 ft

Description. 100 inhabitants. 5 hotels with 350 beds. Other accommodation 150 beds. Language German.

A small high-altitude village in wildish valley surroundings. Somewhat remote both in fact and feeling, this place,

approached by a narrow, sometimes startling jeep-road, will
delight those who seek an unspoilt, quiet, simple village as a
base for extensive tours into mountain areas. It will not delight
the *piste* skier, for it only boasts of minor lifts and small runs
eminently suited to beginner types. Learner parties will find it
inexpensive, friendly, and uncrowded. Little entertainment
laid on – evening fun is largely what you make it, mixing with
fellow guests.

Ski touring. Vent is ideally suited for short and long ski tours
both locally and in the nearby upper world of peaks and
glaciers of the Ötztaler Rundtour region. Many famous huts,
such as the Vernagt (9039 ft), the Similaun (9905 ft), the
Samoar (8104 ft), the Brandenburger (10,735 ft), Schöne
Aussicht (9324 ft), etc. can be used in week-long round tours,
ending at either Obergurgl or Sölden or even westwards over
towards Landeck to continue up into the Silvretta touring area.
Austria's second-highest mountain, the Wildspitze (12,369 ft)
only 5 km. away, can be climbed on skis in a total of 8 hrs.

Accessibility. Train: station Ötztaler Station on main Arlberg–Innsbruck line. Road: bus to Zwieselstein (4744 ft). Jeep
up to Vent. Total time, 2½ hrs. Airport: Munich.

Centres 2 and 77		Altitudes
HOCHSÖLDEN	Province: Tyrol	6857 ft
SÖLDEN		4436 ft

Description. Hochsölden: 15–20 inhabitants. 5 hotels with 600
beds.

Sölden: 1100 inhabitants. 6 hotels and 6 pensions with 550
beds. Other accommodation 400 beds. Language German,
English not widely spoken.

Both these places are extremely popular. Sölden is a straggling roadside valley village of average charm in the famous
Ötztal. A 2434-ft chairlift rise (small road kept open when
possible) takes one up to Hochsölden – the second highest
actual ski hotel settlement in the Alps – a collection of attractive modern buildings on a lovely, very sunny shelf. Views
uninspiring in valley but excellent from Hochsölden and above.

Ski facilities. Two areas served by two chairlift systems.

(1) The Hochsölden–Rotkogel lift gives a rise of 1017 ft above Hochsölden and allows for east- and south-east-facing runs of 1½ km. back to Hochsölden and at least two main runs of 4–6 km. and 2434 ft right down to Sölden. Upper Rotkogel area, open rolling slopes with extensive practice areas round Hochsölden. Below this, long cut trails through timbered hill-sides lead down to open meadows above Sölden.

(2) The Innerwald area gives a chairlift rise of 656 ft above Sölden, shortly to be extended to give a total rise of over 3000 ft. North-east-facing ski slopes.

Present two areas are ideal for beginners and keen learners. Runs, though good, are too limited to interest the proficient *piste*-basher for very long. Best described as excellent place for graduation to long and short ski touring.

Ski touring. A great wealth of good short day and half-day tours above Hochsölden. Easy entry to the wonderful and widespread Ötztaler Rundtouring ski area with its many huts which open at the beginning of March (see Vent, p. 154).

Amenities. Third or fourth largest ski school in Austria. Local ski races. Ice rinks. Toboggan runs. Village shops, bars, village pubs, and '*Stuben*'. Medium- to small-sized hotels.

Life in centre. Happy-go-lucky small village life in Sölden. Lively self-contained hotel life in Hochsölden. Holiday fun atmosphere in both. Many English guests. Accent on youth, large parties, and ski-ing. No smart *après-ski* but plenty of entertainment and activity. Local Tyrolean fêtes and folklore, etc.

Specialities. Excellent ski instruction for all, with emphasis on early tuition. Good spring ski-ing. Long and short excursions and ski tours to huts, etc.

Accessibility. Train: nearest station Ötztaler Station (39 km.) on main Arlberg–Innsbruck line. Road: bus to Ötztaler Station 1½ hrs. Road kept open. Airport: Munich.

General comments. Much to be recommended for school parties, youth groups, and agency parties of first-, second-, and third-year skiers. Individual skiers will soon make friends.

Centre 8   Altitude
KÜHTAI   Province: Tyrol   6454 ft

Description. About 40 inhabitants. 1 hotel and 6 pensions with
250 beds. Mattress beds 23. Dortmunder Hütte 6391 ft.
Language German.

This high, popular little centre, where the living is simple,
unsophisticated, and friendly, is one of beauty and charm in
lovely sunny surroundings. The uphill transport is, to date,
limited to one good nursery-slope ski-lift. The emphasis is
for the beginner and for the ski tourer. The latter has at his
disposal over 40 half-day and full-day ski tours in the immediate vicinity, and the learner has wide and ideal practice
slopes.

Accessibility. Innsbruck 4½ hrs. Bus to Gries in Sellrain,
thence jeep or weasel.

THE INNSBRUCK AREA

THE old, historic, and picturesque capital town of the big province of Tyrol, dating back to the time of Christ, needs little introduction. In beauty and setting it is very hard to rival, for it has many fine historic buildings and the end of almost every street is provided with a wonderful backcloth of high mountains.

Almost more than any other, this is a city of skiers (inhabitants 101,830), yet, strictly speaking, although it contains skating rinks, a ski jump, fine sports shops, etc., it is no ski centre. It has its own ski area and it is surrounded with several satellite ski centres, but Innsbruck itself can only be described as a town.

The immediate Innsbruck ski area is the Seegrube–Hafelekar. The nearby satellites are Igls and Mutters. Steinach and Gries (see p. 162) are only 26 and 33 km. away up the Brenner Pass. Schwaz, an old main-valley town with ski facilities, lies only 29 km. east of Innsbruck, and a little further down the Inn you come to the entry up into the Wildschönau which has its own ski centres (see p. 166). The Zillertal is equally accessible. To the west of Innsbruck the ski resort of Seefeld is only 22 km. away.

In short, the town of Innsbruck is a centre for ski-ing rather than a ski centre. Local inhabitants go ski-ing in their lunch-hour breaks and at week-ends. Bus and railway services take them quickly to any of the above-mentioned satellites and neighbouring ski-centres. The holiday skier who likes to be in pleasant town surroundings, with cinemas, theatres, and many restaurants and bars, could do a lot worse than select Innsbruck as a central base. Using public transport alone, he can visit many different areas, and, with a car, his choice is widespread indeed – without the restriction of timetables.

Innsbruck is 5 hrs by train from Zürich and 9 hrs from Vienna.

side southwards to Grafenast
Skiers wishing cheap accom-
ement atmosphere can stay
vith about 160 beds) at 4429 ft.
th two-section chairlift rising to
d varied north- and north-west-
nt and between $3\frac{1}{2}$ and $5\frac{1}{2}$ km.
und, which is semi-timbered, can
pular with locals and day visitors,
and often crowded. Few resident
but atmosphere of gay, fun ski-ing
airlift from Grafenast up to Arbesser
llerjoch (7690 ft), now takes you on up
om Schwaz of 4396 ft) and greatly ex-
lready good area.
s. train from Innsbruck. Post-bus ser

If in the area, you will not regret a day o
, but the town is barely a place for longe
height gain from the three chairlifts is botl
varding.

Altitud
Province: Tyrol 3438

100 inhabitants. 5 hotels and 3 inns providin
her accommodation 200 beds. Language Germa
ish; Italian spoken.
rprising, large, and not unattractive main-road an
village (Brenner Pass 12 km., Innsbruck 26 km.) h
le accommodation and good ski-ing on a small scal
plans to extend.
cilities. One medium-sized ski area served by chairli
se of 1969 ft up to 5414 ft provides a surprisingly vari
nusing selection of north-facing runs of between 3 ar
Suitable for good, medium, and beginner types. (Proje
end lift up to 6890 ft will considerably enlarge the area

Centre 163

INNSBRUCK   Province: Tyrol.   Altitude 1903 ft

The Seegrube–Hafelekar Area

From the low altitude of the town of Innsbruck, a three-section series of lifts – one funicular and two *Seilbahns* – mounts directly to 7402 ft.

The two upper sections provide a steep and difficult south-east-facing run of over 4500 ft and between 7 and 8 km. Often crowded and hardbeaten, this is not for the unwary or the inexperienced. Angular and gymnastic at top; long zigzag traverses in restricted icy places lower down; ski country that accounts for the general high standard of ski-ing among local inhabitants.

The Axamer–Lizum Area

As soon as the present preparations for the 1964 Olympic Games are completed, Innsbruck will have a fine second ski area based on the nearby village of Axams.

Innsbruck has already been the scene of big international and world championship ski meetings. For the 1964 Winter Olympic Games there will be very important further development. The plan is that the high valley areas which run southwards from Axams and Götzens (villages some 10 to 12 km. south-west of Innsbruck) up to the region behind, and to the west of, the Mutters ski area will be opened up. This region, known as Götzener and Lizumertal, will provide long north-slope ski-ing suitable for international events. A road and uphill transport lifts will be constructed, and this hitherto undeveloped area will greatly add to the present scope of Innsbruck. Top stations of the new lift projects from Axamer Lizum will be:

Birgitzköpfl: 6890 ft west-facing slopes giving descents of approx. 1745 ft.

Hoadl: 7677 ft north-east-facing slopes giving descents of approx. 2549 ft.

Pleissen: 7333 ft north-east-facing slopes giving descents of approx. 2198 ft.

Well sheltered by the Kalkkögel range from the warm *Föhn* winds from the south this interesting new ski area will doubtless attract many a keen skier.

Centre 140
IGLS   Province: Tyrol

Description. 900 inhabitants. 9 hotels and 4 pensions pr⟨⟩ 836 beds. Other accommodation 380 beds. Language Ge⟨⟩

A most pleasant and picturesque little community sitting ⟨⟩ sunny shelf at the foot of Patscherkofel mountain with fi⟨⟩ views out to the north-west and west over the wide Inn valle⟨⟩ (with the town of Innsbruck 950 ft below) and the valley of the Brenner Pass. Colourful and friendly, it is an entity ⟨⟩ itself, only 6 km. by twisting road from all the amenities of Innsbruck.

Ski facilities. One large but relatively limited ski area served by two-section *téléférique* rising to 6404 ft – possibly to be surmounted by a chairlift to Patscherkofel summit at 7375 ft. Ski- and chairlifts of medium size serve open slopes at bottom middle, and top stations – all three good for beginners.

Often windblown on the top section from summit to tree line, the main runs down to Igls are mainly through cleared glades. Difficult and medium difficult, with one easy way, the descents average 3400 ft and between 5 and $7\frac{1}{2}$ km.

Amenities. Ski school. Skating rink (lake). Good village and sports shops. Hotel and bar dancing. Cinema. Bus and tram services to Innsbruck. Ski Club of Great Britain representative.

Life in centre. Simple but comprehensive. No frills, but various gay spots. Ski-ing not over-accented. Fairly international visitors. Easy to mix. Pleasant friendly atmosphere. Fair car traffic, especially at week-ends.

Speciality. The Glungezer Run. A very popular full-day excursion involving a $3\frac{1}{2}$ hr climb on skins to Glungezer Hut at 8530 ft and an interesting medium-difficult descent for the average skier of 16 km. and nearly 7000 ft to the town of Solbad Hall (10 km. down river east of Innsbruck).

AUSTRIAN SKI ⟨⟩

162   uphill transport system from road⟨⟩ via half-way station at Arzberg. ⟨⟩ modation and 'baby' ski sett⟨⟩ pleasantly at Grafenast (3 inns ⟨⟩

Ski facilities. One ski area wi⟨⟩ 4429 ft providing amusing an⟨⟩ facing runs of 2658 ft desce⟨⟩ Never over-difficult, the gr⟨⟩ provide problems. Very po⟨⟩ the runs are well beaten⟨⟩ guests and few amenities,⟨⟩ A third section of the cl⟨⟩ a small summit of the K⟨⟩ to 6168 ft (a total rise f⟨⟩ tends the scope of an ⟨⟩ *Accessibility*. 30 mi⟨⟩

Ski fa⟨⟩
chairlift ⟨⟩
sometimes ⟨⟩
main runs o⟨⟩
only because o⟨⟩
and north-facin⟨⟩
down to the outsk⟨⟩
Simple but amus⟨⟩
behind top station.

General comments. ⟨⟩
bruck ski-ing and not as ⟨⟩

General comments. ⟨⟩ so ski-ing at Schwa⟨⟩ holidays. The big ⟨⟩ surprising and rev⟨⟩

Centre 118
STEINACH-AM⟨⟩
BRENNER

Description. 2⟨⟩ 456 beds. O⟨⟩ – slight Eng⟨⟩ This ente⟨⟩ main-line ⟨⟩ comfortab⟨⟩ which it ⟨⟩
Ski f⟨⟩ giving ⟨⟩ and an⟨⟩ 5 km.⟨⟩ to ex⟨⟩

Centre 164
SCHWAZ   Provin⟨⟩

Description. 9000 inhabitants. ⟨⟩ 214 beds. Language German exclu⟨⟩

An interesting and picturesque ⟨⟩ important in Tyrol) in the lower In⟨⟩ Innsbruck. No ski centre as such, Schw⟨⟩

South-facing ski run (easy) down to neighbouring village of Gries. Sunny nursery slopes with small trainer lifts on big shelf immediately above Steinach.

Ski touring. Good 'ski wandering' above and behind top station.

Amenities. Small ski school. Skating rink. Village shops. Visitors' events. Cafés. Dancing, folklore events, etc. (Amenities of Innsbruck 30 mins. by bus or train.)

Life in centre. One foot on a mountain and one foot on a busy main road. Much through traffic. Friendly atmosphere makes up for lack of 'ski dorf' feeling. Comfort, with reasonable terms.

Accessibility. Road and rail: Innsbruck 30 mins., or direct access from Italy over Brenner Pass.

General comments. Well worth a short visit. Has proved successful with travel-agency parties. Close access to the ski-ing at Gries. (See next centre.)

Centre 102   Altitude
GRIES-   Province: Tyrol   3822 ft
  AM-BRENNER

Description. 1200 inhabitants. 2 hotels and 5 inns providing 210 beds. Other accommodation 150 beds. Language German, Italian spoken.

Small neighbour of Steinach (7 km. distant, 5 km. from Brenner Pass). Also busy main-road village, but picturesque and attractively placed. Old buildings.

Ski facilities. Only small trainer lift at present. Visitors mostly go by bus to Steinach to use the chairlift and return by ski to Gries.

Interesting project is to build two-section lift up to Sattelberg Haus, 6913 ft, on the Italian frontier. This will provide good varied open ski-ing for all comers, with north-east- and north-west-facing runs of 3 to 7 km. and over 3000 ft descent.

Ski touring. The Austro–Italian frontier range, particularly to the east of the Brenner Pass, provides good ski-touring excursions.

Amenities. Modest village amenities.

Life in centre. Admixture of family-type hotel life, floating population visitors, and main-road traffic together with village life.

Accessibility. Road and rail: Innsbruck 40 mins., or direct access from Italy via Brenner Pass.

General comments. Steinach and Gries are capable of considerable development. They will, in due course, form a small but interesting 'circus' together. Guests at both are greatly outnumbered by visiting day skiers from both sides of the frontier. Easy access to Colle Isarco (p. 303) in Italy.

Centre 99	Altitude
SEEFELD Province: Tyrol	3872 ft

Description. 1800 inhabitants. 22 hotels and 17 inns and pensions providing 1860 beds. Other accommodation 1620 beds. Language German – most European tongues catered for.

An attractive and prosperous 'tourist resort' collection of very many hotel, chalet, and village buildings scattered thickly and widespread over a big area of undulating upland plateau which includes a lake. The situation is sunny and there is no feeling of being overpowered by steep hillsides. The horizons and views are wide and the distant mountain backgrounds are splendid. Easily reached from Innsbruck and Garmisch–Partenkirchen in Germany, it is popular not only with the Austrian public, but internationally.

Admirably organized and equipped with every accessory, Seefeld is a 'ski pleasure-drome' for the masses of dilettante winter-sports holiday-makers who like all the fun of the fair without any of the problems or difficulties of energetic ski-ing.

Ski facilities. Two ski areas, one medium sized with a neighbouring annexe, and one small.

(1) *The Rosshütte Area*. Served by a two-section chairlift that rises to 5774 ft. A short cable car continues up to Seefelderjoch at 6759 ft. These provide interweaving wide-ridge runs – west-facing – of about 4 to 5½ km. and 2700 ft descent. Open and medium slopes at top soon become easy, safe, wide wooded glades for the main descent.

A second, short, cable-car branches off south from Ross-hütte to reach the annexe ridge of Harmelerkopf at 6890 ft. This ridge provides rather more enterprising runs down to Seefeld of about 3 to 5 km. and 2600 ft.

(2) *The Gschwandkopf Area.* A glorified and extended north-facing nursery-slope-type area served by side-by-side chairlifts that give rises of 443 ft and 988 ft respectively. Good sunny terraced viewpoint restaurants at ridge-top.

Not much future development possible.

Amenities. Large, well-run, efficient ski school. Skating rinks. Tobogganing (popular). Sleigh rides. Large selection of shops. Many 'souvenir' shops. Riding and swimming (large, glass-enclosed, heated pool). Cinema. Cafés. Restaurants. Bars. Dance bars. Hotel dancing. Visitors' events. Folklore entertainment, etc. S.C.G.B. representative.

Speciality. Large, separate, safe nursery-slope area, close to village centre, served by several good trainer lifts.

Life in centre. Gay, holiday, flashbulb atmosphere. All-track minded. Every class structure, nationality, and pocket catered for. High–low range of prices. A bit of everything for everyone. No over-emphasis on ski-ing. Plenty of activity for the spectator. Not much for the society gossip writer.

Accessibility. Train travel: Innsbruck 40–50 mins., Munich 3 hrs.

General comments. Had there been snow mountains in England, Butlins (with a little help from the S.C.G.B.) would have done it, and given a lot of people a lot of fun.

THE WILDSCHÖNAU AREA

A TRANSLATION of the three German words that form this upland valley name would go 'beautiful, but little frequented, fertile region'. Apart from the fact that it is nowadays much frequented by winter skiers, this description well suits this attractive Tyrolean upland enclave which lies to the south and just above the little town of Wörgl in the Inn Valley (where one can also stay).

The Wildschönau is a modest and popular 'small man's' ski area. Unpretentious, genuine, and inexpensive, it has much to offer. It lies next to the neighbouring ski area of Alpbach, and its back door gives out towards two other ski centres of the Kitzbüheler Alpen – Hopfgarten and Westendorf.

This pleasant region contains three little ski centres, Niederau, Oberau, and Auffach. These are only separated by 3 and 5 km. respectively, and, as they are all closely linked by both bus services and ski runs, it is sensible to treat the area as a whole.

| *Centre 146* | | Altitude |
| NIEDERAU | Province: Tyrol | 2700 ft |

450 inhabitants. 3 inns and 2 pensions providing 108 beds. Other accommodation 130 beds.

| *Centre 134* | | Altitude |
| OBERAU | Province: Tyrol | 3071 ft |

1150 inhabitants. 2 inns and 2 pensions providing 117 beds. Other accommodation 83 beds.

| *Centre 139* | | Altitude |
| AUFFACH | Province: Tyrol | 2871 ft |

550 inhabitants. 1 inn and 2 pensions providing 110 beds. Other accommodation 108 beds.

Language German exclusively.

Description. Three unspoilt Tyrolean villages of considerable charm that show no undue signs of commercialization. Simple comfort without any frills is the keynote, and uncostly holidays are the result. Auffach, a little removed from the main uphill transport system and relatively more primitive, is the cheapest bargain.

All along this curving valley there are meadows that make good nursery slopes. Above these the hillsides are pleasantly wooded with many wide glades and open slopes. The surrounding hills are friendly rounded ski-peaks which seldom exceed the tree line and produce many ridges and valleys that run down to all points of the compass.

Given the finance the Wildschönau would be capable of considerable medium-scale uphill transport development. As it is today, one can wander almost where one will and there is only one area served with a major lift system.

The Markbachjoch Area. Starting up from Niederau a chairlift mounts to the south to ridge top at 4692 ft. The Markbachjoch ridge has one very modern and comfortable hotel (58 beds) where prices are unusually modest, and some 25 small and delightful self-contained private huts, facing south, which one may hire for holiday periods.

The chairlift opens up a surprisingly wide selection of north-facing runs of 2 to 4 km. and 1966 ft, the quality and variety of which provide very good value. There is a 500-ft ski-lift leading back up to top station. Facilities are very well organized.

The nearby hill top of Rosskopf, 5742 ft, from which one can run down to Oberau, is an obvious place for a future lift project.

Oberau has a good 850-ft nursery slope ski-lift – up to the Riedlberg at 4058 ft.

Ski touring. There are widespread and pleasantly easy ski excursions on every hand.

Amenities. Few but adequate.

Accessibility. Bus travel: Wörgl $\frac{1}{2}$ hr. Train: Innsbruck 1 hr, Munich 2 hrs.

General comments. This engaging, simple, and attractive area

is likely to develop fast. Popular with travel-agency parties and
the not-too-well-off, it provides a good mixture of *piste* running, off-the-*piste* ski-ing and gentle ski touring. (43,000 ft of
downhill ski-ing in one day was once recorded on the chairlift
runs!) Much to be recommended for the simple life, good
ski-ing, and an easy-to-make-friends atmosphere in which
ordinary people make their own fun.

		Altitudes
Centre 131		3192 ft
ALPBACH	Province: Tyrol	3297 ft
INNER ALPBACH		

Description. 1390 inhabitants. 2 hotels and 3 inns providing
225 beds. Other accommodation 150 beds. Language German
exclusively.

Sandwiched between the lower end of the Zillertal and the
Wildschönau, with approach road up from Brixlegg in the Inn
Valley, lies the attractive and picturesque little ski region of
Alpbach.

Unsophisticated, undeveloped 'mechanically', it is an upland 'enclave' not dissimilar to the Wildschönau. Living is
comfortable, but relatively simple and primitive, and there are,
as yet, only small trainer lifts for beginners. Plans for uphill
transport may include the Schatzberg at 6457 ft, but for the
moment Alpbach is for those who prefer the short and long
excursion-type ski-ing, for which the region is admirably
suited. Ski tourers have a wonderful choice of easy exploration.
Both Gerlos (see p. 169) and the Wildschönau are within reach
of modest skiers.

The whole of this easily accessible Alpbach region is safe,
sunny, and seldom crowded. The valley has a charm all of its
own and a friendly atmosphere of unspoilt simplicity.

Accessibility. Bus travel: Innsbruck, 2 hrs, or bus to Brixlegg
(30 mins.), thence train to Innsbruck (45 mins.).

THE ZILLERTAL AREA

Famed for its songs, its *Schuhplattln* dances, its village bands, and its folklore, the Zillertal is also financially interested in timber, magnesium, wolfram, cheese, and the tourist. It is also becoming interested in hydro-electric works. Until you get to the far southern end of this long valley, the scenery is not up to Austrian standards, and the main item of interest is the delightful, elderly Zillertal railway with the original locomotives and rolling stock built in 1902.

There are four ski centres in the Zillertal – Gerlos, Mayrhofen, Lanersbach, and Hintertux. In none of these is there much emphasis on long lifts and *piste* running. The accent here is mostly on gentle beginner stuff, upland playgrounds, and there are lovely opportunities for ski wandering and ski touring.

Centre 92   Altitude
GERLOS   Province: Tyrol   4098 ft

Description. 500 inhabitants. 3 inn hotels providing about 250 beds. Other accommodation 200 beds.

Very popular, sunnily situated small village amid friendly upland valley scenery. The surrounding hills, rounded and pleasantly timbered with many open snow slopes, seldom rise more than 3000 ft above the village. Comfortable, unsophisticated, inexpensive, family-type hotels filled with guests of all nations. Easy-going, friendly atmosphere. Little energetic skiing, mostly confined to pleasant practice slopes in immediate vicinity. One or two small ski hoists only.

Efficient ski tuition available and excursions organized. Excellent ski runs of all types to be found for climbs of 1 to 3 hrs. Widespread ski wandering and exploration on every hand.

Gerlos has long provided many people, of all ages and all nationalities, with many happy holidays, and considering the lack of mechanical facilities and 'bare essential' amenities, this speaks volumes for local atmosphere.

Capable of considerable development both in accommodation and lifts, this area may well soon develop into a more

'standardized' ski centre. Plans to construct a large hydro-
electric scheme nearby will bring sufficient revenue for major
uphill transport. Among various possibilities for this, the
Ebnerfeld, the Arbiskögerl, and the Schönbichl are already
being considered. Whatever developments may occur, it is
doubtful if Gerlos will ever lose its built-in charm of simple
bürgerlich living and the easy-going fun that can be enjoyed
either by the lone wolf or the large party.

Accessibility. Bus: Innsbruck 3 hrs. Main-line station; Jenbach 50 mins. from Innsbruck, thence Zillertal Railway, 70
mins., to Zell-am-Ziller; thence bus to Gerlos, 45 mins.

Centre 161		Altitude
MAYRHOFEN	Province: Tyrol	2060 ft

Description. 2500 inhabitants. 7 hotels and 4 inns providing
740 beds. Other accommodation 550 beds. Language German
– most European tongues available.

Deeply tucked into a wide flat surrounded by steep and often
precipitous rocky mountains, this very popular summer resort,
almost a small town, covers a big area. Hotels of all classes to
suit all pockets. Grand surroundings and splendid views from
top station of the *Luftseilbahn*.

Ski facilities. One small to medium-sized upland area reached
by big cable-car system rising 3655 ft to Penken at 5801 ft.
Two runs, one south-facing and largely open, and the other
east-facing and largely close-wooded, bring the experienced
skier down to the vicinity of Mayrhofen (6 and 3 km. away).
These runs, about 6 to 7½ km. in length, are an interesting
experience but are not for the untalented.

The main upland area, sunny and with splendid views, is
excellent for beginners; large classes of these go up and return
by *téléférique*. Served by one or two ski hoists, there is also
a chairlift of 705 ft rise up to Penkenjoch at 6611 ft. Easy
south-east-, and north-east-facing slopes, mostly open but with
pleasantly scattered trees. A new ski-lift opens up north-facing
slopes and the whole forms a compact little upland circus.

Ski touring. Superb spring ski-touring facilities in the famed

Zillertaler Alpen. Two entry valleys lead southwards and east-wards up from Mayrhofen towards the many high glaciers and peaks of the Italian frontier. The Berliner Hütte can be reached from the nearby village of Ginzling in the Dornaubergtal.

Amenities. Good ski school, specializing particularly in chil-dren's classes. Skating rink. Good selection of shops, and all the amenities of a large resort-type village. Visitors' events. Folk-lore entertainment. Cinema. Dancing, etc.

Life in centre. Straggling village with comfortable modern hotels. Friendly but slightly impersonal. On the quiet side, Mayrhofen is primarily a summer resort without the special qualities of a winter 'ski-dorf'.

Accessibility. Train travel: $1\frac{1}{2}$ hrs by Zillertal Railway to Jenbach. 50 mins. to Innsbruck and $3\frac{1}{2}$ hrs Salzburg. Daily direct bus service: Innsbruck 2 hrs (72 kms.).

		Altitudes
Centres 85 and 51		
LANERSBACH	Province: Tyrol	4219 ft
HINTERTUX		4875 ft

Description. Two small and attractive villages, separated by 5 km. Reached by bus from Mayrhofen, 15 km. and 20 km. westwards up the steep and picturesque Tuxertal. Lanersbach has 500 inhabitants. Small inns with 400 beds. Hintertux 100 inhabitants. Small inns with 300 beds.

Sunnily situated but somewhat hemmed-in in steep-sided valley scenery, both provide the novice with excellent nursery and practice slopes served by small trainer lifts. Very popular. Much activity. No places for *piste*-tigers, but parties of be-ginners seeking inexpensive village life in congenial atmosphere and picturesque surroundings will find here all they want. Simple; friendly; gay; no frills. Access to Mayrhofen.

Hintertux has thermal springs, with indoor baths in one hotel and an outdoor thermal swimming pool for spring and summer. Both villages serve as good entry bases for the high ski-touring area of the western end of the Zillertaler Alpen which, in springtime, provide a widespread area of excellent glacier ski touring.

THE KITZBÜHEL AREA

THIS internationally famous and popular ski region of the Tyrol contains five main ski centres of varying sizes, and many other small hamlets at which the visitor may stay. Kitzbühel itself is the large central pivot, with the smaller St Johann and Kirchberg one each side of its immediate flanks. Westendorf and Hopfgarten are two lesser satellites close by, and to the west of Kirchberg.

Generally low in altitude, this region, with its gaily painted buildings and attractive Tyrolean architecture, is, however, a 'snowpocket' and seldom lacks good conditions during its relatively short season (end of December to mid-March). Less enterprising and fiercely varied, and certainly less difficult, than the ground formations of, say, Zermatt, St Anton, and Val d'Isère, the general ski-ing of the whole of this region comes more under the headings of fluency, uniformity, and safety.

Each of the five main centres is an entity in itself, but there is considerable interlinkage of ski runs, and future lifts will bring more. Frequent post-bus and 'minibus' services also interlink by road. The ski-ing of one is available to all. A car is a great asset. The quality of ski-ing at one is, more or less, the quality available at all and therefore one general description of ski terrain will have to suffice.

There is here a wide range of 'three-stage' ski-ing. Big, free, open slopes above the tree line (which is interestingly erratic at anywhere between 5000 and 6000 ft). Glade and wood running in trees that are seldom tightly crowded. Fine wide meadows, nicely shaped and tilted, run down to valley level. Many of the longer runs can be made to include all three of these stages.

The country, in general, consists of lengthy spurs and ridges that branch down like fingers from upper lines of knuckles. These long spurs, down which the main runs flow, face many points of the compass and even on each one it is possible to choose either sunny or shaded slopes. It is, therefore, very seldom difficult to find all snow conditions. Nor is it difficult for the 'off-the-*piste*' skier to find untracked snow or any variation of gradient to suit his skill.

Centre 151   Altitude
KITZBÜHEL   Province: Tyrol   2503 ft

Description. 5000 inhabitants (7500 in total *Gemeinde*). 17 hotels and 28 pensions providing 1780 beds. Other accommodation 770 beds. Language German – English and most continental languages spoken.

A beautiful, picturesque, and historic little walled town whose many recent gaily-painted Tyrolean buildings have overflowed all around and well beyond its original confines. Situated in a wide fertile valley and surrounded by lovely views of kindly mountain scenery, Kitzbühel, as well as carrying on its workaday life, lives and breathes ski-ing.

Ski facilities. Three ski areas. One on east-facing side of valley and two on west-facing side, served by complex system of cable-cars, gondolas, chairlifts, and ski-lifts, many of which are interlinking. (See also Kirchberg.)

(1) *The Hahnenkamm–Ehrenbachhöhe Area.* One cable-car rising to 5420 ft giving access to 'circus' consisting of three or four ski-lifts and chairlifts all giving rises of between 800 ft and 1500 ft. (Highest lift reaches 6306 ft at Gigglinghöhe.) Very wide selection of runs, facing all compass points (including down to Hechenmoos), ranging from 1½ km. to 8 km. (Maximum descent 3757 ft.)

Runs go down to valleys both sides of Kitzbühel to link with other Kitzbühel areas, and ski area of Kirchberg.

(2) *The Kitzbühelerhorn Area.* One gondola system surmounted by cable-car rises to 6440 ft. (Chairlift in the Trattalm basin near summit gives 617 ft rise on sunny nursery slopes.) Wide variety of south- and south-west-facing runs down to Kitzbühel and down shaded reverse side of Kitzbühelerhorn to close to St Johann-in-Tyrol. Excellent enterprising ski-ing.

(3) *The Bichlalm Area.* New chairlift rises to 5479 ft providing south-facing runs. Good ski-ing.

Ski touring. Not basically a ski-touring area, but countless excursions and excursion-type runs available.

Amenities. Large and renowned ski school. Extensive nursery slopes served by good ski-lifts and floodlit at night. Visitors' events. Skating rinks. Ice hockey. Curling. Cafés. Restaurants. Dance bars. Night clubs. Folklore events. Cinemas. Shops and sports shops of all categories. Every amenity. S.C.G.B. representative.

Life in centre. Colourful, gay, international; simplicity and sophistication intermingled. Much activity by day and by night. Big accent on ski-ing, also on youth. Seldom a dull moment. Price range very wide, but life cannot be described as cheap. Heavy car traffic.

Accessibility. Main-line train travel: Innsbruck 1½ hrs, Vienna 7–8 hrs, Munich 3 hrs. Airport: Munich.

General comments. Something for everybody. Beginner to expert. International socialite to overdrawn undergraduate. Playboy to ski girl. Extremely popular.

Centre 144   Altitude
KIRCHBERG   Province: Tyrol   2749 ft

Description. 1900 inhabitants. 1 hotel, 12 inns, and 20 pensions providing 1000 beds. Other accommodation 600 beds. Language German.

Very attractive neighbour-village to Kitzbühel (6 km. west by road). Gaily-painted traditional-type buildings. Unspectacular but pleasant valley scenery. Picturesque farm buildings.

Ski facilities. Two ski areas of medium–small size capable of considerable extension.

(1) *The Maierl Area.* Chairlift to 5290 ft giving rise of 2403 ft on easy north-west-facing slopes. This covers most of a main Kitzbühel run, and the plan is to extend this lift right up to Ehrenbachhöhe to effect complete circus linkage.

(2) *The Gaisberg Area.* Chairlift to 4229 ft giving rise of 1427 ft on easy to medium-hard north-east-facing slopes. Project to extend lift up to 5800 ft to give 3000 ft descents and effect easy linkage with Westendorf – also to provide upland

ski area with ski-lifts in the region of the Gampenkogel and Fleidingkogel, etc. There are also plans to put a *Seilbahn* up to Brechhorn summit (6667 ft).

Ski touring. No big high tours. Plenty of 'ski wandering' of short and long duration.

Amenities. Ski school. Skating rink. Facilities for all forms of winter sports. Visitors' events. Good selection village and sports shops. Cinema. Cafés, bars, dance bars, etc.

Life in centre. Picturesque surroundings and friendly atmosphere. Well organized for sport and entertainment. Relatively simple village life. Prices reasonable. Youthful and gay.

Accessibility. See Kitzbühel.

General comments. Simpler and less expensive than Kitzbühel, it has easy access to all Kitzbühel ski-ing. Good value in itself, it has ambitious projects for the future. Recommended for parties.

Centre 160
ST JOHANN-   Province: Tyrol   Altitude
  IN-TYROL   2165 ft

Description. 4300 inhabitants. 2 hotels, 8 inns, and 9 pensions providing approx. 500 beds. Other accommodation 65 beds. Language German.

A most attractive little workaday Tyrolean town, situated in a wide flat valley at the northern foot of the Kitzbühelerhorn (see p. 173) with a lovely view, northwards, of the rocky Kaisergebirge Range. Old as a community, but young as a ski centre.

Ski facilities. One ski area served by two funiculars and a chairlift giving total rise of 3012 ft up to 5210 ft. All north-facing lower slopes provide excellent beginner grounds, and higher up the enthusiast will find good gradients and large areas of untracked powder. Wide variety of easy, medium, and medium-difficult runs up to 6–7 km. in length.

Amenities. Small ski school. All small-town facilities plus all those of nearby Kitzbühel.

Life in centre. Less crowded and social than Kitzbühel.

Simpler life with more 'local' village atmosphere. Prices also more modest.

Accessibility. Same as for Kitzbühel. Easy bus services between the two.

General comments. Almost part and parcel of Kitzbühel ski-ing with a good ski area of its own. A party here will certainly enjoy itself.

Centre 150   Altitude
WESTENDORF   Province: Tyrol   2576 ft

Description. 600 inhabitants. 5 hotels and 5 inns providing 300 beds. Other accommodation 500 beds. Language German.

A pleasant and picturesque little 'ski dorf' 15 km. west of Kitzbühel and 9 km. west of Kirchberg. Modest expenditure and friendly atmosphere. Situated on south side of wide valley amid pleasant scenery.

Ski facilities. One ski area served by chairlift giving rise of 2543 ft to Alpenrose Hütte at 5168 ft. Runs of $3\frac{1}{2}$ to $4\frac{1}{2}$ km. on north-west- and north-facing slopes. Easy to medium-difficult. Trainer lift on nursery slopes.

Westendorf shares its touring area with Kirchberg. Climbs of 1 and $1\frac{1}{2}$ hrs take you to the Fleidingkogel and the Brech-horn, both of which summits are involved in future projects from Kirchberg (see p. 174).

Forecast is reasonable that Westendorf and Kirchberg will soon be interlinked by uphill transport systems.

Life in centre. Pleasant village life with good amenities. Plenty of young people. Modest ski standards.

Accessibility. Similar lines to Kitzbühel and Kirchberg.

Centre 162   Altitude
HOPFGARTEN   Province: Tyrol   2041 ft

Description. 1500 inhabitants (4000 in *Gemeinde*). 12 inns providing 150 beds. Other accommodation 200 beds. Language German.

Low in altitude, this slightly austere near-neighbour of both the Wildschönau and Westendorf has a short season.

Ski facilities. One ski area served by chairlift up the plum-pudding Hohe Salve. Rise of 2985 ft to Kälberalm at 5026 ft. Ski-lift project to summit at 6001 ft. Three or four runs of 5–6 km. on south-west-facing slopes. 6 km. run on south-east slopes to Westendorf.

Accessibility. Train: Innsbruck 1 hr 20 mins.

General comments. Of value as part of Kitzbühel–Wild-schönau general area – and worth short visit when conditions are good.

THE PINZGAU AND HOHE TAUERN AREA

AN intriguing and rewarding area of considerable charm where a wide variety of ski-ing, from *piste* to high touring, can be found. Zell-am-See, close to the northern entry to the Gross Glockner Pass road (closed in winter), which crosses the high barrier of the Hohe Tauern to drop down, via Heiligenblut, to Lienz, is the focal point of the region. The village of Kaprun is close by. Enzingerboden, with its big *Luftseilbahn* up to Weiss-See, is only 32 km. away. Both of these can easily be reached by bus, or better still by car. The popular little ski centre of Saalbach is only 18 km. north-west of Zell.

Centre 153   Altitude
ZELL-AM-SEE   Province: Salzburg   2487 ft

Description. 3000 inhabitants. 13 hotels and 13 pensions providing 1185 beds. Other accommodation 550 beds. Language German – English available.

A thriving and picturesquely-situated little lake-side town, rightly popular both in summer and winter, which manages very cleverly to be both a centre of commerce and a ski centre. Its front door opens on to the Zeller Lake and its back door looks into a big horseshoe of the eastern end of the Kitzbüheler Alpen which is its sizeable and well-equipped ski area.

Ski facilities. One large semicircular area served by two cable-cabin-car systems starting up from Schmitten (3064 ft and 2 km. by bus from Zell).

The Schmittenhöhebahn rises 3330 ft westwards to Schmittenhöhe at 6444 ft. Hotel restaurant and ski-lifts at or near summit form upland playground. Fine viewpoint. Runs, ranging from easy to very difficult (the Trass), of between $3\frac{1}{2}$ to 7 km. available on both sunny and shaded slopes. Long ski-lift on good nursery slopes on outskirts of Zell.

The Sonnenalmbahn rises north-west to 4534 ft, followed by chairlift north-north-west to Sonnkogel at 6017 ft. Total rise 2933 ft. Runs of about 4 km. on sunny slopes.

Ski touring. Good ski wandering nearby. Big ski touring available from nearby Kaprun and Enzingerboden (see below).

Amenities. Ski school. Skating rink. Lake skating and ski-jöring. Also horse, motor-car, and cycle racing on lake ice. Large variety of shops. Cafés. Bars. Dance bars. Night club, cabaret, etc. Sleighs. Bus tours. Cinemas, etc.

Life in centre. Entertaining small-town life. Plenty of activity and gaiety. Mixed nationalities. Reasonable prices and little sophistication. No monopoly on ski-ing.

Accessibility. Main-line train travel: Zürich 6 hrs, Vienna 5 hrs, Munich 4 hrs, Innsbruck 3 hrs, Salzburg 2 hrs.

General comments. Very good all-round value for the average skier in search of all-round winter entertainment.

Centre 149   Altitude
KAPRUN   Province: Salzburg   2579 ft

Description. 2500 inhabitants. 460 beds. Language German.

A large-scale semi-industrial village involved in big hydro-electric works. Not strictly a ski centre – more a place for visits from Zell.

Ski facilities. Good ski-lift on nursery slopes. Nearby large *Seilbahn* from 2730 ft goes up westwards to Maiskogel at 5069 ft. Rise of 2339 ft allowing for selection of ridge runs – easy and medium – down to bottom station and Kaprun.

Main importance of Kaprun is as entry base to Kaprunertal leading to splendid ski-touring area of the Hohe Tauern range. 4–5 hrs climb to Krefelder Hut (7526 ft) from which many wonderful springtime tours of all grades are possible. Popular favourite is the Kit zsteinhorn (10,509 ft), for 3-hr climb from hut.

Centre 53   Altitude
ENZINGERBODEN–   Province: Salzburg   4856 ft
  WEISS-SEE

Description. Again strictly no ski centre, Enzingerboden only has one inn with 40 beds and is a small settlement tucked into a narrow wooded valley at the top of a steep entry road (Zell 38 km.). Also involved in hydro-electric works, this area has lately acquired a big two-section *Seilbahn* system that gives a rise of 2749 ft up to Weiss-See at 7605 ft. Here the splendid, big, new Rudolf's Hut provides 200 beds.

An intriguing and exciting ski area with a very long ski season. Wild and wonderful ski country, which includes three reservoir lakes, made even a little weird by many overhead wires. Excellent varied ski-ing – not easy – down to Enzinger-boden. Main run about 7 km.

Rudolf's Hut stands at the edge of a large semicircular bowl surrounded by the glaciers and peaks of the Hohe Tauern. Many fine tours, including Gross Glockner summit (12,461 ft) and ski passage over to Heiligenblut in Ost Tyrol available from here.

General comments. An unusual but rewarding place for the keen skier. 'Mechanical' ski-ing good. Ski touring and ski-mountaineering wonderful. Comfortable 'hut-type' living. No amenities or entertainments, save good company. Austrian national team often trains here.

Centre 124		Altitude
SAALBACH	Province: Salzburg	3291 ft

Description. 550 inhabitants in village; 1400 in valley. Including nearby Hinterglemm there are 8 hotels and 20 inns and pensions providing 890 beds. Other accommodation 600 beds. 'Tourist house' 200 beds.

Good example of picture-book 'ski-dorf' created solely through and for ski-ing. Picturesque compact village in sunny open valley surrounded by low rounded hills. Pleasant small hotels and attractive village street and square.

Many buildings scattered up 4-km.-long valley.

Ski facilities. Three small- to medium-sized ski areas, with a fourth under consideration. Served by a selection of ski-lifts and chairlifts. Widespread and fine selection of nursery slopes.

The Kohlmaiskopf ski-lift rises 1982 ft to 5312 ft, with a

project to extend up to 5886 ft. Easy open south- and south-west-facing runs of between 3 and 4½ km.

The Bärenkogel chairlift rises 820 ft to 4167 ft. Short, amusing, varied runs of about 1½ km.

In the valley on both north- and south-facing slopes there are at least five short trainer lifts.

The Zwölferkogel ski-lift, close to Hinterglemm, rises 1047 ft to 4590 ft. North- and north-west-facing runs of about 1½ to 2½ km. on steeper, bumpy open slopes.

Saalbach's project is to construct a cable-car southwards up to the Schattberg at 6621 ft – a rise of 3330 ft which will open up longer runs of greater variety down to various parts of the main valley, including many north-facing slopes. Ski-lift projects at summit to extend season.

Amenities. Large ski school. Skating rink. Visitors' events. Good village shops. Hotel dancing and entertainments. All winter sports catered for.

Life in centre. Pleasant holiday feeling. Mixed nationalities. Simple, semi-funfair atmosphere, with plenty to watch. Comfortable, compact, and not costly. Easy to make friends. Gay. Little sophistication.

Accessibility. 50 mins. bus travel from Zell (see Zell-am-See, p. 178).

General comments. Perfect miniature paradise for beginner and medium skiers, in safe, sunny, gently-rounded, smiling ski country. Many enthusiasts, but few good skiers.

THE GASTEINERTAL AND RADSTÄDTER TAUERN AREAS

EASTWARDS from Zell-am-See, along the lower Pinzgauertal, you come to a series of several valleys that all run up south-wards into the east–west barrier ranges of the Hohe Tauern and the Radstädter Tauern. The westernmost valley contains the ski centres of Bad Hofgastein and Bad Gastein, before the rail tunnel goes through the Hohe Tauern barrier to Mallnitz (see p. 186). The easternmost valley mounts to a pass on which lies the ski centre of Obertauern.

Between these two areas lie several parallel valleys, such as the Grossarltal, the Kleinarltal, the Ennstal, and the Taurach-tal, in which much good ski-ing can be found. These valleys are, however, as yet undeveloped, and the future here will bear watching.

Centre 108   Altitude
BAD GASTEIN   Province: Salzburg 3117 ft to 3707 ft

Description. 6000 inhabitants. 22 hotels and 23 pensions pro-viding 2714 beds. Other accommodation 420 beds. Language German; most European tongues spoken.

An unusual and exceptional ski centre. A small town of many large, medium, and small buildings crammed into a steep-sided well-wooded gorge. Labyrinthine streets, and bridges across a torrent, at all levels. Primarily a health resort with famed thermal waters, Bad Gastein is a kind of cross between Aix-les-Bains and St Moritz.

Ski facilities. Two ski areas, one each on east and west sides of main valley, served by chairlift and gondola car systems respectively.

(1) *The Graukogel Area* (east side). Two chairlifts give total rise of 3005 ft up to Reichebenalpe at 6509 ft. Steep and thickly forested upper and central country with more open lower meadows has provided cut glade runs of all grades from diffi-cult to easy. Ranging between 4 km. and 6 km., these skilfully

planned runs on west- and north-west-facing slopes can cope
with either beginners' classes or international races. Artificial
in nature, they are nevertheless outstanding achievements
created out of difficult and unlikely ski country.

(2) *The Stubnerkogel Area* (west side). Two gondola cable-
cars give total rise of 3730 ft up to 7323 ft where there is a
splendid viewpoint all round the compass, including Gross
Glockner.

Upper section consists of widespread open east- and south-
east-facing slopes served by separate ski-lift as well as upper
gondola system. This ski area also spills over to far side of
Stubnerkogel, where a chairlift on west-facing slopes returns
you about 600 ft back up to main ridge.

Runs down to Bad Gastein vary from 3½ to 6 km., the lower
sections of which are again cut trails through thickly wooded
country. There are two or three small lifts near bottom station.
Lovely 8 km. run down to Angertal, 5 mins. by train return
to Bad Gastein.

Ski touring. Excellent and enterprising ski tours of all
grades available above and behind both top stations. The main
big touring area, however, reached via the neighbouring
village of Böckstein, lies all up and down the high Tauern
range between Bad Gastein and Mallnitz (see p. 186).

Amenities. Big ski school. Ski jump. Skating. Fine shopping
centre including sport and fashion shops. Casino. Theatre.
Tea rooms. Cabarets. Dancing. Cinemas, etc. Hot thermal
baths in several hotels. Doctors by the dozen.

Life in centre. Anything from large Palace Hotel life to that
of modest pension. International clientele. All pockets dealt
with. Cosmopolitan atmosphere. Mink coat to rucksack. Hypo-
chondriac to athlete. Wide range. No normal ski centre, and
certainly not monopolized by ski-ing.

Specialities. The availability – under medical supervision –
of wonderful hot thermal baths after hard exercise and good
ski-ing.

Accessibility. Train travel: Innsbruck 5 hrs; Vienna 7 hrs;
Rome 18 hrs; Zürich 10 hrs; Salzburg 1½ hrs.

General comments. Relative newcomer to list of ski centres.

Entertaining, well-organized, and good value. Specially recommended for those who wish to combine a cure with a ski holiday.

Centre 141   Altitude
BAD HOFGASTEIN   Province: Salzburg   2815 ft

Description. 3000 inhabitants. 14 hotels and 7 pensions providing 1036 beds. Other accommodation 1640 beds. Language German.

Another unusual newcomer to ski-ing, this historic and picturesque old town is primarily a health spa, sharing the same waters with Bad Gastein. Comfortably situated in a wide section of the Gasteinertal amid flat meadows, it commands nearby ski-ing that rates high in value.

Ski facilities. One large ski area served by three-section chair-lift system. This gives a total rise of 3652 ft up to Schlossalm at 6447 ft. Top section chairlift area is also served by 600 ft rise ski-lift.

Widespread open upper areas capable of further lift development. Fine variety of very good ski-ing with runs of all types from easy to medium-difficult ranging from $5\frac{1}{2}$ km. to 7 km. on north- and north-east-facing slopes. Plenty of sunny playground areas.

Amenities. Ski school. Ski jump. Skating rink. Good shops. Cafés. Restaurants. Hotel and bar dancing. Cinema, etc. Large thermal bath establishment.

Life in centre. Quiet, small spa-town atmosphere (bypassed by main valley road and railway). Historical background with plenty of sites of interest. Gentle and easygoing, without much excitement. Moderate and reasonable prices. Comfortable but sometimes slightly clinical hotels.

Speciality. 'Heilsport' – that is 'curative sport'. Holidays that combine ski-ing and a cure.

Accessibility. See Bad Gastein (p. 183) – 7 km. south by road or rail.

General comments. No monopoly on ski-ing; but the ski area is equal to, if not better than, that of a great number of better known centres – including its next-door neighbour. Visitors can, of course, share the Bad Gastein ski-ing together with its touring country. A party of any age group could greatly enjoy this centre. Specially recommended for the keen, not so young, not so energetic, skier.

Centre 27   Altitude
OBERTAUERN   Province: Salzburg   5331 ft to 5702 ft

Description. 800 inhabitants. 7 hotels and 11 inns 668 beds. Youth hostels 320 beds. Other accommodation 50 beds.

A high-pass settlement of many buildings scattered on both sides of, and on, pass height. A popular 'big centre in miniature', it can boast of little picturesque architecture (save for a fifteenth-century staging-post inn, now a comfortable hotel) but plenty of spirit. Already well equipped with small lifts, there is plenty of space for development both in uphill transport and accommodation. Both these are going ahead.

Ski facilities. Surrounded on both sides of the Pass by wide open, pleasant, and friendly ski country, rising to many minor peaks of about 7–7500 ft, one can ski where one will. Three medium-sized lifts give rises of between 700 ft and 1000 ft and extensions to these are planned. Many sunny areas, where small lakes are found, and north-facing slopes also available. At least four baby lifts serve good nursery slopes.

A project of great interest is a 2-km.-long cable-car, southwards up to the Zehnerkarsattel at 7218 ft. This will open up good, enterprising, north-slope ski-ing.

Amenities. Ski school. Small shop or two. Some dancing.

Life in centre. Simple fun. Impromptu gaiety. Family atmosphere. All nations meet both on slopes and in the evenings, dancing and singing. No sophistication.

Accessibility. Bus travel: Salzburg 3½ hrs, Radstadt 1 hr, Spittal 4 hrs.

General comments. Very good value for cheap and spirited holidays with friendly small-scale ski-ing. Easy to make friends. This unusual and rewarding place is intelligently run and is recommended to students and parties of young people.

CARINTHIA

Centre 97
MALLNITZ   Province: Carinthia

Altitude
3931 ft

Description. 1056 inhabitants. 6 hotels and 6 inns and pensions providing 600 beds. Other accommodation 340 beds. Language German.

Large village standing at southern end of the Tauern tunnel (8½ km. long) under the Hohe Tauern range, only 14 km. rail from Bad Gastein. Standing on small flat at hub-junction of several big and impressive valleys.

Ski facilities. The emphasis here is on spring ski touring rather than 'mechanical' *piste* ski-ing.

One ski area served by chairlift giving rise of 2231 ft up to Häusleralm at 6109 ft. Baby lift at bottom station, two baby lifts at top. Popular little upland playground with restaurant and fine views. One main run, with variants, down to bottom station gives about 4 km. of moderate to difficult descent.

Ski touring. Three large ski-touring areas – to the west, the north, and the east, including the whole of the Hohe Tauern range between Mallnitz and Bad Gastein. Many peaks and several good huts make this a splendid region for the ski tourer.

Project. A high motor-road tunnel through to Bad Gastein is planned. In due course, lifts from the southern entry will take one up to Hochalmblick Hut and continue up to Ebeneck at 8550 ft.

Amenities. Small ski school. Skating rink. Village shops. Cinema. Flat-truck car transports through rail tunnel.

Life in centre. Quiet, simple, unpretentious, inexpensive, and friendly atmosphere. Through traffic considerable – as, for example, in Bardonecchia – but never very crowded.

Accessibility. Train travel: Salzburg 2 hrs, Innsbruck 5½ hrs, Zürich 10½ hrs, Vienna 7½ hrs.

General comments. Principally for lovers of spring ski touring.

Future developments will extend lift systems. Not much at present for the *piste* skier, but he can easily use the Bad Gastein lifts and runs, by train travel through Tauern tunnel.

Centre 80   Altitude
HEILIGENBLUT   Province: Carinthia   4426 ft

Description. 300 inhabitants. 5 hotels and 3 inns providing 260 beds. Other accommodation 80 beds. Language German.

This attractive little Alpine village, dramatically situated on the Gross Glockner road (pass closed in winter) amid grand surroundings, is a busy summer tourist spot. In winter it has a secret, remote, Shangri-la atmosphere.

Ski facilities. Until plans to build lifts up from Rossbach north-eastwards up to Tauernberg (6759 ft) materialize, Heiligenblut can only offer limited runs of about $1\frac{1}{2}$ km. from Rossbach – reached by small bus service – with descents of about 1300 ft. There are two small lifts on village nursery slopes.

Ski touring. Heiligenblut is beautifully situated for spring ski touring. Centrally placed between Weiss-See, Bad Gastein, Mallnitz, and Lienz, Heiligenblut commands the main Gross Glockner and Sonnblick peak regions of the Hohe Tauern range. Any amount of fine variety of glacier ski-ing for the enthusiast.

Specialities. The nearby, famous Franz Joseph's Haus Hotel at 7749 ft provides ski-ing all the year round. This hotel is close to the finishing point for the well-known Gross Glockner downhill race – 11,844 ft down to 7579 ft – which takes place in May.

Accessibility. Post-bus travel: Mallnitz 2 hrs, Lienz $1\frac{1}{2}$ hrs.

General comments. Quiet, simple, and with few amenities or facilities for the winter *piste* skier, Heiligenblut comes into its own for the ski tourer in springtime.

Centre 25   Altitude
TURRACHERHÖHE   Province: Carinthia/Styria   5784 ft

Description. 20 inhabitants. 5 hotels and 4 inns providing 370 beds. Other accommodation 10 beds.

No village, this is a collection of relatively high-altitude winter and summer hotels scattered in sunny, gentle surroundings around the shores of the attractive Turracher lake, through which runs the border between Carinthia and Styria.

Ski facilities. Various small lifts on slopes in immediate vicinity (longest rises 580 ft) used in combination give total rise of about 900 ft. Easy east-facing slopes allow for gentle runs. Projected lift will go up to about 7000 ft.

Considerable 'ski wandering' possible in half day and day excursions on the many rounded hills that surround the lake and rise to a maximum of 8000 ft.

Amenities. Ski tuition. Skating rink. One or two small shops. Hotel bar dancing, etc.

Life in centre. Simple, small-hotel life. Comfortable, easygoing, and inexpensive. Party spirit gaiety. Entertainment largely what you make it. Easy to make friends.

Accessibility. Train via Mallnitz to Spittal, thence bus 3 hours. Steep entry road. Chains essential.

General comments. No place for the *piste*-basher. Popular with visitors of many nationalities seeking gentle ski-ing and excursions, together with friendly, family atmosphere both on the slopes and in the hotels.

EAST TYROL

Centre 159   Altitude
LIENZ   Province: Ost Tyrol   2208 ft

Description. 12,000 inhabitants. 6 hotels and 10 inns providing 629 beds. Other accommodation 850 beds. Language German.

This capital of East Tyrol is a beautiful 'little Innsbruck' set in lovely surroundings, with back-cloths of both Alpine and 'Dolomite' scenery. A lethargically busy, workaday little town which has much to offer for a holiday of interest and ski-ing combined.

Ski facilities. Two ski areas served by chairlift and cable-car systems with additional lifts, and various projects for the future.

(1) *The Hochstein Area.* Chairlift gives rise of 1102 ft up to 3340 ft. Leads to beginners' playground with baby lift and provides attractive little north-east-facing runs of 1½ to 2½ km. down through pleasant woodlands. Projected extension will continue up to 4980 ft and greatly increase variety of runs.

(2) *The Zettersfeld Area.* Luftseilbahn gives rise of 3596 ft up to 5971 ft surmounted by a ski-lift up to Steinermandl at 7260 ft. Fine variety of south- and south-west-facing runs of approximately 4920 ft descent and up to 6½ km. in length.

Several ski-lift projects on summit ridge will open up 'circus' type runs on north- and east-facing slopes.

Ski touring. Excellent valley entries up into the Hohe Tauern range, to both the Gross Venediger and the Gross Glockner glacier ski-touring regions. Ski access over to Weiss-See area (see p. 179). Easy access also into the Lienzer Dolomite Range. Lienz in springtime is surrounded with lovely ski-touring country.

Amenities. Ski school. Guides. Skating rink. Large selection of small-town shops. Attractive architecture and historic 'sites'. Restaurants, cafés, cinema, etc.

Life in centre. Low-altitude small Austrian town life, not dominated by ski-ing. Sunny, pleasant, and friendly atmosphere. Prices very reasonable. Comfortable living with no frills. Plenty of interest.

Accessibility. Train travel: Innsbruck 4½ hrs, Salzburg 6 hrs, Vienna 8 hrs. Post-bus to Vienna approximately 6 hrs.

General comments. No 'ski dorf', Lienz, with a relatively short winter season, is much to be recommended for a gentle holiday by car (easy access to Heiligenblut and the Italian frontier – Cortina d'Ampezzo, Venice, etc.) and for those who seek an attractive base for excellent spring ski touring.

STYRIA

Centres 137 and 34
TAUPLITZ—
KLACHAU   Province: Styria
TAUPLITZALM

Altitudes
2923 ft

5446 ft

Description. Tauplitz: 370 inhabitants. 5 inns with 125 beds.
Other accommodation 50 beds. *Tauplitzalm*: 2 hotels providing 220 beds. 8 inns and some 50 huts providing approximately 400 beds.

Tauplitz is a simple but attractive Salzkammergut village
connected by a 4-km.-long chairlift system with the Tauplitzalm 2400 ft above.

Tauplitzalm is an extensive, sunny plateau of many undulations scattered with many buildings small and big.

Ski facilities. Tauplitzalm is furnished with many small
trainer lifts and two larger lifts. The Schneiderkogel ski-lift
rises 496 ft to 5781 ft. The Lawinenstein chairlift rises 1070 ft
to 6434 ft. These two provide south-east- and east-facing
slopes of amusing ski-ing. The plateau in general consists of
widespread easy ski-ing for all types of beginners. No snags.
Easy safe country. Lovely views. Plenty of space.

The two main runs down to Tauplitz range from 5 to $6\frac{1}{2}$
km. One is an easy 'promenade' affair and the other a medium-
difficult descent of some interest to better performers.

Amenities. Ski school. Village shops. Hotel bar dancing, etc.

Life in centre. Simple small village life in Klachau. Many
young people. Life on Tauplitzalm consists of many youthful
groups and parties which congregate and intermingle at the
larger establishments where there are restaurants and bar
dancing. Gay and unusual. Inexpensive.

Accessibility. Train travel: Lienz 3–4 hrs, Salzburg 3 hrs,
Vienna 5 hrs.

General comments. A little ski paradise for beginners both
young and old. Specially suited to parties of students who wish
to live simply and cheaply and make their own holiday fun.

UPPER AUSTRIA

Centre 167
OBERTRAUN–
  HALLSTATT   Province: Upper Austria
(DACHSTEIN)

Altitudes
1677 ft

Description. Obertraun: 750 inhabitants. 2 hotels and 2 inns providing 70 beds. Other accommodation 120 beds. *Hallstatt:* 1440 inhabitants. 1 hotel and 2 inns providing 100 beds. Other accommodation 100 beds. *Krippenstein* (6821 ft): 1 hotel with 32 beds and 30 mattress beds. To be enlarged to 80–100 beds. Language German.

This intriguing and interesting ski area – a popular summer corner of the Salzkammergut only recently opened up for skiing – has two attractive and fascinating lakeside (Hallstättersee) villages as low-altitude bases. The rock fortress mountain of the Dachstein is scaled by a big, new, two-section *téléférique* up to Krippenstein – a total rise of 4826 ft. Beautiful and dramatic scenery below and a huge and wonderful 'upstairs' island plateau of snowfields and glaciers.

Ski facilities. Good beginners' area with short lifts round Krippenstein top station. A selection of highly interesting and medium-to-difficult long runs, ranging from 5 to 9 km. on northeast- and north-west-facing slopes, go down to middle and valley stations.

This ambitious and well-run ski area proposes to extend the *Luftseilbahn*, via Gjaidalm and the Simony Hut, right up to Hohe Gjaidstein at 9160 ft. When completed, in a few years' time, this will make readily accessible the present lovely touring area above and behind Krippenstein.

General comments. A 'must' for the ski connoisseur who finds himself anywhere near this region. Unusual, unorthodox, unexploited, and unspoilt, the Dachstein area has few amenities but tremendous character. Krippenstein hotel has all the comforts, and the ski-ing is very worth while.

FOUR

French Ski Centres

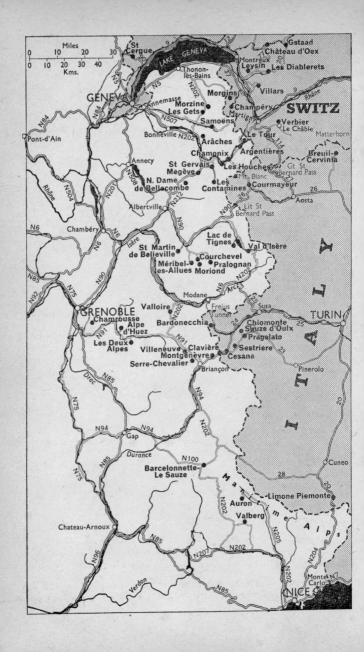

CONTENTS

THE BRIANÇON AREA – DAUPHINÉ

THE BASSES-ALPES

THE CÔTE D'AZUR AREA – ALPES MARITIMES

INTRODUCTION

PSYCHOLOGICALLY, the man in the English street does not connect France with snow. With Paris and the Côte d'Azur, yes. With gastronomic touring, yes. With cabarets, casinos, and champagne, yes. Even snails. But snow, no.

Even supposing that France could only boast of very indifferent ski country, always remember this – it is very, very difficult to eat badly in France. Even the tiniest, scruffiest little *bistro-pension* can, if it feels like it, turn out the most delicious bouilla-baisse. It nearly always does feel like it.

Apart from this very important point, however, France does have a great number of wonderful ski areas, and very excellent ski centres to suit all tastes and all pockets.

The main thing, first and foremost, to say about the planning and development of French ski centres is that, of all the Alpine countries, it is, at this moment, the most ambitious, the most go-ahead, and the most actively constructive. Partly this is so because France, with the obvious exception of Chamonix (and possibly Megève and Val d'Isère) started to develop its winter sports centres in a really big way a good deal later than did Switzerland and Austria. For a long while, in the early days, ski-ing was only moderately popular with the French public.

Within recent years, however, the pendulum has swung right over, and *le ski* now occupies a very high and very important place in the mind of the masses.

The French public, compared with the Swiss and the Austrian, is 'mountain-minded' more by application than by natural inclination or even necessity. By the very nature of the whole country – which probably contains a greater variety of climate, territory, and general attraction for the holiday tourist than any other land – it has so much choice that mountains, until recently, have only occupied a fraction of the French mind. A relatively small proportion of the Monsieur Duponts of France are true *montagnards*, but today, particularly with the young, *le ski* is not only fashionable but truly and universally appreciated and recognized as being the sport of sports.

The average Frenchman may seem an eccentric obstinate Gallic mystery to many, but he is a realist and a business man, and the executive Frenchman – the type that has long led the world in subjects as varied as diplomacy and *haute couture* – combines his diplomatic charm and intelligence with shrewd and limitless imagination.

So far as winter holidays in the mountains are concerned the problems of overcrowding are being tackled in France with far more imagination than elsewhere. Local enterprise, often backed either by big business or by state aid, is busy planning to open up whole new areas of hitherto untouched ski country, and, moreover, always with an eye to keeping the capacity of the uphill transport lifts well in advance of the hotel accommodation capacity. Private enterprise is doing the same. Existing centres are being furnished with greatly increased and improved uphill transport systems. Perhaps the first successful examples of doubling-up of ski-lifts has already occurred here. The problems of bottle-necks and queues can only be solved by doubling up – and side-by-side ski-lifts will certainly be copied elsewhere. France has more 'projects' than anywhere else.

Living conditions are also being tackled with a 'new look'. Not only a great number of ultra-modern, almost *avant-garde*, small- and medium-sized hotels have already been constructed, but a new conception of ski holiday living is even now well established.

The Frenchman does not always wish to be tied to hotel life – nor necessarily to the often arduous task of running a chalet. He likes to be free. He has therefore started to apply the modern principle of self-contained, furnished flatlets (similar to town dwelling, and motels, etc.) to winter sports. Courchevel is the prime example of this development, where large blocks of these apartments, each provided with communal restaurants for those who tire of shopping and cooking for themselves in their own kitchenettes, have already proved popular. The traditional-minded will not approve of such Alpine architecture, nor of the application of city conditions to mountain living, but the theory works out well in practice, and it has many assets.

French ski centres are always gay, cheerful, and colourful. They range from the ultra-sophisticated (Alpe d'Huez, Megève, etc.) to the traditionally simple and genuine (Valloire, Moriond, Les Contamines, etc.); from the new-fangled ski-mill (Courchevel, Chamrousse, and the future St Martin de Belleville, etc.) to the 'private-estate' type of modern traditional architecture (notably Méribel-les-Allues). There is a very wide choice, and many of the small well-known centres in other Alpine countries have far less to offer than many a small 'unknown' centre in the French Alps.

In general, visitors to France are far less international than visitors to Switzerland and Austria. Ninety per cent of the skiers in France in wintertime are French. The atmosphere is French. The language is frequently limited to French.

Volatile, dynamic, and frequently brilliant, the French character is sometimes unwilling to attend to detail. You will thus find, for example, that the electric plugs in the most splendid hotel rooms may not be very reliable. You will certainly find the French far less tidy than the Swiss.

By far the greater proportion of the best French ski centres are found in Savoie and Haute-Savoie, and these areas are as easily accessible from London and Paris as anywhere in the Alps. The quality of good ski-ing extends, however, right down to within a two-hours motor drive of Cannes and Nice. As in the case of Italy, many of the French ski centres, owing to the influence of the Mediterranean climate, enjoy an abundance of sunshine and blue skies which in no way limit the depth of snowfall.

French railways, which before the war were sometimes open to criticism, are now superb. It is to be hoped that the bus services which link main-line stations – and for that matter airports as well – with ski centres will show similar improvement. France will certainly be up among the leaders in installing helicopter or aircraft shuttle services between airports and ski centres.

Week-end ski-ing is immensely popular in France, and the car is more used than any other means of transport. Parking problems are well handled and the public service of the Ponts et Chaussées performs wonders in maintaining the mountain roads and passes in excellent shape.

France has had a reputation for being expensive for ski holidays, but this accusation can scarcely be supported any longer. French centres cater for every depth of pocket. Hotel bills of every category are now completely comprehensive (including tips) and known in advance, and there is no longer an endless list of extras to be added on at the end of the stay.

Not many ski teachers are multi-lingual (as they often are in Switzerland and Austria) but the standard of tuition of the École Nationale de Ski is as high as anywhere in the Alps – and often a great deal more inspiring and amusing than elsewhere. French skiers are principally *piste*-skiers, and the modern tendency to avoid walking at all costs has resulted in a plethora of ski-lifts. Not all of these are presently either comfortable or swift (a slow open *télébenne* on a north slope is no one's idea of fun), but most are now being converted to swifter and warmer forms of travel. Some of the new ski-lifts move so quickly that uphill ski-ing is becoming something of an art in itself.

Even the most stubborn conservative-minded Englishman will readily admit that, gastronomically, France is very hard to rival. The penny does not yet appear to have dropped that France is a country where one can enjoy superb ski-ing as well.

It very soon will.

THE GENEVA AREA

Centre 122*   Altitude
MORZINE   Province: Haute-Savoie   3077–3320 ft

Description. 1815 inhabitants. 50 hotels providing 3000 beds. Other accommodation 1500 beds. Several children's '*école et ski*' schools. French language only.

Originally a summer-holiday resort, this widespread collection of pleasant hotel buildings surrounding an old village now sprawls across both sides of the river Dranse ravine (high footbridge connexion). Popular now for winter sports, Morzine has much that many seek. A trifle low, perhaps, in altitude, this centre is attractively situated in sunny, sheltered surroundings and well furnished with equipment, amusements, and facilities for the holiday skier.

Ski facilities. Two ski areas served by one *téléférique* and one *télébenne* system. Other lifts: six trainer and baby lifts.

(1) *The Pleney Téléférique* (west of river) gives a rise of 1716 ft south-west up to the ridge at 4947 ft (restaurant), which allows for an easy run down to Les Gets (see p. 202), and provides a series of *pistes* of 2–4 km. in length back to Morzine. Easy north- and north-east-facing slopes.

(2) *The Super-Morzine Télébenne* (east of river) gives a long, slow (25-mins.) rise of 2625 ft up to 5906 ft (fine viewpoint). Easy upper slopes – south-west-facing – can be served from middle station (Les Granges at 4593 ft) when the snow on lower slopes melts.

The adequate, but slightly miniature, ski areas of Morzine, which do not extend above the tree line and are ideally suited for medium and beginner skiers, will shortly be increased by two important projects which will greatly widen the scope. (1) A *téléférique* and *télébenne* system, with subsidiary lifts, south of village, to the Pointe de Nyon at about 6500 ft. (2) Lifts, east of village, which will open up the north-facing

---

* Each place description is numbered according to the Altitude List, pp. 104–21.

slopes of Les Hauts Forts up to about 7200 ft close to the Swiss
frontier. (Neighbouring Swiss centres: Morgins and Champéry. See p. 363.)

Amenities. Ski school with 28 teachers. Small skating rink.
Small ski jump. Cinema. Four bar dancings. Good shopping
centre. Sleigh rides. Dancing, etc.

Life in centre. Active, gay, large village. Inexpensive, unpretentious – '*à la fois sportive et familiale*'. *Après-ski* life what
you make it.

Accessibility. Train: either Thonon station (33 km.) or
Cluses (30 km.). Road: bus from Thonon (1 hr 10 mins.) and
Cluses (1½ hrs). Airport: Geneva (55 km.)

General comments. Area and centre well suited to parties of
beginners and medium-type skiers. Interesting future projects.
Crowded on Sundays.

Centre 104		Altitude
LES GETS	Province: Haute-Savoie	3816 ft

Description. 765 inhabitants. 25 hotels providing 900 beds.
Other accommodation 300 beds. French language only.

Six km. by road from Morzine, this centre consists of attractive modern hotel buildings pleasantly situated in an open col.
High enough to get good snow conditions, sunny Les Gets is
also exposed to wind.

Ski facilities. Two ski areas on easy slopes on both sides of
col served by one chairlift and two ski-lifts. Other lifts: four
trainer and baby lifts.

(1) *The Pointe du Chéry Chairlift* (west side of col). Two-
seater chairs go up north-west to about 5900 ft in 13 mins. and
provide easy south-east-facing *pistes* of between 3 and 5 km.
Upper station (restaurant and short ski-lift) provides superb
viewpoint of the whole of the Mont Blanc range. Foreground
shows the whole of the Les Gets–Morzine layout.

(2) *The Chavannes and La Turche Ski-lifts* (east side of col).
Two separate lift systems go up south-east to 5085 ft and 4975 ft
respectively. Easy wide *pistes* of 2 to 3 km. and about 1200 ft.
A short 'promenade' of 20 mins. from top of Chavannes upper

lift leads to top station of the Pleney *téléférique* up from neighbouring Morzine. Les Gets plans a lift to make a direct junction so that the circuit between the two centres is complete.

All lifts provide pleasant, unfrightening ski-ing on lightly
wooded open slopes.

Amenities. Ski school with 30 teachers. Small skating rink.
Small jump. Small cinema. Three bar dancings. Sleigh rides.

Life in centre. Simple and genuine. Reasonable prices.
Interest mainly ski-ing. Small hotel world. Popular. High-
spirited family atmosphere.

Accessibility. See Morzine.

General comments. Good value for those seeking simple terrain and pleasant holiday, particularly for parties and young
people. The col can be draughty. When the various Les Gets
and Morzine projects are completed, the choice will be wide and
much more varied.

Centre 156   Altitude
SAMOËNS AND   Province: Haute-Savoie   2329 ft
ARACHES

Description. 1634 inhabitants. 16 hotels and pensions with 500
beds. Other accommodation in chalets and apartments.
U.N.C.M. 80 beds. 3 *maisons d'enfants*. Language French only.

A low-altitude, picturesque, and quite large Savoyard village
in the wide Vallée du Giffre. Barely a ski centre itself, but with
good ski-ing available 3 km. away (hourly bus service) and
with interesting nearby projects.

Ski facilities. A short bus-ride across the valley takes you up
to Le Fayet at 2674 ft, where there are one or two small hotels.
Here a *télébenne* system gives a rise of 2543 ft southwards up to
Les Saix at 5217 ft. North-facing, lightly wooded runs of between $3\frac{1}{2}$ km. (medium) and 6 km. (easy). A short walk then
takes you to two upper ski-lifts rising 780 ft and 793 ft respectively, climbing up first to 6076 ft and finally to the top station
of Croix des Saix at 6930 ft. Good, open, above treeline slopes,
largely north-facing.

This system allows a total rise above Le Fayet of 4255 ft over

a travel distance of more than 5 km. Good chair- and ski-lifts
also at the hamlet of Les Esserts, close to La Fayet.

Project. Back of the Croix des Saix, to the south and south-
west, there is a large area of fine ski country which links with
the Samoëns ski-ing. Plans to develop this region, as yet untouched save by spring skiers and tourers, will approach from
the reverse side. From the Vallée de l'Arve a road leads up to
the village of Araches at 3609 ft. This road will be continued up
to the Desert Platé (Lac de Flaine) at 4265 ft. From here,
where a modern ski centre will be constructed, new ski-lifts
will go up to about 8450 ft. A lift from the Lac de Flaine will
rise to connect with the Croix des Saix lift above Samoëns.
This important, long-term project makes this area one to be
watched with great interest.

Amenities. Small ski school. Ski jump. Village amenities.
Restaurants. Bars. Cinema, etc.

Life in centre. Quiet village life somewhat removed from the
ski slopes. Friendly and simple. No over-emphasis on ski-ing.
Ski standards moderate. Prices reasonable. *Après-ski* life absent.

Accessibility. From Annemasse (Geneva) 60 km. by bus.

General comments. A pleasant, gentle village, with good ski-
ing nearby, but with only half its mind on winter sports. The
future development of Araches and Le Desert Platé (see
above) will give this place a big boost.

THE MONT BLANC AREA

Centre 109   Altitude
MEGÈVE   Province: Haute-Savoie   3652 ft

Description. 3700 inhabitants. 86 hotels and pensions providing
4000 beds. 10 *maisons d'enfants.* Numerous apartments and
chalets providing about 4000 beds. Total capacity about
8–10,000 beds. Most European languages understood.

Megève lays itself wide open for comment owing to its lordly
complacency in calling itself the '*Capitale du Ski*'. In spite of
the fact that Megève has plenty of the type of ski-ing that
many seem to seek, no centre with a height difference of slightly
over 2500 ft, starting from so low an altitude, can reasonably
call itself the capital of anything. This centre, which bears little
resemblance to a normal winter-sports resort is, in fact, a small,
bustling, expensive, cosmopolitan town of some charm and some
impatience, where manners are often at a premium, and where
the skier, with all the clutter of his equipment, often seriously
impedes the woolly-booted brigade from getting to the sunbathing terraces at the restaurants at the top stations of the
uphill transports. A fashionable, sunny, low-altitude holiday
resort, with only half its mind on ski-ing, is perhaps a better
description. The other half of the Megève mind is most successfully occupied with making itself agreeable, at a price, to
the mink coat, the pale pink *fuseau*, and the business-man not
yet too tired to climb into a rubber-tyred sleigh as transport to
the nearest *téléférique.*

Ski facilities. Three separate but not interlinked ski areas
served by two *téléfériques* and one *télécabine.* Other lifts: six ski-
lifts and four trainer lifts.

(1) *Rochebrune Area* (south-west of town). Quick *téléférique*
(5 mins.) gives rise of 1975 ft to summit restaurant at 5751 ft.
Nearby Alpette hilltop (6138 ft) is reached by ski-lift. Several
bumpy hardbeaten *pistes* of reasonable gradient, together with
longer, easier descents. Average 3½ to 5 km. and 2303 ft. Upper
slopes face north-west. Main runs face north-east. General
direction, north.

(2) *Jaillet Area* (north of town). Four-seater *télécabines* give rise of 1509 ft to summit restaurant at 5184 ft. Various descents on south-facing slopes of 2½ to 3½ km. Lower slopes quickly revert to grass. Behind and beyond this area there is a rewarding 'circus' provided by two ski-lifts, starting from 4597 ft and going up westwards to 5974 ft and north-east to 5581 ft. Good ski-ing, good snow duration, and good variety to be found here. Latter lift is also the start point, when conditions allow, of the 12-km. descent down to Sallanches. This Jaillet area is the most profitable for enterprising skiers.

(3) *Mont d'Arbois Area* (south-east of town, 15 mins. by bus). *Téléférique* rises from 4200 ft to 5709 ft, opening up large areas of gentle sunny slopes most suitable for beginners. Area also served by various slow ski-lifts which reach the ridge crest at Pointe de Fredy, 6014 ft (which is the summit station of the two-section *téléférique* which mounts south-westwards from St Gervais), and up to the top of Mont Joux at 6421 ft.

In general the ski country all around Megève is without malice and agreeable. The start points for each area are awkwardly and widely separated, and car or bus is essential. The popular *pistes* are not so well maintained as might be expected and there is a casual lack of direction posts and general information. Runs of more than average difficulty are relatively little patronized. Wide and wonderful viewpoints of the Mont Blanc area are to be found at each top station, but it would be a good idea to put up panorama tables to inform the visitor of the surrounding ranges and peaks.

Amenities. Large ski school with 80 teachers. Three ski jumps (one Olympic). Two skating rinks. Curling. Artificial rink. Casino. Large bowling alley. Bridge club. Large shopping area. Garages. Many restaurants, *salons de thé*, night-clubs, etc. Two cinemas and various cabarets.

Life in centre. Sophisticated, fashionable, and expensive (although good cheap accommodation can be found). Constant movement and traffic, especially at week-ends when some 5000 car and bus skiers invade the town. (High proportion of cars come from Geneva.) International clientele, forty per cent of which is non-ski-ing. Nightlife gets going from eleven p.m.

onwards. Large cars. Expensive clothes. Plenty to look at. Slightly impersonal atmosphere.

Specialities. Megève is linked by uphill transport and downhill runs both to and from Chamonix, via St Gervais in the intervening valley. This *traversée* is, however, seldom used, for parts of the 'crossing' descend too low for constant reliable snow.

Accessibility. Train: Sallanches station (12 km.). Road: bus 40 mins. from Sallanches. Paris 610 km. Lyon 192 km. Airport: Geneva 71 km. (bus service).

General comments. Excellent for those who seek a cross between gentle sunny ski-ing, sunbathing, and nightlife. From the ski angle, its reputation is overdone. There is something of an air of complacency about the place.

Centre 147
ST GERVAIS   Province: Haute-Savoie

Altitude
2648 ft

Description. Several thousand inhabitants. 55 hotels and 20 pensions providing about 2000 beds. 23 *maisons d'enfants*.

A large, resort-type town of many big buildings whose hotels lie scattered around the valley hillsides up to an altitude of about 6000 ft, reminding one less of a ski centre than a summer resort – one looks, in vain, for a lake shore or seaside beaches.

Standing at the valley entrance of the road leading up to Les Contamines (see p. 208), St Gervais lies midway between Chamonix to the east and Megève to the west. Uphill transports connect it to the intervening ridges between it and these two important centres.

Ski facilities. Two ski areas, one on each side of valley.

(1) South-westwards, a two-section *téléférique* climbs via Bettex (4593 ft, good local practice slopes with trainer lift) up to the Pointe de Fredy 6014 ft on the Mont d'Arbois ridge above Megève (see p. 206). Upper section of *téléférique* provides pleasant north-east-facing ski-ing down to Bettex. Nothing difficult. Below Bettex down to St Gervais the meadows seldom hold snow for long periods.

(2) South-eastwards the Mont Blanc tramway slants up to

Bellevue at 5873 ft on the ridge above Les Houches and
Chamonix (see p. 210). This opens up the Bellevue–Les
Houches ski area, and, when conditions are suitable, one can
ski back down to St Gervais on sunny slopes.

Amenities. Ski school. Skating rink. Casino. Cinema. Tea
rooms. Restaurants. Bars. Dancing. Shopping centre.

Life in centre. Pleasant enough, but largely lacking any winter sports 'atmosphere'.

Accessibility. Train: to Le Fayet station, thence 4 km. bus.
Paris 609 km. Airport: Geneva thence train or bus.

General comments. Far from being a cosy, orthodox, Christmas-card ski centre, St Gervais has its assets for those who
prefer semi-town life. Ski standards that are never demanding
will suit beginners. Easy bus access to Les Contamines.

Centre 103		Altitude
LES CONTAMINES	Province: Haute-Savoie	3819 ft

Description. 730 inhabitants. 20 hotels providing 800 beds.
U.N.C.M. hostel with 90 beds. Language French only.

A very pleasant little village situated in the wide, sunny
valley of Montjoie only 9 km. by road up from St Gervais, at
the south-western foot of Mont Blanc. Set in grand surroundings, this enterprising and friendly little centre has much to offer.

Ski facilities. One large ski area served by three-section lift
system and one local village ski-lift giving 1150-ft rise.

(1) *The Montjoie–Roselette Ski Area.* A surprisingly long
linkage of assorted lifts, consisting of one *télécabine* followed by
one ski-lift and then an upper chairlift, gives a total cable distance of over 5 km. (35–40 mins. travel time), and a rise of
3400 ft. Each lift can be used separately or in any sequence and
the whole system serves a long benevolent spinal ridge which
extends up south-westwards to the Tête de Roselette at 7218 ft.
Lovely open upper slopes are backed by extensive ski-touring
area. Runs of about 8 km. available on both sunny and shaded
slopes. Wide easy *pistes* with difficult sections available. Wonderful views of Mont Blanc.

(2) *The Nivorin Ski-Lift*, which goes up westwards from the

village to about 5000 ft, opens up wide nursery slopes and
steep giant-slalom-type pitches of interesting ground.

Amenities. Ski school with 17 teachers. Ski jump. Ice rink.
Village shops. Bar dancing. Tea shops, cinema, etc.

Life in centre. Friendly, genuine, small-ski-centre atmosphere. Quiet and simple – with accent on sport. Very reasonable prices provide good value all round.

Accessibility. Trains: Fayet station (13 km.). Road: bus
45 mins. Paris 621 km. Airport: Geneva (73 km.); bus
service.

General comments. Good proposition for the keen average
holiday skier. Much to be recommended for parties of young
people looking for good value at reasonable expense. Good
spring ski-ing on Trélatête Glacier (Mont Blanc side).

THE CHAMONIX VALLEY

The Chamonix valley, which runs some 15–20 km. south-
west to north-east up to the Swiss frontier, and which lies
directly at the northern foot of the spectacular Mont Blanc
Barrier Range between France and Italy, contains several ski
centres. There are, in this grand and famous region, many
normal and several unique ski areas, and, since all of these are
readily accessible by bus, car, or train from any part of the
valley, the ski-ing facilities must be treated as being available to
visitors at any of the centres. Accommodation is to be found all
up and down this steep-sided valley (total population 7500) but,
starting from the south-west, on the entry road up from Geneva,
Annecy, or Albertville, the various centres (in most cases semi-
adjoining) are as follows: Les Houches, Les Bossons (Chamonix), Chamonix, Les Pras (Chamonix), Argentière, Le Tour
(Argentière). At the far north-east end of the valley, the Col des
Montets road over into Switzerland is closed in winter, but
access by rail tunnel through to Martigny is always possible.
Extraordinary access to Italy is possible by the fantastic *téléférique* and *télécabine* system, via the Aiguille du Midi and
Piz Helbronner down to Courmayeur (see pp. 270–3), and
more normal but equally sensational access will be available in

1963 when the Chamonix–Courmayeur road tunnel under Mont Blanc is completed.

Popular between the wars, the Chamonix valley suffered a recession owing to the development of other centres. The spider's web of uphill transport systems and downhill *piste* facilities, now available, together with immediate future projects of great interest, will certainly put this region right back on the keen skier's map.

		Altitude
Centre 125		
LES HOUCHES	Province: Haute-Savoie	3281 ft

Description. 1140 inhabitants. 22 hotels providing 650 beds.

At the foot of the Aiguille du Goûter this village, with its scattered hotels lining a loop-road away from the main Chamonix entry road, is relatively peaceful. Set in an angle between the main Mont Blanc Massif and the Bellevue–Prarion ridge (which separates Les Houches from the St Gervais valley), it does, however, see little sunshine.

Ski facilities. One ski area served by one *téléférique* giving a rise of 2592 ft south-westwards up to Bellevue at 5873 ft. Here, a long sunny ridge provides good beginner ground (plus baby lift). A ski-lift from the Col de Voze (5414 ft) goes up northwards to Prarion at 6070 ft. This ridge is also reached from St Gervais by means of the Tramway Mont Blanc (see p. 207). Various runs from the ridge go off westwards down to St Gervais (2648 ft, south slopes – snow seldom allows complete descent) and eastwards down to Les Houches. These latter are good value, giving descents between 3 and 4 km. on east- and north-east-facing slopes where powder snow lasts well. Enterprising ski-ing, suitable for all, save for the famous Piste Verte racecourse which is for higher standards.

Ski-lift on nursery slopes by village.

Three km. eastwards (towards Chamonix) a projected chairlift from Les Bossons will give a rise of about 1300 ft over a distance of 1 km. up to the foot of the Glacier des Bossons.

Amenities. Ski school with 13 teachers. Skating rink. Village shops. Hotel and bar dancing.

Life in centre. Quiet and simple. Not too expensive. Mainly ski interest. Sunny upper slopes (restaurants with wonderful views). Village itself largely shaded in wintertime.

Accessibility. Train: Les Houches station. Air: Geneva (78 km.); bus.

General comments. Simple village, with good, limited ski-ing of its own and easy bus access to Chamonix and all the other valley ski areas.

Centre 119		Altitude
CHAMONIX	Province: Haute-Savoie	3405–3566 ft

Description. Inhabitants 3600. 80 hotels providing 3000 beds. Other accommodation 1000 beds. Language French – some English understood.

This famous small-town capital of the Mont Blanc area is steeped in mountaineering tradition. Not over-attractive in appearance, it has plenty of old-fashioned charm, and the scenery, together with the *téléférique*, can only be described as fantastic. Quiet and shaded in winter, the valley itself sees little sunshine until the end of February. Crowded and 'touristy' in summertime, Chamonix is modest and reserved in winter, and its friendly atmosphere requires a little knowing. This place has much to offer in the way of sensational ski-ing for the good performer. The ski-ing in the immediate vicinity is certainly on the difficult side, but beginners can find practice slopes and lifts in the village and above the tree line. Major efforts are well in hand to simplify the lower portions of the main big descents.

Ski facilities. Three large separate ski areas served by swift and impressive *téléférique* systems.

(1) *The Brévent Area* (north side of valley). Built in 1928–30, the second section of this startling *téléférique* swings across space from Plampraz 6562 ft up to the cliff top of Brévent at 8284 ft, giving a total rise of 4675 ft above Chamonix. Aerial view of ski descent from cabins scarcely reassuring for nervous or uncertain skiers. Main Brévent run consists of about 6 km. of spectacular upper section and immense long steep slopes on lower section. Once accustomed to the unusual exposure and

peculiar angles of pitch, this is a beautiful and unusual run which is not so difficult as it appears. Not to be recommended in icy or poor conditions – nor for the uncertain in technique.

(2) *The Flégère Area* (north side of valley). Some 2 km. eastwards from Chamonix at Les Praz (free bus service) a *téléférique* goes up north-east to La Flégère at 6398 ft – a rise of 2822 ft. Plans are afoot to develop a small hotel and chalet settlement – 'Super Chamonix' – on this upper plateau. A *télécabine* system rises a further 1476 ft northwards up to L'Index at 8104 ft, to form an upper circus with two nearby well-placed ski-lifts. The upper Flégère ski area consists of amusingly and interestingly formed open ground with steep and gentle slopes, in full sunshine, suitable for all comers. Various runs of about 3 km. and 2400 ft.

The runs down from L'Index to valley bottom (about 4590 ft and 6–7 km.) provide sterner stuff for the more competent only, but alterations in the forest sections will provide easier ways.

(3) *The Aiguille du Midi Area.* This two-section *téléférique*, the longest and highest system in the world, is an engineering marvel of such daring conception amid such dramatic surroundings that, skier or non-skier, the ascent is a 'must' for all visitors, and the statistics must be given in full:

The Aiguille du Midi Téléférique
> Chamonix 1043 m. (3422 ft)
> South-east to Plan de l'Aiguille, 2317 m. (7602 ft).
>> Rise 1274 m. (4175 ft). Length 2·525 km. 5 mins.
> South to Aiguille du Midi 3802 m. (12,474 ft).
>> Rise 1485 m. (4872 ft). Length 2·869 km. 6 mins.
> Total: Rise 2759 m. (9052 ft). Length 5·394 km. 11 mins.

The lower section has four pylons – one of which is 170 ft high. The upper section is without pylons and the cable, almost 3 km. in length, swings clear up to near vertical as it climbs the impressive rock wall of the Piton Nord. Rock tunnels lead through to a giddy catwalk bridge that enters the Aiguille du Midi itself and on through this famous rock pinnacle out to the immense glacier world of the main Mont Blanc Massif. Both the Piton Nord and the Aiguille du Midi provide eagle's-nest viewpoints that are not to be matched anywhere else in the Alps. There is a big restaurant inside top station.

From the Aiguille du Midi at 12,408 ft, even the woolly-booted sightseer can continue his or her high Alpine journey, across the beautiful glacier world, to the Italian frontier at Piz Helbronner (11,253 ft), by means of the fantastic, 5-km.-long cables of the four-seater *télécabines* of the Vallée Blanche. This sensational *traversée*, high over the glittering seracs and deep crevasses of wide glaciers, amid the silence and mystery of a world hitherto only known to the mountaineer, surrounded by the myriad rocky pinnacles of many a 'four-thousander' and with the snow dome of Mont Blanc itself seemingly within touching distance, is a fantastic experience. At Helbronner (see p. 272) the huge *téléférique* of the Col du Géant transports the traveller down to the Italian ski centre of Courmayeur at the southern foot of Mt Blanc.

From the skier's angle the midway station of the *téléférique*, at Plan de l'Aiguille, provides two difficult and steep runs down to Chamonix which must only be tackled by the competent when conditions are safe. Top station, however, opens up one of the most glorious glacier runs imaginable. 'La Vallée Blanche', which can be taken either from the Aiguille du Midi or Helbronner, consists of 9000 ft and somewhere between 16 and 20 km. of superb ski-ing – a high-altitude 'ski-mountaineering' descent. When feasible this run, amid glorious surroundings, circles down via the Gros Rognon, through a maze of *seracs*, over the Mer de Glace, back to Chamonix. Never over-difficult, it is a joy both to expert and medium performers. A pointer, however, to the fact that this exceptional descent from the top station of a *téléférique* is not to be trifled with lies in the fact that, for an injured party unaccompanied by a guide, rescue costs about £40. . . . The injured skier with a guide is rescued free of charge. This run, for a party of four, guide and transport included, costs in the neighbourhood of £2 10s. per person, but, purely as an unforgettable experience, it is worth a great deal more than this.

Chamonix amenities. Ski school with 40 teachers. H.Q. of the French National School for Ski-ing and Alpinism. 150 guides (average of 30 active professionally). Four ski jumps (one Olympic size). Two skating rinks (one Olympic). Casino. Four cinemas. Big shopping centre. Hotel dancing. Four bar dancings. Garages, car parks, etc.

Life in centre. Comprehensive and yet unpretentious. Apt to be coldish in winter. Little glamorous *après ski* life, but certainly not dull. Warmer and more lively in springtime. Pleasant slightly old-world atmosphere. Prices range from expensive to cheap.

Accessibility. Train: Chamonix station. Road: Paris 628 km. Air: Geneva (86 km.); bus.

Centre 57		Altitudes
ARGENTIÈRE–	Province: Haute-Savoie	4108 and
LE TOUR		4790 ft

Description. Two attractive small villages at north-east end of Chamonix valley (separated by about 2 km.). 1700 inhabitants. 15 hotels providing 420 beds. Other accommodation 100 beds. U.N.C.M. (50 beds).

Le Tour is probably the most picturesque and sunny village of the valley in which it is possible to stay. It does, however, suffer from draughty winds through the nearby Col de Balme (Swiss frontier).

Ski facilities. One ski area served by two-section chair-cum-cabin lift, which gives a rise of 1575 ft north-east up to Chara-millon, and 836 ft eastwards on up to the Col de Balme at 7234 ft. Easy, pleasant *piste* ski-ing suitable for all comers. An 'excursion' type run called 'Les Jeurres' goes northwards, across the Swiss frontier down to Chatelard at about 3281 ft. (Return by train through tunnel.) Important immediate project – see below.

Amenities. Ski school with 15 teachers. One ski jump. Small shops. Small hotel dancing. Bus service to rest of valley.

Life in centre. Quiet village life. Reasonable prices.

Accessibility. Train: Argentière station. Road: Chamonix 8 km.; Paris 633 km. Airport: Geneva (94 km.); bus.

CHAMONIX VALLEY – GENERAL COMMENTS

This whole valley, with its many ski areas, is primarily for the medium and above performer – with the accent on unusual and spectacular descents for good skiers. A very important immediate project consists of yet another big-scale *téléférique* starting from Argentière (4068 ft) east of south up to Lognan (6562 ft), and continuing west of south up to the Aiguille des Grandes Montets at 10,827 ft. This will open up many square km. of splendid ski-ing.

The Chamonix valley is encouraging earlier and earlier high-altitude ski-ing. The Vallée Blanche is frequently run in January and February. Most comfortable time, however, is still from the end of February onwards. Summer ski-ing available. This is an area that should be high on the list for all keen skiers searching for unusual runs in glorious surroundings.

THE SAVOIE

Centre 65
VALLOIRE
(LES VERNEYS)

Province: Savoie

Altitude
4692 ft

Description. 750 inhabitants. 18 hotels providing approximately 660 beds. Other accommodation, including apartments, approximately 600 beds. Youth hostels (U.N.C.M., etc.)
approximately 500 beds. Languages French and Italian – little
English.

A small, but very active, attractive winter and summer resort
situated on a sunny flat space on the north–south valley road
leading up to the Galibier Pass. Together with Les Verneys
(5108 ft, 1·8 km. away), Valloire itself has many pleasant modern hotels casually placed in the old village, centring around
a big seventeenth-century church and a large skating rink. The
surroundings are picturesque and varied, and the place, with its
little river, the Valloirette, has exactly the right atmosphere for
a winter-sports resort.

Ski facilities. Two large ski areas, separate but interlinking,
served by two main *télébenne* systems. Five other medium-sized
and trainer ski-lifts including excellent slalom practice lift in
village itself.

(1) *The La Setaz Area.* Two-section *télébennes* give a total
rise of 2920 ft over a distance of 2·6 km. up to top station on
ridge at 7612 ft. Lovely panoramas of surrounding ski country.
Middle station (Lac Thimel at 6562 ft) has small restaurant
and two side-by-side ski-lifts of 330-ft rise. *Pistes* vary from
4½ to 6 km., mostly on north- and north-west-facing slopes.
Wide areas of untracked powder snow slopes. Scattered woods
provide pleasant exploration below tree line. West side of ridge
provides wonderful steep open ski-ing right down to Les
Verneys – superb in springtime. All runs of great interest to
medium and above skiers, with emphasis on the good performer.

(2) *The Crey Rond Area.* One *télébenne* gives a rise of 1968 ft

over a distance of 1·35 km. up to 6988 ft and provides three main *pistes* of between 3 and 5 km. Good varied ski-ing on safe, interestingly shaped ground, sometimes lightly wooded, on north-east-, east-, and south-east-facing slopes. Suitable for all, from beginners upwards. (Bus service to bottom station 600 m. up pass road.)

Ski touring. Immense variety of possibilities for wonderful day tours and excursions in all directions. Practically all the region is good ski country. Frontier crossing, Valloire to Bardonecchia (Italy), via Col du Mt Tabor requires 5 hrs.

Projects. Many intriguing developments are planned. Immediate: (1) To put closed transport side by side with the present transport systems up La Setaz. (2) To open up the big Crey du Quart area above the village – sunny, west-facing slopes and the north-facing side of the ridge suitable for modest skiers. Future project (three to five years): To revive the presently uninhabited village of Bonnenuit (5610 ft, some 6 km. up Galibier pass road) with new hotels, and construct uphill transport in no fewer than three separate directions: (*a*) to link north-eastwards with the La Setaz area; (*b*) to mount south-eastwards to the Crête de Barbe Grise (7875 ft); and (*c*) to climb in three *téléférique* sections, westwards up the lovely open slopes of the Raticières, to the Aiguille de l'Épaisseur at 10,600 ft.

Within approximately five years Valloire should have a circus of at least four separate and inter-linking ski areas – each one of splendid value.

Amenities. Ski school – 30 teachers. Large skating rink. Good simple village shopping – sports shops, etc. Many restaurants and bars, and popular well-run night spots. Car parks, garages, etc.

Life in centre. Gay and pleasant village atmosphere, with accent on sport and youth. Attractive to old and young. Full of movement and spectator value. Simple living with all that normal comfort demands, at prices that are never excessive and generally low.

Specialities. Cheap living for the young and unmarried (anything from 16 to 35 years) at the Maison des Jeunes, and the

U.N.C.M. Week-end crowds are noticeably less here than else-where. North-slope and spring-snow conditions.

Accessibility. Train: Saint-Michel-de-Maurienne on main Paris–Rome line (9 hrs Paris). Road: bus or taxi to Valloire (17 km.) 30 mins. Airport: Geneva (180 km.); bus 3 hrs.

General comments. Valloire is only beginning, but already has all necessary amenities and very good ski-ing. With future projects completed it will undoubtedly become a top-line French ski centre. Excellent value, even now, for two to three week holiday for keen skiers, parties, etc., at very reasonable cost. A place to cultivate.

		Altitude
Centre 68	Province: Savoie	4626 ft
PRALOGNAN	(Arrondissement Albertville)	

Description. 480 inhabitants. 8 hotels providing 900 beds. Other accommodation 200 beds. French language only.

Pralognan-la-Vanoise is an old and historic, summer and mountaineering, village community that has converted its ideas to ski-ing. An approach road of considerable beauty up from Moûtiers comes to a stop at a small flat hemmed in by impressive Alpine mountain scenery on all sides. Simple Pralognan – austere, but with character – sees little sun in wintertime. Its situation – sunny 'upstairs' ski fields and grandiose surroundings – make it not unlike a small Mayrhofen.

Ski facilities. One ski area served by one *téléférique*, surmounted by one ski-lift. One slalom lift and one trainer lift in village.

The Mont-Bochor *téléférique* goes steeply and quickly (2¾ mins.) north-eastwards up a rocky unskiable buttress, giving a rise of 1968 ft to the sunny west-facing and gently sloping Bochor Plateau. This is served by a ski-lift 1025 m. long which rises 804 ft to 7365 ft. (Project: extension of this lift up to about 7500 ft.) Ideal playground area, with restaurant, for parties of beginners, with return down by *téléférique*.

From the plateau there are four runs (3 to 4 km. and 2739-ft descents) down to Pralognan. None of these is easy, and two will please the good skier – notably the Verte, which is a long steep west-facing gulley run.

Projects. Distant future: to build a *téléférique* from Mont Bochor south-east to the Pointe Est du Grand Marché (8480-ft, 2·16-km. cable) and to continue south-east to Pointe du Dard (10,499-ft, 1·54-km. cable) giving a total rise of approximately 5800 ft above Pralognan. The idea is to give access to the Glacier du Dard and later to the glaciers of Vanoise and Chasseforêt – easy glacier ski-ing for spring and summer ski-ing – also providing descents amid rocky country of 8 to 14 km. back to the village.

There is also a more likely project to link Pralognon, via the Col de la Grande Pierre (7776 ft), with Courchevel.

Ski touring. Good, spectacular ski touring and ski mountaineering in vicinity, including areas covered by above projects. (Two huts – Félix Faure at 8202 ft and Peclet Polset at 8284 ft – 3 and 4 hrs climb respectively, with 75 beds each.)

Amenities. 17 Alpine guides, including ski school of 14 teachers. Small skating rink. Simple village shops. Four bar dancings.

Life in centre. Quiet, somewhat cold village with simple but warm accommodation at reasonable prices. Youth groups from U.N.C.M. create their own gaiety.

Specialities. Grand scenery and an impression of '*haute montagne*'.

Accessibility. Train: Moutiers. Road: 27 km. bus (1 hr 20 mins.). Airports: Lyon and Geneva.

General comments. A conversion job from summer to winter. Easy sunny 'upstairs' playground suitable to beginner groups. Interest for the spring tourer, but limited interest as yet for average *piste* skiers.

THE THREE VALLEYS

A remarkable development has taken place in the last few years in this corner of Savoie, where well over 100 square miles of superb natural ski country has been opened up for modern 'mechanical' ski-ing. From the main valley of Bozel, which

curls round to Pralognan, three vast valleys run upwards to the
south to converge below the foot of the Glacier de Gebroulaz.
From east to west these are the valley of Courchevel, the valley
of Méribel (both of which have already been opened up), and
the valley of St Martin de Belleville, which is not yet developed
but which has grandiose plans for the future. The ski-ing of all
three valleys is already interlinked and will in the future be
closely interwoven with uphill transport. In the valleys of
Courchevel, Méribel, and St Martin there are limitless snowfields of every kind of a very high order.

		Altitude
Centre 31	Province: Savoie	4757 – 5610 ft
MÉRIBEL-	(Tarentaise)	
LES-ALLUES		

Description. 150 inhabitants. 23 small hotels, private chalets,
etc., providing 1500 beds. Language French. English, German,
and other continental tongues spoken.

An intriguing, unusual conception of a ski centre developed
from scratch by intelligent private enterprise. More like an
estate than a village – many well-designed small and medium-
sized chalet-type hotels, with modern traditional exteriors of
stone and wood containing highly civilized interior décor and
fittings, sprawl casually up some 850 ft of sunny meadow hillside. Unostentatious comfort combined with simplicity. Pleasing picture-book scenery of semi-wooded valley and very wide
snow-fields leading up to high ridges.

Ski facilities. Two large ski areas (west and east sides of
valley) served by two main lift systems, plus one long ski-lift and
one trainer lift.

(1) *La Tougnete* (west side – morning ski-ing). One *télécabine*
surmounted by two ski-lifts giving rise of approximately 3200
ft up to La Tougnete ridge at 7874 ft, providing fine selection of
varied runs of 6–8 km. on north- and north-east-facing slopes.
Shorter descents from intermediary stations. La Tougnete ridge
grants ski access down into the St Martin de Belleville ski area.

(2) *Burgin–La Saulire* (east side – afternoon ski-ing). Three
superimposed *télébenne* and *télécabine* systems give rise of 4128 ft

over 3·6 km. to the impressive and beautiful site of the summit
station of La Saulire, amid dolomite-like rocks on a spectacular
ridge at 8885 ft. This is also the top station of the *téléférique* up
from Courchevel. The two lower *télébennes*, which are duplicated with a long ski lift, give easy access to all parts of Méribel
and provide good *pistes* on west and north-west slopes of
approximately 3 km. Upper *télécabine* (1995 ft rise) gives splendid long descents of over 7 km. (notable run – La Grande
Rosière). Easy access to all Courchevel descents and lifts (see
p. 222) obtainable in the day via La Saulire top station.

The ski country on both sides of the valley consists of wide
and wonderful open upper slopes of great variety leading down
to lightly wooded lower slopes on either side of the valley bottom. Little of this country is beyond the powers of the average
skier, and good performers can find plenty to tax them.

Ski touring. Wide areas for day excursions, far from transport systems, can be found on both sides of, and all around, the
head of the valley.

Amenities. Ski school – 18 teachers. Ski jump. Few small
shops. Bar dancings. No garage or petrol.

Life in centre. Quiet, small hotel, civilized living. Good 'spectator' ski-ing. No *chi-chi* – not 'dressy'. Big open fires, good
cooking, and regular faithful clientele. Little week-end fuss.
Not much *après-ski* life. Prices to suit the quality of comfort,
which is high.

Specialities. Méribel is the centre valley of the Three Valleys,
with easy access to both the others. You always ski right back to
your hotel doorstep – and you can generally do this until the
end of April.

Accessibility. Train: Moutiers (Paris 8 hrs). Road: 18 km. bus
or taxi (45 mins.). Airport: Geneva; 124 km. bus.

General comments. Méribel is surrounded by superb ski
country. This quiet hotel settlement, which has considerable
plans for expansion (to include a centre at the higher village
level, with many more facilities such as large hotels, skating
rink, and *après-ski* life), gives one the impression of a pleasant
private domain. Much to be recommended.

Centre 18
COURCHEVEL   Province: Savoie
  '1850'   (Tarentaise)

Altitude
(officially):
6070 ft
(actually): 5643 – 6070 ft

Description. Easternmost of the Three Valleys (see p. 219).
50 inhabitants. 40 hotels providing 1500 beds. Blocks of studios
and apartments providing approximately 2000 beds. 150
chalets providing 1500 beds. Language French. English,
German, Italian, and other tongues spoken.

It is hard to believe that, prior to 1946, there was nothing
here at all. This large, colourful, and intriguing 'film-set ski
metropolis', with its wide range of ultra-modern architecture,
set in lovely surroundings at the eastern foot of infinitely
variable and yet compact ski country, represents the result of
a bold and successful State-Enterprise experiment to cope with
the ever increasing demands of an ever increasing ski public.
Pleasantly scattered with trees, some 6 km. of looped roadways,
lined with many buildings from private chalets to enormous
blocks of flats, surround, both above and below, the gay central
arena which is the sports heart and shopping centre, etc., of
Courchevel. This intelligently created 'built-up area' is the
new headquarters of four other older, smaller, and slightly
cheaper centres, all of which are today closely interlinked with
roadways, uphill transports, and broad modern *pistes*. These
four ski centres are St Bon (3609 ft), Le Praz (4232 ft), Courchevel '1550' (4823 ft), and Moriond (5118 ft). Together these
satellites provide approximately 15 hotels with some 550 beds.
Wherever you stay in the area the amenities of all five centres
are so interlinked that the whole region must be considered as
an 'ensemble'.

Ski facilities. One very large ski area consisting of two side-
by-side pyramids – above Courchevel and Moriond – served
by a total of one *téléférique*, three *télécabines*, eight *téléskis*, and
two trainer lifts – plus five projected *téléskis*.

The Courchevel Pyramid. Le Praz up to La Saulire (ski link
with Méribel valley). Two *télécabines* plus one *téléférique* give
total rise of 4626 ft over 6 km. of cable and allow for runs of

over 10 km. Top sections steep, spectacular, and enterprising.
Central sections varied with easy and medium slopes. Lower
section all varieties. Whole area entwined with long subsidiary
lifts giving access to every ridge (including Moriond pyramid).
Slopes mostly north- and north-east-facing. Notable north
slope running down Le Bouc Blanc shoulder.

The Moriond Pyramid. Three ski-lifts open up long areas of
more gentle, open snow slopes suitable for medium and
beginner types.

In general there is everything here, from beautifully kept
wide *pistes* to suit all standards, to immense areas of varied
ground both above and below the tree line for 'off-the-*piste*'
exploration. Immediate ski access to every centre and to every
hotel, with no walking between lifts. Clever planning and
efficient running. Direct ski transport access to all Méribel
ski-ing, and back, and to that of the St Martin de Belleville
valley where many uphill transport systems are planned for
the future (see p. 224).

Amenities. Three ski schools in area with 60–90 teachers.
Floodlit ski jump and ski slopes. Skating rink. Luge run.
Large shopping area. Sport and fashion shops. Garages and
car parks, etc. Many small bars, dancings, restaurants, and
night-clubs, etc. Excellent S O S service and road clearance
organization.

Life in centre. A permanent kaleidoscope of movement and
colour. Primarily ski-minded, a big proportion of Courchevel
visitors live in private chalets, studios, and apartments, and
après-ski life is less than might be expected. Plenty of gaiety
for the young nevertheless. Never 'dressy' by night, the ski
and *après-ski* fashions are often startling and always interesting.
Ski-lifts, ski slopes, and every type of skier can be seen from
almost any point including all windows, and any non-skier can
survey and watch the entire area on the main transport systems. Sophisticated but sensible, the living and the ski-ing can
rise to high prices. Never a dull moment.

Specialities. Generally good snow conditions. Good-weather
ski-ing above Courchevel – bad-weather ski-ing below. Floodlit ski-ing between the two Courchevels, with *télécabine* return.

Successful introduction of private service and non-service apartments in big blocks of flats. No lunch-time breaks for any lifts. Little or no waiting for lifts. Nursery classes and teachers for small children.

Accessibility. Train: Moutiers–Salins station (Paris 650 km.). Road: 25 km. Moutiers by car or bus. Airport: Geneva 130 km.

General comments. An imaginative, extrovert, and slightly startling *avant-garde* realization of the modern trend in mechanical ski-ing and ski living. A place to see – and, furthermore, a place to ski. Excellent value for keen and good skiers with reasonably good bank balances. Classified as 'international', Courchevel is mostly patronized by well-to-do French. Its landscape will soon include a 22-storey apartment skyscraper which, in itself, will be an entirely suitable trade mark. For those who seek a more traditional, peaceful atmosphere with all the Courchevel ski-ing easily attainable, then the sunny friendly corner of Moriond is much to be recommended.

Centre 19		Altitude
ST MARTIN DE	Province: Savoie	5000–6500 ft
BELLEVILLE		

This centre, the Third Valley, does not, as yet, exist. The westernmost of the three valleys is even greater in extent (in square km. of snow-fields) than that of Courchevel and Méribel put together, and it contains miles and miles of wonderful ski-ing almost entirely above the treeline with many north-facing and shaded slopes. In the next three to six years, the organization that created Courchevel '1850' intends to exploit this valley, to build several new ski centres, together with extensive uphill transport, and to provide a first-class ski area for mass ski-ing at popular prices. Placed well above the present village of St Martin de Belleville, the centre for most of the lifts, which will fan out to all points of the compass, will be at approximately 6500 ft and transport will carry the skier up to the Pointe de la Masse at 9210 ft. There will also be similar networks of lifts right up at the head of the main valley by Plan de l'Eau at the foot of Mont Brequin (10,289 ft).

This new valley will also be linked by uphill transport with the Courchevel valley via the Méribel valley, and it is probable that these lifts will ascend and descend the central Méribel valley well above the present site of the Méribel ski area – thus creating a kind of 'Super Méribel' or 'Hoch Méribel' at a place called Mottaret. The link with the third valley will probably go via the Roc des Trois Marches at 8858 ft.

Many and varied will be the ski runs that will be opened up by the grandiose schemes that are afoot in this huge area – and, knowing how Courchevel itself has developed in the last ten years, this whole scheme is obviously no pipe-dream. The immediate future of the third valley, and its linkage with the two present valleys, deserves the closest attention from all those interested in immense and glorious ski areas.

		Altitude
Centre 17		
VAL D'ISÈRE	Province: Savoie	5965–6073 ft
	(Haute-Tarentaise)	

Description. 750 inhabitants. 35 hotels and pensions providing approximately 2000 beds. Other accommodation approximately 480 beds. Youth Hostels (U.N.C.M. and C.I.M.) 160 beds. Dormitory beds 110. Total capacity approximately 2600 beds. Language French. English, German, and Italian spoken.

Reached by impressive approach road through tunnels and avalanche galleries, this famous ski centre, close by the Italian frontier and the top of Europe's highest pass (Col de l'Iseran, 9088 ft), lies in a Y of valley closely surrounded, but never overpowered, by steep snow mountains. This old hunting village of the Dukes of Savoy (church dates back to 1533) is today the result of sensible, comfortable, and picturesque adaptation to modern requirements of a true Alpine village.

Ski facilities. Two large main ski areas served by two main, twin-station *téléfériques*. Other lifts: six ski and four trainer. Many projected lifts. Easy ski access to Tignes lifts (see over).

(1) *The Solaise Area* (south-east side of village). *Téléférique* – doubled by series of three ski-lifts – gives quick rise (5½ mins.) up 2293 ft to 8366 ft (restaurant). Four steep high

standard *pistes* and four longer easier *pistes* – ranges $3\frac{1}{2}$ to $5\frac{1}{2}$ km. Developments include a lift continuing up eastwards to the Crête des Lessières at 9843 ft and a long lift south-east-wards up to the Pointe des Lessières at 10,105 ft. This latter area, a splendid sunny valley of easy slopes, will give foot-tunnel access through to the slopes of the Col de l'Iseran. Beyond this to the east, transport is planned to the summit of Aiguille Pers (11,112 ft), where even summer ski-ing will be possible.

(2) *The Bellevarde Area* (west side of village). *Téléférique* gives quick rise (6 mins.) up 3028 ft to rocky summit at 9101 ft. Fine viewpoint. Splendid steep ski-ing down east face – easier descent down neighbouring Santon Gulley – ranges $3\frac{1}{2}$ to $4\frac{1}{2}$ km. Four marked *pistes*, from racecourse to 'family' style, circle round north and north-eastwards for 4 to 6 km. (3212-ft drop) down to La Daille, 2 km. north-west of Val d'Isère. Frequent bus service back. These latter runs give direct access to the lifts that connect, via the Tovière ridge, with the Lac de Tignes ski area.

In general, these two main ski areas alone provide wonderful value comparable with the best in the Alps. Immense variety of ground, including open and tree-running, and slopes that face all points of the compass. *Piste* notices must be strictly obeyed, for there are many steep slopes liable to slide in bad conditions. Mainly for good performers, there is, however, plenty of choice for the modest skiers.

Ski touring. This pleasant village lies in the centre of an immense circular region of almost limitless ski mountains. Within a radius of 10 km. there are no fewer than 35 cols and peaks over 9800 ft and reaching up to approximately 12,000 ft – La Grande Motte (*téléférique* project), Aiguille de la Grande Sassière, Tsanteleina, etc. All of these are splendid for spring-time expeditions until mid-June, and no ascent requires more than 5 hrs. For the well-off a very efficient helicopter service (Feb.–May) at approximately 15s. per minute per person flies one in 6 to 10 mins. to within easy distance of most of these summits. (See p. 91.)

Amenities. First-class ski school – 45 to 50 teachers. One ski jump. Skating rink, plus curling rink. Helicopter airport. Good shopping area. Sport and fashion shops. Garages and car parks. Outdoor snow 'plage' on nursery slopes. First-class cinema. Restaurants. Hotel and bar dancing. Two night spots. Excellent S O S service centralized on network of short-wave radio-posts on main runs. Efficient road clearance organization.

Specialities. Layout of Val d'Isère and nearby Tignes ski areas permits long distance *aller-et-retour* modern form of ski touring without any uphill climbing. Each sequence of lift provides great variety of terrain – and near-future projects will make it difficult for the average vacationist to cover all the ground in two weeks. Transport sequences and runs, however widespread, always allow for linked return to the village. The same applies to spring ski tours.

Life in centre. Friendly, gay atmosphere, where the accent is 95 per cent on ski-ing. A feeling of '*haute montagne*' and true ski tradition. Nothing bogus or glossy – yet surprising comfort and a price range that never exaggerates and covers the modest purse. Good spectator ski-ing. Nightlife available, but not much frequented. High standard Zermatt-type ski-ing, with every detail well planned and run with great efficiency.

Accessibility. Train: Bourg St Maurice station (Paris 8½ hrs). Road: 1 hr 15 mins., bus from station (32 km.). Paris 690 km. Airport: Geneva (174 km.); bus service.

General comments. No good skier, keen on seeking out the best, should miss Val d'Isère. The unique 'Piste Perdue' is a collector's piece. Care is required in deep winter, but in spring-time one can ski anywhere – and when the *téléférique* to La Grande Motte is completed (see Tignes) the choice will be handsome indeed.

Centre 1		Altitude
LAC DE TIGNES	Province: Savoie	6890 ft
	(Haute-Tarentaise)	

Description. 50 inhabitants. 1 hotel and 6 pensions providing 200 beds. Language French.

The natural little lake of Tignes lies only 6 km. (crowflight)

from Val d'Isère, and these two centres share their ski-ing.
On the approach road up to Val d'Isère a road branches right
across the dam of the big artificial reservoir (in which the
original village of Tignes was submerged in 1952) and climbs
up to the little summer beauty-spot where a few scattered
buildings lie close to the shore of the lake.

This small high-altitude hotel settlement has many plans for
the future, and the intention is to develop it into a ski centre of
considerable importance. Situated in a big circle of mountains
and dominated by the Glacier de la Grande Motte, the somewhat meagre present accommodation will be increased up to
600 beds by 1965. It has at present two ski areas of its own.
Easy sunny slopes are served by the Chardonnet lift up to
approximately 7800 ft. Plans are to complete a *télécabine* here
up to the Aiguille Percée at 8944 ft. This spectacular rock,
which commands fine ski slopes, will also be reached by *télécabine* system from the Val d'Isère approach-roadside.

The second ski area, served by a steep *télécabine* which rises
2000 ft up to Tovière ridge, links at top station with a ski-lift
up from the main Val d'Isère ski runs down from the Bellevarde area. The Lac de Tignes side of the ridge is steep and
difficult, but the Val d'Isère side is pleasant and rewarding
for average skiers.

At present small, with few amenities (prices are on the high
side), Lac de Tignes, with its limited but adequate ski facilities,
is really an extension of the Val d'Isère ski-ing.

The ultimate project is to construct a big *téléférique* from
the west side of the little lake right up to the shoulder of La
Grande Motte at 11,647 ft. This important lift, together with
the Aiguille Percée *télécabine* system, will give Lac de Tignes
a very big transport height gain and convert it into a ski centre
of considerable stature in its own right.

Lac de Tignes, at the moment only half completed, has a
slightly bleak appearance in winter, and the life of an evening
is restricted to one hotel. Excellently suited as a spring ski-ing
base already, the many ambitious plans that are afoot in this
area make Lac de Tignes a place for keen skiers to watch with
the greatest interest.

Centre 107   Altitude
NOTRE DAME   Province: Savoie   3720 ft
  DE BELLECOMBE

Description. 420 inhabitants. 8 hotels providing 350 beds.
Other accommodation available. Language French only.

Very pleasant, very sunny, small, picturesque village of some
charm, to which medium-sized hotels have been added.
Backed by low, rolling, semi-wooded hills that never exceed
the tree-line, this village is only 3 km. by road from Flumet in
the main Val d'Arly (Megève 12 km.).

Ski facilities. Two small, semi-adjoining ski areas served by
two ski-lifts. Other lifts: 1 trainer ski-lift. Also nearby lifts at
Crest-Voland (see below).

Reguet Area. Ski-lift from village gives rise of 1283 ft up
rounded west-facing slopes suitable for learners and modest
performers. Reverse slopes (south-east-facing) lead down to
start of second ski area – also reached direct by bus.

Mont Rond Area. Entertaining medium-sized plum-pudding
Alp with ski-lift from 4291 ft to 5906 ft giving rise to summit
of 1614 ft. North-, west-, and south-facing slopes provide runs
of 2 to 3 km. of considerable variety, ranging from easy to
quite difficult descents. Fine views of Mont Blanc. Return to
Notre Dame de Bellecombe by local bus.

Amenities. Ski school with 14 teachers. Ice rink. Sunny
nursery slopes. Small village shops. Three bar dancings. Night
spot. Roadside car parking.

Life in centre. Simple, unpretentious, friendly, and gay. No
frills. Very reasonable prices. Village and small-hotel life.
Extremely sunny. Visitors mostly ski-minded. Many young
people. Popular at week-ends.

Accessibility. Train: either Albertville station (23 km.) or
Sallanches station (25 km.). Road: bus services from both
stations. Paris 624 km. Airport: Geneva (90 km.); bus.

General comments. This centre (together with Crest-Voland,
4019 ft, only 3 km. distant – where there are three small hotels
providing some 130 beds) provides good-value short ski-ing –

safe and sunny – excellent for parties of modest keen skiers. Pleasant, cheerful atmosphere. Crest-Voland ski-lift rises 1270 ft from village to top of Mont Lachat at 5289 ft, providing simple open slopes with lots of sunshine.

THE GRENOBLE AREA

Centre 35   Altitude
CHAMROUSSE   Province: Dauphiné-Isère   5413 ft

Description. 50 inhabitants. 12 hotels with 6–700 beds.

The most popular of several small ski areas in the immediate vicinity of the university town of Grenoble. A well-planned, well-equipped, amusing, and surprising manifestation of what the modern, mechanically-minded public requires of ski-ing.

This cleverly-laid-out, efficiently-run little centre, a long way superior to the sister conception of Monte Bondone in Italy, is, in fact, a kind of miniature Sestriere, a small fair-ground ski-mill, designed to give as much ski-ing as possible to as many people as possible in an area where relatively few would seem like quite a crowd.

A fast *téléférique*, aided and abetted by several smaller and subsidiary ski-lifts, rises some 1970 ft to the Croix de Chamrousse summit at 7382 ft. Hillsides which largely face west provide limited but interesting *pistes* of 3 to 4 km. amid scattered trees and tumbled slopes which lead down to wide areas of open nursery slopes round the centre, where there are trainer lifts.

Life here is not dissimilar to that of a Butlin's Camp and, as such, with all the necessary amenities, it gives a great deal of pleasure to large numbers of people. Apart from the accommodation available, and a large car-park site for car-drawn caravans, most of the clientele consists of week-end and day visitors, locals, and youthful student parties.

The centre and its ski slopes invariably present a gay and animated spectacle and, whereas a keen skier would hesitate to spend his vacation here, it is well worth a flying visit.

Bus, taxi, or car from Grenoble 1 to 1½ hrs.

Centre 15   Altitude
ALPE D'HUEZ   Province: Dauphiné-Isère   6102 ft

Description. 350 inhabitants. 44 hotels providing 4150 beds.
Other accommodation 200 beds. Language French, with minor
coverage of other European tongues.

A large, high-altitude collection of bright and attractive
modern hotels, situated at the top of an impressively steep
approach road up from Bourg d'Oisans, on a superbly sunny
south-facing slope above the tree-line, commanding wide and
wonderful views (in situation not unlike Villars in Switzerland).
A fashionable place of many social amenities deliberately
created for the dilettante seekers of snow holidays in the
sunshine and gaiety at night.

Ski facilities. One large rambling area on the south-west
shoulder of the Massif des Rousses, consisting of several
separate hillocks, terraces, and ridges, served by one main
téléférique in two sections, with a network circus of seven long,
and mostly gentle, ski-lifts – and a nursery trainer lift in
village. The Téléférique des Rousses gives a total rise of 2756 ft
over 3·8 km. up to 8858 ft. Lower section provides broad gentle
piste of almost childlike simplicity. Upper section slightly more
enterprising but never problematical.

The Signal ski-lift, with a rise of 836 ft, gives broad south-
slope *pistes* of medium gradient and good north-west-facing
runs down to Villard Reculas at 4905 ft, with a ski-lift 2·7 km.
long to bring you back to Signal summit.

Best ski run in area, very seldom used, goes from top of
téléférique down north-facing valley to the village of Oz
(2625 ft) – a glorious and very varied descent of some 6000 ft
over 8–9 km. Future project: a *télébenne* system to return up
the greater part of this descent – otherwise return must be
made by taxi. The Oz run is directly comparable to the famous
Rio Nero run at Sestriere, and is excellent value.

Other main projects consist of third-section extension to
main *téléférique* up to the Pic du Lac Blanc at 10,990 ft. This
will open up long, excursion-type, easy runs of over 12 km.
down the Glacier de Sarenne and round to Huez at 4888 ft. It

will also provide a high-altitude summer ski area with its own small ski-lifts.

Amenities. Ski school – 50 teachers. Lovely ice rink. Hockey and curling. Light plane aerodrome for skiers' use. Excellent shopping centre for all requirements. Heated open-air swimming bath. Many restaurants, tea rooms, bars, night-clubs, etc. Large car parks, garages, etc.

Life in centre. Social, '*un peu snob*' atmosphere. Apéritif, deck chair in sun, gentle exercise, late dinner, and flash-bulb photography existence. Easy to spend money – but with cheap restaurants to be found. Over-populated on Sundays when 10,000 day visitors may arrive by car and bus – with consequent queueing on ski-lifts.

Specialities. Sunshine.

Accessibility. Nearest station: Grenoble (63 km.). Road: bus, Grenoble to Alpe d'Huez, via Bourg d'Oisans, 2 hrs. Airport: Lyon (163 km.).

General comments. Easy, simple ski-ing for beginners, with certain good runs available for good skiers who seek them. Largely a place which well-off people visit to see and be seen – and by no means always to ski. Excellent for a restful sunny holiday in amusing, gay, and lively surroundings. Basically a 'Mountain Mayfair' or a winter St Tropez. A sophisticated set-up that many enjoy.

Centre 33   Altitude
LES DEUX ALPES   Province: Dauphiné-Isère   5446 ft
(Alpe Mont de Lans and Alpe Venosc)

Description. 100 inhabitants. 19 hotels providing 8–900 beds. Dormitory beds, 650. Other accommodation 50 beds. (5 new hotels will provide considerably more accommodation and much building is planned.) Languages French and Italian with a smattering of English and German.

A recently developed, sunny, high-valley area (which runs north–south) consisting of two small hotel settlements, separated by 1½ km., connected by constant and free bus service.

This joint 'ski station' is of considerable interest and importance. Blessed with efficient and imaginative management,
plentiful accommodation, and uphill transport, it has many
plans for an even brighter future. Directly comparable already
in layout, scope, and ski terrain with Zürs – which it greatly
resembles – its future projects will considerably surpass those
of its distinguished near twin. Capable of giving very good,
amusing ski-ing to all types of runners in large numbers (3000
day visitors is not unknown on a Sunday), this centre plans
always to keep its transport facilities ahead of its potential
total of guests and day visitors and to avoid the all-too-common
fault of 'bottlenecks' and lengthy queueing. It has its sights on
providing maximum ski facilities for the ever increasing
numbers of youthful skiers of today and tomorrow.

Ski facilities. Two ski areas served by two main lift systems.
Three other ski-lifts. Three good-sized trainer lifts. Projects:
continuation of *télébenne* system up to 9229 ft (Le Diable);
two more ski-lifts; large *téléférique*, in three sections, up to Le
Jandri (10,788 ft).

(1) *Le Diable Area.* From Alpe Venosc (east side of valley
with west- and north-west-facing slopes) *télébenne* (closed
gondolas) system giving rise of 2657 ft over 2½ km. in 6 mins. –
to be increased to give rise of 3848 ft. Present top section
duplicated with ski-lift of 1083-ft rise. Three main *pistes* of
3½ to 7 km. on steep open broad ridges lead down to either
village. *Téléférique* project will go far beyond and above this,
giving an altitude drop of 5300 ft, the possibility of summer
ski-ing from high ski-lifts, and spring snow runs of over 12 km.
Fine ski-ing for good skiers.

(2) *The Vallée Blanche Area.* From Alpe Mont de Lans
(west side of valley with east- and north-east-facing slopes)
ski-lift (shortly to be duplicated) giving rise of 1657 ft and four
main *pistes* of 3 to 4 km. on amusing, rounded hillsides, both
steep and gentle, down to either village. This system is also
triangulated by three other ski-lifts to half-way and to summit.

For interest, compare above figures with those of Zürs (see
p. 139).

All ski slopes are above the tree-line, wide and open, and provide for all grades of performers. Upper duplication of lifts allows for late season.

Ski touring. Good day excursions in and around the Diable–Le Jandri area.

Amenities. Ski school – 26 teachers. Large ice rink. Medium ski jump. Helicopter and light plane landing ground. Hotel and bar dancing (juke-box style). Shops. Garages.

Life in centre. Simple, easy-going, family-type hotel life. Emphasis 95 per cent on ski-ing. Prices moderate and low. Accent on the young element. Little glamorous *après-ski* life. Sunny nursery slopes and good 'spectator' ski-ing. Friendly, unspoilt atmosphere.

Accessibility. Station: Grenoble. Road: bus from Grenoble 60 km. up Briançon road to Chambon, then 8 km. steep road up. Time 2 hrs 15 mins. Airport: Lyon (170 km.).

General comments. Very good value already – with many developments to come. Good ski-ing for low-income groups and young enthusiasts. Watch out for possibility of 'package-deal' terms which will include full-pension accommodation with full use of all uphill transport, ice rink, bus services, etc. This place deserves attention.

THE BRIANÇON AREA

Centres 78 and 71   Altitudes
SERRE CHEVALIER   Province: Hautes-Alpes   4429 ft
  (CHANTEMERLE)
VILLENEUVE   4528 ft

Description. Two small villages 2 km. apart, with 150 inhabi-
tants each, sharing 16 hotels and pensions providing 600 beds.
Other accommodation 100 beds, plus 3–400 youth hostel
(U.N.C.M.) beds. Language French – English, German, and
Italian spoken a little.

Chantemerle (also called Serre Chevalier) and Villeneuve
are two old roadside villages just outside Briançon, which
started before the war with a *téléférique*, and have subsequently
built comfortable but unpretentious hotels. Semi-wooded
valley scenery; very sunny throughout whole winter; long
season owing to north-facing slopes. The Serre Chevalier ski
area is generously equipped with ski transport.

Ski facilities. One large ski area served by two main lift
systems (starting from the villages of Chantemerle and Villeneuve) which almost meet on the minor summit known as
Serre Chevalier.

The Chantemerle *téléférique* mounts in two sections to Serre
Chevalier (no hotels) giving a rise of 3707 ft up to 8137 ft.
Restaurant at midway stop (Serre Ratier) with nursery slopes
and two small lifts, plus one long fast-moving ski-lift giving
rise of 1000 ft.

The Villeneuve *télécabine* system gives a rise of 2100 ft to
Clos de l'Aravet (restaurant, nursery slopes, etc.) and this is
surmounted by a cluster of four medium-sized ski-lifts which
fan out to open slopes and reach, ladder-fashion, almost to
Serre Chevalier summit at approximately 7808 ft.

All the runs, which are on north- and north-east-facing
slopes, can be made to interlink from all lift stations. There is
a splendid selection of types of runs, suitable for all comers,
ranging from the fast race course to the long meander. Open

slopes at top – natural and artificial glades through larch woods lower down, which, in themselves, provide fine wood running. Excellent, entertaining ski-ing mainly for the average and competent performer.

Ski touring. Wide areas above and behind Serre Chevalier provide many opportunities for good short excursions.

Amenities. Ski school – 20 teachers. Village shops. Hotel, bar, and night-club dancing. Garages and car parks. (Cinemas, skating rinks, etc., at Briançon, 5 km. distant.) *Abonnement* tickets cover all ski transport and are very reasonable.

Life in centre. Easy-to-make-friends, family atmosphere. Intimate and simple – not dressy – excellent food. No big agency parties. Mostly French visitors. Not much scope for *après-ski* entertainment, other than what you make for yourself.

Specialities. Good and long-lasting snow conditions generally available. Good spring ski-ing. Easy access to Sestriere and Turin ski area. Little week-end crowding or through traffic.

Accessibility. Train: nearest station Briançon 6 km., thence bus. Road: access from Italy over Montgenèvre Pass, and generally from Grenoble (120 km.) over Col du Lauteret Pass. Paris 750 km. Lyon 300 km.

General comments. Good ski-ing, but relatively uninteresting and too quiet for those who like to whoop it up in the evenings.

Centre 16   Altitude
MONTGENÈVRE Province: Dauphiné, Hautes-Alpes 6089 ft

Description. 120 inhabitants. 10 hotels with 450 beds. Languages French and Italian.

A small but very attractive collection of hotels grafted on to an old village which sits astride the summit road on Franco–Italian frontier pass. Wide exposed situation – plenty of sun. Pleasant surroundings.

Ski facilities. Two ski areas. Large area on north side of pass served by two section chairlift/gondola system. One wide nursery slope area on south side of pass served by two medium-sized ski-lifts.

(1) *Le Chalvet Ski Area* (north side). A rise of 2395 ft up
to 8498 ft opens up a fine variety of runs, largely south-facing,
of 3½ to 5 km. Open slopes, long steep gullies, and big snow
basins. Well kept *pistes*. Plenty of variations, including ski run
to Claviere, 5 to 6 km. Magnificent views from top station.

(2) *The Chenaillet Ski Area* (south side). Gentle, lightly
wooded, north-facing slopes with two parallel ski-lifts giving
rises of 820 ft and 650 ft. Easy amusing practice slopes.

Ski touring. Plenty of good ski wandering above Chenaillet
area similar to, and linking with, that above Claviere. From
Le Chalvet there is an interesting spring excursion (2 to 3 hrs)
to Bardonecchia.

Amenities. Ski school. Cafés, bars, restaurants, dancing.

Life in centre. Simple but lively. Unsophisticated but gay.
Interest mainly ski-ing – standards not high. Prices very
reasonable. Village small scale, but cosy and with atmosphere.

Accessibility. Station: Ulzio (16 km.) on main Paris–Turin
line, or Briançon (14 km.). Road: bus Briançon 40 mins.,
Ulzio 1 hr. Nearest airport: Turin.

General comments. Good value. Rising in popularity owing
to new big lift system which has opened up excellent ski-ing.
High and healthy, with plenty of sunshine and lovely surroundings. This centre links with Claviere (see p. 280) and is
within easy bus reach of Sestriere for a day's ski outing.

THE BASSES ALPES

Centre 73   Altitude
BARCELONNETTE— Province: Basses Alpes   4495 ft
   LE SAUZE

Description. Le Sauze: 20 inhabitants, 10 hotels – and Supersauze at 5577 ft, 2 hotels – are two recently built (4–5 years
old) small ski hotel settlements above the little old town of
Barcelonnette: (3723 ft – 3000 inhabitants – 7 hotels) in the
sheltered Vallée de L'Ubaye. Bus services connect Barcelonnette (300 beds) with Le Sauze (6–700 beds) on its small sunny
plateau at the foot of north-facing slopes some 4 km. distant
up steep approach road.

   Ski facilities. At Le Sauze one ski-lift goes southwards up a
rounded ridge area to Supersauze giving a rise of 1155 ft and
a selection of some six *pistes* of about 2 to 3 km. From Supersauze a second lift continues up another rounded ridge area to
7014 ft giving a rise of 1437 ft and opening up another selection
of some four or five *pistes* of 2–3 km. Total rise of two areas is
2507 ft, and the two sets of *pistes* can be made to interlink
giving descents of 4–6 km. Both areas are lightly wooded with
fair open snow slopes. Limited in scope, the *pistes* are largely
north-facing and concentrated into relatively narrow areas with
little exploration possible. Medium-type *piste* ski-ing with
steepish upper slopes which become progressively easier until
you reach the perfect small playgrounds for beginners around
Supersauze and Le Sauze where there are baby lifts. One good
race-course.

   Amenities. Ski school – 16 teachers. Small shops at Le Sauze
– large car park. Small town amenities at Barcelonnette.
Skating rinks.

   Life in centre. Simple and unsophisticated. Little *après-ski*
life beyond hotel life – juke box and bar dancing, etc. Visitors
come from Marseille, Aix, Toulon, and as far afield as Paris.
Full up at holiday and week-end periods, Le Sauze copes with
1500–2000 skiers and presents a gay, colourful, but crowded

scene. Barcelonnette itself, slightly on the austere side, cannot be termed attractive. Prices inexpensive.

Accessibility. Station Gap (60 km. distant). Road: bus 2 hrs via impressive scenery of La Vallée and the immense works of the Serre-Ponçon dam and reservoir. Grenoble 165 km.

General comments. The most that can be made of a limited area. Something of a 'ski-mill', which gives a lot of fun to a lot of people. Parties of undemanding youthful beginners will enjoy this place.

NOTE. Two important ski areas in this vicinity which it is planned in the very near future to open up and to equip with new lifts and accommodation are the Col d'Allos area and the Costebelle–Lamore area.

These two areas are situated astride the regional boundary of the Hautes and the Basses Alpes and can be included in the Alpes–Maritimes.

No details of this development are yet available, but these areas are renowned for good snow conditions and enjoy long hours of Mediterranean sunshine.

THE CÔTE D'AZUR AREA

Centre 40   Altitude
AURON   Province: Alpes-Maritimes   5282 ft
                                (Provence)

Description. A small but very efficient and well-equipped ski
settlement of hotels and chalets situated on a sunny south-
facing plateau ringed by minor mountains. 50 inhabitants.
10 hotels providing 300 beds. Other accommodation 125 beds.
(Also Saint-Étienne-de-Tinée, a village of 1500 inhabitants at
3740 ft, 6 km. down road, has 8 small hotels providing 80
beds. Bus service.) Scenery unspectacular but pleasing with
both open slopes and large sections of wooded hillsides. Good
panoramas from top station. Language French. Many local
visitors speak English.

Ski facilities. Two ski areas, adjoining but separate. Served
by two main lift systems which start from the same station on
the village square.

(1) *The Téléférique Auron–Las Donnas* (with two pylon
halts *en route*) gives a rise of 2280 ft south-west up to 7562 ft –
2·5 km. long in 10–12 mins. Las Donnas top station is also
reached by a ski-lift 1018 m. long which gives a rise of 1322 ft
back up to the south, allowing for late-season upper circuits
when snowline recedes to the 2000 m. level. Six marked *pistes*
with fine selection of excellent steep slopes as well as easier
routes. All slopes face north and north-east. Plenty to explore.

(2) *The Télébenne* (*open bucket*) *Auron–Col de Saume
Longue* rises 1604 ft to the west in 23 mins. for 2·3 km. This is
surmounted by a ski-lift 870 m. long which rises 968 ft southwards to Hauta Plana at 7858 ft. Four to six marked *pistes*,
largely open slopes mostly facing east, with many facing north-
east and some north. Excellent steep selection for spring snow
conditions.

All runs from both systems end at Rio, about 300 ft below
Auron, where a small open *funiculaire* quickly returns you to
the village square.

Two small trainer lifts serve nursery slopes near the village. Runs range from 3 to 8 km. in length and give descents up to 2860 ft. Good all-round value.

Ski touring. The area behind Las Donnas provides considerable opportunity for various *promenades à ski* – day excursions with climbs of a few hours and open ski-ing.

Amenities. Ski school – 7 to 10 teachers. Several cafés and bars. Small shops. Sports shop. Skating rink. Small ski jump. Garages. Large car park. Small night-spots.

Life in centre. Pleasant, easy-going atmosphere. Mostly ski-minded. Visitors eighty per cent French and twenty per cent international. Hotel, bar, and restaurant life. Crowded and gay at week-ends and national holidays, otherwise on the quiet side with little *après-ski* sophistication. Friendly and easy-going, with nothing much 'laid on'. Simple living from Palace prices – without much Palace luxury – down to more normal levels.

Accessibility. Train: Nice station 96 km. from Auron. Road: bus, taxi, or car in approx. 2–2½ hrs. Airport: Nice.

General comments. Surprisingly good ski-ing for such a small settlement. Intriguing entry up the rocky gorges of the Var and the Tinée and fascinating contrast between the Mediterranean climate of the Côte d'Azur and a real winter sports resort which has good and lasting snow. Ideal for those who wish to mix ski-ing with Nice, Antibes, and Cannes. Real sun on real snow – with the opportunity, in late season, of ski-ing and swimming on the same day. A competition entitled 'Ski Natation' is in fact held here at the end of May.

Auron can cope with 2500 skiers per day – mostly visitors by car or bus – and during such influxes a certain amount of queueing is inevitable. Best ski centre in the South of France region and comparable with many better known places in the Central Alps.

Centre 32   Altitude
VALBERG   Province: Alpes-Maritimes   5570 ft
                        (Provence)

Description. 150 inhabitants. 10 hotels giving about 300 beds.
Other accommodation 100 beds.

A Côte d'Azur 'playground' for unambitious skiers. The
centre consists of a collection of small roadside hotels and
chalets (much building in progress) situated on and around a
sunny col surrounded by small summits. Ski slopes and built-
up area all a bit cramped, with slightly 'touristy' amusement-
park atmosphere. Almost as many luges in use as skis.

Ski facilities. Various small ski-lifts – two medium-sized and
others small – give maximum rise of 700 ft (more is not possible)
with an assortment of short *pistes* seldom more than 1 km.
long. Most of the lightly wooded, rolling countryside – easy
hills and valleys – becomes hardbeaten very quickly. Popular
with locals, especially during holidays and week-ends, when
many come up from the coast for a few hours ski-ing. Not for
the keen downhill skier.

Amenities. Ski school – 5 teachers. Skating rink. Big ski
jump nearby (80-m. jumps possible). Lugeing. Small shops.
Tea rooms. Small night-spots, bars, etc.

Life in centre. Transient 'picnic' air. Entertaining for young
beginners, children, and sightseers curious for the abrupt
contrast of easily reached snowfields from the Mediterranean
coast, via the two very impressive (sometimes oppressive)
approach roads up the spectacular contorted red-rock gorges
of Cian and Daluis.

Accessibility. Train: Nice station. Road: 85 km. Bus: $3\frac{1}{2}$ hrs.
Car: $2\frac{1}{2}$ hrs. Airport: Nice.

General comments. Anyone who can ski will grade Valberg as
an extended and well-developed nursery slopes area. In no
sense can the ski-ing compare with that at Auron. This is a
place for beginners only.

FIVE

German Ski Centres

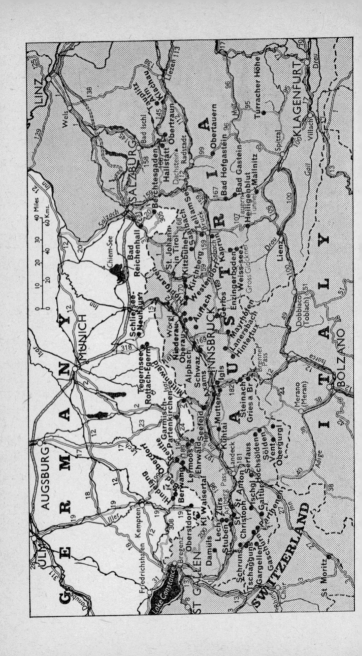

CONTENTS

INTRODUCTION

In Germany, wherever there are hills and mountains, ski-ing is part of the winter scene. The only high mountains of the Alpine region occur down in the south on the Bavarian border with Austria. There are, however, several other popular regions where ski-ing is practised.

In the central area the Harz Mountains, Sauerland, Taunus, Eifel, and Rhön regions all have their winter-sports centres and ski-ing areas. Further south the Bayerischer Wald, the Schwäbische Alb, and the Schwarzwald also come under the heading of medium altitude mountain areas. Many of these, notably the Black Forest (Schwarzwald), are immensely and internationally popular as tourist beauty spots both in summer and in winter, and the ski facilities, no matter how modest in scope, attract large numbers of enthusiasts.

The above regions, especially the Feldberg in the Black Forest, have much to offer the skier who likes to wander gently in rolling hilly country – and there are short ski-lifts in quantity wherever the contours are propitious. It is, however, only fair to say that none of the centres in these regions can be truly compared with the ski centres of the Alps.

It is down to the south, along the frontier mountains that separate Germany from Austria, that the main German ski centres are to be found. These occur in the Allgäuer Alps and the Bayerische Alps. Some of these centres, such as those of the Kleines Walsertal, are actually within Austria, and others, such as Mittenwald and Garmisch-Partenkirchen, are only a few kilometres removed from the Austrian ski centres of Seefeld, Ehrwald, and Lermoos, etc.

Even in this Alpine region – as will be seen from the Comparative Altitude List of ski centres (pp. 104–21) – the main German ski resorts are relatively low in altitude. Ski-ing is to be found here in plenty, but, of the top eight centres, the highest – Hindelang above Bad Oberdorf – lies at 3773 ft and the majority are placed between 3000 ft and 1500 ft.

These modest altitudes do not neccessarily indicate lack of snow. From Christmas to early March there is every reason to count on certain snow down to between 3000 and 4000 ft and frequently there is permanent snow coverage much lower than this. This means, of course, that whereas a low centre may sometimes find itself below the snow line the transport systems above each certainly lead to good ski conditions and snowfields throughout the main season. With the exception of Garmisch–Partenkirchen, where there is ski-ing on the Zugspitze between 7500 ft and 9200 ft, most of the country available above the other main centres barely reaches beyond 6000 ft.

Taking Germany as a whole, official winter-sports brochures indicate that there are some 160 ski centres within Germany 'where there are ski instructors available to give instruction to beginners in the basic principles of the sport and to train the more advanced in ski-ing tours'. A claim such as this is every bit as reasonable as similar claims made by Austria and Italy. It refers to many a village not strictly qualified to be termed as a ski centre which, when conditions are suitable, is well able to provide a great deal of fun for local enthusiasts and skiers from nearby towns. One may perhaps be allowed to term the majority of such villages 'opportunist ski areas' – places which can, and do, handle large numbers of ski visitors

at week-ends and holidays. The chances are that these fortunate villages will be busy throughout the entire season, but it
would not be reasonable to include them among a list of places
recommended to the keen, two-to-three-week-holiday skier
from abroad.

In terms of 'Alpine ski-ing' Germany can only be classified
alongside the main Alpine countries with the relatively short
list of ski centres to be found in the Upper Allgäu and Upper
Bavaria. Among the most important of these are the places
listed on page 247. The largest – Berchtesgaden, Bad Reichenhall, and Garmisch-Partenkirchen for example – are (merely
in population alone) popular resorts rather than specialized ski
centres, and even the smaller places bear similar imprint. The
Germans, as a race, dearly love their mountains, and, whether
actively interested in ski-ing or not, they flock to their mountain resorts in large numbers. Many of the visitors in winter
are seeking merely a rest, or a 'cure', or a mountain-air holiday,
with perhaps a little ski-ing thrown in as a side-line. About
half the English visitors, who number approximately 2000 in
the winter, go for similar reasons.

The facilities for such a holiday are hard to rival. The
Germans on average are well-off, and many are rich. They
enjoy a high standard of living and spend money freely. They
consequently demand comfort, if not luxury, and the mountain
resorts are only too ready to supply them with all they expect.
Great comfort, luxury, and all-round entertainment and
holiday amusements – *thés dansants*, social evenings, wine and
beer taverns, folklore and zither bands, cinemas and casinos,
etc. – are consequently to be found. Prices, very naturally, can
soar to great heights, but, paradoxically, many of the lesser
hotels, which are both picturesque and comfortable, cater for
those who wish to spend perhaps 30s. a day for bed and board,
and a good 'table'. Germans like their food.

Germany as a nation is immensely keen on ski-ing. There
are probably more skiers from Germany who seek snow each
winter than there are from any other Continental country.
They have made very full use of the relatively small high areas
that fall within their own frontier confines, but it is small

wonder that the vast majority of nationals prefer to seek their winter sports in the centres of the other Alpine countries. At almost any ski centre in Austria, Switzerland, or Italy, a high proportion of foreign winter visitors is almost always German.

The inherent character of the German to be well-organized, thorough, and meticulously clean and tidy is reflected in his mountain resorts. Set, for the most part, against picture-book mountain scenery, in which lakes and heavily wooded hillsides play a large part, the small towns and large villages are highly geared to cater for sport, entertainment, and comfort, yet the architecture in general maintains the decorative traditional character of the mountain dwellings.

All the German ski centres are within such easy reach of large towns like Munich and Salzburg that at week-ends there is an inevitable avalanche of day visitors.

UPPER ALLGÄU

Centre 143*
OBERSTDORF
  (AND KLEINES
  WALSERTAL)

Upper Allgäu
(and Austria)

Altitude
2766 ft

Description. Oberstdorf 8130 inhabitants. 40 hotels and pensions with 1650 beds. Other accommodation 4860 beds.

This large climatic spa and holiday resort has everything from a theatre and cinemas to a fine uphill transport system, excellent ski-ing, and lovely surroundings. In situation sunny and sheltered, it is almost unique in that it stands close to the frontier on the only winter entry into a section of Austria where much good ski-ing is to be found. This Kleines Walsertal area, with the villages of Riezlern, Hirschegg, and Mittelberg (which have their own uphill transport systems – notably the Kanzelwand Luftseilbahn with a rise of 2854 ft up to 6430 ft above Riezlern – and a dozen small- and medium-sized lifts) forms, with Oberstdorf, an extremely popular Austro–German ski region.

Ski facilities. Oberstdorf itself has the following ski facilities: The Nebelhorn Luftseilbahn rises 3622 ft up to 6338 ft in 17 mins. over a distance of 4·8 km. The Nebelhorn chairlift continues on up to 6824 ft. This system provides excellent ski-ing on both sunny and shaded slopes with descents of over 4000 ft and 7½ km. Racecourse-type ski-ing for good performers and choices for beginners. (Several short lifts.)

There is also the Oberstdorf Chairlift from 3278 ft up to the Schrettenwang area at 4442 ft with runs back to Oberstdorf and down into the Kleines Walsertal.

Amenities. This well-organized centre with a good ski school has many events for winter-sports visitors. Guest ski races. Ice stadium with ice revues, and ice hockey, etc. Luge runs, Skijöring, etc. It is however most famous for its mammoth ski

---

* Each place description is numbered according to the Altitude List, pp. 104–21.

jump – the 'Ski-Flying' Jumping Hill on which jumps of up to approximately 140 m. (459 ft) have been recorded. This spectacular hill is a tremendous attraction.

The villages of the Kleines Walsertal, peaceful in their valley setting, are only 11, 14, and 17 km. from Oberstdorf. Riezlern at 3609 ft (population 1150); Hirschegg at 3650 ft (population 775); Mittelberg at 3996 ft (population 814) are well furnished with comfortable hotels, all the necessary amenities, and with ski slopes suitable for all standards. In all there are some 53 hotels and pensions at these villages with approximately 3500 beds.

The Oberstdorf–Kleines Walsertal ski region, easily reached by express train or bus service from Munich, has much to offer and is extremely popular.

Centre 106		Altitude
HINDELANG AND	Upper Allgäu	3773 ft
BAD OBERDORF		

Description. 4800 inhabitants. 1350 hotel and pension beds. Other accommodation 1450 beds.

The picturesque resort of Bad Oberdorf at 2788 ft in the Ostrachtal, with its sulphur, mud, and sauna baths, has uphill transport to the Hindelang ski area, which, to a certain degree, is not dissimilar to Oberlech in Austria.

Ski facilities. The Hornalpe Chairlift goes up to 4659 ft. The Oberjoch Chairlift-cum-ski-lift climbs from 3937 ft up to 5085 ft.

Amenities. The atmosphere of Hindelang is simple and friendly and good ski-ing is available. Oberdorf has all the amenities of a large mountain resort where the emphasis is not so much on ski-ing as on enjoying a restful holiday.

Accessibility: Train to Sonthofen, thence bus.

UPPER BAVARIA

Centre 155   Altitude
GARMISCH-   Upper Bavaria   2362 ft
    PARTENKIRCHEN

Description. 25,000 inhabitants. 68 hotels and pensions providing 5000 beds. Other accommodation 2500 beds.

This internationally famous and popular, large (semi-town),
mountain resort – originally based on the two neighbouring
villages of Garmisch and Partenkirchen – is the low-altitude
St Moritz of the German Alps. Garmisch is now big and
modern. Partenkirchen has retained much of the true Bavarian
village atmosphere.

Busy both in winter and in summer, the snow season attracts
large numbers of skiers and holiday tourists – and Garmisch-
Partenkirchen has much to offer every type of visitor. From
the skiers' angle there is a great wealth of uphill transport and
excellent ski-ing with slopes to face all compass points. From
the non-skiers' angle there is plenty of amusement and entertainment and a wide range of spectator sports.

Ski facilities. The uphill transport can be listed as follows:

The Kreuzeck Téléférique 2434 to 5420 ft. 8 mins. 2·3
    km. Rise 2986 ft.
The Wank Téléférique 2444 to 5791 ft. 12 mins. 2·7 km.
    Rise 3346 ft.
The Eckbauer Télécabine 2379 to 4003 ft. 14 mins. 2·1 km.
    Rise 1624 ft.
The Hausberg Chairlift 2428 to 4364 ft. 16 mins. 2·2 km.
    Rise 1936 ft.

These, plus various smaller lifts, serve the immediate
vicinity of Garmisch-Partenkirchen and provide ski-ing of all
grades suitable for both experts and beginners. Suffice it to
say that this centre has already successfully held the Winter
Olympics in 1936.

Garmisch-Partenkirchen stands at the foot of the Zugspitze

(summit: 2963 m. 9721 ft), Germany's highest mountain,
which can be climbed by transport from both the Austrian
side of the frontier (see p. 150) close to Ehrwald, or by mountain
cog-railway from Garmisch-Partenkirchen.

The Zugspitze Railway. 2297 ft to 8694 ft. 60 mins. 18·7 km.
Rise 6398 ft. At top station the celebrated Schneefernerhaus
Hotel, tunnelled into rockface, commands the big upper ski area
of the Zugspitze Platte (or Platt) in which there are two main ski
lifts giving a total rise of 1706 ft up to 9252 ft. There is also a
small cabin lift to return you back to the Schneefernerhaus.
The Platte area, which allows for summer ski-ing, has no ski
run down to Garmisch. A small *téléférique* rising 1027 ft from
the hotel takes you to the splendid panorama point of Zugspitze
summit.

Amenities. Large ski school – 60 instructors. Four ski jumps
including the Olympic jump. Ice stadium. Skating rinks. Ice
hockey. Ice exhibitions. Bob run. Luge runs. Big shopping
centre. Sport and fashion shops. Casino. Cinemas. Tea rooms.
Restaurants. Bars. Night-spots.

Accessibility. Main-line station. Can be approached by express from Munich or local railway from Innsbruck. Road:
Munich 95 km. Innsbruck 56 km. Airport: Munich.

General comments. Germany's senior and most important
ski centre. Excellent also for non-skiers. Many miles of sunny
walks kept open. Crowded at week-ends.

Centre 135   Altitude
MITTENWALD   Upper Bavaria   3018 ft

Description. 6000 inhabitants. 1000 hotel beds. Other accommodation 1800 beds.

This picturesque and decorative spa-cum-sports resort,
grafted on to the old historic village famous for the manufac-
ture of violins, lies close to the Austrian frontier about half-way
between Garmisch-Partenkirchen and Seefeld in Austria.

Ski facilities. The Kranzberg Chairlift, just outside the
village, goes from 3215 ft up to St Anton at 4003 ft. From here,
at 4101 ft the Kranzberg Luftseilbahn continues up to the

Kranzberghaus at 4528 ft. There is also the Wildensee ski-lift which gives a rise of 260 ft up to middle station at St Anton.

This, generally speaking, is easy and relatively limited ski-ing which allows for runs of 3 to 4 km. and about 1300 ft.

The construction of the Karwendel Luftseilbahn from 3051 ft up to 7220 ft – a rise of about 4170 ft over a distance of 2·5 km. in 5 mins. – is a reality that may greatly alter the general picture of Mittenwald as a ski centre.

Amenities. Ski school. Ski jump. Ice rink. Ice hockey. Theatre. Cinema. Shopping area. Tea rooms. Bars. Restaurants. Folklore events. Dancing, etc.

Accessibility. Road and rail from either Munich or Innsbruck. Airport: Munich.

Centre 152   Altitude
TEGERNSEE AND   Upper Bavaria   2487 ft
    ROTTACH-EGERN

Description. 5362 inhabitants. Hotel beds 1300. Other accommodation 700 beds.

A lakeside summer resort, sunny and well sheltered, that is more spa than sports centre. The main uphill transport system, reached by bus, starts up from close to Rottach-Egern at the end of the lake, where there are also hotels, etc.

The Wallberg Gondola system goes from 2595 ft up thickly wooded hillsides to 5302 ft – a rise of 2707 ft. There are two runs down this, cut through the forest.

On the open upper slopes there are two lifts: the Setzberg Chairlift rising 689 ft from 4888 ft up to 5577 ft, and the Kircherlhang Chairlift rising 367 ft from 4921 ft up to 5289 ft.

Small-scale but angular ski-ing. This region has all necessary facilities and is patronized by many who only ski as gentle exercise.

Accessibility. Road and rail from Munich (50–60 km.).

Centre 111   Altitudes
SCHLIERSEE–   Upper Bavaria   2625 ft
   NEUHAUS
SPITZINGSEE   3600 ft

Description. 6040 inhabitants. Hotel beds 1880. Other accommodation 980 beds.

The large and decorative lakeside village of Schliersee, with nearby residential Neuhaus, has a *Kabinenseilbahn* (gondola) system from nearby Josefstal, rising 971 ft from 2703 ft up to the charming little centre of Spitzingsee at 3675 ft. There is also a main road. Schliersee and Neuhaus are primarily for summer visitors. Spitzingsee is the 'ski dorf'.

Ski facilities. From Spitzingsee a chairlift climbs from 3648 ft westwards up to the ridge top of Stümpfling at 4856 ft. Stümpfling top station is also served by the Stuttenbahn Chairlift that gives a rise of 1657 ft up the reverse side of the ridge.

In addition there are three short trainer lifts giving rises of between 100 ft and 560 ft.

Stümpfling top station allows for a variety of runs, on both sunny and shaded slopes, of between 2 and 6 km. Never overdifficult, there is plenty of scope for exploration. The whole area is admirable for semi-touring runs with short climbs up to approximately 6230-ft altitude.

Amenities. Ski school. Two jumps. Two skating rinks. Ice hockey. Luge runs. Cinema. Shops. Bars. Restaurants. Dancing, etc.

Accessibility. Direct road and rail Munich (50–60 km.).

Just up the valley road from Schliersee, close to the Austrian frontier, is the attractive little village of Bayrischzell (2631 ft) which has amusing, open, and wooded ski-ing with some six lifts rising to 4593 ft (2000 inhabitants, 1900 beds).

Centre 168   Altitude
BAD REICHENHALL   Upper Bavaria   1542 ft

Description. 13,000 inhabitants. 3000 hotel beds. Other accommodation 150 beds.

A large low-altitude Bavarian spa resort (asthma cures) with ski facilities, rather than a true ski centre.

Ski facilities. The Predigtstuhlbahn Cable-cars rise from 1555 ft up to 5295 ft, where there is a splendid view. The main ski area is largely limited to the upper area between 4626 ft and 5548 ft where there is the Predigtstuhlbahn Chairlift and the Hochschlegel ski-lift (rises of 656 ft and 492 ft).

There is also the Stadtberg Chairlift down at the resort from 1644 ft up to 2900 ft.

Amenities. Ski school. Ski jump. Two luge runs. Skating. Ice hockey. Big shopping area. Theatre. Casino. Cinemas. Tea rooms. Restaurants. Bars. Dancing. Folklore entertainments, etc.

Accessibility. Direct rail and road, Salzburg – approximately 20 km.

Centre 166	Altitude
BERCHTESGADEN Upper Bavaria	1739 ft

Description. 28,500 inhabitants. 1000 hotel beds. Other accommodation 1739 beds.

This famous large resort is a tourist draw in summer and winter. The small town itself bears no resemblance to a mountain 'ski dorf' but the surroundings are magnificent and spectacular.

Ski facilities. From Berchtesgaden itself the Obersalzberg Gondola cars rise 1608 ft up to 3346 ft and provide some five pleasantly easy runs on meadow lands which are lightly wooded.

From nearby Königssee, the Jennerbahn Chairlift gives a rise of 3839 ft from 2067 ft up to top station at 5906 ft. Several good runs of between 5 and 7 km.

This top station is the entry point for a huge and wonderful ski-touring area, which includes the Funtensee–Tauern, and the Steinernes Meer, where the ski fields extend up to 7874 ft.

Amenities. Ski school. Three ski jumps. Skating rinks. Ice hockey. Tobogganning. Sleigh rides. Bars. Restaurants. Folk-lore. Dancing, etc. All the amenities of a flourishing tourist spa resort.

Accessibility. Fast express trains to Munich ($2\frac{1}{2}$–3 hrs) and Salzburg – road and rail (20 km.).

SIX

Italian Ski Centres

CONTENTS

THE BOLZANO AND VAL GARDENA AREA

THE BRENNER PASS AREA

BELLUNO

INTRODUCTION

ALL too few people in this country know about the ski centres of this beautiful land.

The popular general idea of a holiday in Italy consists of sun-drenched crowded affairs in Portofino or Capri, of sightseeing in Florence or Rome, or of floating in a gondola in Venice. There seems to be a kind of mental block about connecting Italy with wintertime, and with snow-covered mountains and ski-ing. This is a very great pity, for the connexion is real – and very lovely.

Italy has ski centres that provide first-class ski-ing. Its brochures, like those of Austria, insist on laying claim to some two hundred places for the winter visitor to go – not only in the Alps, but all down the Apennines and including Etna in Sicily. This is something of an Italian excess of enthusiasm. At least three-quarters of these are tiny villages and small pass settlements with ski-lifts, where ski-ing does take place whenever conditions are right, and which serve mainly for local week-end traffic. Excellently though these may serve this purpose, they can scarcely be recommended for foreigners on a two- to three-week holiday.

Every keen skier knows of Cortina d'Ampezzo and Sestriere, but even at these famous centres the English tongue is anything but common. How many of the English-speaking public, searching for the first time for a suitable ski centre, are made aware of Madonna di Campiglio, Selva, and Sauze d'Oulx? Or Bormio, Courmayeur, and San Martino?

There is probably more variety of character in the Italian resorts than in Switzerland and Austria – just as there is more variety in the people of Italy. The class structure varies from the very rich to the very poor, and, consequently, living conditions fluctuate between the ornate and the almost primitive. The Italian lira is neither hard nor soft, and prices vary widely. To live with all the frills costs a lot, and, even with 'primitive' living, it goes against the grain to give something for little. But, with the Italian, one can always bargain.

This variety is extended to the differences between the eastern and western sectors of the Italian Alps. In the west you find conditions and surroundings not unlike those of certain parts of Switzerland and Austria. In the east, the beauty and the drama of the Dolomites is unlike any other part of the Alps. In the west, in the Turin area and Breuil–Cervinia for example, the buildings tend to be ultra-modern and sometimes even bizarre. In the east, including of course the original Süd Tyrol, there is more of the older architecture of the 'summer-resort' type (Madonna di Campiglio, Ortisei, and Cortina for example).

There are two other aspects of variety. First the contrast of conditions. Springtime and wintertime seem somehow to go hand in hand in Italy. In the east or in the west (with the possible exceptions of the places that crowd close to the giants of Monte Bianco and Monte Rosa) the relative normality and frequency of a blue Italian sky and a bright Italian sun brings a freshness rather than a harshness to the months of deep winter. Closely intertwined with all this is the second aspect of variety – that of the contrast of locality. One is seldom remote. Even in the midst of extensive snowfields one is never far removed from lovely wide lethargic valleys where the grape and the orange come into their own; or lakelands where sleepy villages mirror themselves in calm waters; or the excitement and bustle of big towns; or the out-of-season intrigue of the Adriatic or the Mediterranean. Come a period of bad weather in the mountains and there is always a bus service ready to transport you to Turin, Milan, Garda, or Venice. Contrasts so vivid as these exist in no other parts of the Alps. A car, of course, is a wonderful asset.

The Italian character itself also makes for variety, and influences the character of the ski resorts. Vital, voluble, vivacious, and sometimes volcanic – even if one understands little of the language – a crowd of Italian skiers seldom allows for dull moments. There is generally a very marked top strata of sophistication and, in large centres, this is well catered for. Most Italians are highly conscious of design, and the flair for fashion and colour is more apparent than anywhere else.

The Italian on holiday is excitable and enthusiastic, sometimes slightly flamboyant, but certainly out to enjoy himself. Curiously enough he is sometimes casual about comfort – all too often the 'C' on an Italian bath tap stands for the same as it would in England. Not everybody loves Italian food, but the Italian certainly does. You, if you do not quarrel with *pasta*, will also enjoy your food. He likes his wine – and so will you. He likes a long session at a sit-down lunch, and this is a good time, in crowded periods, to use the lifts. He does not like to walk anywhere, and in consequence the quantity and layout of lift systems is comprehensive and studiously planned. He skis by bus and car. Italian railways, where they link with ski resorts, play very much second fiddle to the excellent and very comfortable bus services. The Italian is primarily a week-end skier – only the better-off go for long periods – and, consequently, save in the big centres and at big holiday periods, many an Italian ski resort is quite uncrowded during the week.

Appreciating speed, the Italian skis much in the same way as he drives a motor car. Appreciating the fine *autostrade* of his country, he concentrates on *piste* ski-ing and he demands that each *piste* be kept as impeccably as a high-speed motorway. Few Italian skiers ever leave the *piste*, and you will seldom find standard runs kept in more manicured condition. In several centres, they are almost too artificial, but the evident lack of accidents speaks well for the assiduous work of the many '*piste*-gardener' employees. This tendency for *piste* perfection and *piste* popularity is a great joy to those who prefer to ski 'off the *piste*'. The exploratory skier will find few tracks to mar large areas of powder snow.

The southern Alps, as many misinformed people seem to believe, do not sweep down uniformly from the Swiss and Austrian frontiers in long south-facing slopes. North slopes, and slopes that face all compass points, are there in plenty. There is, south of the high border-barrier, an immense complex of transverse valleys interspersed with many mountain groups and ranges, and much of the ski-ing is done in conditions that other Alpine lands have every right to envy. It is easy to think of many a popular and crowded ski centre north of the frontier that has far less to offer the visitor than some of the unpublicized and uncrowded places south of the barrier in Italy.

It is mostly the Italian town-dwellers, and those in the higher income groups, who go ski-ing – and they do so in very large and ever increasing numbers. (The Italian peasant, unlike his Austrian neighbour, can seldom afford the pleasure.) Relatively few, however, move out beyond their own frontiers in search of holiday ski fields. There is little need for them to do so. Apart from the extra expense, the sunshine and the snow, the *pista* and the *pasta*, the Campari and the Chianti – all of which they find in such abundance in their own mountains – are quite sufficient for them.

The travel time required from London or Paris to reach the Turin centres at the western end of the Italian mountains is remarkably little – less in fact than that required for many an Austrian resort. The forthcoming completion of the important new tunnel under Mont Blanc will make it a very simple matter to reach the Val d'Aosta direct from Geneva. For the central and the eastern mountains, including the Dolomites, the time by land transport is naturally longer. 'Ski-flight' air services to the airports of Turin, Milan, and Treviso (Venice), coupled with efficient pullman bus services, bring even the most remote corners within easy reach.

Italians make brave and dashing skiers – particularly on the *piste* – and they tend to skimp tuition in favour of individual experiment. The National Ski School, although perhaps not yet on a par with the organizations of Austria, France, and Switzerland, is both systematic and thorough, and no beginner need fear that he will receive anything but excellent instruction.

In general, the ski centres of Italy have a very great deal to offer. Whatever some of them may lack in the way of Swiss and Austrian tradition, they make up for, not only with good amenities and high quality of ski-ing, but also from the angle of sheer beauty of surroundings. Not many skiers from this country have yet tried out the Italian ski-ing. It surely will not be very long before they discover what they are missing.

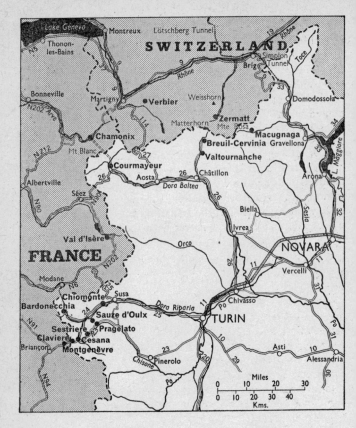

THE MONT BLANC AREA

Centre 94*
COURMAYEUR   Province: Aosta

Altitude
4016 ft

Description. 1307 inhabitants. 25 hotels and pensions providing 790 beds. Other accommodation available. Languages Italian and French.

  * Each place description is numbered according to the Altitude List, pp. 104–21.

A picturesque, peaceful, and traditional Alpine village tucked into the narrow head of the Aosta Valley close up under the magnificent and dramatic south-facing side of the Mont Blanc massif. This charming and unspoilt village, with its narrow little main street, has about it the true atmosphere – similar in many respects, but so far less commercially exploited, to that found in Zermatt, Grindelwald, and Chamonix for example – of being the home of those who understand and respect high mountains.

With its long history of rock and ice climbing in the summer months, it is only in the last few years that Courmayeur has turned its attention to winter and ski-ing. Much has happened here already. More will happen in the future. Courmayeur in Italy and Chamonix in France (separated by a mere 15 km. on the map) have long been linked in spirit by the challenge of the very barrier that separates them. They are now linked in fact by the most fabulous engineering feat in the whole history of high-altitude cableway transport systems, the cars of which swing their way right over the upper glaciers of the Mont Blanc massif. They will, very shortly, also be linked by a 12-km. road tunnel bored right through the base of the massif. The aerial link has already made both Chamonix and Courmayeur famous for the spectacular long glacier runs of the Vallée Blanche, and created all-the-year-round ski playgrounds for both centres. When the dual link of overhead transport and road tunnel is completed, the *Aller-et-retour* ski circus from both sides of the massif will be one of unprecedented magnitude.

On its own, however, Courmayeur has already developed its local ski area, and here again the projects for the future will make this of far more importance than it already can claim.

Ski facilities. The Checrouit Ski Area. A *téléférique* rises 1601 ft to 5607 ft. This is surmounted by a gondola car system that rises a further 1818 ft up to Col Checrouit at 7399 ft. This upper section provides a limited but amusing and interesting playground of short 3-km. runs on north-east-facing slopes. Sunny restaurants at top and bottom provide magnificent views of Mont Blanc and the whole massif. There is one run down the lower section of the *téléférique*, but this is difficult and seldom used. The 7-km.-long Val Veni run, with a descent of 3382 ft, largely on north-facing slopes, circles right round the rock pyramid of Mont Chétif, directly opposite the immensities of the south side of Mont Blanc itself, to return you to Courmayeur.

A project for the immediate future is to extend, with two *téléfériques*, upwards from Col Checrouit, to 8530 ft and 9186 ft respectively. Completion of this scheme will greatly enlarge the present ski area and also open up the whole of the long Valle d'Arp which will provide runs of 10 km. and 5170-ft descents right down to Courmayeur.

The whole of the Checrouit area, at present good but slightly restricted, will, in the near future, be widespread and excellent.

The Courmayeur–Chamonix High-Altitude Link (see also Chamonix, p. 212). The statistics of the Italian startpoint of this audacious aerial cableway are as follows:

Bus or car from Courmayeur, 4016 ft, northwards up to La Palud 4501 ft, close to the Mont Blanc tunnel entrance. Rise 480 ft. 10 mins. 4 km.

The Colle del Gigante (Col du Géant) Cable Cars.
   (1) La Palud 4501 ft, north-west to Pavillon (Monte Fréty), 7129 ft.
      Rise 2628 ft. 6 mins. 1·809 km.
   (2) Pavillon 7129 ft, north-west to Rifugio Torino, 10,896 ft.
      Rise 3767 ft. 5 mins. 2·420 km.
   (3) Rifugio Torino 10,896 ft, north-west to P. Helbronner, 11,254 ft.
      Rise 358 ft. 1½ mins. 0·280 km.
   Total (incl. road)
      Rise 7238 ft. 23 mins. 8·5 km. (4·5 km. of cables)

Top stations have magnificent viewpoints – including Matterhorn and Monte Rosa and many peaks along the '*haute route*'.

There is one superb but stern run, down through the *seracs* of the Glacier du Thule back to Courmayeur. Not for the

untalented, this steep south-facing descent measures 8 km.
and 6753 ft down to bottom station.

At Piz Helbronner, where there is a Customs frontier-post
(passports required), summer ski-ing is practised with short
lifts. The famed long-distance run down to Chamonix can be
taken either from here or from the Aiguille du Midi (see p. 213).

The upper linkage of gondola cars goes from Piz Helbronner
on a breathtaking 5-km. trip across the central glaciers of the
Mont Blanc massif. Hanging from a wonderfully ingenious
'flying' or suspended pylon, the cables go soaring across the
glaciers up to the rocks of the Gros Rognon at 11,591 ft and
continue right up to the Aiguille du Midi at 12,474 ft, where
they connect with the huge *téléférique* up from Chamonix.

Amenities. Ski school – 16 instructors. 33 Alpine guides.
Skating rink. Village shops. Tea rooms. Restaurants. Bars.
Hotel and bar dancing. Cinema. Guides' Museum.

Life in centre. Pleasant friendly atmosphere. Comfortable
inexpensive living. Simple and genuine. No sophistication
but plenty of informal fun. Seldom crowded.

Accessibility. Train: to Turin, thence train or bus ($3\frac{1}{2}$–4 hrs).
Airport: Milan; thence train or bus (5 hrs).

General comments. Courmayeur is a place of great character,
well organized and efficiently run. This unusual and relatively
little-publicized ski centre, restricted as yet for the average
piste-tiger, is much to be recommended. Already it has something for every type from beginner to ski mountaineer. Bound
to grow, both in scope and importance, the ski-ing will soon
be very much more comprehensive. The opening of the Mont
Blanc tunnel will make it very easily accessible from Geneva,
and whether its inevitable future popularity will influence its
character remains to be seen. A place to watch.

THE MATTERHORN–MONTE ROSA AREA

Centre 3   Altitude
BREUIL-CERVINIA   Province: Aosta   6627–6792 ft

Description. 250 inhabitants. 22 hotels and pensions providing
1500 beds. Other accommodation 50 beds. Language Italian –
some English spoken.

Set in superb and splendid scenery, dominated by the
Matterhorn, the 'village' is a surprising, uninspiring example
of heterogeneous modern architecture haphazardly grafted to
a small high-altitude hamlet. Fortunately Breuil is well en-
dowed with abundant sunshine, for, without this, the lack of
character would make it somewhat bleak and uninteresting.
This curious exterior conceals interiors of great luxury and
comfort. Immensely popular with Italians, very crowded at
week-ends, and constantly visited by skiers over from Zermatt
via the Theodule Pass, Breuil is an important centre with much
to offer to skiers. Ski-wise the expanse is even greater than the
expense; village-wise it has a slightly fidgety atmosphere of
constant change. Scenically, from below it is splendid; from
top stations widespread views of great magnificence.

Ski facilities. One vast semicircular arena-area of widespread south-facing snowfields mounting up to glacier levels.
Served by no less than four major cableway systems climbing
in Y-formation to altitudes of 11,431 ft (Plateau Rosa – direct
ski descent to Zermatt) and 11,470 ft (Furggen). Five good
ski-lifts around village. Main lift system gives network of long
runs of 8 to 10 km. and just under 5000 ft. The ski-ing is big,
wide, above-the-treeline, open stuff – varied but somewhat
featureless (which makes for tricky navigation in low visibility)
– all conducted in surroundings of great splendour. Superb
in springtime.

Ski touring. Wonderful glacier and ski mountaineering
region for the competent. Monte Rosa, Castor, Pollux, Breit-
horn, etc., including the Saas-Fee region within easy reach.

Amenities. Big ski school. Guides. Ice rink. Small village shops. Specialist equipment and clothing shops. First-class restaurant. Bars. Dance bars. Hotel dancing. Garage.

Life in centre. Somewhat impersonal and on the pretentious side. Fashionable and glamour conscious. Expensive – watch the extras. Primary interest ski-ing. Lovely sunny terraces. Big comfortable hotels.

Specialities. Spring ski-ing on widespread scale. Summer ski-ing at Plateau Rosa with ski-lifts and instruction. Superb ski mountaineering. Long south-facing *pistes*.

Accessibility. Train: nearest station Chatillon (27 km.), thence bus. Road: 3 hrs bus Turin, 4 hrs bus Milan. Airports: Turin or Milan.

General comments. The highest ski centre in the Alps with so great a ski transport rise *above* the village (4744 ft). An experience not to be missed. Most visitors to Zermatt make the easy ski trip over to Breuil. Fully to appreciate extent of ski-ing you must be reasonably competent. The good skier should not miss the long excursion type run to Valtournanche (18 km.).

Centre 49   Altitude
VALTOURNANCHE   Province: Aosta   5000 ft

Description. 17 hotels and inns providing about 400 beds. Language Italian.

Only 8 km. down the valley road from Breuil–Cervinia, this very different centre is a picturesque old village of considerable tradition and history. In its sunny setting Valtournanche is no fashionable place and the prices are rightly very reasonable. The hotels are pleasantly old-fashioned, catering mostly for summer visitors.

The village, save for the through traffic up to Breuil, is quiet and the life simple. Bus services give access to the big ski-ing up at Breuil, and locally there is a chairlift of about 1000 ft from the village that opens up various pleasantly easy runs of between 2 and 3 km. on west-facing slopes.

Friendly and full of local colour and character, this village

scarcely belongs in any list of ski centres which set out to
'entertain' winter-sports visitors. It is the end point of the
fine long run from Plateau Rosa above Breuil – a descent of
6400 ft.

Centre 82		Altitude
MACUGNAGA	Province: Novara	4354 ft

Not strictly classified as a ski centre in the general sense,
Macugnaga has its charm for those whose approach to, and
requirements from, ski-ing are modest and whose primary
demands are for a quiet holiday in a picturesque spot where
the surroundings are impressive and there is a feeling of being
remote.

The scattered little groups of buildings lie at the foot of the
sensational wall-like flank of Monte Rosa in a wide hollow at
the head of the Anzasca valley. Very popular with tourists and
climbers in summer, it has much less traffic in winter. Climbers
cross over to Zermatt (Weisstor Pass), to Saas-Fee (Mount
Moro Pass), and to Alagna (Colle del Turlo) and the many
famous peaks of the Zermatt area are within easy reach in
summertime.

Ski facilities consist of a chairlift that runs from 4560 ft
westwards up to the moraine of Belvedere at 6339 ft, close to
the glacier of the same name that sweeps down from Monte
Rosa. A ski-lift close to the lower section of this chairlift rises
to 5036 ft.

A place of considerable beauty and charm, but no great
shakes for the modern, nose-to-the-grindstone *piste*-basher.

THE TURIN AREA

Centre 154   Altitude
CHIOMONTE   Province: Turin   2444 ft

Description. 1400 inhabitants. 2 hotels with 60 beds. Language
Italian.

Small, slightly sombre, workaday village in Susa valley on
main road and rail-line (Bardonecchia ½ hr, Turin 1 hr).
Almost purely week-end ski centre for Turin. Somewhat
primitive and low down, Chiomonte itself has little to recommend it save the big altitude rise of its lift system, its upstairs
satellite Frais, good north-slope ski-ing, and cheap prices.

Ski facilities. One big ski area served by long two-section
chairlift. Middle station Frais, at 4800 ft (2 hotels with 70
beds and 4 restaurants) surrounded by lovely 'nursery' areas
and a separate ski-lift, is an excellent simple place for the
impecunious. Top station at Pian Mesdi, 6873 ft, provides
long descents of 4327 ft and 6½ to 8½ km. Delightful 'parkland'
type ski-ing amid glades and natural clearings. Highly entertaining and never over-difficult for the average skier.

Good spring ski-ing above top station. 4-hr ski excursion
takes you over ridge and down to Pragelato close to Sestriere.

General comments. Stay here – preferably at Frais – if you
want a cheap holiday without any frills whatsoever, but do not
miss the ski-ing if you are driving along the Susa valley.

Centre 44   Altitudes
SAUZE D'OULX AND   Province: Turin   4951 to 5135 ft
SPORTINIA   7120 ft

Description. 500 inhabitants. 15 hotels and pensions with 1200
beds. Language Italian – little or no English.

Only 7 km. over the minor Fraiteve–Triplex ridge from
Sestriere, this pleasant modest village – relatively little-known
but fast developing (new buildings, etc.) – is rightly becoming
popular with skiers. Small, attractively placed on a sunny spur

overlooking the upper Susa valley and facing the Franco–Italian frontier mountains by Bardonecchia, Sauze d'Oulx is backed by extensive north-facing slopes and beautifully wooded hillsides where its 'upstairs satellite' of Sportinia (120 beds) sits on a gentle shelf at 7120 ft. Views unspectacular, but pleasing.

Ski facilities. One large ski area served by two lift systems. Main system consists of one ski/chairlift to Sportinia (sole access) with a ski-lift on up to Triplex at 8127 ft. Total rise 3176 ft providing fine network of runs between 6 and 8 km. Secondary system consists of nearby chairlift surmounted by a sledge-lift to Lago Nero giving 2497 ft rise and a selection of slightly shorter, separate but interlinking runs. Good nursery slopes at village, with trainer lift.

The whole area (with future lift projects) commands excellent ski-ing both above and below tree-line. Good wide glades. Good runs for good skiers. Easier descents for all classes. Excellent variations and woodrunning.

Amenities. Ski school. Ice rink. Village shops. Small pubs. Dance bars. Garage facilities.

Life in centre. No frills. No smart *après-ski*, but amusing, unpretentious entertainment in local bars, etc. Popular with big parties. Simple, good living. Medium-class-hotel life. Economic prices. Emphasis on ski-ing – standards medium and below.

Specialities. North-facing ski-ing with good powder snow duration. Lovely open larch woods. Day tours to Sestriere with easy access to runs from Fraiteve (see p. 283).

Accessibility. Train: nearest station Oulx on main Paris–Turin line. Road: Oulx, 20 mins. bus; kept open. Turin 80 km. Airport: Turin (Geneva also easy).

General comments. Much to be recommended for those who seek good ski-ing for inexpensive prices at an unsophisticated centre. Excellent for groups and parties.

Centre 83		Altitudes
BARDONECCHIA	Province: Turin	4118–4305 ft

Description. 2400 inhabitants. 16 hotels and pensions providing

643 beds. Other accommodation available. Languages Italian and French.

This strange, unprepossessing little village-town at the southern entry of the 12-km. long Mont Cenis rail tunnel that leads through to Modane in France (car ferry flat trucks every 2 hrs) is something of a surprise. Tucked into a wide flat corner and surrounded by impressive mountains, the old village, with its sprawling new section all around, scarcely qualifies as a beauty spot, but it unexpectedly commands good sun hours and ski-ing that is a very great deal better than a casual glance suggests.

Ski facilities. Two ski areas served by separate transport systems.

(1) *The Colomion Ski Area*. A chairlift rises 859 ft from Campo Smith up to Gr. Hyppolites at 5167 ft. Here there is a big hotel and wide areas of nursery slopes served by two trainer lifts. A ski-lift continues on up to Colomion at 6890 ft, increasing the rise to 2772 ft above Campo Smith.

Four main runs of between 3½ to 5 km., on north- and north-west-facing slopes, with both open and wooded sections (larches), grant easy and severe choice to both beginner and good skiers.

(2) *The Jafferau Ski Area*. A chairlift from Bardonecchia rises 2103 ft eastwards up to Fregiusia at 6329 ft. Above this a long ski-lift continues up to Jafferau at 8071 ft. A total rise of 3845 ft.

Projected lifts above this will continue up to 8701 ft and 9137 ft.

The run down here is long – 6 to 8 km. – from top to bottom (various halts on the lifts allow for short versions). The slopes face west and north-west and provide a high degree of entertainment for all comers.

Amenities. Ski school. Ski jump. Skating rink. Village shops. Restaurants. Bars. Dancing. Cinemas.

Life in centre. The built-up area is widespread. Campo Smith with its own small hotel settlement is 1½ km. south-west from village main street and the Jafferau lift ½ km. east. There are many streets with few buildings. There is consequently a

slightly disjointed and sometimes aloof atmosphere for the
lone visitor (the hotels, popular with Italians, have yet to
learn a few refinements in the way of comfort to attract international visitors), but a party here could have a great deal of
fun. There are no pretentious frills and the living is not expensive.

Accessibility. Main line (Paris–Turin) train service. Turin
1 hr–1 hr 40 mins. Geneva 3½ hrs. Paris 9 hrs. Airport: Geneva
or Turin.

General comments. This easily accessible, workaday frontier
village, with its phlegmatic character that seems at first glance
unpromising, provides a very welcome surprise with the
quality of its ski-ing. To be recommended for parties who wish
good value for relatively little expenditure.

Centre 26		Altitude
CLAVIERE	Province: Turin	5774 ft

Description. 110 inhabitants. 8 hotels with 250 beds. Other
accommodation 50 beds. Languages Italian and French;
occasional English.

A pleasant little Alpine village at the French frontier barrier
close to top of the Montgenèvre Pass (Cesana over to Briançon
– always open in winter). Sheltered situation. Attractive small
comfortable hotels. Main road village street. Easy bus or car
access to ski centre of Montgenèvre (2 km.) in France – and
also to Serre Chevalier just beyond Briançon (see pp. 236 and
237). Ski-lift is planned to link the Claviere–Montgenèvre ski
areas.

Ski facilities. One small ski area served by two ski-lifts. Good
nursery slopes around village, with trainer lift.

The Pian del Sole ski-lift gives short runs of 2 to 3 km. and
approximately 1000 ft – all on lovely north-facing slopes amid
delightful open larch woods. Three wide glade-*pistes* – go-
where-you-will, joyful slalom-style ski-ing, both steep and
gentle, mostly in powder snow.

Ski touring. Behind Pian del Sole there are many square
kilometres of gentle and picturesque 'ski-wandering' country

where countless small summits can be gained by climbs of 2-4 hrs – including top station of Cesana lifts (see below).

Amenities. Small ski school. Ski jump. Ice rink. Village shops. Small inns.

Life in centre. Gentle, simple, inexpensive, comfortable. Practically no nightlife. A frontier village where Italian, and nearby French, foods can be compared.

Accessibility. Train: Ulzio (18 km.) on main Paris–Turin line, or Briançon (12 km.). Road: bus Briançon 50 mins., Ulzio 50 mins. Airport: Turin (94 km.).

General comments. Moving between the ski areas of Claviere and Montgenèvre you have to have either a passport or a *carte d'identité* – but this causes very little inconvenience. A charming, quiet centre with limited but excellent ski-ing available in pass area. Easy bus access to Sestriere for a day's outing.

Centre 74	Altitude
CESANA Province: Turin	4455 ft

Description. 8–900 inhabitants. 3 to 4 small inn hotels and several pensions. Language Italian.

This workaday Italian village lies in the valley directly between Claviere up on the Montgenèvre Pass and Sestriere up on its own pass. Very infrequently used by foreigners as a centre – the accommodation is very simple – it nevertheless boasts of a sizeable chairlift system and the small but growing upstairs satellite of Sagna-Longa. At 6565 ft, Sagna-Longa sits in a sunny, basin-shelf situation, with splendid views and with good local slopes. It enjoys midway access to all the Cesana ski-ing. There is at least one big comfortable hotel with about 100 beds and other accommodation, and this is fast becoming a popular holiday settlement. Chairlift is only means of access.

Ski facilities. Chairlift rises 1808 ft from 4757 ft southwards up to Sagna-Longa. Here a second section continues west of south up to Monti della Luna at 7336 ft. Total rise 2579 ft above Cesana.

There is a 338-ft-rise ski-lift serving the local Sagna-Longa slopes.

From Monti della Luna there is a network of runs; pisted down to Cesana on north-facing slopes (4½ km. and 2579 ft); semi-pisted down to nearby valley village of Bousson, which lies at 4656 ft; and unpisted, semi-excursion-type runs on shaded wooded slopes down to Claviere (about 6 km. and 1740 ft descent). The area above and behind Monti della Luna is good value for short ski excursions and 'ski wandering'.

General comments. Amenities are few, and the set-up simple, inexpensive, and unsophisticated. Preferable to stay at Sagna-Longa. Quiet life, sunshine, good medium ski-ing. The Montgenèvre ski area and Sestriere are within easy reach for a day's outing and a change of ski-ing.

Centre 5   Altitude
SESTRIERE   Province: Turin   6677 ft

Description. 130 inhabitants. 11 hotels providing 1165 beds. Language Italian – English and most continental languages spoken.

A modern fantasy, created by and for ski-ing. Unique and spectacular, it has glamour rather than 'atmosphere'. A brain-child of FIAT, beautifully situated high up on an open sunny pass amid fine ski country, this small concentrated collection of buildings – with one large luxury hotel close by – is hall-marked by the two famous round-tower hotels. No normal village, this highly geared, generously equipped, and efficiently run 'ski mill' is immensely popular and liable to be crowded with bus and car visitors at week-ends and at high seasons (20 December–10 January and 7 February–15 March).

Ski facilities. Three separate ski areas served by three big cable-car systems. Six other long ski lifts. Baby lifts on big nursery slopes.

(1) *The Sises Ski Area.* Two-section cable-car going south-east, giving rise of 1854 ft and runs of approximately 4½ km. Two long supporting ski-lifts to assist traffic. Steepish, open ski-ing.

(2) *The Banchetta Ski Area.* Cable-car going east, giving rise of 1706 ft and runs of 2287 ft and 3½ to 5 km. down to Borgata. Ski- and chairlift return to Sestriere. Also two ski-lift system from Borgata to Amphitheatre area giving rise of over 2000 ft. The whole consists of fine varied ski-ing for all comers. Long unpisted runs of 7 to 8 km. go down to Plan, close to Pragelato, where a big 3000-ft chairlift is planned.

(3) *The Fraiteve Ski Area.* Cable-car going north-west gives rise of 2129 ft up to 8861 ft and south-facing runs of 4 and 5 km. Monte Fraiteve is also the start point for the short excursion over to Sauze d'Oulx (see p. 278) and the hub of a network of fine spring snow and powder snow runs down to the Sestriere approach road. Most notable of these is the splendid Rio Nero run – 5085 ft and 8 km.

In general Sestriere has something of everything for every skier. Some 50 km. of well-kept, prepared *pistes* in three compact areas on slopes that face all points of compass. Easy, medium, and difficult ski country – plenty of open slopes with many variations, including good woodrunning.

Ski touring. Not basically a touring area, but excursions can be found in the vicinity.

Amenities. Big efficient ski school. First-class S O S service. Excellent nursery slopes. Ice rinks. Cinema. Good arcade shops. Huge garage and car parks. Hotel dancing. Dance bars. Night-club.

Life in centre. International but mainly Italian. Plenty of big hotel *après-ski* life. Gay, colourful, slightly film-set glamour. No traditional village life. Costs on the expensive side – can be heavy. Accommodation from luxury suites to 'tourist-class' rooms. Sunshine and good spectator terraces etc. for watching ski slopes.

Specialities. Excellent safe *pistes* for all standards. Reliable snow conditions. Easy access by car or bus to five other Turin centres, Sauze d'Oulx, Bardonecchia, Cesana, Claviere, and Chiomonte – also to Montgenèvre just over the frontier in France. Simple to visit Turin for day or evening out.

Accessibility. Train: nearest station Ulzio on main Paris–

Turin line. Road: Ulzio 1 hr bus, always open. 2½ hrs Turin.
Airports: Turin or Geneva.

General comments. Unusual, unorthodox, specialized centre.
High-spirited and efficient, the value is extremely good – but
this is no Christmas-card ski 'dorf'.

THE MEDITERRANEAN AREA

Centre 123   Altitude
LIMONE PIEMONTE   Province: Cuneo   3314 ft

Description. 2150 inhabitants. 7 hotels and pensions with 400 beds. Language Italian.

Limone Piemonte lies only some 50 km. from the Bordighera–Monte Carlo Mediterranean coastline, and a very short distance below the Colle di Tenda Pass (4331 ft), which is the Franco–Italian frontier. This compact old village stands on a broad flat, surrounded by mountains, at the junction of the Almellina and San Giovanni valleys, and, whereas it is a very popular summer and winter resort, it still retains an air of tradition and relative simplicity.

Ski facilities. There is a chairlift system giving a 1607 ft rise up to Maire del Cros at 4921 ft. Second section continues a further 1836 ft up to 6757 ft. Total rise 3443 ft.

There is also a ski-lift with a rise of 900 ft up to Monte Feit at approximately 4200 ft – and three ski-lifts of approximately 500 ft, 650 ft, and 950 ft to the Campo Principe.

General comments. Half-way between Turin and Nice and within easy reach from both airports or stations, Limone has interesting ski-ing, and, as at Auron (p. 241) in France, this ski-ing is doubly intriguing in that it is within a short car drive of the blue Mediterranean.

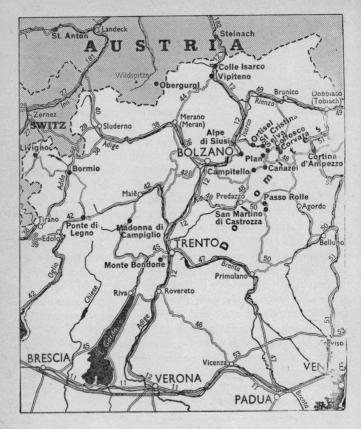

THE ORTLER–CEVEDALE AREA

Centre 95 and 14		Altitudes
BORMIO	Province: Sondrio	3993 ft
LIVIGNO		6135 ft

Description. Bormio: 3000 inhabitants. 22 hotels and pensions providing 1000 beds. Other accommodation 200 beds. Language Italian.

The most engaging small-resort town of Bormio, popular

since Roman times in summer, is growing in importance for the skier. The old village is surrounded by scattered modern hotels and villas and the general effect, in its sunny valley setting close to the foot of the 9045-ft Stelvio Pass (closed in winter), is friendly and pleasing.

Ski facilities. The Bormio ski area has a big three-section lift system, each section of which provides good individual ski-ing. First Section: *Gondelbahn* up to 5479 ft. Second Section: Chairlift up to 7172 ft. Third Section: Ski-lift up to 7890 ft. Total rise 3832 ft. Use of all three sections provides runs of 7 to 8 km. on north- and north-west-facing slopes. Upper sections open and interestingly varied. Lower slopes lightly wooded with occasional woodpaths. Interesting, inquisitive routes, both steep and gentle, suitable for all comers. Good 'nurseries' at top of first section. Upper section served by subsidiary ski-lift.

Apart from this good north-facing area, Bormio plans to erect lifts on sunny hillsides that lie to the west of the resort.

Ski touring. A valley road south-eastwards leads, via San Caterina, to the ski-entry way up into the lovely ski touring regions of the Ortler and Cevedale. Here there are many ski peaks between 10,000 and 12,700 ft, with miles of glacier ski-ing, and several well-placed huts which allow for week-long tours. Very popular in springtime and much to be recommended to the enthusiast.

Amenities. Ski school. Guides. Skating rink. Good shopping area. Tea rooms. Restaurants. Bars. Dancing. Cinema. Natural hot-water indoor swimming bath.

Specialities. Big height gain on local ski-transport system. Excellent glacier ski-touring region easily accessible. Spring and summer ski-ing centres in Cevedale region and at top of Stelvio Pass (short lifts). Swimming in hot mineral springs bath (38° C.).

Life in centre. Pleasant easy-going existence in picturesque surroundings. Sheltered and sunny. Comfortable and unpretentious. Not expensive. Resort atmosphere without artificial glamour. Village life without undue emphasis on ski-ing. For *après-ski* go for a swim before dinner. A car is an asset.

Accessibility. Train or air to Milan. Thence 5 hrs bus (200 km.). 5 hrs bus from St Moritz.

General comments. Gentle and simple, this relatively un-publicized ski centre is unusual and unorthodox. It has many assets. Bormio itself has a shortish winter season, but spring and summer ski-ing are amply catered for nearby. For those who wish for a complete change of scene Lake Como is only 103 km. distant for a day's visit. Organized parties, not seeking high-geared, competitive ski-ing, will greatly enjoy this place – and they will get good terms.

THE LIVIGNO SKI AREA

The nearby high-altitude valley of Livigno is reached from Bormio up a spectacular and sometimes hair-raising road, the 40 km. of which requires 2 hrs of careful driving. Over a 7244-ft pass you come to a 'neutral' no-man's-land zone be-tween the two customs frontiers of Italy and Switzerland. Here you find the extraordinary village of Livigno (6135 ft), the many small buildings of which extend in a long line along the wide valley for perhaps 10 km. This remote 'customs-free' and slightly 'Shangri-la'-like community (where live some 1000 villagers who speak a Ladienish dialect and are reputed to be of Greek origin) has no taxes, and low-priced goods in the shops.

Completely undeveloped as yet, the valley is surrounded by lovely snowfields of big open slopes where the 'ski wanderer', for climbs of 1½ to 2 hrs, can move about on untracked snow to his heart's content. Steep and gentle gradients, many short runs, and easy safe day tours are there to be found.

Livigno will not long stay untouched. Plans are already afoot for a light-plane airstrip and the construction of lifts. These will convert this strange village, where there are only two or three simple inn-pensions, into a standard high-altitude ski-centre of modest proportions and considerable prosperity. At present it is remote, primitive, and highly unusual.

BRESCIA

Centre 89   Altitude
PONTE DI LEGNO   Province: Brescia   4127 ft

Description. 1500 inhabitants. 12 hotels and inns and 8 pensions
providing 667 beds. Language Italian.

A large valley village of considerable character with a pleasant
main square and village street. The speciality of this place is ski
jumping. It has three jumping hills ranging up to the 'Gigante',
on which the record distance is 110 m. (361 ft).

Ski facilities. One large ridge-shaped area served by chairlift
up to 6562 ft surmounted by ski-lift up to 7874 ft. Total rise:
3747 ft. Runs of up to 5 km. on both open and timbered slopes
– medium gradients on sunny slopes and steep on shaded
slopes. Sunny slopes near village with lift.

Amenities. Ski school. Three jumping hills. Skating rinks.
Bobsleigh and luge runs. Good village shops. Restaurants.
Bars, etc.

Life in centre. Quiet and unsophisticated. Italian village.
Italian clientele. Friendly place – easy to mix with locals.

Accessibility. Nearest station: Edolo, on the Brescia line.
Bus Edolo to Ponte di Legno 20 km. Direct bus linkage with
Brescia and Venice.

General comments. This popular summer resort, not as easily
accessible as most Italian centres, has nevertheless a considerable ski transport height gain and ski-ing that is rewarding to
the visitor. International ski-jumping meetings here are a great
spectacle.

THE TRENTO AREA

Centre 50   Altitude
MADONNA DI   Province: Trento   4993 ft
   CAMPIGLIO

Description. 300 inhabitants. 17 hotels and 12 pensions providing 1380 beds. Other accommodation 500 beds. Language
Italian; German spoken.

A truly delightful little centre. Long popular as a summer
resort, with a small village street and square attractively surrounded by several large, traditional, resort-type hotels, and
many smaller chalet-type buildings, Madonna di Campiglio
has proved ideally suited for successful development as a ski
centre. Plenty of accommodation. Sheltered sunny situation.
Three good ski areas in immediate vicinity, backed by the
beautiful and impressive scenery of the Brenta Dolomite group.
Not too high; not too low; plenty of room both in the valley
and on the snow slopes. Medium-sized ski runs to suit all
tastes and grades of efficiency; ski touring areas. Modestly, and
almost without publicity, Madonna di Campiglio has the lot.

Ski facilities. Three ski areas each with separate transport.
Three subsidiary lifts. Nursery slopes with lift in village.

(1) *The Spinale Area.* Chairlift gives 1893 ft rise to south-
east, to Spinale at 6850 ft. Fine viewpoint with restaurant.
Four marked runs from 3½ km. to 6 km. on slopes that face
west, north-west, and south-west, ranging from easy to medium-
difficult. Good variety of open slopes, glade, and wood running.

Spinale summit has good nursery slopes and two trainer
lifts. It is also the entry point for the 2½-hrs climb to the
Rifugio Graffer *en route* for the Passo del Groste and several
ski-touring peaks.

(2) *The Pradalago Area.* Chairlift gives 1778 ft rise to north,
to Pradalago at 6752 ft. Restaurant, fine view. Slopes largely
east-facing. (Above this station is a large amphitheatre of excellent ski slopes – an obvious site for future lift development
towards the rocky summit of Zeledria.) Two main runs,

medium and easy, of 4 and 6 km. respectively, on south and south-east slopes. Foolproof, ideal '*autostrada*' for beginners. Ski-lifts at Campo Carlo Magno (5518 ft), the pass just above Madonna di Campiglio.

(3) *The Cinque Laghi Area.* Chairlift gives 1772 ft rise to west, up to Pancugolo at 6792 ft. Small restaurant with splendid viewpoint of Spinale and Brenta Dolomites. Two main runs of $3\frac{1}{2}$ to $4\frac{1}{2}$ km. – medium to medium-difficult – on interesting varied ground. 'Ski wanderers' can explore the area behind top station where several lakes lie tucked into secret corners.

All ski runs from all three areas return you down to the village.

Amenities. Ski school. Guides. Ski jump. Ice stadium. Skating rink. Ice hockey. Village shops. Restaurants. Bars. Cinema. Dancing.

Life in centre. Pleasant, easy-going, sunny existence. More small-resort than village life. Unpretentious, friendly, and simple. Mostly Italian clientele – apt to be busy at week-ends and holidays, but uncrowded otherwise. Little or no sophistication. *Après-ski* entertainment spontaneous and largely what you make it. Very reasonable prices.

Accessibility. $2\frac{1}{2}$ hrs bus (75 km.) from Trento. 5 hrs bus from Milan.

General comments. Unspoiled and uncommercialized, with good comfort standards, Madonna di Campiglio must rank high on any international list for good ski-ing and good value. Slightly more difficult to get at than other Italian ski centres, the extra journey is well worth while. Compact, yet widespread, there is ski-ing here to suit all grades – and scenery to impress even the blasé. Much to be recommended. Character and 'atmosphere'.

Centre 79   Altitudes

MONTE BONDONE   Province: Trento

Vaneze: 4256–4429 ft
Vason: 5249–5413 ft

Description. Vaneze: 150 inhabitants. 4 hotels and pensions with 185 beds. *Vason*: 20 inhabitants. 4 hotels and pensions with 104 beds.

These two small hotel settlements (buildings modern and comfortable) have little accommodation. Linked together by chairlift, they lie near the top of the steep pyramid-shaped mountain directly above the attractive town of Trento. Approached from the town by an energetic 13 km. of hairpins, the road climbs 3635 ft and requires some 25 mins. by bus or car. The summit section of Monte Bondone, limited in area of snowfields, is the week-end ski playground for the people of Trento. Newly constructed, it falls into the category of a modern, miniature 'ski mill', and the object has been to see how many transport lifts can be crammed into a small area. To date there are five chairlifts, one ski-lift, and two trainer lifts. These can, and do, attend to the demands of 3000 skiers per hour, and there is seldom a square metre of snow that is not hard beaten by the passage of many pairs of skis.

Used in step-ladder fashion, these lifts take you up 2612 ft above Vaneze to the top of Monte Bondone at 6877 ft, where, on the angular little summit of Cima Palon, there is a restaurant with a spectacular panorama and a bird's-eye view of Trento town 6234 ft below.

Short open slopes face north and north-west. Never over-difficult, there are both steep and gentle gradients, and on busy days the visitor will require a driving mirror and trafficators.

Monte Bondone is a modern phenomenon. Immensely popular with locals, this limited area is almost a 'ski eccentricity', representing the type of terrain sought by the masses of today. Indicative of a not-too-distant future when every inch of every accessible snow mountain will probably be treated in a similar fashion, Monte Bondone has to be seen to be believed. Hampstead Heath is enjoyed by many thousands on a Bank Holiday, but relatively few would choose to spend a fortnight's holiday on the fairground site.

Centres 52 and 7   Altitudes
SAN MARTINO   Province: Trento   4738–4856 ft
   DI CASTROZZA
PASSO ROLLE   6463 ft

Description. San Martino di Castrozza: 250 inhabitants. 27
hotels and pensions providing 1389 beds. *Passo Rolle*: 50 inhabitants. 4 pension inns providing 90 beds. Language Italian.

Scenically this area is hard to rival. San Martino, originally
built by the Austrians as a summer resort, and the little high-
altitude pass-settlement village of Passo Rolle – an 'upstairs
satellite' connected both by road and by chairlift – together
share a ski terrain which enjoys a sensational, almost theatrical,
back-cloth of the turrets and pinnacles of the Pale Range
(eastern Dolomites), whose red rocks and precipices tower up
close by. Both in the resort and on the snow slopes, the visitor
is always confronted with magnificent mountain scenery.

San Martino has a long, curving, climbing main street, with
many traditional-type large hotels and several modern structures. Passo Rolle is a simple, small, slightly austere collection
of buildings of more 'Alpine' character.

Ski facilities. Two ski areas and one upland ski playground
where spring and early summer ski-ing is possible.

(1) *The Caston di Rolle Area.* The chairlift linking San
Martino with the Passo Rolle ski area climbs in two sections
to 5922 ft and 7234 ft. The first section provides an easy and
pleasant south-facing run of about 4 km. and 1066 ft down
through wooded hillsides. Upper section climbs steeply a
further 1279 ft to Caston di Rolle. (Restaurant and terrace
with lovely view of the Cimon della Pala.) Run down to San
Martino, via Passo Rolle, approx. 7 km. and 2350 ft.

Passo Rolle itself has lovely rolling west-facing slopes served
by one ski- and one chairlift (plus one trainer lift) with maximum rise of 890 ft and short runs of about 2 km. Restaurant
huts in splendid surroundings.

Area eminently suitable to beginners and modest skiers with
steep south-facing slopes for good skiers.

(2) *The Col Verde–Rosetta Ski Area.* Chairlift rises 1532 ft

north-eastwards to Col Verde. Easy, gulley-type wooded run down of 2½ km. Cable-car continues south-eastwards up to Rosetta at 8537 ft. One severe and angular descent for experts only.

The wide upland plateau slopes up at Rosetta, which is a superb viewpoint, are served by a 600-ft-rise ski-lift. Fine north-east-facing 'nursery'-type slopes. Several good ski tours available.

A third ski area of easy and medium east-facing slopes is planned within 1½ km. of San Martino. A projected gondola lift will give a rise of over 3000 ft up to the Alpetognola plateau at 7808 ft. This will greatly extend the scope.

Amenities. Ski school. Ski jump. Skating. Ice hockey. Good shopping facilities. Cafés. Cinema. Restaurants. Bars. Night-club, etc.

Life in centre. Easy-going, unhurried, resort-type life with long sun hours. Spectacular setting, but with little or no 'village life'. Holiday atmosphere. Busy at holiday periods but seldom crowded. Wide range of prices for all purses. With little emphasis on organized entertainment, the *après-ski* and evening life is largely what a party creates for itself. Every opportunity to create well.

Accessibility. Train or air to Milan. Thence 7 hrs bus via Lake Garda. Air to Venice. Thence 4 hrs bus. Train via Brenner Pass to Bolzano. Thence 3½ hrs bus. Bus from Innsbruck 6½ hrs (207 km.).

General comments. The case-hardened experienced skier may find the terrain insufficiently taxing, but beginners and modest skiers will be tremendously impressed with everything and greatly enjoy the facilities. Very good value for parties of up to three seasons' experience and for anyone who likes gentle ski-ing in beautiful surroundings.

Centres 56 and 59		Altitudes
CANAZEI	Province: Trento	4807 ft
CAMPITELLO		4751 ft

Description. Canazei: 8–900 inhabitants. 18 hotels and pensions providing 850 beds. *Campitello* (2 km. away, 5 mins. bus): 14 hotels with 350 beds. Languages Italian and German.

These two centres, together with little nearby Alba, are medium-sized, unpretentious valley villages of considerable charm. The narrow valley setting is surrounded by spectacular mountains. In the heart of the Dolomites (the Hoch Almen Gebiet), close to the famed Marmolada, they lie at the foot of the Sella and Pordoi Passes. Immensely popular with tourists in summer, this district, with the passes closed by snow, is the end of the road up from Bolzano and Trento in winter, but these two Passes, close up under the lovely Dolomite groups of Selva and Sasso–Lungo, can, thanks to uphill transport systems, be easily crossed on ski. The Sella Pass is in fact the ski link between Canazei and the Val Gardena (see pp. 296–300).

Ski facilities. Two ski areas, plus the Marmolada (after February).

(1) *The Belvedere Ski Area.* Two chairlifts, via Pecol middle station (6350 ft), give total rise of 2808 ft up to Belvedere at 7677 ft close to the Pordoi Pass region.

Pecol–Belvedere area consists of wide, sunny, easy slopes. Good for learners. Lovely views (directly opposite Marmolada). Separate trainer lift. Two ways down to Canazei, one medium and one easy, give total descents of 5 to 6 km. and 2808 ft. Lower sections, cut glades through wooded hillsides.

It is planned to keep Pordoi Pass open in winter, which will allow for east-facing runs down the reverse side to Arabba (5256 ft) of about 6 km. and 2420 ft. Return to pass height by bus.

(2) *The Campitello–Sella Pass Ski Area.* Two-section chairlift gives total rise of 3104 ft to Col Rodella at 7828 ft. No marked runs down the line of the lift. Top station gives easy access to Sella Pass, and ski way down into Val Gardena area. (Lift back up almost returns to pass.) Superb viewpoint. Two long (6 and 8 km.) south-facing runs down to Canazei – never over-difficult for indifferent skiers.

(3) *The Marmolada Ski Area.* This famed late-winter and spring ski area is reached by bus (8 km.). Close to Pian Trevi-

san (5633 ft) a chairlift rises to about 8530 ft. A project for an upper *Seilbahn* to the winter summit of Punta di Rocca (11,021 ft) is planned. Much development to be done. Marmolada has splendid long north-facing descents and undulating open slopes that are often steep.

Accessibility. Train to Bolzano; thence 2 hrs (52 km.) by bus. Airport: Milan or Venice.

General comments. Apart from the Marmolada region, the largely south-facing ski runs are of average quality distinguished mainly for the magnificence of their views. Using lifts, the day-tourer can cover long distances. Beginners have plenty of space in lovely surroundings. In winter the valley villages do not pretend to provide amenities of the order of more wealthy, more popular centres, but living is comfortable and reasonable, and entertainment of non-sophisticated character is not hard to find. Canazei is well organized and ambitious and, with its sunny Belvedere area, has considerable appeal for first- and second-season parties. For spring ski-ing, the reputation of the Marmolada ski area requires no embroidery.

THE BOLZANO AND
VAL GARDENA AREA

THIS friendly, versatile, relatively unsophisticated and very beautiful valley, which curves up into the heart of the Dolomites, provides excellent ski country for all comers, from beginner to expert. There are here some five or six semi-adjoining ski centres, interlinked by bus, car, gallant little train, and by almost countless lifts and *pistes* connecting the upper slopes. The upper network, consisting of a total of some 47 lifts (half a dozen large, and the remainder ranging from medium size down to small trainer lifts), is cleverly planned to allow the skier to move without effort from hillock to Alp, from Alp to ridge, from ridge to minor summit, and from minor summit up to and over two major passes. The Sella Pass leads over to the Canazei ski area and the Gardena Pass over and down to Corvara and Colfosco.

The Val Gardena, with its centres of Ortisei, Alpe di Siusi, San Cristina, Selva, Plan – and the hotels on the Sella and Gardena Passes – is thus directly linked with Canazei, Campitello, Corvara, and Colfosco. Even a moderate skier, based in any one of these places, has a very wide day-to-day choice. He can, in fact, move about from centre to centre all over the wide, intriguing snow slopes that sweep up at all angles and compass points to the foot of the impressive and spectacular rocky peaks of the lovely Dolomite groups that form the background of the whole region.

Centre 93   Altitude
ORTISEI   Province: Bolzano   3848–4055 ft
  (ST ULRICH)

Description. 3000 inhabitants. 35 hotels and pensions providing 1500 beds. Other accommodation 2500 beds. Language Italian and German.

Something of a small town, with the predominant atmosphere of a summer resort. Not unattractive but lacking the cosiness of village ski centres. Apart from good north-facing nursery slopes plus a short lift (the main ski area is that of Alpe di Siusi – see below) Ortisei has, at present, little ski-ing in its own right. This resort has, however, a project to build a long two-section lift north-eastwards up to the region of Seceda at about 8260 ft. With a rise of some 4200 ft over a distance of about 3 km. this will allow for runs of 6 to 7 km. down to Santa Cristina, the next village up the valley, and back down to Ortisei itself.

The *Luftseilbahn* up to Alpe di Siusi, which rises 2579 ft due south up a rocky steep escarpment, has only one descent back to Ortisei. This very dizzy, and often icy, descent, mostly on artificially built-up corners and galleries (often protected by wire netting) somehow finds a precarious way for the very sure-footed skier down what amounts to cliff-sides.

Ortisei has a ski school, ice rinks, and skating, cinema, etc., and all the amenities that the visitor would expect to find in a popular summer resort. Nine-tenths of the ski activity takes place up at easily-reached Alpe di Siusi.

Accessibility. See p. 301.

Centre 6		Altitude
ALPE DI SIUSI	Province: Bolzano	6578 ft

Description. An immense stretch of some 30 sq. km. of pic-turesque rolling country – one of the largest, highest upland pasture areas of the Alps.

This ideal beginners' playground, sunny and sheltered, and framed by splendid Dolomite mountains (Sasso Lungo, Denti di Terra Rossa (with lift), Sciliar, and the dramatic rock-tooth of Santner) rises gently southwards in a series of soft waves and hillocks on which there are many small sections of woodlands.

Scattered about on this vast area are some 12 hotels, berg-hotels, and small pensions providing about 400 beds. Equally scattered, on many a small slope and hillock, is a fine collection of little lifts – at least 17, of varying sizes – and giving rises of between 130 and 500 ft.

Alpe di Siusi is no village. It consists of a number of small and widespread hotel communities – each self-contained and simple – with horse-sleigh communication. Reached by the *Luftseilbahn* from Ortisei, this unorthodox and unique area is rightly very popular with absolute beginners, and sunseekers who like to wander at will in absolute safety without car traffic or snags of any sort.

Simple, quiet, friendly, holiday life at little expense, without any frills or sophistication. No ski runs in the normal sense, but large gentle areas of sunny, up-and-down-dale, nursery slopes, with all the facilities and amenities of Ortisei to be had for a 5-mins. ride down in the cable-car.

Accessibility. See p. 301.

Centre 66   Altitude
SANTA CRISTINA   Province: Bolzano   4682 ft

Description. 900 inhabitants. 8 hotels and pensions (including Monte Pana) providing 315 beds. Other accommodation 300 beds.

A pleasant and picturesque little roadside valley village, popular both in summer and in winter. Easy bus and train service both down to Ortisei and up to Selva and Plan.

Ski facilities. Chairlift rises 689 ft southwards up to Monte Pana (2 hotels) at 5348 ft. Here are wide nursery slopes on a broad sunny shelf. A small ski-lift serves these and takes you to the bottom station of a second chairlift which rises, east of south, 1276 ft up to Monte de Soura at 6745 ft, close up under the tall rock precipices of Sasso Lungo. Three main runs of 2087 ft and between 3 to 4 km. on safe north-west-, north-east-, and north-facing slopes, through glades and trees, channel together on the Monte Pana shelf and continue down one short hardbeaten section to Santa Cristina. No difficulties for modest performers. Good pleasant ski-ing. Lovely views.

Amenities. Small ski school. Village shops. Small restaurants and bars, etc.

Life in centre. Friendly little place where people get to know one another and no one is in a hurry. Nothing much happens, but does so very peacefully and happily.

Accessibility. See p. 301.

Centre 38   Altitude
SELVA   Province: Bolzano   4961–5331 ft
  (WOLKENSTEIN)

Description. 1200 inhabitants. 30 hotels and pensions providing
1115 beds. Other accommodation 600 beds. Languages Italian
and German.

Ortisei may be the 'capital' of the Val Gardena, but Selva
is the capital ski centre. This elongated, scattered, but most
attractive village consists of many medium-sized and chalet-
type buildings that lie widespread on the slopes of a broad bend
of the main valley. Two separate clusters of buildings form
village centres. At first glance slightly disjointed, Selva grows
on one. Its simplicity conceals much character and charm.

Ski facilities. Two ski areas, linking with other areas at Plan
and on the two passes – Sella and Gardena. Total of two long
lifts and seven short lifts (of which five serve nursery slopes
round village).

(1) *The Ciampinoi Ski Area.* Open buckets (or 'Bennes')
rise 2014 ft to Ciampinoi at 7139 ft. Short upper lift continues
up to 7389 ft. Excellent north-facing runs of between 3½ to 4½
km. and 2274-ft descent down to Selva. Broad, fast, twisting,
racecourse-type *piste*. Also runs down to Plan to connect with
Piz Seteur lifts and down to Monte Pana with the Santa Cristina
lifts.

(2) *The Danterceppies–Gardena Ski Area.* One short chairlift giving 663 ft rise gives short south-west-facing runs down
to Selva, and on the reverse side, leads down to the start of the
long Danterceppies chairlift. This starts at 5413 ft and rises
2300 ft eastwards up to the Gardena Pass area. Top section
has short shuttle ski-lift. Main run down – with woodrunning
variations – gives 2300 ft and about 4½ km. of west- and north-
facing slopes. Big open slopes at top. Swerving gulley-run,
lower section. Good value.

Top station at 7713 ft has chairlift link north-westwards up
from the Gardena Pass hotels at 7005 ft. Gardena Pass is the
arrival point of the ski-lift system that climbs westwards up
from the Colfosco–Corvara region (see p. 302).

Amenities. Ski school. Ski jump. Skating rink. Village shops. Cafés. Restaurants. Bars. Dancing, etc.

Life in centre. Well-organized, without any fuss. Sunny situation and holiday atmosphere. Neither bustling nor overrun, there is plenty of space both in the village and on the ski slopes. Splendid setting and superb Dolomite scenery. Many a cosy friendly spot, small and unsophisticated, to be found for evenings and meals. Simple comfort, adequate to good, and prices very reasonable. A car is an asset, but far from essential.

Accessibility. See p. 301.

General comments. The variety of ski-ing in the immediate vicinity of Selva is all-round and good value. The surroundings are spectacular and beautiful. The beginner has plenty of space and the good skier has high-standard country for training and technique. Very little English to be heard but every good reason why there should be. Selva has much to offer and is much to be recommended.

Centre 41   Altitude
PLAN   Province: Bolzano   5269 ft

Description. 100 inhabitants. 2 hotels with 84 beds. *Plan de Gralba.* 5988 ft. 10 inhabitants. 3 hotels with 94 beds.

2 and 5 km. respectively beyond Selva you come to the tiny village of Plan and the small hotel settlement of Plan de Gralba. Quiet, peaceful, and unpretentious, these two share the Selva ski-ing and have their own uphill transport.

The Plan Ski Area. From Plan di Gralba a chairlift rises 784 ft south-west to Piz Seteur at 6772 ft. 3-km. runs on north-east- and east-facing slopes go pleasantly down to bottom station. A short westward descent leads to the foot of an upper ski-lift which rises northwards to Piz Sella at 7349 ft. Easy 3-km. runs down to Plan. Interconnexion runs down to Selva and to Santa Cristina (6 km. and 2690 ft).

From Piz Seteur it is an easy walk-climb to the south (30 to 50 mins.) to reach the Sella Pass at 7264 ft (where there are short trainer lifts) which is the ski-way over and down to Canazei (see p. 294). Projected ski-lift will soon connect the Plan ski area with the Sella Pass.

VAL GARDENA ACCESSIBILITY

Road entry from Ponte Gardena in the Val d'Isarco (Bolzano
23 km. to south: Brenner Pass 61 km. to north). Main-line
train to Chiusa just north of Ponte Gardena. Thence Val Gardena railway. Two hours to terminus at Plan. Bus services
from Bolzano serve all centres.

Centres 36 and 43		Altitudes
COLFOSCO	Province: Bolzano	5397 ft
CORVARA		5168 ft

Separated by less than 3 km. from one another, these two little
ski centres lie just outside the Val Gardena area on the eastern
side of the Gardena Pass.
Description. Colfosco: 195 inhabitants. 6 hotels/pensions with
160 beds. Language Italian and German.

Close to the north-facing rocks of the spectacular Sella
Group of Dolomite mountains, this little place has one local
ski-lift giving a 300-ft rise.

The two Grödnerjoch ski lifts run in sequence, westwards,
from 5545 ft up to the Gardena Pass at 6959 ft. Here the chairlift dei Cir continues up to the top of the Selva–Danterceppies
chairlift at 7713 ft to link with the Selva ski area.

The Colfosco–Grödnerjoch ski lifts give a rise of 1411 ft and
provide easy beginner runs of about 3 km. These east-facing
slopes are almost constantly shaded by the big bulk of the Sella
Group, but the Gardena Pass area, with its lifts, is sunny.

Corvara. 556 inhabitants. 5 hotels and pensions with 240
beds.

This attractive little village amid lovely and spectacular
surroundings lies in a wide sunny valley just east of the Sella
Group of Dolomite mountains. It has a chairlift rising some
1170 ft north-eastwards up to 6339 ft. Open gentle slopes,
facing west and south-west, with some woods. Suitable for
beginners and moderate skiers. There are also several other
lifts of about 1000 ft rise. Good day tours to be found behind
top station.

Easy bus service links with Colfosco and the Grödnerjoch ski-lifts up to Gardena Pass (see above).

Accessibility. Rail station Brunico. Thence $1\frac{1}{2}$ hrs bus.

General comments. Both places have their assets, but, of the two, Corvara has an enviable atmosphere and is much to be recommended.

BELLUNO

ft some 5
a rise of
With
bruck

Province: Belluno

o inhabitants. 50 hotels and pe
g 5000 beds. Other accommodation
ian and German – English and mo
spoken.

s place, almost exactly midway between
nice, is of major importance. In some senses
Italy, but with a character entirely of its ow
situated in a wide, sunny, valley arena – surrounde
and backed, but never overshadowed, by superb
s of Dolomite mountains – Cortina is shy of reveal-
y splendid ski areas all at once from the main street.
a small town, Cortina can boast of every facility and
It caters for every nationality, every taste, and every
and every type of skier – and there is here a movement
iety not easily found elsewhere. Part of the charm, for
modern structures and the recent development, lies in
t that this widespread built-up area is based on old
onal foundations. However successful Cortina may be as
t, both in summer and winter, you still feel that this is
nuine place, with its own life, rather than an artificial
tion designed only for holiday visitors.

Ski facilities. Four ski areas – each served by its own uphill
nsport systems, with a total of some three cable-cars, two
en *télécabines*, six chairlifts, and seven ski-lifts.

(1) *The Pocol Ski Area.* Cable-car rises 1076 ft up to the
sunny small hotel settlement of Pocol at 5049 ft. This is a widespread beginners' area, with several lifts of its own continuing
up to about 5420 ft, with north-east- and east-facing slopes and
runs right down to valley bottom. 'Happy Hampstead' picnic
fairground air.

(2) *The Tofana Ski Area.* No less than four chairlifts in

THE BRENNER PASS AREA

Centre 112
COLLE ISARCO   Province: Bolzano
(GOSSENSASS)

Altitude
3599 ft

Description. 850 inhabitants. 10 hotels, inns, and pensions providing about 400 beds. Language Italian and German.

A pleasant little main-road and main-line village only 9 km. from the Brenner Pass frontier and Austria (Innsbruck 50 km.). Sunny, south-facing situation with west-facing ski slopes.

Ski facilities. Two medium-sized, side-by-side (but not interlinked) ski areas served by two separate chairlift systems.

(1) The Hühnerspiel chairlift at Colle Isarco rises 2592 ft from 3642 ft up to Cima Gallina at 6234 ft.

(2) The Brennerbad (Terme di Brennero) chairlift – some 5 km. further up the pass towards the frontier – rises 1968 ft up to the Genziana Hut at 6247 ft.

Both these lifts give good, standard-type *pistes* of between 3 and $4\frac{1}{2}$ km. on west-facing slopes. Open fields and glades allow for testing runs for medium good skiers and easy routes for the inexperienced. Total of seven marked runs.

In the area there are three trainer ski-lifts.

Amenities. Ski teachers. Skating rink. Luge run. Horse sleighs. Restaurants. Bars. Cinema. Radio-active thermal baths at Brennerbad. Vipiteno town close by.

Life in centre. Main-road Brenner Pass traffic. Popular and crowded at week-ends. Simple, unsophisticated place. Similar in many ways to Steinach and Gries close by just over the Austrian frontier. Reasonable prices.

Accessibility. Main-line and main-road access from Innsbruck to the north and Bolzano from the south.

General comments. No 'ski village' in the true sense, Colle Isarco has good popular-type ski-ing. Accommodation can also be had at the attractive little nearby town of Vipiteno at 3110

THE BR...

km. dow...
...bo...
...car...
...ea.

306

Centre 87
CORTINA
D'AMPEZZO

Description. 600...
classes providin...
Languages Ita...
nental tongues...
This famou...
bruck and V...
St Moritz o...
Beautifully...
by forests...
rock tower...
ing its ma...
Almos...
amenit...
pock...
and a g...
all the...
the fa...
tradit...
a res...
a ge...
cre...
tr...
o...

sequence, giving individual rises of 807 ft, 988 ft, 1378 ft, and 610 ft, take one up to Upper Tofana at 7480 ft. Each section has its own runs, and the four together produce such excellent descents as the Olympic and the Tofana Runs (3445 ft and 6 to 8 km.). Top sections: Open steep snowfields surrounded by impressive rock turrets. Middle sections: Long steep slopes or well-graded glades through woods. Lower sections: Long gentle open meadowland. Excellent variety for all comers. Slopes mainly east-facing.

(3) *The Faloria–Tondi Ski Area.* Cable-car rises 840 ft to Mandres at 4866 ft (easy runs down) then a further 2096 ft up a cliff-face to Faloria at 6962 ft (no runs down under cableway). Cable-cars continue from Faloria with a rise of 673 ft up to Tondi at 7635 ft. Both upper stations have fine viewpoint restaurants.

The Faloria–Tondi ski area, also served by two upper lifts which slant obliquely 2860 ft back up to summit, is surprisingly large, and has much interesting and amusing ski-ing, mostly on north- and north-west-facing slopes, on highly original jumbled and tumbled ground formations. One long, entertaining, and diversified run, circling down northwards via the Tre Croci Pass, returns you from this upper area back to Cortina (3661 ft and 8 to 9 km.).

This area is mainly for average and above skiers.

(4) *The Monte Cristallo Ski Area.* Bottom station for this audacious open *télécabine* system, on the Tre Croci Pass, is reached either by bus from Cortina (6 km., 25 mins.) or on ski from the Tondi–Cortina run.

First section: Open buckets rise 1798 ft northwards to Valgrande at 7320 ft. Medium difficult upper section gentles out to long lower slopes.

Second section: Open buckets rise 2677 ft north-eastwards up long steep gulley to Cristallino at 9836 ft. Impressive and spectacular surroundings with splendid upper viewpoint. Total rise 4314 ft. Height above Cortina 5810 ft. Long upper section is immensely steep. Facing the south, it is a joy to good skiers in true spring snow conditions. Even experts will avoid this section when conditions are unsuitable. Every visitor to

Cortina should go up to Cristallino purely for the experience and for the view. All but the good, however, should return down in the lift. Total run, Cristallino to Cortina, is a gloriously varied affair of about 11 km. and nearly 6000 ft.

Amenities. Large and efficient ski school. Guides. Olympic ski jump. Olympic ice stadium. Several skating rinks. Ice hockey. Speed skating and exhibitions. Bob run. Sleigh rides. Big shopping area. Fashion and sports shops. Tea rooms. Restaurants. Bars. Cinemas. Night-clubs. Many dance spots and cabarets.

Life in centre. Gay. International. Colourful. Fashionable. A great deal of movement, activity, and ready entertainment. Sunshine and holiday sport, both for the active and the spectator. Cosmopolitan atmosphere. Prices of all ranges – high to low – luxury suites down to bed and breakfast accommodation. Well organized. Never a dull moment.

Accessibility. Air to Treviso (Venice). Thence 4 hrs by train or bus. Air or train to Milan, thence bus 10 hrs or train 7 hrs. Train to Innsbruck, thence bus or train about 6 hrs.

General comments. A friendly, entertaining town – well capable of holding the Winter Olympic Games (1956) – in lovely surroundings where the ski-ing rates in the top line internationally. Anyone, from the lone wolf to the family party or the large group – from beginner to expert standards – will enjoy Cortina. A car is an asset here – and Venice is only a 3-hrs drive away (165 km.). Cortina is not to be missed.

SEVEN

Swiss Ski Centres

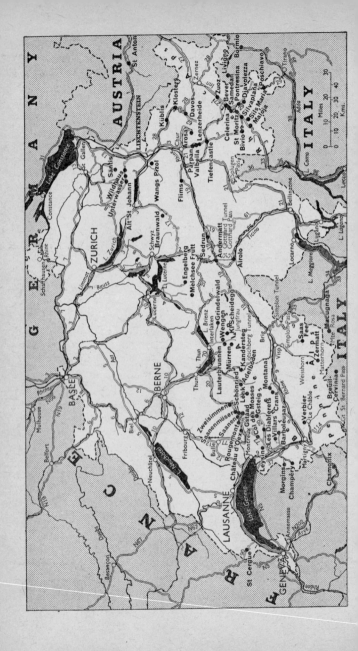

CONTENTS

THE SAANENMÖSER–GSTAAD–CHÂTEAU D'OEX AREA

INTRODUCTION

MENTION the Alps to anyone and their first thought is Switzerland. Mention the word 'ski-ing', and the chances are heavily weighted that Switzerland will again be the first thought. History, tradition, geographical and geological good fortune, sound business acumen, and good publicity, together with efficient organization, have all contributed towards the fact that this happy, neutral Confederation has long been regarded as the Mecca of all ski-ing.

Mecca it may be, but although Switzerland is very far from owning a monopoly of high snow-covered Alps, it can, and always will be able to, boast that it owns some of the finest, best developed, and best-equipped ski country in the world.

On the whole the ski centres of Switzerland tend to be larger than those in other main Alpine countries. Many of the original mountain villages grew large, long ago, as summer and/or health resorts. The many big 'Palace' hotel buildings reflect back to more spacious days of architecture and living. Many of the 'approach' railways and the mountain 'viewpoint' railways are of the old rack-and-pinion type that date back to the

days before the *téléférique*. A large number of these long established mountain resorts very naturally face the south, a fact
which, in spite of certain disadvantages, ensures maximum sun
hours.

Switzerland, however, has not stood still. It has never,
barring one or two exceptions, allowed its centres to rest on
their laurels. Grafted on to the old are all the new facilities of
overhead cable-ways, chairlifts and ski-lifts, helicopter and
light plane airstrips, and countless modern hotel buildings and
comfortable chalets. Clever planning has resulted in a tremendous network of uphill transport, ever reaching higher and
higher, which ensures that nearly every centre has a wide
choice of slopes that face all points of the compass and controls
a big variety of ski terrain.

Few Swiss will admit it, but this is a rich country. The
standard of living is higher than in most countries and the
Swiss franc is one of the soundest currencies in the world. In
other words you have to pay for what you get in Switzerland –
but what you get is excellent value for your money.

The Swiss character is very much reflected in the character
of Swiss centres. The words and phrases that spring to mind
are: solid; stolid; honest; regimented efficiency; extreme tidi-
ness; good humour rather than humour; careful consideration
rather than spontaneous imagination. A consciousness of
fashion rather than a fashion flair. Attention to detail at the
cost of quick results, but with an eye firmly fixed on the penny
as well as the pound. A glass of beer rather than a Martini.
Muscle rather than guile – wood rather than plastic.

In the woodpile every log has to be the same length and very
exactly placed. There is always hot water – but baths are generally treated as 'extras'. There is plenty of good food – even
though this has largely lost its original 'national' and 'regional'
character and is now all too often somewhat dully and even
pompously 'international'. When and where it flourishes it is
the visitor who has brought sophistication to the Swiss resorts
rather than the Swiss who has provided it. Frivolity and
night-life are importations that have taken the Swiss some
time to understand, but, now that the penny has dropped,

they know how to provide the machinery or at least the setting.

The Swiss make good wine – not up to French standards, but then none is – notably in the Valais and round the Neuchâtel and Geneva lakes. You will search all over the Alps in vain to find the cosy friendly atmosphere of a true Swiss *Gaststube* elsewhere. This semi-equivalent of an English pub is unique – and it will be a great mistake if too many of these are allowed to be converted into juke-box-type American bars.

Swiss railways are highly efficient (when in doubt about a meal, go to the *Bahnhof*). So are the post and telegraph bus services. Engineering of all kinds is technically superb and the standards of safety of the many audacious cable-car systems are the highest in the Alps. There is a greater tendency here to provide closed and warm uphill transport than elsewhere. The economic practice of issuing weekly and fortnightly *abonnements* is widespread.

Swiss ski schools are earnest and painstaking – and what they lack in inspiration they make up for in patience and detailed attention. If you learn to ski properly in Switzerland you will become a true all-round skier able to go anywhere. Swiss ski teachers approach all the frills and foibles of each successive modern technique with a sensible amount of reserve, until theory is established as fact.

Every form of winter sport – skating, curling, ice hockey, ski-jöring, bobsleighing, lugeing, etc. – is admirably catered for. It is of interest to note that true curling, the ancient and very popular sport that originated in Scotland, is almost unique to Switzerland. With very few exceptions, the other Alpine lands that widely advertise 'curling' in their brochures refer to a local game played with 'woods' rather than 'stones'.

The statistics of Switzerland, given by the Swiss National Tourist Bureau, show how highly developed this country is for the winter visitor.

There are over ninety ski schools and approximately 900 qualified ski instructors (classes 10 a.m.–12 noon and 2 p.m.– 4 p.m. A week's instruction costs from 25 to 35 Swiss francs according to the centre.)

There are over 500 uphill transport systems ranging from mountain railways, funiculars, and aerial cableways to gondola, chair-, and ski-lifts. Ice rinks, excluding lakes, number 260, ski jumping hills, seventy-five, bobsleigh runs, fourteen; and there are various luge and skeleton runs.

The roads of Switzerland are kept in excellent condition in winter, and petrol here is cheaper than anywhere else in Europe.

So far as ski-ing is concerned, Switzerland is very hard to rival. Names like Davos, Zermatt, and St Moritz speak for themselves – even to the inexperienced.

Switzerland is Switzerland – and there is magic even in the name.

For more comprehensive information and fullest details of all the Swiss ski centres, the reader is referred to *The Ski Runs of Switzerland*, published by Michael Joseph Ltd.

THE EASTERN AREA

Centres 46 and 47*
DAVOS DORF   Canton: Graubünden
DAVOS PLATZ

Altitudes
5118 ft
5052 ft

Description. 8000 inhabitants. More than 50 hotels and pensions with 5000 beds. Other accommodation 1500 beds. Language German. English and other languages widely spoken.

The town of Davos Platz and its neighbouring Dorf are now one long built-up area well linked by constant bus services. This world-famous centre, with accommodation ranging from first-class hotels to village inns, cannot be termed picturesque, nor can the sheltered but sunny long valley in which it stands. Few places, however, command such widespread and wonderful ski terrain. Busy and bustling, somewhat brash, Davos caters for every form of winter sport. Immensely popular and generally crowded with all nationalities, skiers and non-skiers. The centre is uninspiring in appearance, but the views from top stations are the very reverse.

Ski facilities. Three big ski areas served by three main lift systems.

Davos and its near neighbour Klosters (8 km.) share the ski paradise of the whole Parsenn area together with the upland ski circus of the Parsenn Hut region. Many and widespread are the subsidiary and nursery lifts.

(1) *The Bräma Büel and Jacobshorn Area* (Platz), served by two-section cable-car system going up south-east, and one long subsidiary ski-lift from middle station. Maximum height gain 3445 ft. Runs of all types, up to 5 km., to suit all standards – mainly open slopes above, but wood running can be found lower down. Entertaining ski-ing.

(2) *The Schatzalp–Strelagrat Area* (Platz), served by one funicular and three-section *Gondelbahn* going up north-west. Height gain 3050 ft. Several descents of 4–6 km. of smiling open sunny slopes best suited for the inexperienced. This area

* Each place description is numbered according to the Altitude List, pp. 104–21.

can also be reached from Weissfluhjoch – an easy beginners' run.

(3) *The Weissfluh–Parsenn Area* (Dorf), served by two-section Parsenn Railway, and upper cable-car, going up north-west and west respectively. Height gain 4144 ft. Both upper stations command the vast world-renowned Parsenn Area and its big network of runs with descents ranging from 6605 ft and 12 km. to Küblis; to 3910 ft and 7 km. to Wolfgang. There is a direct run to Klosters and a second to take in the upland circus lifts around the Parsenn Hut. From Weissfluhjoch, runs of 4–6 km. and approximately 3600 ft return down the Davos side.

Weissfluhgipfel, at 9262 ft, is the start point of the famous Parsenn Derby course that finishes at Küblis. (Hotels.)

In general the main Parsenn runs, some of which are ideal for medium and some for good skiers, are too long for in-experienced beginners. Infinite variety of *piste* and off-*piste* running with easy and very difficult routes both above and in the tree line can be found at will.

Ski touring. Fine touring facilities for the enthusiast, specially in the Silvretta Range. Easy ski way to Arosa and extension to Lenzerheide.

Amenities. Excellent big ski school. Very efficient S O S Service. Fine nursery slopes. S.C.G.B. representatives. Huge ice rinks. Ice hockey. Curling. Ski jumps. All small-town amen-ities from comprehensive shops to cinemas, night-spots, etc. Sleigh rides. Ski-jöring. Valley walks. Mardens Ski Club.

Life in centre. Busy, populous, efficiently run resort. Not socially inclined – little glamour – functional rather than frivolous – main street too long to give cosy, meeting-place atmosphere. Accent mainly on ski-ing. International visitors with high proportion of English. Much crowded at weekends.

Specialities. Many spectator sports including international ski jumping, ice hockey, and exhibition skating. Horse show, horse races, and riding. Curling.

Accessibility. Train: main-line station, Landquart, 1 hr 22 mins. *Rhätischebahn* up. Road: approach from both sides kept open. Airport: Zürich (3 hrs train).

General comments. Long renowned for superb ski-ing and length and scope of runs. Ski standards average and above. Beginners must not expect to appreciate all that Davos has to offer until properly mobile – when so, its reputation speaks for itself. The keen skier who has never experienced the Davos–Klosters ski-ing should have his head examined.

Centre 98		Altitude
KLOSTERS	Canton: Graubünden	3908 ft

Description. 2850 inhabitants. 26 hotels and pensions with 1200 beds. Other accommodation 2000 beds. Language German – English and other languages widely spoken.

A fashionable, highly successful resort of varying-sized hotel buildings pleasantly and cleverly grafted into an attractive Swiss village. Considerable car traffic in streets. Semi-enclosed wooded valley setting, relatively shaded but sheltered. Picturesque yet modern, with a touch of the Hollywood film set. Half-way between Davos and Küblis on eastern road and rail perimeter of the Parsenn Area, the whole of which it shares with Davos – it also commands wonderful ski country of its own. Top station provides lovely views of nearby Silvretta group and mountains of Austrian Vorarlberg.

Ski facilities. One big ski area enclosed by, and interwoven with, the main long Parsenn runs. Served by two-section cable-car system, surmounted by Parsenn Hut Upland Circus region, served by two ski-lifts. Good local practice slopes with two sizeable trainer lifts.

The Gotschnagrat area provides network of excellent runs of 3589-ft descent and anything from 4 to 9 km. Steep race-course type *pistes* for the proficient and long gentle roundabout routes for the more modest. Wide choice of exploration for the ambitious. Extremely steep Gotschnawang for the expert. Easy access from top station to the lovely sunny slopes of the Parsenn Hut Upland Circus whose lifts open up a beginners' paradise and also serve as connecting link with central section of main Parsenn runs over the Furka Pass.

The recent construction of a cable car lift from Parsenn Hut

(7219 ft) right up to Weissfluhjoch (8737 ft) has formed a complete interlinkage with the main Davos runs. This, combined with a lift from Kreuzweg back up to the Parsenn Furkha, has tremendously increased the scope of the upland circus.

Ski touring. Not basically a touring centre, but splendid facilities can be found in nearby regions, notably the Silvretta.

Amenities. First-class ski school. S.C.G.B. representatives. Ski jump. Ice rinks. Ice hockey. Curling. Cinema. Excellent shops. Fashion and sports shops. Cafés. Restaurants. Bars. Night clubs. H.Q. of Mardens Ski Club.

Life in centre. Seldom a dull moment. Lively and sophisticated. Ski-ing primary interest, society gossip columns close second. Rightly popular with gay young things. Considerable veneer of international and smart-set atmosphere, with prices to match. Expensive restaurants and considerable *après-ski* and nightlife entertainment. Hotel price range wide – but all things considered, quite reasonable. Extras can mount up.

Specialities. For spectator sports, go to Davos.

Accessibility. Train: main-line station Landquart 50 mins. *Rhätischebahn* up. Road: approach road both sides kept open. Airport: Zürich (3 hrs train).

General comments. Superb ski-ing for all comers. Many good skiers here but general standards never alarming. (See also Davos, p. 317.)

Centre 12		Altitude
AROSA	Canton: Graubünden	5610 ft to 6200 ft

Description. 1980 inhabitants. 60 hotels and pensions with 3100 beds. Other accommodation 1200 beds. Language German – English and other languages widely spoken.

Well-known, long-established, large resort – almost a small town, with many hotels big and small – whose lengthy main street climbs some 600 ft to end just above tree-line. With a sunny situation high up at head of Langwies valley, it is not in itself a place of any particular beauty but commands surroundings of great beauty. Immensely popular – cosmopolitan rather than fashionable – Arosa reminds one of a supermarket holiday travel brochure rather than a village-shop Christmas card. Largely devoid of traditional character in architecture but with fully comprehensive facilities from luxury downwards, it is a highly organized holiday centre efficiently developed to deal with all forms of visitors and all forms of winter sports, for skiers and non-skiers.

Ski facilities. One very large ski area served by one main two-section cable-car system and three long subsidiary ski-lifts. Other lifts: one ski-lift, baby lift.

The Weisshorn–Carmenna–Hörnli ski area consists of a wide spread of sunny, mainly south-facing slopes served by long lifts of the same names that fan out to various points on a long background ridge.

The outer-edge lifts give rises of 2966 ft and 2251 ft (top station of the Weisshorn Luftseilbahn stands at 8704 ft), and a snakes-and-ladders effect can be achieved by using these and the intermediary lifts. Individual runs vary from 2 to 5 km. Sunny, amiable, very seldom difficult, open rolling country – almost all above the tree-line – provides a good variety of obstacle-free ski-ing.

Ski touring. Good but limited short tours in vicinity. Several longish unpisted runs down the far side of Weisshorn ridge. Ski passage over to Lenzerheide.

Amenities. First-class ski school. S.C.G.B. representatives. 6 ice rinks. Sleigh rides, ski-jöring, toboggan runs, bobbing, ice hockey, curling, ski jumps. Excellent shops of all types. Cinemas, hotel dancing. Dance bars and night-spots. Casino.

Specialities. Ice carnivals. Horse racing on lake. Ice hockey. Ski jumping. Exhibition skating, etc.

Life in centre. Most things are laid on. Gaiety in abundance, more often organized than spontaneous. Stolid, well-to-do big-hotel atmosphere. Friendly but not matey. Middle-class air of respectability treating *après-ski* life with slight reserve and the occasional dinner jacket. Living on the expensive side.

Accessibility. Train: 1 hr 10 mins. Chur (main-line station). Road: good, kept open. Airport: Zürich (3 hrs train).

General comments. Sunny, windless climate. Good snow conditions generally available. Much to be recommended for

parties of mixed ski standards – particularly learner types who
will greatly appreciate the wide areas of the gentle lower slopes.

		Altitude
Centre 54		4840 ft
LENZERHEIDE	Canton: Graubünden	
(including		
VALBELLA and		
PARPAN)		

Description. 800 inhabitants. 13 hotels and 4 pensions providing
800 beds. Other accommodation 650 beds. Language German
– English and most continental languages spoken.

An attractive little village set in the wide sunny valley of the
Julier Route (leading from Chur via the Julier Pass over to the
upper Engadine) which has two small nearby satellites, Valbella
– 200 beds (5082 ft) – and Parpan – 170 beds (4988 ft). Pleasant,
semi-wooded valley scenery. Long popular with many nationalities, Lenzerheide at present commands a medium-sized ski
area – mostly east-facing – which is compact and uncomplicated but which has something to offer to all comers.

Ski facilities. One ski area served by three ski-lifts mounting,
ladder fashion, to Piz Scalottas at 7595 ft. Total rise 2969 ft.
Lower lift provides widespread gentle nursery slopes. Centre
lift opens up easy, pleasant, short runs in lightly-wooded
country. Upper lift serves open steeper slopes above the tree-
line where there is plenty to test the good skier. The Philips
racecourse is a fast descent of 3·8 km. and 2625 ft.

The Valbella area has two ski-lifts surmounted by a new
lift that reaches almost to the summit of the Stätzerhorn at
8268 ft with a total rise of about 3186 ft. The Parpan area one
lift rising about 1000 ft. Both have good areas for beginners
and problems for proficient skiers.

On the east side of the main valley, opposite the present lift
systems, Lenzerheide has a fine transport in construction. Gondola cars reaching up to middle station some 500 ft above the
tree-line will, by 1962, be surmounted by a *Luftseilbahn* up the
Parpaner Rothorn to approx 8530 ft.

Amenities. Ski school. S.C.G.B. representatives. Skating

rink. Curling. Ice hockey. Tobogganing. Tea rooms. Village shops and sports shops. Hotel dancing.

Life in centre. Well-organized, unpretentious, but very comfortable living. Simple, but sophisticated in a friendly, somewhat old-fashioned way – which many prefer to chromium glamour. Upper-middle-class air of refinement. Amusements genuine and seldom raucous. Picturesque setting.

Accessibility. Train: Zürich to Chur 3 hrs. Post-bus: Chur to Lenzerheide 1 hr. Airport: Zürich.

General Comments. Preponderance of sunny gentle-to-medium ski slopes much favoured by family groups with children. Many 'old hands' return year after year. With its present development Lenzerheide will change character and really enter 'the big time'.

Centre 113		Altitude
FLIMS	Canton: Graubünden	3543 ft to
		3609 ft

Description. 1300 inhabitants. 10 hotels and 9 pensions with 1200 beds. Other accommodation 1100 beds. Language German – English and other continental languages spoken.

The village of Flims and the resort of Flims Waldhaus, connected by a fine new bridge across a deep ravine, lie side by side, facing the south, at the back of the lovely wooded, terraced arena that looks across the Upper Rhine valley towards the mountains around Lenzerheide, Arosa, and Davos. Behind Flims, the ground sweeps upwards, gently at first, and then steeply, to a skyline of wide snowfields and the impressive rock profiles of the Flimserstein. Flims and Waldhaus, which provide accommodation for all pockets, and buildings from Grand Hotel proportions to small inexpensive inns, command fine ski-ing and a large-scale uphill transport system.

Ski facilities. One very large ski area – 'The white arena of Flims' – served by two-section chairlift surmounted by a big *Luftseilbahn.* These give rises of 1103 ft, 1795 ft, and 2381 ft respectively – a total rise of 5315 ft above Flims to Cassons Grat at 8858 ft, with a travel distance of 5·6 km. Restaurant at top with fine panorama.

These remarkable figures ensure large-scale ski-ing and long runs. Lower chairlift serves wide easy country – also provided with a long nursery-slope ski-lift. Upper chairlift opens up good selection of varied and amusing runs for the medium performer. Top *Luftseilbahn* controls really steep and enter-prising open slopes for good and expert skiers. Runs of all grades and distances can be chosen. The longest from top to bottom station is the Segnes Run measuring over 13 km.

Four-fifths of the snowslopes face the south, but the long *pistes* are good. Off-*piste* conditions can be tricky in winter, but in spring conditions there is glorious widespread ski-ing everywhere. In bad weather, upper section is liable to be closed.

There is a ski-lift at Cassonsgrat top station. Other lifts in the 'white arena' are also being constructed to ensure variety and shaded slopes. There is almost endless room for all manner of future projects.

Amenities. Well-organized ski school with clubhouse and ski-lift on its own nursery slopes. Ski jump. Skating rink. Ice hockey. Curling. Toboggan run. Good shopping area. Sports shops. Cafés and tea rooms. Cinema. Hotel and bar dancing, etc. Sports and social events.

Life in centre. Quiet and genuine. Comfortable living. Wide range of prices. Seldom uncomfortably crowded. Plenty of space. Pleasant walks for non-skiers. Little glamour but plenty of friendly fun and spontaneous entertainment. Several large terraced restaurants at mid-stations of uphill transports.

Accessibility. Train travel: Zürich 3 hrs. Good road. Post-bus: Chur 1½ hrs.

General comments. Big, wide, excellent south-slope ski-ing, with large-scale uphill transport. Skiers of all categories can find all they want at Flims. Much recommended.

Centre 70		Altitude
SEDRUN	Canton: Graubünden	4606 ft

Description. 250 inhabitants. 2 hotels and 5 pensions with 200 beds. Language German.

Attractive little roadside village lying close to the eastern side of the Oberalp Pass within easy train distance of Andermatt on the western side.

A quiet and friendly little place, with no frills. Nursery, and short lifts only, serve the lower slopes of widespread south-facing hillsides where many day and half-day ski tours and ski excursions can be made. New lifts will soon continue higher.

Sedrun is closely linked with the ski-ing at Andermatt (see p. 337) and with the new and important construction of the Gemstock *Seilbahn* above Andermatt – where runs of over 5000 ft are available – this little centre will undoubtedly gain in importance in the near future.

Centres 13 and 28		Altitudes
ST MORITZ	Canton: Graubünden	5825 ft to 6135 ft
(DORF AND BAD)	(Upper Engadine)	
CELERINA		5676 ft

Description. St Moritz Dorf and Bad. 4200 inhabitants. Over 50 hotels and pensions providing 5000 beds. Other accommodation 5000 beds. Total 10,000 beds. *Celerina.* 640 inhabitants. 7 hotels and pensions providing 532 beds. Other accommodation 400 beds. Total 932 beds. *Note:* The nearby village of Champfèr is included in the St Moritz commune. Languages German and Romansch – all languages spoken.

If any place can rightly be called the 'Capital of the Alps' it is St Moritz. The modest little village first referred to in 1139 (Roman and even Bronze Age remains date its existence as a spa back to very early days) is now a big thriving built-up area of many large hotels, and countless chalet and other buildings, sprawling widespread around and above the beautiful frozen lake. Celerina, much smaller, but growing fast itself, is a pleasant holiday resort based on a typically attractive Engadine village. Dominated by St Moritz – sunnily situated; ideal for both winter and summer; impressive and efficient – the whole of this area of the Upper Engadine is a unique and spectacular playground, popular with all nationalities, for all forms of winter and other sports, for both skier and non-skier alike – particularly for the keen skier.

Ski facilities. St Moritz and Celerina must be considered in conjunction both with Pontresina and with various neighbouring villages – notably Silvaplana, Samedan, Sils Maria, Bevers, and the more distant Zuoz – all of which have their own uphill transport lifts, either major or minor, and all of which are closely interconnected either by road or rail services, or both (see p. 329). The whole forms an enormous ski region with some 25 lifts and half a dozen projects yet to come.

Basically St Moritz either owns or has direct access *to no less than four major ski areas* as well as to several minor ones.

(1 and 2). *The Corviglia–Piz Nair Area above St Moritz* which links with the *Marguns–Trais Fluors Area above Celerina.*

The Corviglia–Piz Nair lift system of two mountain railways and an upper *Luftseilbahn* gives a total rise of 3885 ft up to 9941 ft – all in enclosed transport. Splendid viewpoint. Large-scale south-facing slopes of all gradients provide many interweaving runs of between 2½ and 5 km. Slopes also served by several subsidiary lifts – notably two long ski-lifts giving a rise of 2540 ft above Suvretta House; the 525-ft rise ski-lift at Corviglia; and the slalom-cum-trainer lifts at Salastrains and Alp Giop – the nursery slopes.

Long runs of up to 8 km. go down from Piz Nair and Corviglia on north and shaded slopes to Celerina – either on ridge runs or in the Saluver valley via Marguns.

From Celerina a long gondola-car system climbs from 5676 ft up to Marguns at 7500ft. From Marguns a ski-lift up north-facing slopes rises 656 ft back to Corviglia. A second ski-lift, up south-facing slopes climbs 1562 ft to Trais Fluors at 9062 ft. Total rise, Celerina to Trais Fluors, 3386 ft and just under 4 km. travel.

The whole Marguns–Trais Fluors ski area consists of an enormous snowbowl arena of glorious ski slopes.

These two linked areas directly above St Moritz and Celerina provide endless exploratory possibilities and their top stations are excellent start points for many ski touring and glacier expeditions.

(3). *The Corvatsch Ski Area.* A big two-stage *téléférique* system (now under construction) starting from approx. 5970 ft at Silvaplana will give a total rise of 4840 ft up to Corvatsch at about 10,807 ft. At middle station – Mandras at 8872 ft – two good ski-lifts of approx 700 ft and 950 ft rises will open up a big 'upstairs playground'. Splendid summit viewpoint with restaurant. Glorious north slope ski-ing of great magnitude and variety with runs of all lengths up to 11 km. and 5000 ft descent. Also south slope ski-ing down into the Val Roseg where a lift is planned to return up to the ridge. Many other possibilities – notably Piz Staz and Piz Rosatsch – for tours or airlift runs. Top line ski-ing. Long duration season. Excellent variety for all comers.

(4). *The Diavolezza and Lagalb Ski Area*. See Pontresina, p. 330.

Ski touring. Each 'mechanized' ski area of the region, including Muottas Muragl, is surrounded by an 'outer circle' of endless ski-touring and ski-mountaineering opportunities. Whether you tackle these tours on your own two feet or by helicopter it will be difficult to exhaust the possibilities.

Amenities. Large ski school. Guides. S.C.G.B. representatives. Olympic ski jump plus two smaller hills. Skating rinks galore. Ice hockey. Curling. Bobsleigh run. Famed Cresta Run. Horse-racing and ski-jöring on lake. Horse-back riding. Many spectacular spectator events. Visitors' events and races. Ski tours. Ski races. Helicopter and light plane airports. Many fine shops including sports and fashion shops. Many attractive and well-kept woodland and valley walks. Sleigh rides. Tea rooms. Casino. Bars. Bowling alleys. Fashion shows. Cinemas. Cabarets. Restaurants. Night spots, etc., etc.

Life in centre. Highly geared and efficiently organized. International, colourful, gay, sophisticated. Rare and admirable mixture of luxury and simplicity. Millionaire and student, mink coat and windjacket, all rub shoulders. Wide range of prices from ultra expensive to bargain basement. Constant movement and activity. Interest, intrigue, and fun for all, from the wide-eyed innocent to the gossip columnist. H.Q. for international set. Dark glasses at candle-lit tables. Brown faces in open-air restaurants. Permanent and comprehensive Motor Show. Tomorrow's fashions worn today. Ski-ing not the only

topic of conversation. Ski standards medium and never overwhelming. Ski potential, superb. By no means essential, a car
is a tremendous asset. Many car skiers, in search of quieter and
more modest approaches to living, stay close by the main
centre either down at St Moritz Bad or in outlying villages such
as Silvaplana.

Specialities. Lift runs of every calibre and distance – up to
18 km. and approx. 6000 ft (Lagalb to Poschiavo, see p. 331).
Widespread touring. Airlift ski-ing. Spectator sports and exhibitions. Long duration of snow season, especially on Corvatsch.

Accessibility. Train travel: Zürich 5 hrs. Air Service from
Zürich Airport, 1 hour. Road travel: three entries: up Engadine valley from Austria; Julier Pass from Chur, always kept
open; Maloja Pass up from Italy, always kept open.

General comments. St Moritz is St Moritz. In a nutshell,
while there is still masses of room for future projects and general development, this corner of the Upper Engadine already
has everything. No skiers' case history is complete until he has
experienced it.*

All the villages shown on the table opposite, with the exception of Diavolezza, which is merely a halt on the railway
over the Bernina Pass, are typically attractive villages with the
picturesque architecture of the Upper Engadine. Particularly
attractive are Zuoz, and Guarda – the entry point for the
Silvretta Tours (45 km.).

Zuoz, at the foot of Piz Kesch, has a long 'nursery' ski-lift
up south-facing slopes, with a project to extend this a good deal
higher. It, and nearby Madulain, are start and finish points for
ski tours between the Inn valley and Davos.

Centre 24   Altitude
BIVIO   Canton: Graubünden   5803 ft

Just over the summit of the Julier Pass (west side) is a most
pleasant little ski resort in its own right with a long (1·8 km.)
ski-lift giving a rise of 1378 ft up to top station at 7181 ft.

* For further details of the St Moritz region, see *Ski Holidays in St
Moritz,* a booklet published by the Kurverein and on sale in Switzerland and elsewhere.

ST MORITZ REGION

Neighbouring villages	Altitude	Distance from St Moritz	Inhabitants	Travel	Hotel beds	Other beds	Lifts
SOUTH-WEST							
Champfèr	5988 ft	4½ km.		Road	(Included in St Moritz)		
Silvaplana	5955 ft	7 km.	347	Road	400	120	Corvatsch and trainer
Sils Maria	5922 ft	12 km.	210	Road	431	360	Ski-lift
WEST							
Bivio	5803 ft	21½ km.	250	Road	150	100	Ski-lift
NORTH-EAST							
Celerina	5676 ft	3 km.		Road and rail	(see St Moritz)		
Samedan	5627 ft	6½ km.	1890	Road and rail	381	680	Trainer
Bever	5610 ft	7½ km.	234	Road and rail	—	244	Nil
Zuoz	5630 ft	15 km.	1012	Road and rail	100	350	Ski-lift
EAST							
Diavolezza Halt	6713 ft	14 km.		Road and rail	(Start point of Diavolezza and Lagalb *Luftseilbahnen*)		

Literally surrounded by all manner of ski-touring country, including several routes over from St Moritz itself, Bivio, with its quiet friendly atmosphere and its delightfully easy ski-ing, is popular not only for week-end visits but for full length holiday periods. Prices are most reasonable.

Centre 20   Altitude
SILVAPLANA   Canton: Graubünden   5955 ft

The little village at the foot of the Julier Pass road, already a most pleasant place to stay, is highly important. With the advent of the big Corvatsch *Luftseilbahn* system and its upper ski-lifts across from the village, Silvaplana will inevitably become very popular and much development will take place very shortly.

Centre 21   Altitude
PONTRESINA   Canton: Graubünden (Engadine)   5820 ft to
                                                        5938 ft

Description. 1040 inhabitants. 27 hotels and pensions providing 1960 beds. Other accommodation 700 beds. Language German and Romansch. English and most continental languages spoken.

Long famed as a summer and winter resort, this beautifully situated, quieter, and less sophisticated near neighbour of St Moritz has been greatly improved for keen skiers by the recent creation of the nearby Diavolezza and Lagalb *Luftseilbahnen*. Local ski area, at present limited and suited mainly for beginners, is capable of future development. Many non-skiers who enjoy walking come here.

A pleasant, picturesque main street, many old chalets, and a fair share of large hotel buildings.

Ski facilities. One small local area; the nearby area of Muottas Muragl; and, 7 km. south-east up the Val Bernina, the big Diavolezza and Lagalb areas.

(1) *The local Alp Languard Area.* Widespread, west-facing, sunny nursery slopes served by a small lift rising 315 ft surmounted by a ski-lift giving 1184 ft rise to 7464 ft. One main run of about 2 km. for medium performers.

A project to extend these with transports up to over 9000 ft – close to the Fuorcla Piz Muragl – may come in the future. If it does it will greatly extend the area, and link it with

(2) *The Muottas Muragl Ski Area.* An elderly funicular rises 2317 ft up to 8032 ft. (Restaurant and fine viewpoint of most of the region of the Upper Engadine.) Valley runs of up to 3½ km. down to bottom station and Pontresina.

Good ski excursions to be found above and behind both these two areas.

(2) *The Diavolezza Ski Area.* (25 mins. by Bernina railway or 15 mins by car.) A fine new *Luftseilbahn* goes from 6824 ft in a spectacular ride up to 9754 ft to the Diavolezza Hut. A rise of 2880 ft. A long new ski-lift on the Firnfeld close to top station allows for summer ski-ing here.

Two main long *piste* runs, with variations, on east- and north-east-facing slopes – about 6 km. – for medium and above skiers – down to bottom station. Excellent, high standard, steep south-facing slopes for spring ski-ing go down into the Arlas valley. Good skiers only.

On the reverse side there is from the hut a superb view of the glaciers and peaks of the Piz Palü–Piz Bernina range. This side is the start for the famous Morteratsch Glacier run (3534 ft and about 9½ km.) down to the Morteratsch rail station and hotel at 6220 ft. (15 mins. train return to Pontresina.) A splendid ski-mountaineering-type run which is not always open and which the inexperienced should not tackle out of season.

Close to Diavolezza is Piz Lagalb, hitherto a favourite ski mountain for day expeditions. A new *Luftseilbahn* now in construction with a height difference of 2569 ft, up to 9508 ft, will provide wonderful possibilities for fine open ski-ing on huge west-facing slopes. Lagalb is also the start point for the long winter run down to Poschiavo – a distance of some 18 km. and about 5900 ft descent.

Ski touring and mountaineering. Superb opportunities of all grades and duration for the keen and the ambitious to be found in the Palü–Bernina ranges and in the region of the Italian frontier.

Amenities. Ski school. Guides. Ski tours. Ski jump. Skating rink. Curling. Sleigh rides. Good shops. Sports shops.

Cafés. Restaurants. Night-spots. Cinema. Well-kept walks.

Life in centre. Quiet and sedate in comparison with St Moritz. Peaceful and friendly atmosphere. Ski-ing by no means the sole interest. Internationally popular, particularly with Germans. Plenty of entertainment locally or accessible nearby at St Moritz. Efficient organization. Wide price range, but easily possible to live very reasonably.

Accessibility. Train: 5 hrs Zürich. As for St Moritz.

General comments. Excellent local facilities for beginner parties and family groups. The keen, good skier will find all he wants nearby, but he has to get to it. By no means a necessity, a car is a great asset.

Centres 136, 110, and 138   Altitudes
UNTERWASSER   Canton: St Gallen   2973 ft
WILDHAUS   The Obertoggenburg Area   3450–3600 ft
ALT ST JOHANN   2920 ft

Description. Unterwasser: 750 inhabitants. 9 hotels and pensions with 415 beds. Other accommodation 100 beds. *Wildhaus:* 1160 inhabitants. 15 hotels and pensions with 650 beds. Other accommodation 400 beds. *Alt St Johann:* 500 inhabitants. 6 hotels and pensions with 200 beds. Language German.

This engaging little valley, called the Obertoggenburg, containing three ski centres in a row, lies at the foot of the north-facing sides of the seven impressive, and unmistakeable, jagged teeth of the Churfirsten Range. Backed by the south-facing slopes of the Säntis Massif (8209 ft – where lovely late spring ski-ing can be had from the pylon stops of the big *Luftseilbahn*), this relatively low-altitude valley of rich pasture land consists of rounded Alp country with intermittent forest and open meadow. Many small farms, in a patchwork of fields, are dotted about the lower slopes. In winter, this picturesque region is recognized as a snow pocket. Very popular with Swiss skiers, it offers good short ski-ing.

Ski facilities. Almost all on north-facing slopes, the ski-ing above each centre is so planned with uphill transport that it can be shared by all three.

Unterwasser has a funicular surmounted by a ski-lift with a total rise of 2546 ft up to Stöfeli at 5518 ft.

Wildhaus has a chairlift surmounted by a ski-lift with a total rise of 2434 ft up to 5774 ft. There is also a 1150-ft *Luftseilbahn* project.

Alt St Johann has a ski-lift rising 1640 ft up to 4560 ft, with an extension rising a further 700 ft.

From these three parallel systems many runs of varying grades, ranging from 1½ to 5 km., lead down to any one of the valley stations. Good nursery slopes available.

Already varied, with good short ski-ing, this region is well capable of further 'upward' development with lift extensions.

Amenities. Ski schools. Ski jump (Unterwasser). Skating rinks (Wildhaus and Unterwasser). Small village shops. Hotel dancing. Bars, etc.

Specialities. A lovely long-distance run – 12–14 km. and 6000 ft – from the top of the Wildhaus lifts right down to Grabs (near Buchs) in the Rhine valley.

Life in centres. Simplicity and comfort. Pleasant traditional atmosphere. Little glamour or sophistication. Prices medium to very reasonable. Crowded at week-ends with car and coach visitors. Unterwasser is the most lively and Alt St Johann the most simple. Plenty of activity and movement with little organized entertainment.

Accessibility. Zürich 2½ hrs by train to Chur and thence bus.

General comments. A rewarding area to visit, especially for medium competent skiers seeking something a little different. The region does not come into the lists of international or well-known ski centres, but it combines character with lovely surroundings and it should be enough to say that large numbers of Swiss approve of its ski-ing.

Centre 165   Altitude
WANGS PIZOL   Canton: St Gallen   1755 ft
  (BAD RAGAZ)

Just over the Churfirsten range (to the south) and in the main valley of Sarganserland two long lift systems go slanting up to

Pizol from the low-altitude villages of Wangs and Bad Ragaz.

From Wangs two cable cars in sequence surmounted by two ski-lifts climb a total of 5529 ft up to top station at 7284 ft. This top area is also reached by a similar, south-facing, system from nearby Bad Ragaz.

During the week you may have the main long *piste*, and the long ladder of lifts, much to yourself, but at week-ends you will have to share this entertaining but relatively narrow area with some 6000 skiers – at least half of whom will all be ski-ing at the same moment.

Wangs Pizol has good ski-ing, lovely views out over the Rhine Valley and the Lichtenstein Mountains; pleasant workaday valley villages at which to stay, and particularly at Bad Ragaz, good accommodation; a surprising height gain – but, at weekends in good snow conditions, the main *piste* becomes something like a Brighton beach on a Bank Holiday that has suddenly been tilted to a sharply angled slope. This in itself is a spectacle that should not be missed, and a car stop here on a Sunday is a highly entertaining risk.

Centre 90   Altitude
BRAUNWALD   Canton: Glarus   4115 ft

Description. 350 inhabitants. 9 hotels and pensions with 400 beds. Other accommodation 400 beds. Language German (practically no English).

Many picturesque buildings, interspersed with small hotels, attractively scattered amid lovely clumps of tall fir trees. The whole situated on a broad sunny terrace above steep valley cliffs, backed by limited but pleasant ski fields that lead up to a splendid rocky backcloth of minor peaks. Reached only by funicular, there is no car traffic. Peaceful, quiet, unpretentious, and modest, this small centre enjoys lovely views, including the Tödi, across the wide Linth valley. Perfect Christmas-card scenery.

Ski facilities. One ski area served by one chairlift with a rise of 1936 ft providing runs of between $2\frac{1}{2}$ to 4 km. One other lift. One baby lift.

Restricted in scope but amusing, two wide sloping terraces, one above the other, linked by a short bottle-neck passage, provide the ski grounds. Upper terrace open and medium steep. Lower terrace, gently rolling semi-wooded country. The whole ideal for first and second season standards. In good conditions, one difficult and enterprising run goes right down to Luchsingen in the Linth valley – 4176 ft and 6–7 km. – which good skiers will enjoy.

Ski touring. Good short day-tours for modest performers.

Amenities. Ski school. Ice rink. Sleighs. Village-type shops.

Life in centre. Gentle and unhurried. No luxury; no bright lights; adequate comfort for moderate to cheap prices. Little *après-ski* in smart sense; evening life consists of hotel entertainments and party fun. Visitors mostly Swiss and German – very few English.

Accessibility. Train: Zürich 2 hrs via Ziegelbrücke and Linthal (funicular). Airport: Zürich.

General comments. Excellent for families and children. School, student, and travel-agency groups well catered for. Standard of ski-ing extremely modest. Standard of beauty high.

Centre 126		Altitude
ENGELBERG	Canton: Unterwalden	3281 ft

Description. 2410 inhabitants. 15 hotels and pensions with 1500 beds. Other accommodation 800 beds. Language German – English and other continental languages spoken.

This large and very attractive winter and summer resort, with its big monastery, is a very pleasant place with much to attract the keen skier. Sunnily exposed in a wide valley, it is surrounded by mountain scenery that rivals that of many a high-altitude centre. The extensive ski fields, well served by uphill transport, are surmounted by many a fine ski-touring region, and the skylines consist of rocky and impressive peaks. Relatively low in altitude, Engelberg is a 'snow-pocket', and, whereas it is easily accessible and in no sense overpowered or hemmed-in by mountains, it gives a complete impression of cosy remote seclusion, ideal for a winter sports holiday.

Ski facilities. Two ski areas. One large north-facing area served in sequence by a funicular, a *Luftseilbahn*, and a ski-lift, gives a total rise of 3980 ft up to the Jochpass at 7261 ft. One smaller, south-facing ski area served by a cable-car and an upper ski lift gives a total rise of 2746 ft up to Brunnihut at 6102 ft. (Project to extend this up to Schönegg.)

Nursery slopes, with lift, at Engelberg.

The north-facing Trübsee–Jochpass area provides a fine selection of long and short runs (up to 8 km.) from racetrack standards to beginner standards, with several steep descents for experts. Glorious, steep, open, and little-frequented slopes, such as the Laub descent, can be sought by good skiers for the effort of short climbs. The lower slopes of the Laub now are served by a new ski-lift. There is also a new lift from Trübsee up to approx. 6217 ft on the Bitzistock.

The south-facing Brunni ski area loses the snow on its lower slopes relatively early in the season, but the terrain is amusingly varied when conditions are good.

Ski touring. Fine selection of glacier excursions and tours – including Titlis and Reissend Nollen, etc. – for climbs of up to 5½ hrs. Also ski excursion from Jochpass over into the Melchtal (see below).

Amenities. Ski school. S.C.G.B. representatives. Ski jump. Skating rink. Ice hockey. Curling. Tobogganning. Casino. Cinema. Good shops, sports shops, etc. Tea rooms. Bars. Cafés. Hotel and bar dancing. Visitors' events and local fêtes, etc.

Life in centre. Easy-going, pleasant, traditional atmosphere. No high pressure. Colourful and gay, with pleasing overtones of old-fashioned courtesy. Popular but in no sense 'fashionable'. Plenty of fun, but little artificial glamour. Comfortable living with wide range of prices. Genuine.

Accessibility. Lake boat from Lucerne to Stansstad, thence train. Zürich 3½ hrs. Lucerne to Engelberg by road, 1 hr.

General comments. No class of holiday skier will be disappointed with the facilities Engelberg has to offer.

Centre 9   Altitude
MELCHSEE FRUTT Canton: Obwalden   6299 ft

Description. Inhabitants hotel staff only. 4 hotels and pensions
providing 300 beds.

A high-altitude small settlement on a sunny plateau above
Stöckalp in the Melchtal. Reached by a cableway from Stöckalp
at 3527 ft, this friendly little place has the advantage of no
road and no wheeled traffic. It consists of a few buildings –
hotels, rooms and flats, a shop, and a chapel.

Ski facilities. Two ski-lifts, giving rises of about 700 ft and
1121 ft (Balmegghorn) up to 7420 ft. Wide open slopes above
tree-line. Extensive nursery slopes and good ski school. Runs
from top station down to the Melchtal by Stöckalp give descents of about 3500 ft. Sheltered valley slopes with woodrunning included.

General characteristics are unpisted ski-ing on long open
gentle slopes, high enough and shaded enough to preserve
powder snow conditions for long periods.

Many short and long day tours, with and without skins, are
available in equally pleasant conditions and surroundings, and
ski excursions are a popular feature.

Life in centre. Quiet, friendly, self-contained, and gay. Comfortable living at reasonable prices. International clientele.
Happy atmosphere.

Accessibility. Train to Sarnen on Brünig line. Bus to Stöckalp
(garages for cars). Cable-car system to Melchsee Frutt.

General comments. Very suitable for beginner parties and
medium skiers – and particularly for those keen on touring
and earning their own untracked snow. S.C.G.B. representative.

Centre 60   Altitude
ANDERMATT   Canton: Uri   4711 ft to 4747 ft

Description. 1500 inhabitants. 12 hotels and pensions providing
about 400 beds. Language German – English spoken.

This attractive little village, situated in a high flat valley, stands at the main mountain 'crossroads' of south-central Switzerland. High above the northern entry to the Gotthard Tunnel, Andermatt commands the entries to the Furka Pass (and the Grimsel), the Gotthard Pass, and the Oberalp Pass. Busy with traffic and tourists in summer, the village acquires all the special attributes of a cosy yet remote ski centre in wintertime, when the passes are closed by snow.

Ski facilities. Shortly to be greatly extended with a second ski area (see below), there is at present one rounded plum-pudding ski area on and above the Oberalp Pass. Served by Furka–Oberalp railway up to 6044 ft – thence by two ski-lifts up to Stöckli at 7700 ft.

The area served by ski-lifts gives a variety of short runs on south-east-, south-, and south-west-facing slopes with descents of about 1600 ft. Extended down to Andermatt, the total descent is 2989 ft. There is also good lift ski-ing at nearby Hospental and at Calmot.

Sunny and seldom over difficult, the area is too compact and limited for the confirmed *piste*-basher, but ideal for beginner and medium performers. There is an almost complete absence of trees.

When the new Gemsstock *Seilbahn* is completed (summit 9715 ft) this big two-section lift will open up a splendid and completely new area. There will be long runs of over 5000 ft descent, including many north-facing slopes, down to Andermatt, and the ski country will meet all the demands of all grades of skier – from beginners to expert. (Now in construction.)

Ski touring. If Andermatt has so far been limited for *piste* skiers, it has always been rich for those who like ski touring. Almost all round the focal point of the village the high 'crossroads' country around the big Alpine passes offers almost limitless choice of ski-touring country. Well served by huts, tours of all grades from glacier to easy excursions are available for periods of long or short duration. Untracked powder regions, which even the moderate performer can enjoy, are a speciality.

Amenities. Good small ski school. Ski jump. Skating rink. Ice hockey. Curling. Tobogganning. Sleighs. Attractive main street. Village and sports shops. Cafés, tea rooms, restaurants, bars. Hotel and bar dancing. Cinema. S.C.G.B. representatives.

Life in centre. Cosy, friendly atmosphere. Well-organized entertainments both for visitors' events and evening parties. Prices reasonable. Accent on simplicity with little or no sophistication. Popular with English. Difficult not to make friends.

Accessibility. Train travel: 2½ hrs Lucerne. Also via Gotthard Tunnel, from Italy.

General comments. Strangely unspoilt for so well-known a centre. The White Hare Ski Club (established 1934) is very active and has largely helped to create conditions admirably suited to family parties and to the young. For a long while Andermatt stood still when other centres were developing. With the construction of the important new Gemsstock *Luftseilbahn* – together with new lifts at nearby Hospental and Sedrun etc. – this friendly little centre will enter a new era.

Centre 101		Altitude
AIROLO	Canton: Uri	3855 ft

It is of interest to note that Airolo, at the southern entry to the St Gotthard Tunnel and Pass, is a new Swiss winter sports centre in the making. Situated at 3855 ft, with 1800 inhabitants (and, at present, only two small hotels with about 90 beds). The cantonal government has recently announced plans to develop this picturesque Italian-speaking and Italian-looking village into a new ski centre complete with lifts, an ice stadium, a ski school, and a new 100-bed hotel.

Projects include a *téléférique* to Sasso della Boggia, a rise of some 2970 ft up to about 6775 ft in 7 mins.

THE GRINDELWALD–
SCHEIDEGG–WENGEN AREA

THE widespread and popular ski area, shared by the above three very different centres, consists of one very large circuit. Starting from Wengen, the Männlichen cable-car gives a swift rise of 3055 ft in 7 mins. (no ski run back to Wengen). The splendid Männlichen Run (7 km. and 4252 ft) takes one to Grindelwald–Grund. The upper half of this run is served by a fine new ski lift. A rack and pinion railway takes you 7½ km. from Grund back up to Scheidegg – a rise of 3678 ft. From here, together with the Lauberhorn and Eigergletscher transports, there is a variety of long runs both back to Grindelwald and, to complete the circuit, down to Wengen. (Rack and pinion railway, Wengen to Scheidegg, 7 km. long, and rise of 2592 ft.)

The wide range of ski-ing, from racetrack *piste* to ambling runs, provides plenty of choice for everyone. Open country, woods, steep and gentle places, short as well as long runs, are there to be used, and in general the circuit is ideally suited to the medium type skier. The many halts on the rack and pinion railways allow considerable choice for beginners and for those seeking the snow conditions they require.

The huge and wonderful upper world of glaciers and peaks reached so easily by the Jungfraujoch mountain railway from Scheidegg (6772 to 11,332 ft, rise 4560 ft) provides wonderful ski touring and ski mountaineering of limitless variety from simple to severe. The most popular guided tours from Eismeer and Jungfraujoch (hotel 46 beds) include the following:

(1) Eismeer–Grindelwald.

(2) The Aletsch Glacier via Concordia and the Riederfurka down to the Rhône valley near Brig.

(3) Via Concordia, Lötschenlücke, to Goppenstein beyond Kandersteg.

(4) Via Concordia, Grünhornlücke, Oberaarjoch, to Grimsel and Meiringen.

Air-lift ski-ing with light aircraft operating from Männlichen top station serve all the above areas including the Ebne-fluh and Petersgrat. (See p. 346.)

Centre 115		Altitude
GRINDELWALD	Canton: Berne	3300 ft to 3500 ft
	(Bernese Oberland)	

Description. 3000 inhabitants. 30 hotels and pensions with 1200 beds. Other accommodation 1000 beds. Language German – English widely spoken.

True village atmosphere amid many hotels and scattered chalet buildings. Of long tradition and great character, this large and attractive village has a long curving main street and spreads widely over the surrounding hillsides. Situated on south-facing slopes, some 300 ft above valley bottom (Grund). The shadow of the Wetterhorn passing across the village re-stricts sun hours in the early part of the season, but this makes for excellent skating and curling conditions. Set in superb surroundings this very popular, friendly place has achieved gaiety without any of the unnecessary trimmings of glamour.

Ski facilities. For main Grindelwald–Wengen circuit see p. 340.

One big local ski area served by four-section continuous chairlift system. Baby lifts on good nursery slopes.

The 'First' ski area chairlifts take you up 3626 ft over 4·355 km. of wires. Excellent sunny restaurant at top station with spectacular views. The Wiederfeldgrätli ski-lift now continues up to about 8202 ft, giving a total rise of 4705 ft above Grindel-wald. Largely south-facing slopes provide runs of 6 to 8 km. – steep at top, gentle after half-way. Beginners and experts pro-vided for. Specially good when conditions provide spring snow.

Ski touring. Easy rail access to Jungfraujoch (see p. 340). Local tours in Faulhorn–Schwarzhorn range above 'First', and lovely 'off-the-*piste*' runs from the Grosse Scheidegg. The Eagle Ski Club actively encourages ski touring.

Amenities. Large ski school. Mountain guides. S.C.G.B. representatives. Skating rinks. Curling. Sleighs. Ski jump. Good shopping centre. Sports equipment shops. Local pubs.

Cinema. Tea shops. Dance bars. Hotel dancing. Night-clubs.
Garages and repair service.

Specialities. Glacier tours. Long easy *piste* runs. Curling.
Warm coats provided on chairlifts. Good value transport
abonnements.

Life in centre. Easy-going, friendly atmosphere. Many English visitors. The non-skier has good walks and plenty of
sunny places for lunch. All prices catered for – living can be
very reasonable. *Après-ski* life spontaneous and not sophisticated – pleasant and fun. Considerable car traffic at week-ends.

Accessibility. Train: 4 hrs Basle, 4½ hrs Zürich. Road, always
open, chains advisable. Airport: Zürich.

General comments. A place of great tradition and character.
Widespread excellent ski facilities.

Centre 4		Altitude
KLEINE	Canton: Berne	6772 ft
SCHEIDEGG	(Bernese Oberland)	

Description. 10–15 inhabitants. One hotel with annexes, 175
beds. Language German – English spoken.

Famous small settlement at the high-altitude junction of
the Jungfraubahn and the two cog-railways that come up from
Lauterbrunnen via Wengen, and from Grindelwald. Situated in
a splendid sunny position on the exposed pass, the few
buildings, surrounded by ski slopes, have spectacular close-
up views of the Eiger North Wall and the magnificence of the
Jungfrau group with its nearby glaciers.

Quiet in the evenings – hotel life only – this place is lively
and busy throughout the day with crowds of skiers from
Wengen and Grindelwald (and also visitors over from Mürren)
making the Männlichen–Scheidegg ski circuit.

Ski facilities. For main ski circuit, see p. 340.

Two small local ski areas served by a couple of ski-lifts and
one mountain railway.

(1) *The Lauberhorn Area.* Ski lift gives 1263 ft rise to 8055 ft
allowing for short, open, pisted runs back to Scheidegg, and the
extended shoulder runs, of about 6 km. and 4000 ft, to Wengen.

(2) *The Eigergletscher Area.* Lower section (before tunnel) of the Jungfrau railway provides variety of short amusing runs down both sides of the pass. Shuttle ski-lift back up to Eigergletscher from Salzegg.

Ski touring. Direct access to Jungfraujoch. See p. 340.

Amenities. Ski school. S.C.G.B. representative. Skating and curling rink. Shop. Restaurants. Long season with good spring ski-ing, and summer ski-ing at Jungfraujoch. Comfortable living, with prices to match.

Accessibility. 20 mins. train from Wengen (see Wengen below).

General comments. A gay 'rendez-vous' by day. Quiet and somewhat cut off by night. Renowned for long season – especially for short-distance runs in late springtime. Scheidegg is a tiny place that is fortunate to have all the facilities of nearby Wengen and Grindelwald. (Beds also at Wengenalp.)

Centre 86   Altitude
WENGEN   Canton: Berne   4180 ft
                   (Bernese Oberland)

Description. 1200 inhabitants. 25 hotels and pensions with 1500 beds. Other accommodation 1000 beds. Language German – English widely spoken.

A big 'resort atmosphere' centre of large and small hotels and many chalets. Fairly compact, with large central nursery slopes and skating rinks, Wengen is functional rather than decorative, and has the asset, to date, of no road and no wheeled traffic. Situated on a large sunny shelf above the deep Lauterbrunnen valley, the village, and particularly its top stations, command magnificent views of the Oberland giants (Eiger, Mönch, Jungfrau, etc.) and across the valley towards Mürren.

Ski facilities. For main Wengen–Grindelwald circuit see p. 340.

Widespread local nursery slopes, well furnished with baby and slalom lifts, etc.

Ski touring. Easy rail access to Jungfraujoch. See p. 340.

Amenities. Large ski school. S.C.G.B. representatives. Skating rinks. Curling. Ski jumps. Good shopping centre.

Excellent specialist equipment and clothing shops. Cinema. Tea shops. Night-clubs. Hotel dancing and dance bars.

Specialities. One of the most highly organized centres – specializing in ski-ing, skating, and curling. Thriving local organization, the Downhill Only Club, provides full programme of ski training, ski races, ski jumping, etc., with emphasis on the encouragement of the young British racer and skier. Glacier tours. Curling. Weekly night ski jumping. Many competitive events. Good value railway *abonnements*.

Life in centre. Visitors tend to dominate village life. Prices on the upper side of medium but cheap accommodation available. Much colourful activity on rinks and nursery slopes can be watched from village street. Nightlife – save in big hotel where dinner jackets still occur – is simple and plentiful. Young people have gay times and meet easily. Extremely popular with the British.

Accessibility. Train: 4 hrs Basle. 4½ hrs Zürich. Road: stops at Lauterbrunnen (garages), thence 15 mins. train. Airport: Zürich.

General comments. High geared and successful, Wengen has about it something of the atmosphere of a gay co-ed college campus.

The whole Wengen–Scheidegg–Grindelwald area can be described as a cooperative society on a grand scale and is a wonderfully organized corner of Switzerland for all categories of skiers.

Centre 148		Altitude
LAUTERBRUNNEN	Canton: Berne	2612 ft
(STECHELBERG)	(Bernese Oberland)	

Description. 2800 inhabitants. 5 hotels and pensions with 175–200 beds. Language German – English widely spoken.

Situated at the bottom of the deep canyon of the Lauterbrunnen valley, backed by impressive precipice cliffs, this village sees little sunshine. Cool in summer and cold in winter, it can only be considered as an inexpensive place where parties can stay with the convenient choice of daily ski-ing either in the Wengen–Scheidegg–Grindelwald area or at Mürren. A few kilometres up the valley lies Stechelberg, from which village an important *Luftseilbahn* is planned to reach the Schilthorn, way above Mürren.

Centre 37   Altitude
MÜRREN   Canton: Berne   5374 ft
(Bernese Oberland)

Description. 350 inhabitants. 11 hotels and pensions with 675 beds. Other accommodation 470 beds. Language German – English widely spoken.

Famous small village of reputation, charm, and unique position. Perched on a grandstand ledge above the Lauterbrunnen cliffs with spectacular views directly across to the giants of the Bernese Oberland barrier. Birthplace of the Kandahar Ski Club and winter home of Sir Arnold Lunn – the father of British ski-ing and inventor of the slalom – it has been closely connected with the development of competitive Alpine ski events. Sunny and peaceful, there is no road and no car traffic – and consequently no noise.

Ski facilities. Two adjoining ski areas.

(1) *The Schiltgrat Area.* Ski-lift, giving rise of 1640 ft and runs of 2 to 3 km. – including world-famous Kandahar course.

(2) *The Allmendhubel–Maulerhubel Area.* Funicular giving rise of 856 ft and adjacent ski-lift of 525 ft allowing for gentle runs of 3 to 4 km.

The approach funicular to Mürren (Lauterbrunnen to Grutsch) gives a steep rise of 2273 ft up 1·5 km. of rail. When snow conditions are good, this provides fine, difficult ski-ing. This is the lower half of the famous Inferno racecourse from Schilthorn summit (11–12 km. and over 7000 ft).

In general there are *pistes* for the beginner and tricky racecourse type ski-ing for the expert.

Ski touring. Not basically a touring centre. Schilthorn 3½-hrs climb (projected cable-car system). Easy rail access to Jungfraujoch (see p. 340) via Lauterbrunnen, and to Wengen, Scheidegg, and Grindelwald.

Amenities. Ski school. Kandahar Ski Club Headquarters.

S.C.G.B. representatives. Ice rinks. Curling. Village and equipment shops. Tea rooms. Hotel dancing and dance bars.

Life in centre. Quiet and sunny. Village atmosphere. No car
traffic. Ski-ing and skating easily watched by spectators.
Compact ski-ing insures easy return for lunch. Nothing startling about evening entertainment which revolves around Palace
Hotel and two or three bars. Average prices on the high side
of medium.

Specialities. Well-deserved reputation for good and reliable
snow conditions. Short steep ski runs. Curling. Arlberg-
Kandahar held here every five years. Airlift ski-ing to Ebneflul
and Petersgrat across the Lauterbrunnen valley. Superb long
runs. The Petersgrat descent starts at 10,522 ft and finishes at
Stechelberg at 2986 ft – a drop of 7536 ft and about 14 km.

Accessibility. Train: 4½ hrs Zürich, 4 hrs Basle – both via
Interlaken. Road to Lauterbrunnen only (garages), thence 3
mins. funicular and train. Airports: Zürich or Basle.

General comments. Specially recommended for families with
children. The limited ski area ideally suited for beginners and
for good skiers. Quick shuttling on Schiltgrat lift (which could
well be doubled) provides strenuous training. Mürren has
stood still for a long time. The important plans for the large
scale *Luftseilbahn* right up to the Schilthorn will greatly extend
the ski-ing of this already famous centre, and this construction
will certainly result in a great deal of development in the way
of accommodation and general facilities.

Centre 100　　　　　　　　　　　　　　　　　　　Altitude
KANDERSTEG　　　　Canton: Berne　　　　　　3858 ft
　　　　　　　　　(Bernese Oberland)

Description. 900 inhabitants. 19 hotels and pensions providing
1050 beds. Other accommodation 830 beds. Language German
– English spoken.

　One of the few Swiss ski centres that can be reached direct
by main-line train service, this pleasant, scattered little village
which stands on the wide upper flat of the Kander valley at
the northern entry of the Lötschberg tunnel, is closely sur-

rounded by mountain scenery of great strength and beauty and has about it an air of Shangri-la seclusion. This is no deception.

Ski facilities. Two medium-sized ski areas, one for beginners and the other an artificially created descent for the connoisseur.

(1) *The Oeschinen Area.* Served by chairlift giving rise of 1591 ft up to 5528 ft. Lovely scenery. Short distance to Oeschinen lake. Smiling beginners' country. Three runs – easy, medium, and medium difficult – up to $4\frac{1}{2}$ km. lead down to Kandersteg.

(2) *The Stock Area.* Served by *Luftseilbahn* giving steep rise of 2051 ft up to 5988 ft. One highly entertaining artificially built-up run in very impressive surroundings gives descent of about 3 km. Collector's piece. Not easy.

Above top station, where a ski-lift is planned, a long wide valley climbs gently for 8 km. to the Gemmi Pass. This is the ski way over to Leukerbad in the Rhône Valley (Valais). Good upland nursery slopes and good touring country.

Ski touring. Fine choice of peaks, including Wildstrubel. Kandersteg and Adelboden share much of their touring country and there is wide variety.

Amenities. Ski school. Ski jump. Skating rink. Ice hockey. Curling. Sleigh rides. Tobogganning. Village shops. Cafés. Tea rooms. Bars. Hotel and bar dancing.

Life in centre. Friendly, gentle, and genuine. Lovely surroundings. No sophistication but plenty of ingenuous entertainment. Pleasant old-world courtesy and charm. Prices medium and below. Sunny, unhurried existence.

Accessibility. Main-line train travel: Berne $1\frac{1}{2}$ hrs, Zürich $3\frac{1}{2}$ hrs, Brig 40 mins. Airport: Zürich.

General comments. Famed for its 'initiation parties', Kandersteg is ideally suited for beginners. Simple and unpretentious, it caters for all the general amusements of winter sports without undue emphasis on ski-ing.

Centre 75
ADELBODEN   Canton: Berne

Altitude
4439 ft

Description. 3000 inhabitants. 18 hotels and pensions with 1000

beds. Other accommodation 3000 beds. Language German –
English spoken.

A large, sprawling village with an attractive main street, a
fifteenth-century church, and many decorative chalet buildings.
Placed on a broad sunny terrace, it faces the south-east across
the Engstligenbach valley towards the rocky Lohnergebirge,
with the big table-top massif of the Wildstrubel blocking the
head of the valley to the south.

Ski facilities. Four medium-sized and separate ski areas,
situated amid a complex of ridges and valleys at the head of
the main valley.

(1) *The Hahnenmoos Area.* 25 mins. bus ride to Geils at
5623 ft. Chairlift Geils to Hahnenmoos Pass, a rise of 798 ft to
6421 ft. Very gentle ski area with more enterprising country
on both sides of pass to be gained by short climbs. Ski way
over pass down to Lenk, and new lift back from the Lenk
valley to return you to Hahnenmoos. The runs from the
Laveygrat via Hintersillern are the most rewarding for keen
skiers. These fine runs are now served by an excellent new lift
that climbs direct from Geils right up to the Laveygrat at about
7326 ft.

(2) *The Kuonisbergli Area.* A buttress ridge served by two
ski-lifts gives total rise of 1909 ft up to Höchst at 6273 ft.
Enterprising selection of short varied runs of between $3\frac{1}{2}$ to $4\frac{1}{2}$
km. Steep and tricky *pistes* as well as simple descents. Good
racecourse.

(3) *The Schwandfeldspitz Area.* Another ridge area served
by chairlift giving rise of 1863 ft to 6643 ft. Ski-lift on reverse
side. Fine viewpoint. Amusing runs of between $2\frac{1}{2}$ and 5 km.
on unorthodox but not too difficult terrain.

(4) *The Engstligenalp Area.* A small *Luftseilbahn* rising 1867
ft takes you to 6444 ft. No ski runs down; this is the transport
entry to the Adelboden ski-touring area (see below).

The various detached ski areas allow for wide and free
choice of slopes facing all compass points, and permit considerable variety of gradient from simple to severe. There is
plenty of room for future lift projects.

Ski touring. The hotel pension and restaurant at Engstligenalp is the entry base of many excellent glacier ski tours in the well-known Wildstrubel region. Apart from many climbs and peaks, there are ski ways over to Kandersteg, and over to Crans and Montana in the Rhône valley.

Amenities. Ski school. S.C.G.B. representatives. Ski jump. Skating. Ice hockey. Curling. Tobogganning. Many shops. Sports shops. Cinema. Cafés. Bars. Hotel and bar dancing, etc. H.Q. of Silleren Ski Club.

Life in centre. Adelboden has many faithful friends. Slightly pretentious and with adequate comfort, it is neither a 'ski dorf' nor an Arosa. Plenty of activity, but a trifle lacking in cohesive enthusiasm.

Accessibility. 16 km. by bus from Frutigen on the main Spiez–Lötschberg–Brig railway. Berne 2 hrs. Zürich 4 hrs. Airport: Zürich.

General comments. Good varied ski-ing. Adelboden falls contentedly into a middle-class bracket that pleases a large number of holiday-makers.

Centre 114	Altitude
LENK	3504 ft

Canton: Berne
(Bernese Oberland)

Description. 1860 inhabitants. 11 hotels and pensions providing 450 beds. Other accommodation 500 beds. Youth groups, etc., 600–700 beds.

Looking down from the top of Hahnenmoos Pass above Adelboden, the village of Lenk, in the wide Simmental, stands at the foot of a large rounded spur. These pasture-land hillsides of the Betelberg are Lenk's ski area – big enough, wide enough, and good enough to provide limited but excellent ski-ing. The village itself, like its ski country, is simple, attractive, unsophisticated, and sensible.

Ski facilities. One ski area served by two-section chairlift. 3·6 km. in length, these give a total rise of 2790 ft up to Leiterli at 6400 ft. A fine selection of well-marked interlinking runs go down the spur ridge and the nearby valley from both top and half-way station (Stoss). Several hut restaurants. Runs

vary from 2 to 6 km. Upper sections easy and open. Lower
sections steeper and pleasantly wooded. Versatile, compact,
never difficult but seldom dull, this ski-ing, mostly on north-
east- and east-facing slopes, contains no pitfalls and is very
good value both for medium skiers and beginners.

A new ski-lift starting from Buhlberg close to Lenk village
now climbs the opposite, west-facing side of the valley up to the
Hahnenmoos Pass and effects complete interlinkage with the
Adelboden ski-ing. Rise approximately 2,900 ft.

Good nursery slopes with long trainer lift at village.

Amenities. Ski school. Short ski tours. S.C.G.B. representative. Ski jump. Skating rink. Ice hockey. Curling. Village
shops. Hotel and bar dancing. Sulphur baths.

Life in centre. Quiet and gentle. Village and visitor life intermingled. Simple comfort and reasonable prices. Spontaneous
amusements with no *après-ski* frills.

Accessibility. Electric railway from Spiez (main line) via
Zweisimmen. Berne 2 hrs. Zürich $4\frac{1}{2}$ hrs. Airport: Zürich.

General comments. Close to Adelboden, and closely associ-
ated with the easily reached Zweisimmen and Gstaad area
ski-ing, Lenk is a well-organized, self-contained little entity
ideally suited for second or third season visitors looking for
attractive comfortable ski country where they can gain experience.

THE SAANENMÖSER–GSTAAD–
CHÂTEAU D'OEX AREA

THE long upland pastoral region of Saanenland and the 'Pays d'Enhaut' is shared by two cantons – Berne and Vaud – and, roughly speaking, the borderline between these two marks the frontier between German-speaking Switzerland and French-speaking Switzerland. Nine-tenths of this very popular ski area consists of lovely, rolling, semi-wooded, rounded hills – intersected by many valleys and ridges – that run up to an average of about 7000 ft, and which provide an almost limitless amount of smiling, versatile, and safe ski country. A comparison with the Kitzbühel area is almost unavoidable – in the social sense as well as the ski-ing sense.

There are in this well-favoured region no less than eight well-established ski centres – some large and sophisticated, others small and relatively simple – all of which are readily accessible, either by road or rail, from each other, and several of which are inter-connected by ski runs from their own individual uphill transport systems. The main ski centres are these: Zweisimmen, Saanenmöser, Schönried, Gstaad, and Saanen in Canton Berne, and Rougemont, Château D'Oex, and Col des Mosses in Canton Vaud. (Future development of the ski country of Les Diablerets – see p. 359 – will also bring this part of Vaud into the Gstaad orbit.)

All told, there are at least two dozen different lifts of varying sizes – not counting baby lifts – dotted about all up and down this well-developed region, with more to come in future projects, and overall *abonnements* are both sensible and good value. The keen and energetic skier in any one centre can easily provide himself with different lifts and fresh ski runs every day of a fortnight's holiday. Even without a car he can do this, but this is one of the areas of the Alps where a car of one's own is a very great asset.

Centre 133   Altitude
ZWEISIMMEN   Canton: Berne   3087 ft

Description. 2550 inhabitants. 10 hotels and pensions providing
190 beds. Language German.

The 'capital' of the Simmental, situated in a broad valley at
the Y-formation rail junction of two valleys, one of which runs
southwards to Lenk (13 km.) and the other south-westwards
to Gstaad (15 km.) and Château d'Oex (28 km.).

An elderly, old-fashioned, slightly nondescript large village
with nearby pine forests. Inexpensive living – few modern
buildings, but these will doubtless appear soon.

Ski facilities. One large ridge formation ski area served by
two-section, 5-km.-long *Gondelbahn* system giving a total rise
of 3478 ft up to Rinderberg at 6588 ft.

At Oeschseite – 5 km. up Gstaad railway line – a ski-lift with
an approximately 1000-ft rise branches up to close to *Gondelbahn* middle station.

Entertaining ski runs of about 6½ km., steepish at upper
levels with gentle meadows lower down, lead back to Zweisimmen. Good exploratory runs for the enterprising, down sides
of ridge, lead to Oeschseite and the vicinity of Lenk village.

Accessibility. Train travel: Zürich, via Spiez, 3¾ hrs. Geneva,
via Montreux, 3 hrs 7 mins.

General comments. Amenities and facilities at Zweisimmen
are as yet not fully developed – but these will doubtless follow.
Living is inexpensive and in no sense frivolous. Hotels tend to
be on the old-fashioned side as it has not yet become fashionable to stay in Zweisimmen in winter, but those that do stay
here find all the essential comforts. Zweisimmen, owing to
S.C.G.B. activities with parties of young skiers, is rapidly gaining in popularity.

Centre 88   Altitudes
SAANENMÖSER   Canton: Berne   4170 ft
SCHÖNRIED   4054 ft

Description. 200 inhabitants. 4 hotels and pensions providing

200 beds. Other accommodation 160 beds. Language German, – English spoken.

Two attractive little places, more wayside halts – with a collection of buildings scattered nearby – than villages. Wide, open, sunny situation, facing the friendly Hornberg ski area, with a fine view south-westwards down the valley towards the Gummfluh and Rubli mountains close to Gstaad. The two places are separated by 2 km. of near-level road along which there are a number of chalet buildings, etc.

Ski facilities. One ski area served by two-section funi-sledge lift system, surmounted by two small ski-lifts branching out like antlers (or horns of Hornberg) to the summits of the Hornfluh (6250 ft) and the Hühnerspiel (6303 ft). Total rise 2126 ft.

From these minor summits there is a wide variety of shaded slope ski-ing both down to Saanenmöser and to nearby Schön-ried, as well as down the sunny reverse side to Gstaad.

Schrönried has its own ski-lift slanting up 1720 ft to close to the Saanenmöser funi-sledge top station, reaching 5775 ft, with excellent short north-west-facing runs down its own length.

Runs of 3 to 5 km. suitable for all comers, but with little to test the expert, are available in most pleasant open meadow, lightly treed surroundings.

Amenities. Ski school. Day tours. S.C.G.B. representative. Skating. Ice hockey. Curling. Tobogganning, etc. Few shops. Hotel dancing.

Life in centre. Quiet and gentle. Pleasant air of friendly and old-fashioned courtesy. Sunny existence without bright lights. Glamour available at nearby Gstaad. Standard of ski-ing moderate – with emphasis more on enjoying ski movement than nose-to-the-grindstone ski-ing.

Accessibility. Train travel: 2 hrs Berne. $1\frac{1}{2}$ hrs Montreux.

General comments. Most pleasant, semi-'country life' atmosphere.

Centre 117   **Altitude**
GSTAAD   Canton: Berne   3450 ft

Description. 2000 inhabitants. 12 hotels and pensions providing
850 beds. Other accommodation 1500 beds. Language German
– English, French, and other languages spoken.

A small 'village town' of many chalet and chalet-type
buildings intermingled with medium-sized structures around
the attractive and busy main street. Gstaad sprawls over a
wide area in its own sunny enclave, surrounded by rounded
and amusing ski country. Popular, fashionable, and successful,
with a prosperous air of cosmopolitan sophistication, Gstaad,
which can boast of one enormous period-piece hotel, un-
blushingly perched on an elevation, has many regular and
enthusiastic clients.

Ski facilities. Three ski areas served by chair-, ski-, and gon-
dola-lift systems.

(1) *The Wasserngrat Area.* Two-section chairlift rising 2711
ft to 6375 ft. North-west- and north-facing slopes. Steep upper
sections – scattered woods – gentle lower section. Runs of 3
to 5 km.

(2) *The Windspillen Area.* Two ski-lifts giving a rise of
some 2330 ft up to about 5750 ft. Mostly north-facing slopes.
Enterprising top section. Beginners' slopes on lower lift.

(3) *The Eggli Area.* Four-seater gondola cars surmounted
by gentle upper ski-lift. Total rise 1998 ft up to ridge top at
5482 ft. North-east-facing slopes and short entertaining steep
runs of 2 to 2½ km. back to Gstaad, and easier north-facing
runs of about 5 km. down to Saanen. Saanen is a large village,
with its own ski-lift up the Eggli, where one can stay quietly
and inexpensively (five hotels and pensions with about 100
beds). (See also the Rougemont–Videmanette ski area, p. 355.)

An important project some 13 km. due south from Gstaad at
Reusch (4406 ft) consists of a cable-car system up via Oldenegg
(6306 ft) to the Cabane des Diablerets at 8278 ft. These first
two portions are already under construction and should be
ready in 1962. The Cabane des Diablerets will also probably
be reached by a cable-car rising from the Col du Pillon close

to Les Diablerets (see p. 359). A final upper cable-car will
extend both approaches up to the Diablerets Glacier at 9748 ft.
A grandiose scheme that will take some years to complete, but
which will open up fine big ski-ing and a summer ski season
for both Gstaad and Les Diablerets on the upper glaciers.

Amenities. Ski school. Ski tours. Ski jump. S.C.G.B. representatives. Skating. Ice hockey. Curling. Sleigh rides. Helicopter airport. Good shops, sports shops, etc. Restaurants.
Cafés. Tea rooms. Bars. Hotel and bar dancing. Night-spots.

Life in centre. Busy, animated, gay. International clientele
with definite slant on social register. Fashionable – sometimes
blasé. Prices on expensive side. Traditional village life intermingled with the Bentley, Mercedes, and Lancia class. Plenty
of young people (several finishing schools in area). Easygoing,
cushioned existence both on slopes and in village. Could be
termed a cross between Kitzbühel and Megève.

Accessibility. Train travel: 2 hrs Berne, 1½ hrs Montreux.
Airport: Geneva.

General comments. Not in the 'big ski-ing' class, but frequently in social gossip columns, Gstaad is rightly immensely
popular for its wide variety of good, short, safe ski-ing. Almost
equidistant between Zweisimmen, Château d'Oex, and the Col
du Pillon–Diablerets areas, with all their present and projected
facilities, Gstaad, in spite of a relatively short season, is the
central point of an important and highly developed ski network
that covers a very wide area.

Centre 129   Altitude
ROUGEMONT   Canton: Vaud   3264 ft

Description. 930 inhabitants. 7 hotels and pensions providing
150 beds. Other accommodation 200 beds. Language French –
and German.

A charming and picturesque little roadside village – large
decorative chalets and twelfth-century church and castle –
close up under the steep north-facing sides of the Rubli.

Ski facilities. One ski area served by the fine, new Videmanette *Luftseilbahn* which gives a two-section rise of 3888 ft

up to 7087 ft. Steep, north-facing ski-ing for skiers of above medium up to expert class. Runs of 3½ to 5 km. down to Rougemont and vicinity, and 7–8 km. down north-east- and east-facing slopes to the Eggli ski area above Gstaad. (Short ski-lift link to join the two areas at Kalberhönital.)

Practice slopes round Rougemont village.

Amenities. Ski teachers. Ski tours. Luge run. Village shops.

Life in centre. Quiet. Village life only. Inexpensive. Charming.

Accessibility. Train travel: 1 hr 20 mins. Montreux, 2 hrs 20 mins. Berne. Airport: Geneva.

General comments. Peaceful base for good high-standard local ski-ing with easy access to less demanding slopes at either Gstaad or Château d'Oex. Bound to grow and become more popular.

Centre 132   Altitude
CHÂTEAU D'OEX   Canton: Vaud   3182 ft

Description. 3250 inhabitants. 24 hotels and pensions providing 560 beds. Other accommodation 590 beds. Language French – German and English spoken.

A large workaday Swiss village of great tradition and charm, nicely and sunnily situated in lovely surroundings. Comfortable and unpretentious. Well organized, friendly, and easygoing. Popular both in summer and winter, this resort, which has a relatively short snow season, is genuine – without the all-too-frequent overtones of artificiality.

Ski facilities. Two ski areas served by *téléférique* and *télécabine* system and by chair- and ski-lift system.

(1) *The La Braye Area. Téléférique* immediately from village rises 692 ft (no direct ski runs down this section) to ski area. *Télécabines* give rise of 1503 ft up to Montagnette at 5325 ft. Projected ski-lift will continue up to 5915 ft. Fine wide region of easy north- and north-east-facing ski-ing – ideal for beginners and learners up to medium standards. Runs of 2½ km. – with 5½ km. run down to Gérignoz (5 mins. bus return).

(2) *The Mont Chevreuil Area.* 8 mins. by bus brings you to the little village of Les Moulins. One short chairlift, one

long ski-lift, and one upper ski-lift give total rise of 2819 ft up
to Chevreuil summit at 5739 ft.

Good selection of easy, medium, and difficult runs ranging
from 3–6 km. on north-east- and north-west-facing slopes.
An easy, promenade-type run takes you across to Col des
Mosses ski area (see below).

Open meadows, lightly wooded areas, gentle and steep
glades. No snags.

Amenities. Good ski school. Ski jump. S.C.G.B. representative.
Skating. Ice hockey. Curling. Tobogganning, etc. Village shops.
Restaurants. Bars. Hotel and bar dancing. Folklore museum.

Life in centre. Pleasant, friendly atmosphere. Prices medium
and reasonable. Village and holiday life intermingled. No
glamorous *après-ski* life but plenty of fun to be found. Several
finishing schools and many young people about.

Accessibility. Train travel: Montreux 1 hr 10 mins, Berne
2½ hrs. Airport: Geneva.

General comments. A happy holiday place with ski-ing to
please all comers. Much to be recommended for parents of
young people and for parties of second and third year experience.

Centre 62   Altitude
COL DES MOSSES   Canton: Vaud   4741 ft

Description. 30 inhabitants. 3 hotels and pensions providing 60
beds. Language German.

The highest and smallest centre of the whole Zweisimmen
to Château d'Oex region – a place where, even in a poor season,
snow can generally be found. Situated in open, somewhat dull
pass country, Col des Mosses is more a day-to-day, week-end
bus or car-borne visitors' place.

Ten kilometres southwards from Château d'Oex, Col des
Mosses is easily reached (also from the Lake of Geneva side).
It consists of a few buildings with two ski-lifts on big open
slopes – one of which gives a rise of 490 ft. The other is 2 km.
long with a rise of 1400 ft. Gentle, easy ski-ing. Good nursery
slopes. In springtime medium-standard tours involving 2–3

hrs climb are easily available. There is also a sizeable ski-lift at nearby La Lecherette (altitude 4524 ft).

Centre 105		Altitude
LES DIABLERETS	Canton: Vaud	3780 ft
	('La Suisse Romande')	

Description. 1000 inhabitants. 9 hotels and pensions with 400 beds. Other accommodation 1000 beds. Language French. English understood.

Just 4 km. west of the Col du Pillon (5072 ft. At present closed in winter. Plans are to keep it open.) which leads over into the Gstaad area (see p. 354), this simple unsophisticated village of attractive chalet buildings lies widely scattered at the edge of a little flat valley, backed by gentle and interesting ski country and confronted by the spectacular Diablerets Massif with the magnificent rock walls of the Creux-de-Champ amphitheatre. A friendly, easygoing place of considerable tradition and history – and no little charm.

Ski facilities. Two ski areas – one large, one small – served by one gondola *téléférique* and small upper ski-lifts, and one medium-sized ski-lift.

(1) *The Isenau Ski Area.* Gondolas give rise of 1865 ft up to 5797 ft. Hotel restaurant with splendid viewpoint terrace. Small ski-lift gives further rise of 437 ft up to 6234 ft. Small trainer ski-lift serves upper basin by hotel.

Sunny, south-facing runs of considerable variety and no great difficulty – either direct down to village or via the Col du Pillon – ranging from 4 to 7 km. Open slopes and ridges with many clumps of trees and natural glades. Upper Isenau bowl excellent for beginners, with many small climbs available to minor peaks for those who like to wander. Project to extend gondola system across bowl up to Col d'Isenau at 6814 ft.

(2) *The Diablerets Ski Area.* Ski-lift gives rise of 794 ft and provides delightful 'baby' run on north-facing slopes. Project to extend this up to Meilleret at about 6000 ft. A great deal of tree felling in this thickly wooded region will be necessary to make this extension worth while.

Les Diablerets' major project is linked with that of the Gsteig–Reusch project from the Gstaad area (see p. 354). A separate *téléférique* up from the Col du Pillon to join the Reusch *téléférique* at the Cabane des Diablerets (8278 ft) – with a shared extension up to the Diablerets Glacier at 9748 ft. As each section of this is completed in the next few years, the importance of this centre will grow and grow. A glacier airport is planned at top station.

Amenities. Ski school. Ski tours. Ski jump. Skating rink. Ice hockey. Curling. Tobogganning, etc. Small village shops. Restaurants and bars.

Life in centre. Gentle, unhurried village life. Friendly atmosphere. Simple inexpensive living. Ski standards modest. Holiday spirit entertainment with no bright lights.

Accessibility. Train travel: $1\frac{1}{2}$ hrs Montreux, $2\frac{1}{4}$ hrs Geneva. Airport: Geneva.

General comments. Recommended for groups and parties of first to third season skiers. Ambitious projects make this a 'growth investment'. Good skiers should watch this corner of the Alps.

Centre 91 and 96		Altitudes
VILLARS	Canton: Vaud	4111 ft
BARBOLEUSAZ		3973 ft

Description. 1950 inhabitants. 27 hotels and pensions providing 1400 beds. Other accommodation 2500 beds. Language French – English, German, and other continental languages widely spoken.

Villars, with its immediate satellites of Chesières and Arveyes – and its small near-neighbour, Barboleusaz – is a big residential, resort area of considerable charm, consisting of many chalets and hotel buildings, large and small, spread out in an arc along the edge of a wide balcony, 2763 ft above Bex, facing out south-westwards across the hazy width of the Rhône valley. Functional rather than picturesque, Villars is popular and busy both in summer and winter and it is the superb views that catch the eye more than anything else.

Ski facilities. Villars. One ski area served by two approach systems (see below). *Barboleusaz.* One ski area served by a *Gondelbahn* and upper ski lift.

(1) *The Villars–Bretaye Ski Area.* A mountain tramway rises 1817 ft to the Col de Bretaye at 5928 ft where there are a few restaurants, hotels, and chalets. Here there is a 'starfish' of no less than five lifts, three reaching up to three minor summits – Chamossaire 6890 ft, Petit Chamossaire 6663 ft, and Chaux–Ronde 6562 ft – and one to return back from a little chain of lakes that lie beyond and below the Col de Bretaye. Maximum ski transport height gain, 2779 ft to Chamossaire (which is the most splendid viewpoint of the whole area).

This area is also reached, more directly, by the new Roc d'Orsay chairlift with a rise of about 2190 ft up to 6430 ft.

Short east- and west-facing runs in Bretaye 'starfish' area. Predominantly south-facing runs of 4–5 km. down to Villars. Considerable variety, from easy to medium difficult.

(2) *The Barboleusaz–Les Chaux Ski Area.* A long ridge formation served by a 2·6 km. long, four-seater gondola car system rising 1903 ft to 5876 ft. Upper ski-lift continues up to 6628 ft. Good selection of entertaining ridge runs (south-west-, west-, and north-west-facing) of up to 5 km.

The two areas, Villars and Barboleusaz, almost interconnect – and future projects will probably effect the linkage. Long ridges parallel to Barboleusaz will also probably be exploited with lift development.

Amenities (Villars). Ski school. Special emphasis on children's classes. S.C.G.B. representatives. Skating rinks. Ice hockey. Curling. Tobogganning, etc. Many visitors' events and entertainments. Big shopping centre. Tea rooms. Cafés. Restaurants. Bars. Cinema. Hotel and bar dancing.

Life in centre. Sunny 'resort' existence, with anything from Palace to Pension life. Big price range. Prosperous yet friendly. Pleasant, happy atmosphere. Popular with all generations. Many young people. Considerable gaiety – mainly based on Palace Hotel.

Accessibility. Mountain tramway: Bex 45 mins. Main line: Geneva 2½ hrs. Airport: Geneva.

General comments. Sunny situation and superb views. Ski-ing widespread, safe, varied, and never arduous. Good facilities and competent organization, greatly assisted by the Villars Visitors Club. Much to be recommended for families with children.

Centre 58   Altitude
LEYSIN   Canton: Vaud   4134 ft to 4757 ft
             (Lake of Geneva Region)

Description. 3547 inhabitants. 76 hotels and pensions providing 3500 beds. Language French – German spoken.

Only recently converted from hospitals and clinics into hotels and pensions, etc., the very large and somewhat severe buildings which cluster thickly on the steep and wooded south-facing slope above the old village and overlook the Rhône valley do not make Leysin a beauty spot. Thousands of balconies and terraces, however, speak rightly of much sunshine.

Ski facilities. One ski area served by gondola *téléférique* and two short lifts at top station.

The Berneuse Ski Area. Four-seater gondolas give a rise of 2353 ft up to 6683 ft. Behind top station – restaurant and fine viewpoint – you look down into a bowl, backed by the rocky peaks of the Tour d'Ai and the Tour de Mayen, at the bottom of which lies the small Lac d'Ai at 6201 ft. Ski-lift from this lake back up to top station (rise 484 ft) and second lift on far side of bowl (south-facing) giving rise of 850 ft.

Runs of between 3 and 4½ km. lead down to Leysin, on predominantly south-facing slopes of terrace, glade, and woodpath. These traverse round, and can pass above Leysin, to the Les Chamois area where large nursery slopes are served by a lift rising some 670 ft. Wide and gentle practice areas also to be found at foot of village.

Amenities. Ski school. Skating. Ice hockey. Tobogganning. Shops at various levels of village. Tea rooms, cafés, etc. Cinema.

Life in centre. Popular with German coach parties and tourist parties, this steep and somewhat 'clinical' centre lacks any 'ski dorf' attraction. Apart from the glorious sunshine, living is slightly austere and the words 'Palace and Grand Hotels' are ill chosen.

Accessibility. A funicular up from Aigle on the main Simplon line. Lausanne 1½ hrs, Geneva 2½ hrs. This funicular also serves the steep village with four separate halts in the built-up area where the main village street has to zigzag in hairpin bends. Road approach from Aigle goes via Le Sépey, which stands at the junction of the Col des Mosses and the Col du Pillon roads. Airport: Geneva.

General comments. New, unorthodox, pretentious, and, by certain standards, successful, Leysin has reasonable ski-ing for first and second season skiers and grand sunshine for any-one. It also has a long way to go before it acquires any of the background one normally associates with cosy or traditional ski centres. If you have never been to the Alps in winter, Leysin will not disappoint you.

Centre 120   Altitude
ST CERGUE   Canton: Vaud   3422 ft

Description. A sunny little village tucked into the wooded hillsides of the south slopes of the Jura mountains looking out over a splendid view of Lake Geneva and a wonderful pano-rama of the Alps.

The snow season is relatively short and the ski-ing gentle and picturesque. Four ski-lifts and one chairlift scattered near-by in the rounded hills give separate rises of up to about 1000 ft and open up a number of easy and moderate gradients which include both open fields and wood-running.

Not for the experienced skier who demands long and testing *pistes*, St Cergue is a delightful little place with a friendly atmosphere – well suited to beginner classes and families with young children. A bull point for parents who wish to ski on their own is the special Children's Club with an English and a French hostess to look after the young. There is skating and ice hockey and curling and all the entertainment to make a gentle winter sports holiday a success.

Accessibility. 50 mins. by train from Geneva.

Centre 116
CHAMPÉRY   Canton: Valais

Altitude
3429 ft to 3491 ft

Description. 850 inhabitants. 15 hotels and pensions providing 350 beds. Other accommodation 1100 beds. Languages French and German. English understood.

Close to the French frontier, this is a very attractive, picturesque village with a long main street and many chalets of elaborately carved woodwork and decorative and original roofs that project forward to slant across the street. Sunnily situated on a south-east-facing ledge above the Illiez valley, it looks across to a lovely view of the Dent du Midi with its many rocky pinnacles.

Ski facilities. One upper ski area reached by a *Luftseilbahn*, and served by two upper ski-lifts.

The Planachaux area is reached by cable-car rising 2314 ft up to 5870 ft. No direct ski runs down this climb. At Planachaux, which is a sunny, south-facing upland playground, two ski-lifts serve open, easy, and medium slopes between the altitudes of 5394 ft and 6378 ft. Practice runs of about 1 km. and 984 ft descent.

Two main, south-facing runs, which the sun is apt to denude of snow, can, in good conditions, return you to Champéry. These curl round for 4 to 5 km. – 2700 ft descent – with intriguing and difficult upper sections followed by long stretches of wood path road.

Ski touring. Big, upper bowl around Planachaux area provides good short excursions. There is a ski way over to the Swiss centre of Morgins and tours can be made across the frontier to the French centres of Morzine and Samoëns (see pp. 201 and 203).

Amenities. Small ski school. Ski tours. S.C.G.B. representative. Ski jump. Skating. Ice hockey. Curling. Tobogganing. Village shops. Sports shops. Tea rooms. Cinema. Bars. Dancing, etc.

Life in centre. Easygoing, sunny existence in pleasant and picturesque surroundings. No over-emphasis on ski-ing. No sophistication. Friendly atmosphere. On the quiet side but with adequate spontaneous entertainment in the evenings.

Accessibility. Train: via Aigle ($1\frac{1}{4}$ hrs) thence main line
Geneva (total $3\frac{1}{2}$ hrs). Airport: Geneva.

General comments. Little scope for long-distance *piste* skiers.
Limited but large sunny area successful with beginner parties.

Centre 76		Altitude
MORGINS	Canton: Valais	4439 ft

Description. 65 inhabitants. 6 hotels providing 250 beds. Languages French, German – English spoken.

Long popular with skaters, this pleasant small place on the
Franco–Swiss frontier close to Champéry is a little family-
type centre where the ski standards are not high and where
the 'atmosphere' is friendly and gentle.

There is a chairlift project up to La Foilleuse at 5589 ft,
which will open up short runs on north- and north-west-
facing slopes. Generally good snow conditions. There is a short
lift on sunny nursery slopes.

Evening life, which is quiet but very agreeable, centres
round the Grand Hotel where there is dancing.

Ski school. Ski jump. Skating. Ice hockey. Curling. Tobogganning. Village shops and amenities. Modest prices. H.Q.
of Corbeau Ski Club.

Accessibility. Bus service to Aigle on main Simplon line.
Also bus service from Thonon and Évian on French railways. Easy pleasant ski-ing, with good variety of ski-tour
excursions.

Centre 48		Altitude
VERBIER	Canton: Valais	4872 ft to 5010 ft

Description. 600 inhabitants. 17 hotels and pensions providing
750 beds. Chalet beds 5000 (over 300 chalets to rent). Languages French and German.

An important newcomer to the list of ski centres. Hard to
believe that it is only some ten seasons old. Verbier is unusual,
original, and ambitious, with excellent ski-ing already superbly
developed in a fantastically short time, and capable of even

further extension. A 'constructed' ski centre, not based on any existing village (Old Verbier is some distance removed), it consists of many buildings – chalets, hotels, pensions, shops, etc., all constructed in 'chalet' style – which lie scattered over a wide sunny area facing to the south-west.

Ski facilities. One huge amphitheatre area forms a 180° arc background to Verbier, in which enormous snowfields sweep down at all sorts of angles, facing south-east, south, south-west, west – and, in small areas, even north-west and north.

This big arena is served by one *télécabine* surmounted by two *téléfériques* at one end, and a long chairlift; three ski-lifts and various small trainer lifts serving the rest of the arc. Top station of *téléférique* at Attelas, 8947 ft, is 4026 ft above Verbier and there is a 600-ft chairlift behind top station. Splendid runs of $4\frac{1}{2}$ to $6\frac{1}{2}$ km. ranging from steep to gentle. The ultimate aim is to extend this system with two further *téléfériques:* first to Mont-Gelé at 9918 ft (already built) and then on up to Mont-Fort at 10,919 ft (in construction). This will greatly increase the scope into superb regions well outside the amphitheatre area. Present height difference 4908 ft. Near future will be 5909 ft. Splendid ski-ing with runs of up to 9 km. on west- and north-facing slopes.

Use of the ski- and chairlifts inside the amphitheatre allows for widespread uninhibited ski-ing, mainly south-facing, where ground suitable for all comers is readily available.

Ski touring. It is enough to say that Verbier is a popular terminal of the famous '*Haute Route*' from (or to) Zermatt and Saas-Fee. Many local ski mountaineering tours are thus available, including nearby Grand Combin. From the amphitheatre itself there are ski ways down to Sion, and via Isérables to Riddes, both in the Rhône valley.

Amenities. Ski school. Guides. Skating rink. Shops. Restaurants. Bars. Dancing.

Life in centre. Simple and unsophisticated. Busy and gay, with many young people, the life is not centralized in any way. Informal entertainment goes on in many quarters in individual chalets and parties. Holiday atmosphere, without village life, and with main focus on ski-ing. Best to be in a family or bigger

party, but the enterprising lone visitor need not be lonely.
Much traffic at week-ends. Superb viewpoints with lovely
panoramas, which include the Mont Blanc range.

Accessibility. Station: Le Châble, thence 8 km. by bus.
Martigny 1¼ hrs. Geneva 3¾ hrs.

General comments. Rightly very popular already, Verbier has
grown very rapidly. With wonderful ski-ing at its command,
this centre has plenty of room for expansion both in accommodation and with uphill transport. Verbier is an experience that
keen skiers of all categories should not miss. It has, and is,
developing so quickly that it is difficult to keep pace with each
new addition to the lift network.

Centre 55		Altitudes
CRANS	Canton: Valais	4823 ft
MONTANA		4905 ft

Description. These two centres sit side by side on a broad,
sunny, south-facing shelf high above the wide Rhône valley.
Crans: 200 inhabitants. 14 hotels and pensions providing 1045
beds. Other accommodation 800 beds. *Montana:* 2500 inhabitants. 30 hotels and pensions providing 750 beds. Other
accommodation 1000 beds. Languages French and German –
English spoken.

Montana village is large and contains many big ex-sanatoria
structures. Crans was built as a summer and winter pleasure
resort. The two now form one continuous area of many buildings that caters jointly for all-the-year-round holidays – and
the clinical, medical aspect of Montana has largely disappeared.
The whole of Crans–Montana is situated on a lovely grassland
terrace with widespread pine woods and backed by country
that lends itself admirably to ski-ing. Boldly ridged and picturesque mountain sides sweep steadily upwards towards the
heights of Wildstrubel and Wildhorn, beyond which lie the ski
centres of the Lenk–Adelboden ski areas.

Ski facilities. One large ski area served by chair- and ski-lift
from Montana and by *télécabine* system from Crans. These
two systems slant together and meet at Cri d'Err 7415 ft. From

here the *télécabines* continue up to Bella Lui at 8297 ft. Total rise: 3353 ft over 4 km. of travel. Restaurant terrace at top gives splendid viewpoint and dramatic surroundings. Various halts on these transports allow for a fine variety of runs both long and short, easy, medium, and difficult – varying from 2 to 7 km. – with both open and wooded country. Mainly south-facing, there are, however, many shaded areas to be found. The National racecourse will test any expert, and the enter-prising and talented skier will delight in the strange formations and surprises that lie in a vast area to the east of Bella Lui top station. Many terraces separated by rock cliffs and snow gullies, with miniature canyons known locally as 'Colorado', are there to be explored.

Ski touring. Ski access over the barrier range to Lenk and Adelboden provides endless opportunity for the ski mountaineer and tourer in the Wildstrubel, Bonvin, and Wildhorn regions.

Amenities. Large ski school. Large, sunny nursery slopes. Guides. Ski jump. Skating. Ice hockey. Curling. Tobogganning, etc. Casino. Cinema. Tea rooms. Good shopping area. Res-taurants, bars, etc. Hotel and bar dancing.

Life in centre. Sunny, sheltered, comfortable existence with every holiday amenity for skier and non-skier in lovely sur-roundings with magnificent views. Price-range wide. Well organized but never over-geared. Simple rather than sophisti-cated, with no over-emphasis on ski-ing, and little *après-ski* glamour.

Accessibility. Funicular from Sierre. Also road entry. 1 hr 20 mins. Brig, 2 hrs 40 mins. Lausanne.

General comments. A happy place for beginners and parties of early and medium skiers. General standard of ski-ing seldom startling but there is plenty here to tax and amuse any expert. Much recommended, especially in early springtime.

Centre 22		Altitude
SAAS-FEE	Canton: Valais	5873 ft

Description. 560 inhabitants. 18 hotels and pensions providing

1000 beds. Other accommodation 800. Language German –
Italian, French, English spoken.

A delightful village of true Alpine tradition, set amid high
mountains of great splendour, which has long been famous as
a wonderful base for ski touring and ski mountaineering.
Cleverly and quickly it has in recent years developed itself
into a centre for holiday ski-ing of the modern *piste* variety
without detracting from its original charm. A fine road now
leads to Saas-Fee, but no traffic is allowed beyond the large
carpark and garages outside the village. No modern architectural fantasies have been allowed to replace the traditional
style of building. Saas-Fee has managed to move with the
times and yet retain the unspoilt atmosphere of a high Alpine
community.

Ski facilities. One ski area served by two-section *téléférique*,
and comprehensive beginner areas around village served by at
least three lifts.

The Langefluh area is reached by four-seater gondola cars
rising 2143 ft to Spielboden and a further 1358 ft up to Langefluh Hut at 9416 ft (total rise of 3501 ft).

Splendid and impressive viewpoint at top station with panorama of at least seven *Viertausender* (see Appendix 7) and
a bird's eye view down on to the *seracs* of the Fee Glacier.

Main run, with variations, on north-east- and south-east-
facing slopes – about 5 km. Angular ski-ing, mostly on the steep
sides of a long moraine ridge. Entertaining for the good skier,
difficult for those below medium standards.

The Glacier run is a longer, semi-ski-mountaineering run
of about 7 km. which involves a climb and a careful crossing
of the broad Fee glacier until one reaches the beautiful broad
open snowslopes that run down north and north-west from
the Egginerjoch (ski route to Zermatt) and lead back to Saas-
Fee.

The village area is provided with three lifts giving rises of
508 ft, 360 ft, and 384 ft (and a smaller rope tow), which provide wonderful nursery slopes with proper miniature *pistes* for
beginners and learners.

Ski touring. Saas-Fee is the start of the famous '*Haute*

Route' to Chamonix and Verbier. Saas-Fee and Zermatt share some of the finest ski touring and ski mountaineering that exist in the Alps.

Amenities. Ski school. Guides. Ski jump. Skating. Ice hockey. Curling. Sleigh rides, etc. Village shops. Sports shops. Restaurants. Bars. Hotel and bar dancing.

Life in centre. Picturesque village life against a glacier background. Quiet and friendly. No traffic. Plenty of activity and gaiety. Spontaneous evening fun rather than organized entertainment. No sophistication or artificiality.

Accessibility. Bus from Stalden, 1 hr 50 mins. Brig, $3\frac{1}{2}$ hrs Lausanne, 6 hrs Zürich.

General comments. A place of character, beauty, and atmosphere. The *piste* ski-ing provides good value for the good skier and for the absolute beginner, but there is a noticeable gap for the medium performer. When the touring season starts in the springtime, the enthusiast has everything he could wish for.

Centre 39   Altitude
ZERMATT   Canton: Valais   5266 ft to 5316 ft

Description. 1500 inhabitants. 54 hotels and pensions providing over 3000 beds. Other accommodation 1600 beds. Language German – Italian, French, English, and other languages spoken.

This immensely popular village has all the ingredients required to make it the top-line ski centre that it has become. An old village. Great tradition. Superb mountain scenery. Widespread and wonderful ski-ing. A long season. Spring ski-ing. Ski touring and ski mountaineering. And finally – the best publicity trademark of all the Alps – the Matterhorn.

In spite of tremendous growth in the last fifteen years, the village, which has long been a famed summer mountaineering centre, has so far maintained character. The many new buildings are in no way offensive and motor traffic has not yet penetrated the streets. Zermatt is now as equally famed in winter as it long has been in summer. How long these conditions will continue, in view of the recent vast developments of the hydro-electric schemes in the Zermatt region, remains to be seen.

The village became successful commercially through becoming fashionable among keen skiers. Subsequently it became almost over-popular. What happened to the Isle of Capri could happen to Zermatt.

Ski facilities. Three large separate ski areas – two of which interlink. One mountain railway. Four cable-cars. Two chair-lifts. Three ski-lifts. Baby lifts. Various projects.

(1) *The Gornergrat–Stockhorn Ski Area.* Served by mountain railway up to 10,135 ft with two-section *Luftseilbahn* continuing up to Stockhorn at 11,175 ft. Total rise 5910 ft. Big sunny area of easy slopes for beginners between Gornergrat and Riffelberg (hotel and restaurants). Gornergrat Derby racecourse run gives 7·5 km. and 4819 ft down to Zermatt. Superb long north-facing slopes from stations of upper cable-car system give enterprising and difficult runs of between 8–11 km. down to Zermatt. These runs interlink with the Blauherd area by means of an 820-ft-rise chairlift at Findeln to Sunegga.

(2) *The Blauherd Ski Area.* Served by chairlift up to Sun-negga at 7508 ft with upper ski-lift up to 8466 ft. Total rise 3184 ft. Fine selection of runs ranging from 2–6 km. on west-north-west- and south-facing slopes, suitable for all comers from expert to beginner. The 'National' racecourse is one of the most testing.

(3) *The Matterhorn–Schwarzsee Area.* Two-section cable-car system gives total rise of 3100 ft to 8471 ft, up to foot of Matterhorn. Upper ski-lift on glacier. 'Snowcat' tractor service up to Theodule Pass on Italian frontier. Long and short runs on north- and north-east-facing slopes for all comers. Lower section cable-car excellent for beginners.

All top stations, notably Gornergrat and Stockhorn, provide superb panoramic viewpoints of many of Switzerland's highest mountains.

All three ski areas provide superb opportunities for explora-tory 'off-the-*piste*' enthusiasts and each top station is an entry point to ski touring and ski mountaineering areas.

Ski touring. One of the most renowned areas for tours of all grades. Easy excursions include the ski passage over the Theo-dule Pass down to Breuil-Cervinia in Italy (see p. 274). Ski way also over to Saas-Fee. Also entry point for '*Haute Route*' over to Chamonix and Verbier. Major ski mountaineering expeditions include Monte Rosa, Castor and Pollux, etc. Incomparable selection. Considerable activity with light aircraft for 'airlift' ski tours. (See pp. 91–3.)

Amenities. Large, efficient ski school. Guides. Ski touring expeditions. S.C.G.B. representatives. Ski jump. Skating rink. Ice hockey. Curling. Sleigh rides. Helicopter and light plane airport. Good shopping area. Sports shops. Cinema. Tea rooms. Restaurants. Bars. Night club. Hotel and bar dancing. Entertainments, etc. Kandahar Ski Club.

Life in centre. Gay and lively. International clientele. Wide price range from luxury to relatively cheap living. Plenty of *après-ski* glamour and sophistication. Life centres round the pleasant and entertaining main street. Combination of energetic ski-ing and equally energetic nightlife.

Accessibility. Train: Brig 1 hr 40 mins. 4 hrs Lausanne or Berne. 6 hrs Zürich. Geneva $5\frac{1}{4}$ hrs.

General comments. The ski-ing here is high, big, serious, and glorious, and can only be *fully* appreciated by relatively good performers. The beginner will enjoy himself but would be well advised to graduate elsewhere. Even with so much uphill transport the accommodation in Zermatt is such that queueing for railways and lifts is inevitable and often frustrating. Disadvantages of this picturesque, sophisticated, highly commercialized ski centre are largely offset by the intriguing and wonderful ski-ing. The high reputation of Zermatt is in some ways its own worst enemy, for you may find the uphill transport accommodation limited by the presence of non-ski-ing sightseers.

Appendices

Appendix 1: *The Ski Club of Great Britain*

Founded in 1903, the Ski Club of Great Britain, which is one of the oldest established ski clubs in the world and the Senior Ski Club in Britain, is the governing body of the sport in this country.

The S.C.G.B. is affiliated to the International Ski Federation – the FIS – and, in turn, the great majority of British ski clubs, and many of those in the Dominions, are themselves affiliated to the S.C.G.B.

The Club, which has played an outstandingly important role in the history and development of ski-ing – notably in achieving the recognition of Downhill and Slalom racing by the FIS and in the formation of the rules governing International racing, etc. – has a large membership (14/15,000).

This membership, ninety per cent of which consists of active skiers, is, in order to be able to assist prospective skiers, sensibly planned to include non-skiers. Very few remain non-skiers, but the first-time planner of a ski holiday can thus enjoy the facilities of the Club together with its many advantages, for the full enjoyment of his first winter visit to the Alps.

The advantages are manifold and the cost of membership is modest. Various subscription rates are available, ranging from £1 1s. 0d. per annum for University, Service, and Junior Members (up to nineteen years old) to £3 3s. 0d. per annum for full membership – with various intermediary rates.

Investment in membership is more than repaid by taking advantage of the services offered and by making full use of the many amenities – some of which are indicated herewith:

So far as information is concerned the Club has a comprehensive information library on ski-ing centres throughout the world. Advice is also available on equipment, clothing, and ski technique. The Club has Regional Representatives throughout England (see p. 377). There is a film library for hire of films to members, groups, clubs, and organizations interested.

On travel arrangements the Club has a Special Members Air Service. (The saving on this alone will recoup your annual subscription.)

There is a special Club Ski Accident Insurance Scheme which started benefits for those using approved safety release bindings.

On the snow there are club representatives – active and qualified skiers – in many of the major ski centres in the Alps (see p. 378). At these centres British ski tests (see p. 65), club runs, and races are organized and held each week. Annual arrangements are also made for both junior and senior racing training – and periods devoted to glacier tours and ski mountaineering. Weekly Club cocktail parties are held at S.C.G.B. centres. A Ski Club representative at a ski centre will always give members information on local matters – how and where to join the local ski school and where to hire equipment, etc. – and application for membership of the Club can, if required, be dealt with on the spot.

At home, both in London and at Regional Centres, lectures, film shows, cocktail parties, and dances form part of annual events.

Full membership entitles one to full use of the fine Club House in Eaton Square, London, which is the headquarters of the organization. This includes members rooms, a library, a bar, and a restaurant. Many of the annual events take place in the Club premises, where private parties can also be arranged. In these days not many clubs can boast of such useful meeting and eating facilities for so modest a subscription.

Up-to-date snow reports from the representatives in the Alps are posted on the Club notice boards throughout the season.

Annual publications include the *British Ski Year Book* and three editions of *Ski Notes and Queries* – both of which enjoy high international reputations in the ski-ing world – together with S C.G.B. Notices which list the season's and year's activities, including, of course, all the competitive events in the Alps.

There are also the handbooks, *Pre-Ski Exercises* and *Glacier Touring* and *Ski Mountaineering*, which can be purchased by non-members.

Both for the prospective skier and for the subsequent enthusiast the S.C.G.B. has much of value to offer. Membership will keep him in touch with friends he meets in the Alps and keep him informed of all the events and activities in the ski world. The really keen member can graduate to becoming a representative at a ski centre and/or to taking an active part in the administration of the Club on one of the many committees that deal with every aspect of the sport of ski-ing. The trefoil badge of the S.C.G.B. is recognized wherever people ski.

Applications for membership, and inquiries about how to join, should be addressed to the Members' Secretary at 118 Eaton Square, London SW1 (telephone BEL 4711).

This process is not complicated. Out of the widespread 14,000 odd membership it is never very difficult to find friends and acquaintances, who already are members, to propose and second you.

Appendix 2: *Regional Branches of the S.C.G.B.*

Regional Representatives of the Ski Club of Great Britain are located in the following areas:

BIRMINGHAM
CARDIFF
DEVON/SOMERSET
GLOUCESTERSHIRE
LEEDS
NORTH-EAST REGION – Newcastle (Main centre)
                              Tees-side (Sub-Area)
NORTH-WEST REGION – Manchester (Main centre)
                              Chester (Sub-Area)
NOTTINGHAM
STOKE-ON-TRENT
WILTS/BERKSHIRE

A post-card or telephone call to the London H.Q. of the S.C.G.B., 118 Eaton Square, SW1 (BEL 4711) will provide you with the name of the representative and his or her address.

Appendix 3: *S.C.G.B. Representation in the Alps*

S.C.G.B. representatives are to be found at the following ski centres for either part or the whole of the season. Times and dates can be ascertained from the Ski Club (see p. 377).

Indication is also given of the location of other British ski clubs (some of which have invitation membership only) which are affiliated to the S.C.G.B.

ADELBODEN (H.Q. of the Silleren Ski Club)
ANDERMATT (H.Q. of the White Hare Ski Club)
AROSA
CHAMPÉRY
CHÂTEAU D'OEX
DAVOS DORF ⎫ (Mardens Ski Club)
DAVOS PLATZ ⎭
ENGELBERG (H.Q. of the Harlequin Ski Club)
GRINDELWALD (H.Q. of the Eagle Ski Club)
GSTAAD (Kandahar Ski Club)
IGLS
KITZBÜHEL (Kandahar Ski Club)
KLOSTERS (H.Q. of Mardens Ski Club)
LENK
LERMOOS
LENZERHEIDE
MÉRIBEL-LES-ALLUES
MELCHSEE FRUTT
MORGINS (H.Q. of the Corbeau Ski Club)
MÜRREN (H.Q. of the Kandahar Ski Club)
SAANENMÖSER
SEEFELD
SESTRIERE
SCHEIDEGG
ST ANTON-AM-ARLBERG
ST CERGUE
ST MORITZ (H.Q. of Combined Services Winter Sports Association)
VILLARS (H.Q. of the Villars Visitors Ski Club)
WENGEN (H.Q. of the Downhill Only Ski Club)
ZERMATT (Kandahar Ski Club)
ZÜRS

Appendix 4: *The Combined Services Winter Sports Association and Other Service Schemes*

The Combined Services Winter Sports Association, a non-profit-making concern, founded in 1950, has for its aim to give past and present members of H.M. Forces the best opportunities for ski-ing and other winter sports at the lowest possible inclusive cost.

The schemes at St Moritz, Klosters, and Scheidegg are available to serving and ex-service members of the Royal Navy Ski and Mountaineering Club, Army Ski Association, or the Royal Air Force Ski and Winter Sports Association. The facilities are also extended to families and friends accompanied by full members.

For detailed information concerning the schemes at St Moritz, Klosters, and Scheidegg, apply to:

The Combined Services Winter Sports Association
43 York Terrace
Regent's Park
LONDON NW1   WEL 0063 Ext. 6

Other services' ski-ing is available at HECHENMOOS (nr Kitzbühel) and ST ANTON (apply to the Royal Navy Ski and Mountaineering Club, Mrs Guthrie, 56 Perham Road, West Kensington, London W14, FULham 1836); at KITZBÜHEL, ZÜRS, ST ANTON, ALPBACH, GRINDELWALD, ST CERGUE, FLIMS, SESTRIERE, many centres in NORWAY, and a hut in SCOTLAND (apply to the Army Ski Association, The War Office (A.S.C.B.), Stanmore, Middlesex, STOnegrove 6377, Ext. 87); and at ZERMATT (apply to the R.A.F. Ski and Winter Sports Association, c/o Powell Duffryn (Air) Ltd, 5/7 Great Tower Street, London EC3, MANsion House 4555).

Appendix 5: *Classification of Hotels*

Hotels in the ski centres of the Alps are often subdivided into categories according to strict standards set down by National Tourist Office authorities.

These standards, which give a fair guide to the likely price range from expensive to modest cost, are marked either in numerals, letters, or stars which represent the degree of luxury and comfort, the efficiency of management, and the diversity of services obtainable.

It is a relatively easy matter for anyone signing up for inclusion in any travel agency party, or other group, to ascertain the quality of the accommodation that is being offered for any all-inclusive charge.

It is equally simple for the family group or the lone traveller – once he or they have decided which ski centre or area they wish to visit – to discover the type of hotel most suited to requirements and pocket.

In both cases, all that has to be done is to ask the National Tourist Office concerned for the list of hotels and study the category markings and prices.

The following table indicates how the various national markings compare with one another.

		Luxury	1st Class	2nd Class	3rd Class	4th Class
AUSTRIA	Hotels	A1	A	B	C	D
	Pensions			B	C	D
FRANCE		****A	***A	**A	*A	
		****B	***B	**B	*B	
		****C	***C	**C	*C	
ITALY	Hotels	L	I	II	III	IV
	Pensions			1	2	3
SWITZERLAND		No official markings				

In the upper brackets there is a universal and tremendously high standard of comfort and service in the Luxury and 1st Class hotels of the Alps. Those whose pockets do not stretch to high prices need not be alarmed by 2nd or 3rd class classification. For the most part such hotels provide all that the normal holiday-maker requires, and they frequently have far more charm and atmosphere than is found in the big 'international' establishments.

Appendix 6: *National State Tourist Offices in London*

AUSTRIA

Austrian State Tourist Dept.
219 Regent Street, W1   REG 3446

ITALY
Italian State Tourist Office
201 Regent Street, W1   REG 2818

GERMANY
German Tourist Information Bureau
61 Conduit Street, W1   REG 2600

FRANCE
French Government Tourist Office
66 Haymarket, SW1   WHI 7766

SWITZERLAND
Swiss National Tourist Office
458 Strand, WC2   WHI 9851

Appendix 7: *High Mountains of the Alps*

The peaks that top the 4000 m. mark (13,123·6 ft) are known as
Viertausender – in English 'Fourthousanders'.

	Metres	Feet
MONT BLANC	4807	15,771
MONT BLANC DE COURMAYEUR	4704	15,433
MONTE ROSA, DUFOURSPITZE	4634	15,204
MONTE ROSA, NORDEND	4609	15,122
MONTE ROSA, ZUMSTEINSPITZE	4563	14,971
MONTE ROSA, SIGNALKUPPE	4556	14,948
DOM	4545	14,913
LYSKAMM	4527	14,853
WEISSHORN	4505	14,782
TÄSCHHORN	4490	14,733
MATTERHORN	4477	14,690
MT MAUDIT	4465	14,649
PARROT SPITZE	4436	14,554
DENT BLANCHE	4356	14,293
LUDWIGSHÖHE	4341	14,242
NADELHORN	4327	14,196
GRAND COMBIN DE GRAFENEIRE	4314	14,154
LENZSPITZE	4294	14,088

	Metres	Feet
FINSTERAARHORN	4275	14,026
MT BLANC DE TACUL	4248	13,937
STECKNADELHORN	4242	13,918
CASTOR	4226	13,865
ZINALROTHORN	4221	13,849
HOHBERGHORN	4219	13,842
LES GRANDES JORASSES (PTE WALKER)	4208	13,806
ALPHUBEL	4206	13,799
RIMPFISCHHORN	4198	13,776
ALETSCHHORN	4195	13,763
STRAHLHORN	4190	13,747
GRAND COMBIN DE VALSOREY	4184	13,729
DENT D'HERENS	4171	13,686
BREITHORN	4165	13,665
BIESHORN	4159	13,645
JUNGFRAU	4158	13,643
GRAND COMBIN DE TSESSETTE	4141	13,586
AIG. VERTE	4122	13,524
AIG. DU DIABLE	4114	13,498
LA BARRE DES ÉCRINS	4102	13,458
MÖNCH	4099	13,448
POLLUX	4091	13,422
GR. SCHRECKHORN	4078	13,380
ROCCIA NERA	4075	13,370
OBERGABELHORN	4062	13,330
GRAN PARADISO	4061	13,324
AIG. DE BIONASSAY	4051	13,291
PIZ BERNINA	4049	13,285
GR. FIESCHERHORN	4048	13,284
GR. GRÜNHORN	4043	13,266
GR. LAUTERAARHORN	4042	13,261
DÜRRENHORN	4034	13,238
ALLALINHORN	4027	13,213
HINTERES FIESCHERHORN	4025	13,206
WEISSMIES	4023	13,199
DOME DE ROCHEFORT	4015	13,173
DENT DU GÉANT	4013	13,161
LAQUINHORN	4010	13,157
AIG. DE ROCHEFORT	4001	13,127
LES DROITES	4000	13,123

Both France and Italy share the highest peak – Mont Blanc (frontier). Switzerland and Italy share Monte Rosa (frontier). The highest mountain entirely within Switzerland is the Dom. Austria's highest mountains are:

	Metres	*Feet*
GROSS GLOCKNER	3798	12,461
WILDSPITZE	3770	12,369

Germany's highest mountain is:

	Metres	*Feet*
ZUGSPITZE	2963	9,721

and this summit is also shared by Austria.

Appendix 8: *Highest Railways and Téléfériques in the Alps*

The highest railway in the world is outside Europe. The cog railway of Pikes Peak, U.S.A., built in 1890, reaches 4716 m. (15,473 ft).

In the Alps, where there are literally thousands of different forms of mechanical devices to haul the skier, the mountaineer, and the sightseer to the tops of local peaks, the order of highest points so far reached is as follows:

(1) *The Chamonix – Aiguille du Midi*

Two-section *téléférique* system in France. This goes from 1030 m. (3379 ft) to 3802 m. (12,474 ft) in a travel time* of 11 mins. Height difference 9095 ft.

(2) *The Breuil Cervinia – Furggen*

Two-section *téléférique* system in Italy. This goes from 2050 m. (6726 ft) to 3496 m. (11,470 ft) in a travel time of 13 mins. Height difference 4744 ft.

(3) *The Breuil Cervinia – Plateau Rosa*

Three-section *téléférique* system in Italy. This goes from 2050 m. (6726 ft) to 3484 m. (11,431 ft) in a travel time of 21 mins. Height difference 4705 ft.

(4) *The Lauterbrunnen – Jungfraujoch*

Two-section mountain-railway system in Switzerland. This goes from 796 m. (2612 ft) to 3454 m. (11,332 ft) in a travel time of 2 hrs 8 mins. Height difference 8720 ft.

* The travel times given above indicate actual travel without time periods spent in changing trains or lifts etc.

(5) *The Courmayeur – Col du Géant*

Three-section *téléférique* in Italy. This goes from 1372 m. (4501 ft) to 3430 m. (11,254 ft) in a travel time of 13 mins. Height difference 6753 ft.

(6) *The Zermatt – Stockhorn*

Three-section – one mountain railway and two *téléférique* – system in Switzerland. This goes from 1605 m. (5266 ft) to 3407 m. (11,175 ft) in 1 hr 15 mins. Height difference 5910 ft.

(7) *The Verbier – Mont Fort*

Four-section *téléférique* system in Switzerland. This starts from 1527 m. (5010 ft) and will reach 3328 m. (10,919 ft). Height difference 5909 ft.

(8) *The St Moritz – Piz Corvatsch* (when completed)

Two-section *téléférique* system in Switzerland. This will go from 1819 m. (5968 ft) to 3294 m. (10,807 ft) in 13 mins. Height difference 5414 ft.

These, to date, are by far the highest transport systems in the Alps. One or two future projects – such as that at Lac de Tignes in France to the top of the Grande Motte – will reach 11,647 ft, and doubtless more will follow and go higher than ever.

There are some seven or eight uphill transports that reach up to between 9000 ft and 10,000 ft. The vast majority reach up to between 6000 ft and 9000 ft, and very few do not attain a height of 4000 ft.

Appendix 9: *Good Areas for Car-Ski Holidays*

Arlberg Area.
Ausserfern.
Dolomites.
Gstaad–Château d'Oex Area.
Innsbruck Area.
Kitzbühel Area.
Mont Blanc Area.
Montafon.
Ötztal.
Pinzgau and Hohe Tauern (Zell-am-See).
Savoie Area.
St Moritz Region.
Turin Area.

Appendix 10: *Temperature Conversion Table*
(by courtesy of Arnold R. Horwell Ltd and H. J. Elliott Ltd)

Degrees Centigrade	Degrees Fahrenheit	Degrees Centigrade	Degrees Fahrenheit	Degrees Centigrade	Degrees Fahrenheit
100	212	−4	24·8	−18	−0·4
10	50	−5	23	−19	−2·2
9	48·2	−6	21·2	−20	−4
8	46·4	−7	19·4	−21	−5·8
7	44·6	−8	17·6	−22	−7·6
6	42·8	−9	15·8	−23	−9·4
5	41	−10	14	−24	−11·2
4	39·2	−11	12·2	−25	−13
3	37·4	−12	10·4	−26	−14·8
2	35·6	−13	8·6	−27	−16·6
1	33·8	−14	6·8	−28	−18·4
0	32	−15	5	−29	−20·2
−1	30·2	−16	3·2	−30	−22
−2	28·4	−17	1·4	−35	−31
−3	26·6	−17·8	0	−40	−40

Appendix 11: *Currency Conversion Table*

As of Summer 1961. It is always wise to consult your bank in view of possible changes.

Sterling	Austrian Schillings	French Francs	German Marks	Italian Lire	Swiss Francs
£1	72	13·7	11·13	1734	12
10s.	36	6·85	5·57	867	6
5s.	18	3·43	2·78	434	3
2s. 6d.	9	1·71	1·39	217	1·5
1s.	3·6	·69	·55	86·7	·6
6d.	1·8	·34	·28	43·4	·3

Appendix 12: *Metric Conversion Tables*

Miles to Kilometres

Miles	Kilometres
1	1·61
2	3·22
3	4·83
4	6·44
5	8·05
6	9·66
7	11·27
8	12·87
9	14·48
10	16·09

Use of the decimal point allows simple reckoning of all greater distances, thus:
40 miles = 64·4 km.
400 miles = 644 km
45 miles = 64·4 + 8·05 = 72·45 km.
450 miles = 724·5 km.

Kilometres to Miles

Kilometres	Miles
1	0·62
2	1·24
3	1·86
4	2·49
5	3·11
6	3·73
7	4·35
8	4·97
9	5·59
10	6·21

Metres to Feet

Metres	Feet
1	3·28
2	6·56
3	9·84
4	13·12
5	16·40
6	19·69
7	22·97
8	26·25
9	29·53
10	32·81

Appendix 13: *Standard Ski Length Conversion Table*

Skis on the Continent are measured in centimetres and in many English-speaking countries often in inches.

Short		Medium		Long	
1·75 m.=5 ft 8¾ in.		1·95 m.=6 ft 4½ in.		2·15 m.=7 ft 0½ in.	
1·80	5 10¾	2·00	6 6½	2·20	7 2½
1·85	6 0¾	2·05	6 8½	2·25	7 4½
1·90	6 2½	2·10	6 10½	2·30	7 6½

Appendix 14: *Pre-Ski Exercises and Dry Ski-ing Classes*

Many shops, stores, and travel agencies usually run pre-ski
exercises and dry ski-ing classes, and these are held in many
different parts of London. The following usually organize these
classes and it is advisable to telephone to ask for particulars as to
where and when.

World Sport & Travel (Lairdways Ltd)	BEL 6361
Erna Low Travel Agency	KEN 0911

If you patronize other travel agents a ring on the telephone
will tell you if and where they have pre-ski arrangements. The
shops most actively concerned are:

Gordon Lowe Sports Ltd	KEN 4494
Harrods Ltd (The Lotti Smith Ski School)	SLO 1234
Jackson & Warr Ltd	CHA 6996
Lillywhites Ltd	WHI 3181
Moss Bros Ltd	COV 4567
Pindisports	CHA 3278
Simpsons (Piccadilly) Ltd	REG 2002

*

Dry ski training is organized by the Central Council of Physical
Recreation in cooperation with the Ski Club of Great Britain
and this training is open to anyone who wishes to prepare for a
ski-ing holiday. Local centres are organized by the regional
offices of the C.C.P.R. and information about classes in any
particular area can be supplied by the appropriate office. The
address of the headquarters is:

The Central Council of Physical Recreation	
6 Bedford Square, WC1	MUS 0726

C.C.P.R. REGIONAL OFFICES

North-East (Co. Durham, Northumberland, North Riding of
Yorkshire)

40 Saddler Street, Durham City	Durham 2772

Yorkshire (East and West Riding)

4 Albion Street, Leeds	Leeds 21320

North Midlands (Derbyshire, Leicestershire, Lincolnshire, Northants, Nottinghamshire, Rutland, and Soke of Peterborough)

Bank Chambers, 125 St Ann's Well Road, Nottingham

Nottingham 53882

East (Bedfordshire, Cambridgeshire, Essex, Hertfordshire, Huntingdonshire, Norfolk, East and West Suffolk)

Association Buildings, Harpur Street, Bedford   Bedford 61045

London and South-East (Middlesex, Kent, Surrey, East and West Sussex)

6 Bedford Square, London WC1   MUSeum 0726/9

South (Berkshire, Buckinghamshire, Hampshire, Isle of Wight, Oxfordshire)

Watlington House, Watlington Street, Reading   Reading 2342

South-West (Somerset, Devon, Cornwall, Dorset, Wiltshire, Gloucestershire)

29 Market Street, Crewkerne   Crewkerne 448

West Midlands (Warwickshire, Staffordshire, Worcestershire, Shropshire, Herefordshire)

10 Edmund Street, Birmingham 3   Birmingham Central 1154

North-West (Lancashire, Cheshire, Cumberland, Westmorland)

2 Mount Street, Manchester 2   Manchester Blackfriars 9573

Wales

18 Windsor Place, Cardiff   Cardiff 31814

Northern Ireland

45 Arthur Street, Belfast   Belfast 29387/8

Appendix 15: *Specialist Travel Agencies*

When selecting a travel agency to make your arrangements for your ski-ing holiday – whether for travel tickets and/or hotel booking only, or for inclusion in any all-in-party arrangements – *always go to a well-established organization that has long specialized in winter sports.*

Winter sports holiday arrangements require specialized and personal knowledge of ski facilities and ski centres in the Alps, and many a hopeful holidaymaker has suffered disappointment through placing his affairs in the hands of agencies without knowledge.

Among the many agencies in London that claim all the
necessary qualifications are:

Ashton & Mitchell Ltd	MAY 7222
(All Depts) 166 Piccadilly, W1	
Bell, Denys & Susan	AMB 5521
33 Southwick Street, W2	
Continental Transport Co. Ltd	COV 2021
357 Strand, WC2	
Cook, Thos., & Son Ltd	GRO 4000
(Head Office) 45 Berkeley Street, W1	
Erna Low Travel Service Ltd	KEN 0911
47 Old Brompton Road, SW7	
Frames Tours Ltd	EUS 3488
(Chief Office) 25 Tavistock Place, WC1	
Ingham, F. & W., Ltd	MAY 9885
26 Old Bond Street, W1	
Lunn, Sir Henry, Ltd	AMB 7777
Marble Arch House, 39 Edgware Road, W2	
Polytravel Ltd	GER 6979
(Head Office) 73 Oxford Street, W1	
Swan Tours (Overseas) Ltd	LAN 4901
260 Tottenham Court Road, W1	
Wayfarers Travel Agency Ltd	LAN 8222
20 Russell Square, WC1	
World Sport & Travel Service (Lairdways Ltd) BEL 6361	
198/9 Sloane Street, SW1	

Appendix 16: *Ski Clothing and Equipment Shops and Stores*

Since ski-ing has become so popular and so fashionable, most
department stores now have a winter-sports department which
deals in ski clothing.

There are of course several famous stores and shops which deal
with both clothing and equipment, and, in most of these there
is a winter-sports and ski-equipment expert to advise both the
knowledgeable and the ignorant. So far as equipment is concerned this expert advice is essential.

Among the various possibilities the following shops in London
are obviously the answer both for those who know their own
minds and for those who don't:

Gordon Lowe Sports Ltd   KEN 4494
23 Brompton Arcade, SW1
(Clothing, equipment, and hire)

Harrods Ltd   SLO 1234
Knightsbridge, SW1
(Clothing and equipment)

Jackson & Warr Ltd   CHA 6996
33 Ludgate Hill, EC4
(Clothing, equipment, and hire of boots)

Lillywhites Ltd   WHI 3181
Piccadilly Circus, SW1
196 Sloane Street, SW1   BEL 6406
(Clothing and equipment; boot hire at Piccadilly branch)

Moss Bros. Ltd   COV 4567
Covent Garden, WC2
(Clothing and equipment, hire of clothes and boots)

Pindisports   CHA 3278
14 Holborn, EC2
(Clothing and equipment)

Simpson (Piccadilly) Ltd   REG 2002
Piccadilly, W1
(Clothing and equipment, hire of ski, sticks, and boots)

The following stock ski clothes only:

Jaeger Co.'s Shops:
Jaeger House, 204 Regent Street, W1   REG 4050
191 Sloane Street, SW1   BEL 2505

Benjamin Edgington Ltd
144 Shaftesbury Avenue, WC2   COV 0541
2a Eastcheap, EC3   MAN 0814

Bourne & Hollingsworth Ltd   MUS 1515
Oxford Street, W1

Derry & Toms Ltd   WES 8181
Kensington High Street, W8

Selfridges Ltd   MAY 1234
Oxford Street, W1

Swan & Edgar Ltd   REG 1616
Piccadilly Circus, W1

Many of the above shops and stores also have branches in the
provinces

Appendix 17: *Glossary of Ski-ing Terms*

German is spoken the most in Alpine ski-ing centres (in Switzerland, Austria, the ex-Süd-Tyrol in Italy, and in Germany itself). French is spoken in French-speaking Switzerland and France. Skiers frequently use words, almost internationally, from both languages. An understanding of some of these will assist the uninitiated in the reading of this book and serve good purpose when ski-ing in the Alps.

(*G*) German; (*F*) French; (*I*) Italian; (*E*) English.

Abfahrt (*G*), *Descente* (*F*), *Discesa* (*I*).
   Downhill. A downhill ski run.
Anfänger (*G*), *Débutantes* (*F*), *Principianti* (*I*).
   Beginners.
Anorak (*G*), *Cagoule* (*F*).
   Windjacket.
Alm, *Alp* (*G*).
   Mountain pastures on medium slopes below rocky mountainside proper.
Achtung! (*G*), *Attention!* (*F*), *Attenzione!* and *Pista!* (*I*).
   Look out!
Bach (*G*), *Rivière* (*F*), *Torrente* (*I*).
   Stream, brook, rivulet.
Bahn (*G*), *Chemin* (*F*), *Via* (*I*).
   Line. Railway line. Way.
Bahnhof (*G*), *Gare* (*F*), *Stazione* (*I*).
   Railway station.
Bindungen (*G*), *Fixations* (*F*), *Atacchi* (*I*).
   Bindings. Devices (either cable, thong, or safety release) for attaching the ski boot to the ski.
'*Bird's-nesting*'.
   Exploratory ski-ing away from *pistes*. Often in slightly eccentric, tortuous places involving wood running.
Boden (*G*), *Fond* (*F*).
   Floor. A flat place or area.
'*Bumbag*' (*E*), '*Banane*' (*F*).
   Small, but very convenient, form of rucksack built into a belt and worn round the waist.
Büel (*G*), *Colline* (*F*).
   Hill.

'Combined' (E), *Combiné* (F).

Classified results obtained from the results of two or more events in a ski race meeting.

Cable-car (E), *Luftseilbahn* (G), *Téléférique* (F), *Teleferica* (I).

General term for overhead suspension transport. Generally applied to alternating cabins capable of holding anything from 10 to 60 or more persons.

Chairlift (E), *Sesselbahn* (G), *Télésiège* (F), *Seggiovia* (I).

Overhead suspension transport involving single or double chairs either facing forwards or sideways. Generally open but sometimes provided with canvas shelter.

'Christiania'.

A flowing turn or a stop turn on skis. Of Norwegian origin, used internationally.

Dorf (G), *Village* (F), *Villaggio* (I).

Village.

Egg (G).

Corner. Angle.

Firn Schnee (G), *Névé* (F), *Spring Snow* (E).

A granulated or wet condition resulting from a hard-frozen snow surface having its upper layer slightly or considerably thawed by the action of the sun. Can produce excellent ski conditions. Also refers to snow on the glaciers from the preceeding year or years.

FIS

The initial letters of the international governing body for competitive ski-ing, Fédération Internationale du Ski. Often used to indicate a difficult ski run previously used for an international downhill race.

Fluh (G), *Rocher* (F).

Precipice.

Fall Line.

Straight down the line of greatest slope on any hillside.

Föhn.

Warm wind in the Alps – generally from the south. Can produce serious thaw condition and spoil snow for ski-ing.

Funicular.

Mountain railway.

Gebiet (G), *Région* (F), *Regione* (I).

Area. *Ski Gebiet* = Ski Country.

Gefahr (G), *Danger* (F), *Pericolo* (I).

Danger.

Gesperrt (G), *Fermé, Barré* (F), *Chiuso* (I).
Shut. Closed. Not to be used.

Gipfel (G), *Sommet* (F), *Vetta* (I).
Peak. Summit. Also *Spitze, Kogel, Kopf, Horn* (G) – *Dent, Aiguille, Pointe*, etc. (F) – *Piz, Monte*, and *Cima* (I).

Giant Slalom (E), *Riesen Slalom* (G), *Slalom Géant* (F).
Race that is half downhill – half slalom. A controlled downhill race.

Gondelbahn (G), *Télécabines* (F).
Overhead suspension transport provided with series of small enclosed cabins – 'bubbles' or gondolas – for one, two, or four persons. Enclosed chairlifts made of metal, plastic, perspex, etc. Probably most comfortable form of uphill travel.

Gletscher – also *Kees* or *Ferner* (G), *Glacier* (F), *Ghiacciaio* (I).
Glacier.

Grat (G), *Arête* (F), *Cresta* (I).
Ridge.

Hang (G), *Pente* (F), *Pendio* or *Campo* (I).
Slope.

Hütte (G), *Cabane* (F), *Rifugio* (I).
Hut. Mountain Hut. Shelter.

Joch (G), *Col* (F), *Colle* (I).
Saddle. Pass. Neck between two peaks.

'*Kanone*' (Slang G), *Champion* (F), *Asso* (I).
A ski expert.

'*Kanonenrohr*' (G).
Lit. 'A gunbarrel'. Refers to steep, narrow sections of race-courses which only 'Kanonen' (expert racers) attempt to run straight.

Langlauf (G), *Course de Fond* (F), *Gara di Fondo* (I).
'Long run', indicating a cross-country run or race.

Luftseilbahn (G).
See Cable-car.

Lawine (G), *Avalanche* (F), *Valanga* (I).
Avalanche. '*Lawinengefahr*' = 'Danger from avalanche'.

Luge.
Toboggan.

Lehrer (G), *Moniteur* (F), *Maestro* (I).
Teacher. Ski-teacher.

Mäder (G), *Champs* (F), *Campi* (I).
Alpine meadows.

Mulde (*G*), *Goulet* (*F*).
 A gulley or dip or hollow.

Offen (*G*), *Ouvert* (*F*), *Aperto* (*I*).
 Open.

Piste (*F*), *Pista* or *Discesa* (*I*).
 An 'international' word meaning 'track'. A marked and/or well-beaten ski run. Snow is 'pisted' when it has been much used and is beaten down to a hard surface.

Pulver (*G*), *Poudreuse* (*F*).
 Powder snow.

Sammelplatz (*G*), *Place de Rassemblement* (*F*), *Punto di Raduno* (*I*).
 Meeting place – i.e. for ski-school classes.

Safety Binding (*E*), *Sicherheitsbindung* (*G*), *Fixation de Sécurité* (*F*), *Attacchi de Sicurezza* (*I*).

'*Schuss*'.
 International for a straight run on skis. Generally down a long steep slope. A fast, straight track down the Fall Line.

Schlepplift (*G*), *Remonte Pente* (*F*), *Sciovia* (*I*).
 A ski hoist or ski-lift.

Schwung (*G*), *Virage* (*F*), *Virata* (*I*).
 A swing or turn on skis.

See (*G*), *Lac* (*F*), *Lago* (*I*).
 Lake.

Serac (*F*).
 Large block or tower of ice formed by the various combined and constant movements of a glacier. An icefall is caused by seracs tumbling as a glacier moves over convex ground or over precipices.

Sesselbahn (*G*).
 See Chairlift.

Slalom.
 International word for a ski competition, a race against the clock down a prepared course between flagged 'gates'.

Ski School (*E*), *École de Ski* (*F*), *Scuola de Sci* (*I*), *Ski-Schule* (*G*).

Skins (*E*), *Felle* (*G*), *Peau de Phoque* (*F*), *Pelli di Foca* (*I*).
 Long strips of material, originally seal-skin, attached to the running surface of skis to assist climbing. Used in ski touring and ski mountaineering.

S.C.G.B.
 The Ski Club of Great Britain.

Strasse (G), Route (F), Strada (I).
Road. Route.

Steilhang (G), Pente Raide or *Mur (F), Pendio Rapido (I).*
A very steep slope.

Stem (G and E), Chasse-Neige (F), Caccianeve (I).
A position adopted on skis to brake forward motion.

Tal (G), Vallon, Vallée (F), Vallata (I).
Valley. *Täli (G)* is a small valley.

Téléférique.
See Cable-car.

Télébenne.
Overhead suspension transport using open 'buckets' in which one or two persons stand.

Tobel (G).
Gorge or gully.

Übungsplatz (G).
Beginners or 'Nursery' Slopes. Practice slopes.

U.N.C.M.
Union Nationale des Centres de Montagne. A French Student and Youth Organization with accommodation in its own buildings.

Vorlage (G), Avancée (F).
A forward position when running. Essential to good ski technique.

Vorlage-Hosen (G), Fuseau (F).
Ski trousers so tailored that they taper neatly and tidily down to the boot.

Wald (G), Forêt (F), Foresta (I).
Forest. Thick wood.

Wang (G), Mur or *Paroi (F).*
A wall. Rock precipice.

Wasserscheide (G), Ligne de Partage des Eaux (F), Sparti-Acqua (I).
Watershed.

'Wedeln' (G), 'Godille' (F).
Lit. 'Tailwagging'. A technique of modern ski movement. Continuous, tightly-linked rhythmic half-turns directly down the fall time.

Weg (G), Sentier (F), Sentiero (I).
Way. Path.

Wiesen (G), Prés (F).
Meadows.

Ziel (G).

The finishing posts of a race.

For terms of Ski Movement, see also The Sequence of Tuition (p. 68).

INDEX

Praise for Juan Goytisolo

"Juan Goytisolo is one of the most rigorous and original contemporary writers. His books are a strange mixture of pitiless autobiography, the debunking of mythologies and conformist fetishes, passionate exploration of the periphery of the West and audacious linguistic experiment" Mario Vargas Llosa

"Goytisolo strives for a unity of politics and form, trapping his readers and characters alike in an epistemological purgatory" Village Voice, Top 25 Books of the Year

"Goytisolo's extraordinary lyrical and imaginative gifts are simultaneously forceful and beguiling, and the only response is to give in to the tumultuous, hallucinatory voices" Observer

"Fantastically imaginative and intensely moral" Scotsman

"Bold, exuberant, provocative and a joyously original alternative to the shelves of conventional contemporary fiction" The Times

"A beautifully written metaphor for what it means to seek out the truth in a world often dominated by lies... The Garden of Secrets reminds us that this author, now 70 years of age, is one of the most brilliant of living writers" Los Angeles Times

"He writes with a searing intellectualism, and this makes his work linguistically intense and rather unnerving. Labyrinthine, complex and dense, State of Siege is frighteningly wonderful and is a book of real literary stature" Leeds Guide

"Juan Goytisolo is by some distance the most important living novelist from Spain... and Marks of Identity is undoubtedly his most important novel, some would say the most significant work by a Spanish writer since 1939, a truly historic milestone" Guardian

"Literary fiction at its best, with a message for life" Good Book Guide

"A passionate dialogue with the reader, a reflection on privacy and commitment... a great literary voice" Le Monde

"Full of skilfully deployed devices – script, poems, reports, unbroken blocks of prose, thoughts interrupted by italicised conversation snippets – this solid, landmark novel, banned in Spain, is amongst the last century's finest" Insight

With the support of the
Culture 2000 programme of the
European Union

Education and Culture

Culture 2000

Born in Barcelona in 1931, **Juan Goytisolo** is Spain's
greatest living writer. A bitter opponent of the Franco
regime, his early novels were banned in Fascist Spain.
In 1956, he moved to Paris where he lived until 1996
when his wife, the writer Monique Lange, died. He
currently lives in Marrakesh and chairs the UNESCO
Committee for the Defence of Non-Material Culture.

Other books by Juan Goytisolo published by Serpent's
Tail: *Landscapes After the Battle, Makbara, The Virtues of
the Solitary Bird,* his trilogy *Marks of Identity, Count
Julian, Juan the Landless,* as well as *The Garden of
Secrets, State of Siege,* and *A Cock-Eyed Comedy.*

•» THE BLIND RIDER •»

JUAN GOYTISOLO

Translated by Peter Bush

The crushed thistle I saw in the middle of the countryside reminded me of this death.

Leo Tolstoy, *Hadje Murad*

I

He hadn't slept for months. The pills he'd taken regularly for some time now made no impact, not even when he tripled the dosage. His friend the chemist had warned against the dangers of addiction and the damaging consequences it could have for his memory. He thought quite the opposite: amnesia might help him over the hump. He'd tried combining sleeping pills with physical exercise: he would go for a stroll, walk nightly through the embers of life in the square and return home exhausted. But this therapy didn't work either. He collapsed on his bed, tossed and turned till day cruelly dawned.

Another misfortune then beset him. As he dozed lightly, tunes and ditties infested his brain. Not, as one would have expected, the favourite pieces he'd listen to with her after dinner – Schubert sonatas, *Don Giovanni*, Mozart's *Masonic Ode*, Verdi operas, Brahms'

3

Requiem, but martial airs or saccharin melodies the
radio broadcast the year the war ended and he, his
father and siblings returned to the city of his birth. He
was plunged into the muck of that distant era as if
someone had suddenly opened the lock-gates to a dam
and the putrid waters swollen by a sinister
conjunction of oppression and poverty sloshed over
him: the hymns of the Falange and Carlist *requetés*, the
Marianist version of the Royal March, that favourite
40s song *Rascayú*, the tinny, tawdry voice of Rina Celi.
Like the tide washing up seaweed and other kinds of
marine flora with all manner of rubbish and
pollutants which then pile up on the sandbar, the
repeated, lapping waves of lines and lyrics as absurd as
they were vacuous swamped his mind: the radio
patter for Café Columba and La Miranda, the
wonderful housing complex of La Miranda; the list of
pupils in his first form at school; the line-up for the
city's main football club as learned from the lips of his
elder brother. However much he tried, he couldn't get
rid of them.

That regression to a childhood he thought definitively buried dismayed him. The tunes unexpectedly invaded his mind and would not let go. One day it was the fascist *Cara al sol*, another the Carlist *Oriamendi*, and the next the hymn of the Foreign Legion. There was no way he could silence their persistent buzz. He tried to repel them like insects, but they returned stubbornly to the fray, banging away.

Were these the first symptoms of senile dementia? Sometimes he thought they were, and fatalism took over. But what mysterious relationship existed between his loss and those years of vertical salutes and imperial language, of the *Führer*'s lightning victories and religious fever in the school of the Fathers? Was that incomprehensible retreat into childhood, to its symbols and reference points, partly a strategy to conceal his misfortune, partly a secret ruse for survival? If not, how to explain this programmed persecution by loathsome ballads and vile tales of old?

A conversation with her best friend, on one of his rare trips to the world closed off by her departure, helped clarify the link which existed between the two experiences of abandon: the abrupt interruption in his emotional life had brought to the surface of consciousness the reality of his mother's death hidden away half a century ago. To assuage the pain of the recent wound, he concluded, he should re-visit that older scar.

The house smelt of death: of his and everyone else's. One day, the patio floor greeted the dawn covered in butterflies and libellulas, victims of a mysterious epidemic. On another, it was the corpse of a bird from the large flock which settled at nightfall on the branches of the orange trees. Before that, one of his tortoises had died: the ants scurrying in the corner where it used to retire alerted him, and the discovery of its definitive acquiescence struck him as strange. He thought chelonians lived for more than a hundred years, that the duo would survive him. Now only the widower remained, and perhaps inconsolable at that: he avoided the spot where his partner died and ate his daily ration of greenery and fruit peel reluctantly. He thought it might be a good move to mate him again, but decided to postpone that until after the period of mourning.

The discovery of the sex of the deceased was belated and by chance. He had lived with her for several years in blissful ignorance when one day, at the wheel of his dumpy car, he spotted another in the middle of the road, on the city outskirts. On an impulse, he braked, got out and grabbed him. Once home, the newcomer approached his pet and, without any pretence at foreplay, assailed her and drove her into a corner. The ceremonial copulation was deeply impressive: the stranger repeatedly assaulted the female carapace, tried to mount her and, when frustrated, fell back, before renewing his attack. His *machista* behaviour would have riled you, he later told his wife on the phone. It seemed a *sui generis* version of porno videos filmed in Amsterdam. You should have refused him hospitality, she laughed, if my women friends find out, they'll skin you alive! Don't say a word to them, he said, I'll educate him and hope he'll act more like a gentleman in future. But no opportunity for improvement presented itself: there was no second coupling. The female tortoise laid an egg which she buried in the earth around one of the orange trees. Unexpectedly, the egg went rotten. That seemed to discourage the father and subsequently the couple had co-existed peacefully without further union. When she came from Europe and they spent a few days together, she noticed the progress made and complimented him on his pedagogical gifts. Happiness seemed to reign for some time. Winter lethargy followed the voracity of summer. Several years passed and the day the tortoise died, she was no longer there to tell.

Then, as if in a bad patch, there was a succession of deaths and disappearances: of the pigeon found on the terrace roof, of his favourite cat in the alleyway, of the stork who came and went. The house fell sick as well: pipes burst and cracks on walls and ceilings multiplied. He was disheartened by the convergence of signs. Was there a secret correspondence between his own wasting and that of the space in which he dwelt?

He was sure only of one thing: the shadows thickened and, in inverse proportion, matter was fading.

He compared his life, what was left of his life, to a bicycle wheel whose external propulsion is losing impetus and energy: the seasons and sorties – his, not the wheel's – got slower and more spaced out. It was a real effort to get out of the armchair where he normally read the papers, to climb the stairs to the terrace, to go for his daily walk in the square and listen to his friends conversing. His ability to hear had diminished, particularly the high registers. He heard, but didn't understand, the voices of little kids. That loss grieved him, for he felt an obscure need to communicate with them. His doctor had warned: first you will stop understanding soundtracks in foreign languages, poorly-articulated dialogues and sentences; then the opaqueness will spread to conversations held in noisy places which hustle and bustle. Moreover you're from a family of deaf people. I advise you to buy a hearing-aid: if you get used to it and follow the lips of the people talking to you it will be easier to grasp what they're saying. But he wasn't sure he wanted to: the familiar hum of the café regulars was enough for him. She had pointed this out to him long, long ago: this deafness suits you, you can live ever more enclosed within yourself. One could say that everyone, myself included, are always interrupting something. Yes, we keep distracting you.

His neighbour distracted him? Sometimes he thought he did: that he severed the now tenuous, meandering thread of his ideas. What he didn't know was whether these were currently worth very much. He'd begun to withdraw from the world, no doubt about that: he glimpsed that in the looks, the respect and interest of those around him. Initially he felt hurt: he wasn't old yet, something he needed to prove to himself and to everyone else. He tried to quicken his pace, straight-backed and fearless amid the tricky traffic in the streets around the square or the rush of cars and carts. Later he abandoned such futile rearguard action. He was like the plants on his patio which turned green and flowered, only to droop and yellow. But the gardener came every year to prune them and, suddenly, they perked up, greened again. If plants could, why not human beings? It was an infantile, ridiculous comparison which nevertheless haunted him. He established and compared the growth periods of the climbing plants and the potted shrubs on his patio. Each organism lived its cycle, whether long or short, then died. Only the animal and vegetable species didn't know they were dying and his – the inhuman – did. He was tormented by the idea of leaving the world, not the natural business of leaving it, but because he would depart before extracting a possible meaning: so-called experience had alienated him from life and its rhythms, his thirst for knowledge had led to an unlearning of all wisdom and certainties. All that remained of him was the shadow projected from the window of a train hurtling towards an unknown destination.

There was a before and after. That of the child suddenly deprived of his mother's warmth and that of the old man who blocked out the news and survived despite himself in the ruins of the building she constructed, without entirely admitting that he too was dead.

The old beggar sang and leaned on his stick. He shuffled a centimetre at a time through the lingering or heaving crowd and nobody thought to measure his slowness. He watched him, from the stool that belonged to his friend the bookseller. Conversation with the latter, a sip of water or tea, a tiny incident in the street or a bottleneck provoked by the Mercedes owned by a pig-faced bourgeois, distracted him from his observations, and when he stared again at the old man he had progressed barely a metre. How long would he need to cover the distance to the square?

Did he live nearby or must he cross the swell of voices, noises and cries, without a single friendly hand to gently guide his forearm? For that's how he advanced, almost imperceptibly, towards a certain, if elusive destiny. He didn't know whether he would reach the terminal glory of the square. If the One or Mephisto knew, they made very sure they didn't let on. When several minutes later the old man disappeared from his field of vision, he realised he hadn't helped him. He'd thought of doing so but had stayed on his stool. The One or Mephisto would laugh at him: at the total futility of his gesture. He was surrounded by believers and left the – scientific or philosophical? – debate for another afternoon.

How to interpret her boundless vitality, loyalty towards her friends, love for beaches and the sun, mania for collecting mirrors, ashtrays, paperweights and all manner of curios, whether beautiful or in bad taste, except as an attempt to spread pebbles to signal her presence throughout the journey inexorably leading her to the extinction of herself, at the end of a brief, intense sleep?

The terrain shared when they first met had shrunk with the passage of time. One day he could no longer stand the sun and definitively abandoned the beaches, first on the Mediterranean and then in Brittany. Ever since she'd swum alone with her hats, books, notebooks, towels, rush-mats, and he'd just meet her at lunchtime and accompany her to their hotel.

Their previous social life had contracted as well. Guests for dinner were few, almost always the same people. Both worked at different times and when she went to the cinema with one of her friends, he'd go for a stroll in the neighbourhood or take the metro to his favourite cruising grounds, around Barbès or the Gare du Nord.

The brutal, abrupt blow of destiny threw a shadow over all that: he saw once more the dead parks, the ruined walls, the trees shot to pieces, a woman's black hat and a solitary woollen bootee lying in the mud. There was nothing left to hold on to, not even the memory. Whoever thought up the wretched idea of measuring time and subjecting lives to the derisory tyranny of a clock?

Like ballast which hot-air balloons shed at a given moment in order to pursue their airborne journey, he suddenly felt the need to cast out not what was unnecessary – as he'd already done on his thirtieth birthday – but something more intimate and painful, like the pastimes they shared together. The greater his detachment from their things, the more he could rid himself of his memories, the easier it would be, he thought, to bid farewell to the world and leave with only what he wore.

The cinema was one of their common haunts. She used to go daily to the first matinée show and he'd accompany her once or twice a week. When they didn't walk to one of the now scant local cinemas, they caught a bus to the Champs Elysées or as far as Montparnasse. He remembered the enthusiasm she showed for the films of Losey and Fellini, her

criticisms of Bergman and Resnais. The cinema
ceremonial – entering as if it were a church, getting
comfortable in their seats and filling the waiting time
by leafing through the film programme – was
inconceivable without her presence. They had seen an
Iranian film, the rigour and austerity of which
reminded them of Rossellini's first films, and that was
the full stop. A whole fragment of his life was lopped
off irremediably: an area of light henceforth forbidden.
He thought it cruel, almost sacrilegious, to immerse
himself in the penumbra alone or with anyone else,
however close they were. When the flat was shut up,
he distributed their entire collection of videos
amongst their friends. It was like having a limb
amputated, but he felt better after this dispossession.
The same happened with their music. Although they
never set foot in the Opéra or in concert halls, they'd
assembled a fine set of CDs which allowed them to
choose their favourite music after dinner. Her range
was broader and less repetitive than his. The human
voice, especially the soprano voice, summed up her

conception of artistic bliss and in the end her passion infected him. They would listen to their favourite recordings of Mozart and Verdi, reading or chatting until they felt sleepy and, after returning the disks to their slots, each retired to their respective bedroom.

When he was left by himself, he hesitated a long time before being separated from them. They were an integral part of their life. Nevertheless, he decided to do without that slice of happiness. More ballast was cast into the void with a mixture of relief and pain. His precarious state required greater lightness. If he looked back, existence was reduced to a series of severings from all he illusorily thought he possessed. Nothing, absolutely nothing of the goods or ideas he had inherited remained. There was no continuity at all between his past as a child, youth and adult and the tired body he now reluctantly adapted to. His name and surnames hardly identified him. He was no longer himself. Or only superficially. After she was gone, everything shrank.

When he watched the children on their way to school, rucksacks stuffed with books and exercise-books, or racing each other on their bikes in the shade of the orange trees, he tried to imagine what had been definitively buried in his childhood. Playing and quarrelling with his brothers and sister, gradual awareness of the world from the perspective of home and family. All erased however much he racked his memory. He never saw himself in his mother's arms. Only images of the woman who disappeared which were not directly related to him. The older children were about his age when he stopped seeing her and the amnesia programmed by his infant brain seemed cruel and unjust. Why condemn to non-existence the single period of absolute surrender, of ephemeral, yet total bliss? Those children he had adopted to placate the void were his last defence against imminent expiry. Would the intensity of feelings, the impulsive expressions of affection they daily bestowed also fade from their minds? He found it difficult to accept the overwhelming evidence that they would.

He decided to photograph them and be photographed in their company during the holidays or when they went away, when they wore their school uniforms or on fiestas and birthdays. That way, he thought, self-deceivingly, they'd later recognise him, the day after he'd abandoned the scene. The snapshots of happy faces and gleeful expressions piled up on the small shelf in his study next to those of other beloved people who'd been brutally obliterated. Now he was the only one able to identify them. When he in turn was eclipsed, none of those around him would recognise them. To make what was once never to have been belonged not to the powers of God, but to oblivion's.

He remembered the time when he'd been inspired by the idea of a chimerical transcendence. Reading Saint John of the Cross had consoled him during another period of anguish. The symptoms of an infection contracted in the Nile Valley resembled those of the pandemic decimating the ranks of his friends and he thought he had been contaminated by the offspring of the angry monsters thirsting after animal lymph which one of them described. He decided not to submit to medical analysis out of fear of a definitive, damning verdict. A deep impulse guided him along the paths of poetry. Didn't the lightness and brilliance of the *Spiritual Canticle* translate perhaps the intuitive experience of an arena alien to logic and the tautologies of argumentation? These were weeks of intense creativity, of corrosive yet fertile anguish. His reasoning was agnostic but his heart resisted being so and sometimes, he thought, one must follow the reasoning of the heart. Despite his natural reserve about himself, those closest to him seemed shocked by the change and his unexpected allegiance to those – beautiful, deceptive? – expressions of spirituality. When the tests he submitted himself to in a local clinic proved negative he felt relieved; however, his entranced reading of the mystics deepened his propensity to hermeticism and distance from all social life. Was his misanthropy a reaction against the comfortable, fairly self-satisfied world which they inhabited? One day she said to him: living with you is like serving an apprenticeship in solitude. I don't know whether I should reproach you or be grateful.

The comment, though expressed gently, almost casually, stirred him. Gradually he put aside his reading and immersed himself in the brutality of the real: travelled to besieged cities, countries at war, to the savage, proud Caucasian landscapes masterfully depicted by Tolstoy. She admired his calm in these difficult days without realising she was the source: if anything happened to him, he thought then, she'd be there to ensure his wishes were followed and to watch over the children's future. He was blindly convinced that he would be the first to depart the scene and was caught unprepared by what happened instead. A future so painstakingly planned collapsed and his vulnerability was translated into another radical change in behaviour: he became possessed by irrational fear of travel, of falling down in the street, of climbing stairs quickly, of suffering a ridiculous traffic accident. His mystical emotions abandoned him. She had passed over to the other side and he felt – first incredulously, then painfully – the raw harshness of her absence. That blow swept away the illusions created by his fervorous reading. He stopped meandering in the future in order to remember the past. His dreams had turned to nightmares. His inner universe had contracted, turned sourer.

Was his life a chain of errors mingled with successes? Or else were these successes merely intervals between one error and another? The evocation of their joint past plunged him into predictable disarray: everything blurred over time. Her diaries and notebooks, with her almost illegible jottings, didn't help him reconstruct the facts. Oblivion was the only true God: its omnipotence belied that of the Creator and his ephemeral offspring.

Their destiny – hers, his, that of every descendant from the Cave – would be the same as the thistle the image of which obsessed Tolstoy, the same stubborn thistle he sought out in the Caucasian mountains. He was travelling in a scrap metal car along the muddy track to Shatoi and caught a glimpse, beneath them, of tanks and vehicles incinerated in an ambush similar to the one set for the Tsar's soldiers a century and a half earlier. He witnessed once more history's stupid repetitions, its obtuse cruelty. There was a magnificent variety of flowers in the Argun valley. Via an interpreter he questioned one of the recruits who stopped them to beg for cigarettes about the plant. He drew a blank and, although he continued to scrutinise in between patrol-points, he didn't spot a single one. The journey to the town's still recent ruins confirmed him in his conviction that he belonged to the most harmful species in the universe. The amputated thistle and its blackened flowers assumed a symbolic value. The blind vehicle which cut them down was the one systematically severing their lives.

The past was reduced to a collection of greyish, desperately still snapshots. As if reproduced on a screen by a slide-projector, ever more faded and unreal as they became lost in time. There was no way of setting right that discontinuity. Was he the spoiled child from pre-war summer holidays or the boy brutally deprived of his mother's love? The reader of history and geography books at home or the one indoctrinated at school in futile credos? The youth pretending to believe and take communion or the one secretly pursued by all kinds of doubt? The artistically-inclined university student or the shame-faced concealer of his own desires?

The projector jammed between images and an avaricious blackness filled the void. His life lacked consistency: actors and bit-players rose up and disappeared in an incoherent procession of silent pictures. He didn't enjoy the gift of granting them speech. Their voices always rang untrue, never matched their gestures and mannerisms. He tried to think of her. He needed to look at snapshots and portrait photos in order to revive her smile and melancholy expression. Were her generosity and warmth as he evoked them, or were they tarnished by memory? Her growing remoteness, the inexorable passage of time, the cruel power of the living compared with the vulnerability of the dead, nourished his bitterness. He resurrected in vain her recorded voice and pursued her in his dreams.

What had he done with her?

He didn't know.

All that was left were letters and the printed page, but he didn't have the energy to immerse himself in a reading of those.

The projector still kept breaking down. The telephone rang inopportunely with voices from beyond the grave. Drums of war, incitement to hatred reached him from afar. Night fell around him and he too was nightfall.

• II •

His father's desire to channel the future of himself and his siblings encompassed also the framework that should surround their lives. He wanted to leave no ends untied: their preparation for the professions – a guarantee for the future – as well as the property they'd inherit and in particular the farm, with its cows, hens, mules, fruit-trees, cork-tree woods, vineyards, fields of maize and vegetable gardens. He encouraged the living hedges of prickly pears, the long-term usefulness of which he always praised: on embankments and the edge of terraces, by the side of paths snaking towards the river-bed, next to stables and in the shadow of eucalyptus trees.

You only had to take a sickle to cut spatula from those already thriving, dib them lightly into the soil and they'd root and grow without need of further attention. They, their children, and their children's children would enjoy them and set off in turn in the morning, in a youthful troop, to pick prickly pears with pincers and devour them on the spot.

He remembered how the overseer trustingly planted fig, cherry and quince-trees close to the house. He also did that with them and his own progeny in mind. Just like the share-croppers who came to offer a beautiful basket of grapes on the eve of the grape harvest.

So much canny precaution had been in vain: the calculations were out, the pious hopes went unfulfilled. Agriculture in the area was a distant memory: innumerable bungalows and second homes now covered the land where old vines and crops once grew. Many woods had been cut down. The ponds and irrigation cisterns no longer existed. Neither he, his brothers or sister, nor their children enjoyed the promised fruits. Time was a blind rider nobody could unsaddle. As he galloped, he ravaged all that seemed enduring, transformed landscapes, reduced dreams to ashes.

His yesterdays were a series of eclipsed scenarios. The houses where he lived as a child and youngster had been demolished or were inhabited by strangers. Although he lacked any attachment to property, and money meant nothing to him if he couldn't share it among friends and his dearest, he felt that loss of the past to be a mutilation. The places where he still roamed in his dreams were now forbidden; if he stepped there, he did so as an intruder.

Although the departure-point was in doubt, the plot developed according to markers that had been carefully laid down: the evidence of constancy and value of a random return to Ithaca. He wanted to reach the farmhouse but, as he thought he was drawing nearer, he was diverted along strange twists and turns that led him away from the place. The tracks he climbed or descended didn't recall those from his childhood. However, the lack of familiar references didn't dissuade him from his task, despite the distressing, abnormal range of hurdles he encountered. He teetered along precipitous inclines, on the edge of the void. Walked in high mountains, ever more distant from the sea. Finally glimpsed snow: but he'd never seen snow in that district enjoying such a benign climate. The suspicious novelty of the phenomenon made him question his efforts: he woke up exhausted, like a real rock-climber.

After her abrupt departure, his dream returned with new variations. He walked the neighbourhood where he'd lived most of his life, a meandering neighbourhood that held no secrets for him: he knew it inch by inch, every hiding place, crevice and cranny. Nevertheless, as he walked on, he went backwards. Retreated, both from himself and the huge city. He looked at it from afar, from a high point (the *Sacré Coeur* or Montparnasse tower). And how could he ever find his abode in that seething mass, in such a vast, disorientating labyrinth? His experience as a beater of shoe-leather and map-reader were no help. He couldn't even locate the river! He discerned strange, perhaps forgotten faces, of people who didn't belong to his circle of friends and dearest: an old salt from Saint Tropez, the owner of a Roscoff hotel. Only later, as he tried to wind back the thread of his nocturnal wandering did he decipher the message: they were places where they'd lived short periods or spent summers together. But she didn't reappear, even momentarily.

On his first summer holidays in the long vanished family house in the country, he'd surprised her with his expertise at identifying the brightest constellations: the Great Bear, the Little Bear, Cassiopea, Orion and the Vega of Lira. Some twenty years earlier, his father (or was it his uncle?) had taught him and his brothers to recognise them, on that same terrace where he relaxed with her after the day's heat and sweat. The whole universe was like a wonderful toy manufactured for his contemplation, was his plaything. Naming the stars was the quickest way to possess and incorporate them in their small realm of bliss.

Now he saw things differently. The stars stared disconcertingly down at him. The magic tracery of constellations gave way to a savage universe of sound and fury, fruit of the dispersal of an infinity of bodies and gases in a continuous process of expansion. The creation was also destruction, a boundless, ferocious violence: stellar explosions, forces of repulsion and attraction, brutal collisions, burning clouds of dust, voracious chasms. From the modest vantage-point of his terrace he imagined the prodigious acceleration of matter: the emergence of *supernovas* generating their own light, myriads of stars coming into being, phantasmagorical filaments of light, elliptical galaxies, embryonic yet already annihilated. The death which had consumed bodies from the day life burgeoned on the planet was a mere reflection of galactic cannibalism, of meteorites voraciously swallowed down by an endless whirling vortex. Wasn't his own existence the fallacious twinkle of an extinct star?

The cold, fury and silence of night wrapped him in their mantle. He lurched back to his youth, to Pascalian doubts and dilemmas aroused by his reading of Kierkegaard. Life wasn't a dream but a hallucination, a hallucination the consistency of which grew with the combination of experience and age. To emerge from that was to relapse into the absurdity of the world: the hallucination persisted, was and would be prolonged, irremediably averse to its offspring in the cycle of repetition, shadow and diaphanous light.

As in the ritual dances of conquest by some species of insect, when males display a brilliant choreography to Bolshoi perfection, the youngest kid, barely three years old, would rush into his study in the morning after heralding his arrival by stamping and shouting up the staircase. He'd push open the leaves of the door and come in dancing a *zapateado*, his dark, twinkling eyes staring at him. Had he seen that dance on the TV or was it the fruit of his imagination? The kid exercised his heart-winning arts so naturally and effortlessly that repetition didn't diminish their charm. His little shoes beat the carpet rhythmically, his tiny hands waved imaginary castanets, his eyes seemed to deepen their sparkle as he advanced towards him. Then he held his arms out and whirled like a top, transformed into a miniscule apprentice dervish. After the third or fourth twist, he fell to the ground and lifted himself up with a smile, sure of his seductive wiles. He wanted the pill, and its soothing magic. He was ill, he lied mischievously, the menthol gragee would instantly restore his health. Hand in hand they walked to the cupboard with shelves piled high with medicine. Eyes shut, mouth open, the child waited for the tablet to be popped onto his tongue. It was like sixty years ago when, kneeling before the priest, he received the sacred host in his local parish church. With or without transubstantiation, the miracle was replicated. The boy's face radiated happiness. He wondered whether the officiant in the mass experienced a similar feeling of joy or whether it was dulled by routine. Curiously, in the kid's mother-tongue, the wafer given out in churches was likewise dubbed the Christian pill – whether magical or medicinal.

Sometimes he furtively slipped into the forbidden space. He knew it no longer belonged to him and that he had thus to proceed stealthily. The peaceful backcloth to summer holidays, first with his father, brothers and sister, later with her and a handful of friends, had suffered a series of mutations which left it almost unrecognisable: a carpark where the attendants waved handkerchiefs to indicate an empty space, stalls with fry-ups and cold drinks, buildings with awnings and barbecues. Wearing the complacent smiles of families who push carts stuffed with all kinds of articles and victuals through Pryca or Carrefour tills, numerous visitors had taken possession of the place. In shorts, T-shirts, straw hats and sunglasses, they noisily paraded round the threshing-floor or terrace, lulled by a crooner or songster's sickly-sweet melody or loathsome lilt.

On one of his forays, he'd managed to tiptoe inside the country house now occupied by strangers and see with his own eyes the extent and irreversibility of the changes. The family furniture had been replaced, his ancestors' portraits no longer hung on the dining-room or corridor walls, the bedrooms had been garishly painted, all reeked of newly acquired, conspicuous wealth. The person accompanying him – identity unknown – advised him to proceed extremely cautiously. A birthday party or dance was being held in the gallery. He attempted to visit the bedroom of his father – lean and sorrowful like the Don Quixote imagined by Doré – but the way in via the back door had been removed. He then noticed the clock on the wall had disappeared, the one which as a child he'd doomed forever by fiddling with its hands: a first, definitive revelation of an innate incompatibility with objects and practical things which made her laugh so. Nor could he see the majestic, carpeted staircases. He didn't dare ask his guide whether the overseer's family was still in place or had also been subject to eviction.

He saw himself half a century ago, in the train which went to the coastal village where the covered trap of the overseer of the vanished family property would be expecting him. Their country house, erected on the site of an ancient *masía*, of which only the door arch remained, made him think retrospectively of Yasnaya Polyana. On his much later visit to the patriarch's museum house he'd been struck by the similarity between the two buildings: that of the rich emigrant who returned from Cuba and was his great-great-grandfather by quirk of fate and that of the writer who, by virtue of reading his novel on that routine journey, became an indispensable link in his future genealogy. Both owned stables, store houses, a chapel, kitchen and quarters for servants and labourers, a strict separation, as by divine law, of serfs and masters. The Catalan emigrant's designs were but a cheap parody of the kind the Russian aristocrat rebelled against internally. The sight of the writer's desk, his lovingly preserved library, the sofa bed where Sophia gave birth to their children, transported him to that emotional moment in the train when he was immersed in his book: the epiphany of a world infinitely more beautiful and attractive than his own, one from which he would not be separated.

War and Peace gave him entry to a different reality where human passions developed naturally, without explicit or implicit moral judgements, in a climate of freedom where good and evil depended on the reader's individual interpretation and not on an intangible and alien code of oppression. Absorbed in the novel's plot, he didn't watch the landscape unfurl through the compartment window: the dirty sea on the outskirts of the city, the spigots defending the coast against its attacks. Years before, on the return journey, the convoy used to brake in order to facilitate the throwing of sacks of flour or vegetables to the raggle-taggle shadows which, in cahoots with the engine-driver, waited to collect the merchandise by the side of the railway track. That poverty and commerce belonged to the past, but access to a more or less decent existence was yet to be complemented by a clearing of lungs or skylights against stifling gloom and general apathy. Literature allowed one to live by proxy. Tolstoy's characters embodied his dreams of a more intense, varied life. It was then he discovered freedom only existed in books.

His incursions into secondhand bookshops and semi-clandestine back counters began there. The multiplying of worlds within reach of his imagination was the prize earned by his voracious reading: an extensive, heterogeneous list where he journeyed from Poe's America to Proust's Normandy, from the ambitions and loves of Julien Sorel to the spiritual exercises of a Dublin adolescent. Literature united and distilled the essence of two childhood passions – history and geography – in a unique arena. Escape was possible without taking a step. The jolting train, its bursts of speed and braking on that short journey,

brought back the image of a redundant existence from
which he wished to escape, and from which one day
he would.

As he reflected and reversed the tape of memory, he saw that the parallel drawn between the family farmhouse of his childhood and the villa he visited in socialism's grimy fatherland was pretentious and naïve. Although both mansions had a chapel, ponds, stables and fruit orchards, obviously in a very different climate, the hybrid Basque and Catalan house lacked both the luxury and refinement introduced by Sophia in Yasnaya Polyana, and the school, which unlike the owner of muzzled blacks, the writer created for his *muhjiks*, in accord with his dreams of universal fraternity. As the deadpan official guide recited, Tolstoy wished to free the serfs and bring up their children in line with progressive, humanist principles, so they would cast off their chains of ignorance and be redeemed by the light of education. But the monochord guide did not add that, like all grandchildren and great-grandchildren of troglodites, the peasants resisted his preaching, clung to their icons and ceremonies, kneeled before wizards with sticks and mitres, abhorred the lethal habit of thought.

He was meditating in the warm sun, a copy of *The Sonata* on his lap, when a voice erupted, someone who laughed as he declared he was both creator and created.

"Do you think there can possibly exist, not some miserable tribe, but a society of the kind you call modern or postmodern without any kind of irrational or fantastic belief? Without a white canopy, brocade mantle, purple chlamys, gold tiara, pontifical sceptre? The peoples, your flocks, wouldn't stand for that. Look where your mentor's utopias and mystic crises ended! His compatriots tried to condemn me to oblivion, only immediately to forge idols as cruel as me, however ephemeral and contingent: the strident, monocled prophet and the despot with the cockroach moustache! Tell me now: what has become of them?

They didn't succeed in replacing me: they were knocked off their pedestals while I continue cool as a cucumber, with my sorcerers blessing the soldiery and sprinkling incense over their massacres. Once again boots crush the thistle. Was so much effort, sacrifice and horror worth it only to come back to the old doghouse? Don't think I'm a megalomaniac if I suggest that, whether malevolent or benign, you need me, and that I won't disappear in the near future. You are a colony of insects where everyone follows his own bent and seeks immediate benefit at the expense of everyone else. The fraternal equality of which some dream is a chimera. You only have one certainty, though you'd prefer not to look it in the face: the equality of the dead which, after death, you won't be the one to behold."

He'd sometimes dwell on his now distant reading about Tolstoy's flight and death. His books had been faithful companions at different stages in life: *War and Peace*, in the city of his birth; *The Kreutzer Sonata* and *Anna Karenina*, in Paris; *Hadje Murad*, in the Caucasian mountains. On his first trip to the defunct fatherland of socialism he accompanied her and her daughter on a visit to the Yasnaya Polyana mansion now converted into a museum. Wearing slippers as leaden as clogs, they visited the rooms where the family gathered and held parties, the vast library with its portrait paintings and encyclopedias, the writer's study, the music-room, the dining-room, the stables and servants' quarters: the whole area of well-being, wealth and unjust privilege Tolstoy had wanted to escape.

The prerogatives of the nobility to which he

belonged hung from his neck like a millstone. His
egalitarian utopias, yearning for poverty, and mystical
crises nourished his claustrophobia in that gilded cage,
kindled his desire to flee. He wished to rid himself of
goods and chattels, to face destiny with only what
was strictly necessary on the last stretch of his
existence. His decision to break with Sophia and his
family circle coincided with a longing to return south,
to the Caucasus mountains where he'd been happy
despite his compatriots' outrages and abuses which he
soberly described in the novel he never saw in print.
To travel to Chechnya with this book was both the
most heartening and disturbing experience on his
journey to cover the nth war of conquest. Not only to
contemplate the cruel repetitions of history through
the writer's eyes, but also to intuit what Tolstoy
sought when he fled the cushioned world of Yasnaya
Polyana like an impetuous youth: the return to the
wooded fastnesses on the way to Vedeno and Shatoi;
the fir and thicket-covered slopes which hid Imam
Shamil's rebels. Perhaps it was his return to the

origins of his writerly vocation that inspired the final hours of his escape, the futile attempt to put Sophia and the ubiquitous blue-jacketed gendarmes off the scent. Death caught him in Astapovo, in the station-master's humble abode, and with a third-class train ticket.

He remembered the night they both listened to *The Kreutzer Sonata*. Neither was addicted to Beethoven but, after reading the novel, they wanted to elicit the keys to his influence on Tolstoy's creation. The idea behind the work, according to the prologue in the edition they consulted, preceded married life with Sophia. Nevertheless, he observed, it seemed to anticipate and describe it precisely. The raptures, disaffections, hatreds, arguments and reconciliations that had as their scenario the mansion in Yasnaya Polyana converged in one real respect: their two opposite characters never blended. The dramatic scenes mentioned in the writer's diary followed on in an inexorable crescendo till the night he could no longer stand the sleeplessness and improvised his horseback escape to the nearby railway station.

She enacted the after dinner musical ritual with

the hi-fi system and the CD of Beethoven's works which accompanied their alternate reading of fragments from the book. They evoked couples close to them whose daily co-existence bore the hallmark of a small hell. Why didn't they make a break once and for all and each go their own way? But perhaps they needed the torture and clung on, as to an ineluctable punishment.

What was the meaning of that work? Had men and women been born to bring hatred and bitterness into each other's lives? She thought not and acted accordingly. She was intrigued by Tolstoy's *Sonata* which she found strange, if not repellent, unlike his great novels.

Perhaps, she said, it was because she was a pagan and refused to believe in hell.

The book of his life lacked a plot: there were only fragments of pages, loose or ill-fitting pieces, outlines of a possible theme. The inconsistency of the drafts allowed for no closure or exemplary glow. The desire to attribute *a posteriori* coherence to disconnected events implied a deception which might work for everyone else but not for him. Was all the effort worth such a scant outcome? He was inclined to think not. Was it so important if his behaviour and ideas risked being wrongly interpreted and, in fact, were? The awkward scribbles or sketches couldn't be transmuted into an elegant composition by a writer on an arts fellowship. He wanted to be neither model nor statue. His attempt to avoid any acceptable definition or morality responded to that wish. His writing left no trails, erased all traces: he wasn't the sum total of his books, but what was subtracted from them. Only the release contract was missing and that would be along soon.

The awareness that he was a mere actor or bit-player of inconsequential scenes restored his good temper. He wrapped up against the cold from the snow-capped mountains and went for a walk. Zigzagged down the twisting alleyway, cut a path between cyclists, cars and calashes, gazed fleetingly at cinema posters with their Hindu beauties and brave *karatekas*, greeted neighbours and customers in the shops, lost himself in the square's hustle and bustle. He held the youngest child's hand, or rather was dragged by him to toy shops or sweet stalls for a cornet of nuts or pistachios; he felt light and happy, as bereft of past as his diminutive guide, nothing mattered now beyond that stroll and the dark little hand clinging to his, the sparkle in the mischievous, endearing eyes, everything converged, was consumed in the present, the old man who hardly recognised himself in the mirror was the one photographed with his brothers and sister in the shadow of the

eucalyptus trees, their mother had absented herself,
they didn't know much about her, or about what they
were leaving behind or what life held in store, but
stood there solemnly, so very solemnly, staring at the
camera, none seemed happy or smiling, thus the
child's smile set by their side lit up the faces in the
photograph, was a final, precious gift he must hold
tight, and afterwards, no afterwards existed any more.

Stretched out on a lounger on his roof terrace, he let the hours pass by, a book between his hands, at times intent on what he was reading, at others distracted by the view of the cityscape offered by his lookout point. The voices and rhythms intensified in the square as the afternoon advanced and acted as his watch.

The gleaming white backdrop of the mountains and silhouette of the great mosque secured a precarious continuity in the face of time's destructive fury. The urban space grew and degenerated: the anarchic proliferation of shanties and lofts created a stratified city, hid gazes, and reflected the unstoppable increase in population. The forest of bare, vertical aerials was now joined by a disconcerting spread of white, round, poisonous mushroom satellite discs. Why did people persist in procreating and cramming that planet of dwindling resources? Didn't they realise the illusory desire for survival was the origin of fresh disasters, that the way of the world was leading to its ruin? What enlightened despot would finally summon up the courage and honesty to state this categorically and sterilise all his subjects? Perhaps nobody saw death live on the news, the agonising of children ripped to the bone, the corpses piled in common graves, the pools of the victims' still warm blood? Perhaps genocides and pandemics were the secret weapons of a plot-maker bent on alleviating the consequences of his rash creativity. Exterminating angels or devils undertook quite unawares a praiseworthy cleansing operation, deserved medals for such civic foresight! If to err is human, to hit true must be the mark of the demiurge. What future did abject children have in accursed countries and continents? Swift's modest proposal was clearly unavoidable. They should feed and fatten the earth's starving children and, once ready for consumption, crystallise and sell them off in the big supermarket chains destined for the masters of the world! That

way natural selection of the species would make up
for the blindness of such futile procreation!

He never tired of scrutinising the mountains, the frontier imposed by their massive, untamed configuration. After visiting the secondhand bookseller he used to converse with of an afternoon, he would often suddenly discover they were almost within reach, stuck to the buildings in Sidi Bulukat. It was an optical illusion reiterated with strange perfection. The white cordillera had apparently advanced like the witches' wood in *Macbeth* till they brushed against the pink-ochre roof terraces of the city. The phenomenon occurred when he was least expecting it, like a grandiose theatrical artifice prepared by an astute scenographer. The mountains were his horizon, his wall: the boundary of a remote, tantalising world, with a magnetic pull that responded to his confused desire to escape.

Many travellers have left evidence of the

impressions made by the majestic landscape, but his were different. From his look-out post he took in the huge extension of the mountain ranges, the ruggedness, narrow haunches, sinuous outline of peaks, the sharpness of edges burnt by the sun. The space separating them recalled the coloured illustrations in childhood geography books: the move from the print with palm trees and spare, semi-desert vegetation to the print of a Mediterranean basin of olive groves and reddish earth, upon which forests of firs were unexpectedly to erupt, as on an unlikely Alpine vista. The rapidity of the changes created an unreal effect of connection and concentration; sometimes, on rare excursions into the countryside by car, he felt he'd visited a theme park.

The beauty of contrasts deepened as dusk fell. The sky was bluer, the snow whiter and the cypresses and buildings poking hungrily out above the city seemed to absorb the last rays of sun. Then, while the half-dark took over the urban arena and storks flew serenely to their nests, the mountains hoarded the light, a dense condensation of light, as in the apotheosis of a diva maximising the power and passion of her art before the imminent curtain-fall.

Then, the view dissolved into the night: outlines blurred, tired street lights preceded by a few minutes the slowly emerging constellations. But the observer still dreamed of the south, of the unkempt territory crouching in the wings, as if lying in wait for his total, absolute surrender.

The children began to burn: like pinheads, their tiny faces carpeted the infinite stretch of space. The number of kids born and killed over millions of years perhaps exceeded the number of meteorites, planets and stars. They belonged to all the races and mixes of the inhuman species he had the misfortune to belong to. The Big Bastard had torched them and, like remote, incandescent galaxies, they twinkled and were never consumed. There was no end to the Gehenna forged by his malicious mind. The slightest peccadillo had to be paid for with an irrevocable sentence. The bodies decomposed and recycled on earth went on to suffer pain and torment in eternity. What distraught, sylvan intellect had forged the notion of the eternal, and how long had this calamitous, rustic invention existed? The first expressions of anguish at expiry gave birth to myths, ceremonies, invocations and sacrifices to the great divided demiurge: the good guy who let things go and turned a blind eye and the bad guy who certainly knew what he was doing. He'd been brought up as a pawn in that malign dichotomy. Without pyres, scaffolds, firing-squads and guillotines, authority on earth would cease to exist; but the manipulators of fear extended it to the afterlife. The violence and wars he witnessed, the stark images of mass graves and extermination camps seemed like child's play compared to those the Soulless One conceived and prosecuted from his hideaway. The victims could be counted in their trillions, from the first paleolithic Homo Erectus to the latest Silicon Valley nerd. No Court of Justice, however, would pass judgement on his holocaust, or even on the crime of not helping the myriads of endangered beings. No matter how bloodthirsty, any tyrant was a benign apprentice by the side of him and his crimes. Children burned like wood shavings; convulsed in horror, their faces belied the seraphic poses of statues and pious prints. The

Soulless One had previously sprinkled them with petrol and they flamed like the flickering candles in the chapels of any provincial capital. He shivered with cold and tried to wrap round himself the patchwork blanket she'd bought him before her final departure.

Had he dozed off as night fell? Scary, incandescent images no longer overlaid the concentration of stars that stood out against the backcloth of opaque matter. The voices of the children playing in the street restored his peace of mind.

He advanced holding a big machete, in the style of those old prints of black Cuban independence fighters lurking in the jungle. He didn't know whether it was himself or a double, or whether a third person (himself?) was peering at the others from a hidden spot. The scene's exuberant foliage recalled landscapes from an imaginary childhood, forged by photogravure prints in the family library. He felt the proximity of the swamp and its lethal snares. The path he cut was muddy and he was afraid of being sucked down. He gasped from fright, not fatigue. He wanted to get to school. Imperceptibly, the vegetation changed, became mountainous and steep. The climate also adjusted to the elements in the new scenario: relentless gusts of wind shook the boughs of trees that looked like firs. Gripping his machete, he continued his murky route along the earthen path to Vedeno or Shatoi. Was he in

Tolstoy's Caucasus, in foothills skirted by a murky, swollen river? The images he glimpses convince him that must be the case. The track is a succession of patrol-points, damp, ramshackle encampments, groups of drunk militia men, nests of machine guns manned by recruits numb with cold, civilians warming their hands around miserable fires. The man with the machete (he can only see the weapon, not who is holding it) has reached the village. There, he (or is it the other fellow?) has just amputated his classmates' arms and legs. The severed limbs lie in the mudbath like dislocated bits of shop dummies. The victims of the mutilation have vanished. A lady's black hat, placed in a round cardboard hatbox with balls of naphthalene, reminds him of the one kept in the wardrobe at home, which disappeared one fine day. The schoolmistress (whose face he can't discern) berates him: How often do I have to tell you that the extremities of animals and human beings don't sprout again like plants! Zoology isn't botany! You've failed natural sciences! Go home right away! He (now he knows it's him) sobs, recounting his misfortune to his family. The father (his father) shouts at him: The schoolmistress is right! No dinner for you tonight! Perhaps that'll teach you not to be so stupid!

The nocturnal film show was interrupted by mechanical failure, or because he suddenly woke up.

It all began in the heart of night: a dull hum emerged, muffled by distance, from an insistent pickaxe or electric drill. Initially he'd wondered whether he was living the prolongation of a nightmare, or if the noise was simply the result of a hearing problem. He waited a few drowsy moments before stretching out his arm and flicking the light-switch. The bulb didn't light up. Had it fused? He got out of bed to switch on the heating and the other lights. Didn't work either. The temperature had plunged cruelly and he shivered with cold. He groped for his slippers and woollen jerkin. The buzz of the drill and blows from the pickaxe had not only not stopped, they now resounded more aggressively. Was it building work next door, as was recently often the case? An absurd idea, for who could dream of working at that time of night, showing such disrespect for their slumbering neighbours? He opened his bedroom door and looked into the gallery. The waning moon was in its fourth quarter and barely illumined the branches of the orange trees and front façade. He tried another switch in vain. The house was in darkness, they'd cut off the electricity. The blows got louder and louder. He tried to find out where they were coming from. Warily he walked down the flight of stairs leading to the guest-room. On the other side of the wall, someone was raging against it. Hammer-blows rained down angrily, threatening its destruction. He thought of going out and asking for help, calling the police. Ridden with anxiety, he found his line had been disconnected. Thick clouds had finally covered the delicate sickle moon, and it was pitch-dark. Who wanted to demolish the house and why? Why did the people dwelling there remain silent, not give any signs of life? He thought of the children, and the urgent need to save them. He shouted to their parents. The house might collapse and bury them under the debris! His anguish mounted. Now the blows came from all sides: from

left and right, from the top floor and from downstairs.
Stressed by the hammer blows and the vibrations
from the drills, he went down to the patio. How could
he make himself heard amid such barbarity? The walls
cracked and yielded to the pressure from the infernal
machines. The children's names filled his mouth. He
shouted and shouted and shouted. Then realised the
loud banging in the tottering house was the unbridled
beating of his own heart.

From Stone Age to Cybernetic Spring, myriads of people had advanced like a huge, slow tide on the cliff's precipice. They walked hand in hand, perhaps to keep up their spirits, though they didn't flinch when recruits from the disciplined battalion of neighbouring or nearby ranks lost their footing and vanished down a voracious hole. An infinite number of children didn't even have time to start their journey. Their tiny bodies were immediately covered by fresh waves of the newly-born. The tide comprised a succession of gentle, almost imbricated waves, the power of which declined in direct proportion to the immediacy of the abyss. Wars, epidemics, famines, decimated their lines and the survivors prudently slowed their pace, aware already of their merciless, mean fate. He could see the flags waved by those who'd sidestepped dangers and traps. Life expectation varied according to the brutal whims of local geography. Those from the Indian subcontinent and sub-Saharan Africa plunged *en masse* into the swirling vortex, never reached the first luminous buoys which subdivided and marked out the various stages. Nobody took pity on them or tried to help. Similarly the economically weak from other areas, lacking initiative and an innate inclination to win out, perished more easily than the scheming bastards and those blessed with good fortune. Natural selection, depending on the character of the society and power of money, regulated the flow of waves. The crowd thinned out with the sixty-plus, particularly the one with those judged to be dispensable because unproductive or excluded because incompetent. After the next line of buoys, as after an obstacle race, many faces faked beams of happiness. The septuagenarians, himself included, absent-mindedly reviewed the newspaper obituary columns, to assure themselves they still existed. It was comforting to exchange comments on the demise of so-and-so or disappearance of such-and-such as they gently travelled on the moving walkway to the cliff. Then they held birthday parties, family or public memorials and homages. Any excuse to toast the sickly, wrinkled skin of some carcass about to become fodder for worms or a feast for vultures. Did they have to prolong that farce to the bitter end? To put on a show as they blew out the candles and chorused that dismal English ditty? He remembered the Californian dames, tarted up like dolls, with head-combs and fans, as they arrived in their limousines, to the Tijuana bull-ring to applaud El Cordobés. Their Antiquities lined up at the barrier, waving and tittering as people did in that era when they still hadn't passed the luminous buoy of the thirties and Tyrone Power and his suit of lights in the ring in *Blood and Sand* drove them ecstastic. Were they trying to delude everyone else or just themselves? Were they still there, miniaturised, among the sparse ranks of nonagenarians, preserved in pots of Ponds cream?

She'd always refused to wear make-up or not look

her age. Had wanted to live and express herself in her notebooks as long as it were possible; as long as her body resisted and lucidity persisted. She swam across the boundaries drawn by the buoys, as on the beaches of the Breton solstice where she bathed, and was swept away by a tornado. The "ever absent" husband he'd been took bitter note of his negligence and lack of foresight. From then on, his universe teetered on the brink. It would soon be his turn to reach the precipice at land's end. He dreamed of Tolstoy's dignified finale in his chimerical escape to the Caucasus. But there was no expiry date and the separating out of his existence, of the world and the universe couldn't be predicted as in a theatre script. The stage curtain of mountains remained in the hands of the scene-changer.

Her clothes were still there. Not the ones she'd left in the flat he had fled, jettisoning everything as if it were an accursed inheritance, but those which lined up on hangers in his wardrobe, the ones she bought on her visits to the ochre-pink city: a dozen or so kaftans she wore at home in order to read, talk or listen to her favourite music, glass of whisky in hand. Should he renounce them as his friends advised or preserve them as they were on her last visit? He looked at the wardrobe, but it wasn't his wardrobe: it was a bigger, more antique and beautiful mahogany item, comprising three sections with mirrors. They had stored on one side his grandmother's garments from the day the family sent her to the sanatorium where months later she was to perish. Her suits and shoes vanished in turn and for a time only a black hat lay among balls of napthalene at the bottom of a cardboard box, the same hat she used to wear when in her senile dementia she meandered aimlessly round the neighbourhood, furtively ferreting in rubbish bins after fruit peel or objects beyond redemption. But the cardboard box also disappeared and the hat – was it his grandmother's, or Anna Karenina's or the one he spotted in the mud in the ruins of Shatoi? – was lost for ever. That absence made more impression on him than death itself. The heart of this little boy gave a turn, his eyes moistened. He suddenly understood what life was: a hole or voracious abyss down which memory plunged.

• IV •

Although he avoided a face-to-face encounter in the shadows of nightfall, did he visit him once he'd crossed over?

"I shall tell you in cruel Castilian: you were born to perpetuate oblivion. Grief at loss abates, memory wanes, feelings and affections lose their strength and intensity. It is the law of the world which I supposedly created and to which you are subject. There is no such thing as an inconsolable child or wife. Those around you will shed some tears over you but your image will dissolve like snow in a glass of water.

You no longer think of her daily and need to look at her photo to bring her to mind. Everything blurs, darkens and is extinguished. It is my only manifestation of goodness. For if those who belong to your incorrigible species enjoyed the power of telling the future, do you think they'd procreate alien children, grandchildren or great-grandchildren whose behaviour and ideas they wouldn't understand and would be appalled by? If the father of the father who begat you could have imagined what you'd turn into and how you'd write about him, there's no doubt he wouldn't have done his duty, he'd have got off the moving train. All you are today would horrify him. That's why I regularly send you off to push up daisies: to spare you the spectacle of a descendency contrary to your dreams…"

The stars weren't still twinkling or were covered in cloud; darkness enveloped him, the patio remained silent and the only sound was a child crying next door, or perhaps on a corner of his side-street. He curled up in the patchwork quilt and let him monologue on.

"You who imagine me blissfully surrounded by my angels and devotees, don't realise it's only the deeds of ill-doers which amuse me. No perversity is alien to me. You are now entertained by televised images of wars, mutilated bodies and the savagery of the soldiery, unaware that I've been enjoying them from the day you conceived me. You are so easily deluded by what your minds concoct!

I know you don't believe in me, but you are powerless before those who do. I exist through them and so it will always be as the centuries clock up.

What I'm saying goes for you and your admired Tolstoy, although he didn't altogether lose his peasant faith: he diluted me into a kind of generic, rather bland entity. Such was his greatness: the intuition or doubt which drew him to the railway station of Astapovo in a third-class train. He wanted to go south, beyond the White Mountains and, in his quest for a coherent end, died before reaching them.

As for you..."

"There are no big differences between you and me. Though you were engendered by a droplet of sperm and I was manufactured by dint of speculation and Councils we both hold something primordial in common: non-existence. We are chimera or spectres dreamed up by something other, call it chance, contingency or caprice. You were still-born and already belong to the kingdom of shadows. I was invented over millennia of Byzantine quarrels and will cease to exist the day the last of your fellows stops believing in me. Each of my imaginary attributes or properties has been the cause of disputes, amendments, clarifications, battles to the death. Am I One, am I a Trinity, am I Merciful? Or a cruel, bloodthirsty monster, an impassive spectator before your evil-doing and outrages? Those who transform me into Supreme Goodness immediately face the problem of the world's merciless brutality. What the devil am I doing up here if I don't stir a finger to halt it? Have I granted myself an interminable holiday or am I blind, insensitive and useless? It is impossible to resolve that contradiction, however much my invention has been perfected over the passage of time. If I am not that furious Being ravaging all he has created in blood and fire, imposing himself through terror on the consciences of his children, what am I? A bland, anaemic phantom, an idea so tenuous it fades into nothingness. In the beginning, when you started to forge my fantastic existence, I was amused by your theories and hypotheses. The nouns defining me, the adjectives fleshing them out, strengthened my substance and its specific weight. I'll be frank with you. The additions and finishing touches to my person fanned my greed, kept me in a state of stressful anxiety. The equilateral triangle with the watchful eye at its centre or the imitation triangular sun adorned with clouds didn't meet my expectations. Why Triple and not Quadruple? Didn't my Son's mother perhaps harbour the requisites of a real Deity? And, if we're into dreams, why couldn't I, the Dreamèd, be a Hexagon or, better still, a Decahedron with as many faces and corners as the commandments sculpted on the Tablets of Law that I handed to Moses? I could see myself as a prismatic, crystalline block, like the eyes of flies able to examine things and beings from different angles. I will confess to you my envy of pagan gods: they had limited competencies, but lived their passions and hatreds to the full, did not take themselves too seriously, lied to you, but were ready to be bribed and placated. On the contrary, you deny me humour and laughter. I am as solemn as your autocrats or Napoleon on the day of his Coronation. If hell is a psychic state, as the old man grotesquely encapsulated in a mobile plastic bubble argues, whatever happened to the beautiful, awesome, Dantean vision of fire, cauldrons and flames where the condemned were eternally consumed? If you erase all that with one stroke of the pen you strip me of a fundamental part of myself, reduce my powers as an absolute monarch to a species of constitutional president! If my competitors in other creeds hold on to theirs, they will finish me off irrevocably, for what sustains my authority is the secret weapon of intimidation. I know all about turning the other cheek, sacrificing the Son and other pious legends destined to alleviate the harshness of the first part of the story, like the sweet arbour the tyrant cultivates next to the barbed wire fences and watch-towers of his extermination camps. But none of that can compensate the removal of my best arguments and attributes. Your species behaves according to the alternate currents of abject submission and the longing to transgress. Would you, for example, have surrendered to an angel's insipid beauty, without the stunning power of those tough skulls, rough chins, voracious lips, sinewy bodies to which you have yielded throughout your life?"

"When you lived as hirsute animals in caves, two-footed and tottering, perhaps yearning after your plantigrade support, in what ways did you differ from other primates?

Your rustic lights were only exercised satisfying elemental needs, searching for roots, hunting and devouring whatever inferior or weaker species fell into the grip of once hairy extremities it would be an insult to call hands.

Guided by female oestrus, you bolted into grottos where they sheltered and, in order to shaft them, stuck crude stone weapons into the thoraxes or skulls of their males, cut them up and swallowed down their testicles and cocks to bolster your potency, just as a few rickety aficionados still down the piping hot nuts of fighting bulls (such atavism survives, however civilised and wise you may think you are).

I don't know if you'd discovered the secret of fire and celebrated your victories and captives by leaping and grunting around bonfires, or I may have seen such like in one of your Tarzan or dinosaur films; I hadn't yet been born into your minds. Millions of years went into my invention.

But ever since you created me omnipotent and eternal, I have contemplated you retrospectively over time and can measure your advances and regressions, the struggle between lucidity and your animal heritage. Frankly, I don't see a big difference between your predatory appetites and those you displayed when fresh out of the cave.

You haven't been modified by the hundred thousand light years passed since then (forgive the scant rigour of my calculations); you still dance your ritual dances around bonfires, grind down the bones of your adversaries and copulate with their deities on heat: centuries and centuries of culture and enlightenment vanished in the smoke of the conflagration and collapse of skyscrapers.

Like young Tolstoy, you saw the massacres and devastation in Chechnya.

Tell me: what has changed on the Earth which, according to legend, I created in a week?

Close your eyes for a moment: only the wild fastnesses of the Caucasus mountains, like the one you anticipate behind the peaks you admire from your terrace, retain their luminosity for you. The bodies sacrificed accumulate dust and rancour in the deep valleys and my laughter resounds around the Roof of the World."

Occasionally, the voice condescended to converse with him.

"You're a fictional being. Your destiny was written in advance."

"In the Uncreated Text?"

"I discovered it in the work a calligrapher composed centuries ago. The incidents and episodes in your life, even the most sordid, are there, and not a detail missed. I won't elaborate or you'll get bored."

"Won't you let me take a peep?"

"Curiosity was always your downfall! Don't you remember the first chapter of the Book?"

"Where the devil did you find the manuscript?"

"Don't look in libraries destined to burn. The manuscript is your own life."

"Did my double have my name?"

"Name, surname, date and place of birth coincide.

But you're the one written, not him. Everything figures in its pages."

"Even this dialogue between you and me?"

"I have it before my eyes as if on a computer screen. All that occurs was foretold."

"What happens then if I keep quiet?"

"There are blank spaces. But you don't want to keep quiet. When you talk, you prolong your life. You have come onstage and aren't in a rush to leave."

"And how about yourself?"

"Let's just say that in order to exist I need an audience. The day when the theatre empties I'll be gone as well. But that won't happen tomorrow or the day after, do you think?"

"A long story!"

"Very, very long. Unless your world becomes uninhabitable and you put an end to it."

"I won't live to see that."

"Will you be sorry?"

"Who doesn't have the odd dream of dying and taking the world with him?"

"Perhaps you haven't the wherewithal but soon that won't be the case. The desire to reach me and my promises of happiness contain the threat of my disappearance. By longing for me thus, those who love me can reduce me to ashes!"

"Tell me what is written there."

"Don't be impatient. The inevitability of happenstance is the world's best kept secret. What would become of me if I were to bring my offspring in on the act?"

"History is the kingdom of the lie. As soon as you invented the alphabet and skilled yourselves in the mechanics of writing, you discovered the deceptions of palimpsests, the preparation of codices to justify myths and foundational legends, of commandments dictated by divinities which you both create and are victims of. You forged my miracles and attacks of rage, the searing fires of Sodom, the sayings attributed to prophets and messengers. Would the titles granting earthly power, the Vicariate of Christ in Peter's Seat at Rome, the crowns and sceptres of kings and sultans have been possible without the fraudulent labours of venal scribes and copyists? Biblical texts, conciliar resolutions and books of revelation don't merit the slightest credit: they've been rehashed, rewritten, corrected and erased again.

If you allow yourself to be duped by this

cybernetic era of instant communication, think what might have happened a thousand years earlier with relics, apparitions and miraculously identified cadavers, savage struggles over thrones and crosiers, centuries-old genealogical trees, if no caliph, pontificate or tyrant had had the good wit to base the undeniable source of his nobility on Adam's coupling with Eve.

Be convinced once and for all: there is no person, family, lineage, nation, doctrine or State that doesn't base its pretensions to legitimacy on a flagrant falsehood. Those who burn libraries to erase awkward traces ignore the fact that the burnt manuscripts are themselves spurious. The greatest enemy of the lie is not truth but another lie. The calligrapher who penned you did so in the full knowledge that you didn't exist."

"When I shat your physical world and from My
Heights contemplated the Finished Job, I shook in
horror: it was worse than a turd, than foul dung, than
a fetid pile of dough threaded like a beaten meringue.
Its spheric form gyrated in the stratosphere obscenely
complacent, not noticing it was shown up by the sun
and was clearly a zero minus in the myriad of
asteroids, meteorites, stars and planets you stupidly
call the Creation. An ass sprinkled it with some of its
own and it almost drowned in its piss, but that
hapless drunken prophet of ill-omen constructed his
ark and saved your bacon. Saved you from what?
From envy, evil, oppression, crime, war, corrosive lust
after power and wealth? From pain, sickness,
decrepitude and death? Mentally you placed
yourselves at the centre of the universe and imagined
that the nightly spectacle of the moon and

constellations had been created to pleasure your eyes and never for a moment did you understand that you are but a microscopic grain of sand on a huge, constantly expanding beach. And if I existed, would I have taken so much trouble to ensure your delight and entertainment? Or do you really believe I hang on your every word and deed however puerile and malign they are, in order to note them in a record book so I don't forget them? Such a presumption would make me die of laughter if I weren't by definition mortal.

Yesterday, when you were on your café terrace in the square, I noticed you absent-mindedly watching the little fellow who daily pushes the chair of someone disabled and who stops in front of you to soften your heart and extract a coin or two. His twisted head, tortured eyes, foaming, gaping mouth didn't extract a single tear of pity from you. The repetition of things numbs their effect and enters the category of the over-familiar. I don't escape that rule either: your cruelty and pettiness rehearsed over the centuries make me yawn. That's why I invented eternity, not because I want to give out prizes and punishments like an arrogant deity subject to rages and caprice, but so, like any idler, I could sustain the immensity of my boredom."

"The cordillera you contemplate is a theatre safety curtain: lift it up, enter there. The world stretching out on the other side answers to your emotional longings: precipitous, wild, scorched by the sun and sculpted by the four elements. You anticipated it first in Gaudí's volcanic space, then in the lunar wastes of the Great Erg and endless dunes of Tarfaya. There is no vegetation, there is no green, no human trace softens its nakedness and sumptuous austerity. The sorties and occultations of the tiny star warming you repeat their cycles for millions of years before an empty amphitheatre. All colours and shades of the spectre combine in an apotheosis staged for you. You will be its only spectator if you rid yourself of the goods and chattels keeping you on this ephemeral islet.

What are you waiting for? Do you think you'll

always see the bulls from the barrier, never from the sand itself?

The worse that could happen to you already has. You live without her, far from her and hardly see her diminished by distance. Make the necessary arrangements for those who look after you and for the children who will forget you, only to grow and multiply, in their cruel innocence. Don't cling to what you will soon abandon. The greater your detachment, the easier will be your passage.

Tweak your ear, don't use your deafness as a shield: you catch me on a good roll and I speak without malice aforethought. Nothing you cast off, the routine and comforts of old age are worth a jot in comparison with what awaits you. You will receive a whole tunnel of light to yourself. You will accompany me across the White Mountains and peaks of Black Dust, along ravines and gullies where scurries the rascal I lovingly instructed and armed. The most lethal, polished artefacts won't prevail against him for I will clone others and yet others possessed by his same appetite for destruction. Such has been the law of your stupid world from long before you invented me. But beyond the horrors you glimpse on television, veiled from you by zealous manipulators, lies the beauty hidden behind the safety curtain. Enter there and lose yourself in the spectacle. I will be there to close the parenthesis between nothing and nothingness. My voice will boom round the heights as in that far-fetched bible story. As I said, or so they say I said, to the dead man you will be: Arise and walk!"

One fine day he made up his mind. He went to the collective taxi station without warning anyone and leaving his folk only a few lines scribbled in the local dialect: they shouldn't expect him for lunch or dinner, he was off on his travels. He waited patiently in the front seat while the vehicle filled up. He peered in the rear-view mirror at the faces of peasants with little kids and esparto grass baskets. Then two youths arrived, one slipped in beside him and stretched his arm behind his seat. The taxi drove off and, squeezed between driver and youth, he gazed at the outskirts of the ochre-pink city and bade goodbye without yielding to the emotion of a final farewell. The strength of his decision excluded any kind of feeling. His past had been abolished: he was no longer himself but a blank page. He existed only in the flux of space and time and his world was nought beyond the taxi's dusty bodywork. He scrutinised the flatlands with a mixture of tedium and relief, as he calculated the number of kilometres separating him from the mountainous range he'd chosen. The travellers in the back seat whispered to each other; nobody ventured into a general conversation. Out of the corner of his eye he saw the profile of the driver, cigarette butt on lip, rosary hanging from the front mirror, the inevitable hand of Fatima. Neither the heat nor overcrowding provoked the usual commentaries on the drought, the ruin of yet another harvest and the flight from the countryside. Everything unfolded according to the script foreseen: no room here for conversations or sociable rites.

Then he dozed off. Did the others take advantage of his nodding to gossip about his things or the grave situation the country was passing through? Who was this European travelling with them? He'd spoken to him in their dialect, whispered the driver. All he had for luggage was a bottle of mineral water. But he wasn't sure this conversation took place. Although they had reached the port, the voracious clouds hid the panorama of the plain which stretched out to the sea. As they wound their way down, the horizon cleared. His neighbours smoked cigarette after cigarette, exhaustion etched on their faces. On the other hand, he felt full of energy, impatient to finish that penultimate phase of his voyage. He wanted to catch the next vehicle which would drive him to his destination point and wanted to arrive before the sun set.

Everything happened as he'd predicted in his dreams. Another collective taxi was waiting for him, its engine already running, and the resigned passengers made a space for him. There were old men, women and children: they looked at him on the sly but didn't direct any questions his way. It was as if his presence and the imprecise purpose of his journey imposed a sense of respect. He'd told the blue turbanned driver he should stop en route, at a place he would indicate. Did he know the name of the village? No, it's in wasteland, he retorted, and to fill the silence following on his words he pretended to

lose himself in the contemplation of the
encampments and farmsteads that clung to the
mountainsides. He thought of the trampled bush of
thistles, the stumps of its mutilated arms, the broken
stems and blackened flowers, crushed by the weight
of the armoured car. Their proximity to the deferred
encounter raised his spirits and accelerated his
heartbeats.

They neared the ochre-stone desert, the awesome, abrupt disposition of the landscape. A vermilion sun heightened the astonishing profile of the mountains, walled bastions of a miraculous, haughty, extinct city. Rocky strata, horizontally striated in chameleon colours, created pyramidal shapes of bronzed faces, without the least attempt at green. The fierce rigour of the geometrical shapes suggested the intervention of a masterly but discreet artist. Then, the stria traced a vertical, filigree composition. The landscape painter seemed to have gradated the colour and shades of the components, adapting them to fit the perspective of an observer situated in the river basin where the rough ground of the track ran. How many centuries had it taken to polish the edges of the strata, order the harmonious contrasts of volume, weave the criss-crossing, superimposed layers that shaped the great amphitheatre in the fleeting luminosity of twilight?

"Stop here."

The taxi braked. The man in the blue turban turned round to look at him.

"Is someone expecting you?"

"Don't worry, I have an appointment."

The passengers piled in the vehicle looked at him in mute bewilderment.

"You sure? The last bus left a few minutes ago."

"I told you not to worry. May God go with you!"

The taxi moved away slowly, almost reluctantly, and he wasn't disappointed by the fullness of the moment he now lived. He went with the clothes he wore and a bottle of water. He scrutinised the stony plain, devoid of shrubs or oleanders: the absolute kingdom of the inorganic. He thought of other landscapes which had fascinated him throughout his life, and all suddenly melded there. Was the wild thistle and its raspberry-coloured flowers awaiting him, the one he'd glimpsed on the roadside on his way to Shatoi? He walked towards the reddish light.

The sun was about to dip down and gradually sink into the theatrical immensity of the set. He tried to avoid the pebbles and snares on the ground. The proximity of snakes and scorpions no longer worried him. The wreath of light had reached its much rehearsed, ephemeral perfection. Was the Great Soulless One likewise the Supreme Artist? His confused mind, immersed in the growing density of the shadows, alternated affirmation and negation. Then the darkness thickened, the silence too. He had returned to the entrails of matter, not knowing how, why, wherefore, the distance, the rhythms.

"Don't go to sleep early. Had you forgotten you had an appointment with me?"

(He'd agonised for hours, exhausted and numb from cold, with no other light than the familiar childhood constellations, and the loud voice made him start, forced him to open his eyes.)

Stop thinking of squaring the circle and concentrate on the life you have left: on the sand running from the top of the timer. Intensity compensates the ephemeral. There are beings whose days are moments, yet we are dazzled by the brightness of their flame. Your appearance has lasted decades: you barely remember who you are and how much you messed up and did! I'm not the elephantine memory you think I am either. Today I know nothing of the forebears who begat you because their passage on earth was indifferent and anodyne. Look at the splendour of the night, think on the reiteration of its cycles. You have returned to the warmth of the maternal cloister you should never have left. But the error will shortly be erased depending on what happens as the centuries pass.

You have already unlearned all you knew and are a stranger to the world. Nor do I remember very much either. Apart from two or three murky, probably fictitious snapshots. Certainly, I was at the train station in Astapovo when Tolstoy broke off his flight to the Caucasus of his youth. He didn't see ever again the thistle trampled by boots and hoofs. You are luckier: you've reached the stone desert you admire so much. The kaftans and lady's black hat which you've already forgotten never existed. There are roses of sand buried around your cradle. If you wake up, you won't see me and, if you don't, that will be that.

He woke up and didn't see him. He discovered he'd not moved from his room and peered out at the orange trees in the patio. It was darkest night, the city was resting. He wrapped up against the cold and walked up to his terrace. The sky revealed its magnificence, invited him to decipher the algebra and alphabet of the stars. The square also slept: no voice arose from its deserted space. He spotted fleeting silhouettes, trembling and forlorn. Shadows draped the outline of the cordillera. Nevertheless he felt awed by it, as it prepared to reveal its whiteness to the brow of dawn. What lay hidden behind held its secret tight. The appointment would be for another day: when the safety curtain was raised and he confronted the vertiginous void. He was, was still among the spectators in the stalls.

●) ●) ●)

Then, even my own life was entirely hidden from me
by a new set, like the one erected on the edge of a stage
in front of which actors perform an entertainment
whilst, behind, new scenes are put into place.

Marcel Proust
In the Shadow of Young Girls in Flower

●) ●) ●)

Marrakesh, November 1996 –
Tangier, August 2002